BREAKING NEW G
IN LAO HISTORY

BREAKING NEW GROUND IN LAO HISTORY
ESSAYS ON THE SEVENTH TO TWENTIETH CENTURIES

EDITED BY

Mayoury Ngaosrivathana

AND

Kennon Breazeale

SILKWORM BOOKS

This publication was made possible by a grant from the Toyota Foundation.

ISBN 974-7551-93-4

First published by Silkworm Books in 2002

Silkworm Books
104/5 Chiang Mai–Hot Road, M. 7, T. Suthep
Chiang Mai 50200, Thailand
E-mail address: silkworm@loxinfo.co.th
Website: http://www.silkwormbooks.info

Cover photograph by Catherine Raymond. Mural of *Balasankhaya Jataka* in Sisaket
Monastery, Vientiane, by an unknown artist, c. 1819–24.

    The *Balasankhaya Jataka* is an extracanonical text that was popular in Lan Sang and
Lan Na. Its hero, King Bokkharaphat, entrusted affairs of state to a thief, who was more
honest than the ministers. This mural shows the king and the thief hiding on a roof one
night, preparing to steal gifts given by the king to his ministers.

Typeset by Silk Type in Garamond 11 pt.
Printed in Thailand by O. S. Printing House, Bangkok

CONTENTS

LIST OF MAPS

INTRODUCTION

This book was produced by an international group of scholars, each with an individual approach to the central Mekong basin. The essays encompass nearly 1,400 years of history and draw upon materials in more than a dozen languages. The bibliography demonstrates the richness of the sources for research. And yet, books on Lao history are not very numerous. This volume illustrates some of the reasons why the subject is not well developed.

Language are foremost among the obstacle. Primary sources are abundant, but they are written in many languages and are scattered around the world, in archives that have not been well explored. Some materials are available only in languages understood by few Lao historians, such as Chinese, Dutch, Italian, Latin and Portuguese. The vast majority of materials, up to the middle of the twentieth century, are in French and unpublished. Primary sources in the Lao language itself are very limited, and few materials have been translated from other languages into Lao for use by Lao scholars and students. Indeed, successful explorations into some subjects in Lao history will depend on cooperative efforts among researchers who can contribute a knowledge of several languages each. They must also apply a variety of other skills.

The first chapter of this book is by Martin Stuart-Fox, the author of three essential works: a historical dictionary of Laos, a history of twentieth-century Laos and a study extending back to the earliest recorded Lao history. He draws from his broad knowledge to explain basic structural problems in writing Lao history and to introduce major historical themes. He offers two approaches: the first focuses on geographical areas inhabited by the Lao-speaking lowland people and their political structures throughout the centuries; the second stresses cultural diversity and the continuity of ethnic interaction between lowland and highland peoples. These approaches provide background for a theme that arises in subsequent essays: that of defining what we mean by Laos at various times in history.

The geographical theme is taken up in the second chapter. For the study of mainland South-East Asia in the seventh and eighth centuries, we rely heavily on Chinese records. But their meaning is not always clear. Western textbooks have perpetuated tentative ideas proposed a century ago by scholars who were trying (not always successfully) to interpret these records. Tatsuo Hoshino examines the original texts in the light of archaeological discoveries of recent decades, combined with his first-hand knowledge of the countryside in the central Mekong basin. Using these resources, he constructs a new theory about the locations of numerous small political entities mentioned by the Chinese. This theory enables him to describe the political, diplomatic, and economic networks in the interior of South-East Asia, from the mid-600s to the end of the 800s. Once the map of these long-known Chinese place-names is more accurately determined, this structural contribution will facilitate the work of archaeologists.

Hoshino discusses the antecedents and origins of the early Lao political entities. Souneth Phothisane continues the discussion of early history prior to the emergence of the kingdom of Luang Prabang in the fourteenth century. He completes the chronological overview of the book by reviewing Lao sources from the fourteenth to the twentieth centuries—the period for which records in the Lao language itself have been preserved.

Souneth introduces readers to a specific tradition of historical writing—the Luang Prabang chronicle—comparing all known versions of this work and discussing its potential uses for research. He points out how successive generations of annalists have reinterpreted historical events and the roles of individuals, and how they have continuously rewritten their history. The chapter by Bernard Gay pursues a similar theme by comparing twentieth-century authors and their opposing interpretations of Lao history.

In terms of sheer volume, sources for the study of Laos are mostly European, but these become regular and numerous only in the 1860s. Contemporary European sources for the precolonial period are very limited and are discussed by Mayoury and Pheuiphanh Ngaosrivathana. Prior to 1864, only two eye-witness descriptions of the Lao appeared in Europe: one by an Italian priest (1663) and one by a Dutch merchant (1669). Despite this, European knowledge of the central and upper Mekong basin dates back to the early European explorations of coastal South-East Asia in the 1500s, and for several centuries information about the Lao continued to trickle through to Europe. The Ngaosrivathanas provide a comprehensive survey of European publications prior to the mid-nineteenth century, including attempts to represent Laos on early maps, and they discuss how Western writers imagined and depicted the Lao-speaking region of the interior. After the 1660s, almost all new information available to Europeans came from coastal areas, and the contacts between the coast and the interior provide evidence of economic and political interactions in every direction around the landlocked Lao territory.

One landmark among European sources is the *Universal History*, published in London in 1759. It attempts to give its readers an encyclopaedic view of the world, and it was compiled near the half-way point in Europe's 500-year acquaintance with the Mekong valley. Its chapter on the Lao kingdom is reproduced in this volume for two reasons. First, the anonymous compilers demonstrate the quality and extent of knowledge about the Lao available in the West at the time of writing, including some of the problems of what they meant by 'Laos'. Second, copies of the original edition are almost unobtainable today, and this reprint will make it readily available.

Meg O'Donovan provides an introduction to this work and a critical review of it, in the context of Western scholarship in the mid-eighteenth century. Despite its severe limitations, this work is still useful, given that so very little contemporary documentation has survived in Laos itself and in surrounding countries.

Most records have vanished because of the fragile nature of the writing materials, either through decay or the devastations of warfare. For example, as a result of wars in Laos and Vietnam at various times from the 1770s to the 1820s, most day-to-day government documents were destroyed. A small but unique archive, however, was maintained by successive Vietnamese officials stationed near the Lao border. Some of their documents were concealed in a family shrine, until Tran Van Quy found them. Tran describes his discovery and translates some of the texts concerning the Lao. Although small in number, the documents are invaluable, because some of the information they contain is recorded nowhere else.

The officials who maintained the archive resided along the Quy Hop trail, which Tran describes as the best natural trail crossing the cordillera into Laos. It fell into relative obscurity in modern times, because French engineers in the early twentieth century selected the trail to the north by way of Na Pae, and the one to the south by way of Muya, when they began to build the motor roads that link the seacoast to the Mekong.

Both Tran and Hoshino lead us on journeys in our mind's eye, crossing the cordillera in two different eras separated by a thousand years. We cannot be sure, but the trails they describe could be one and the same: a geographical continuity of communications into the twenty-first century, with Mekong traders on foot still carrying their goods on horses and pack-cattle to sell in areas with access to the sea.

Among the devastating wars noted above, the Tay-son movement in the 1780s and 1790s overthrew the old order in Vietnam and led to the formation of a complex but temporary network of international alliances and hostilities. Kennon Breazeale assesses the newly discovered Vietnamese documents, along with evidence in Lao, Thai and French records, in an attempt to reconstruct the basic pattern of Lao-Vietnamese relations during this period. He re-examines the arguments made by Tran and comes to very different conclusions about the warfare that spilled over into Vientiane's territory in the early 1790s and the consequences of an ill-timed Lao–North Vietnamese alliance during the protracted civil war in Vietnam. This essay also complements the next one by providing details of a precolonial millenarian movement and its political consequences.

Bernard Gay introduces readers to Lao millenarian movements, the 'holy men' of the colonial period and French efforts to suppress them during the first four decades of the twentieth century. He provides much new material about internal resistance to colonial rule, drawing on unpublished records in French archives. After establishing the chronology and character of events, Gay compares modern Lao writers' interpretations of these movements and investigates the discourse behind their divergent approaches to history.

This book begins with continuities and discontinuities in history, and the final chapter illustrates both. It shows how the territory of Laos, as we know it today, came to be defined no more than a generation or two ago. Kennon Breazeale briefly reviews the well-known international treaties between Britain, China, France and Thailand—the colonial powers that carved up the Mekong valley during the late nineteenth century. He then discusses the French legislation and administrative decrees that gave Laos its present shape by adding territory to the country or taking it away. He divides the resulting international boundary into eighteen segments and discusses the legal instruments that define them. Citing unpublished archival materials, he concludes that the process of defining modern Laos, in the territorial sense, was a series of illusions, contradictions and much abuse of power by colonial authorities.

All of these essays raise questions. The authors believe that their work breaks new ground, and that it will stimulate new ideas and will lead to further research on these and related subjects. They also hope that this book will be informative to all readers who are interested in the central Mekong basin.

CONTRIBUTORS

KENNON BREAZEALE is a projects coordinator, East-West Center, Honolulu, Hawaii, United States.

BERNARD GAY is a researcher at the Centre National de la Recherche Scientifique, Paris, France.

TATSUO HOSHINO is an independent researcher, Yokohama, Japan.

MAYOURY NGAOSRIVATHANA is the general manager, Drs. Mayoury, Pheuiphanh and Sons, Legal Counsel Office, Vientiane, Lao PDR.

PHEUIPHANH NGAOSRIVATHANA is a national policy and law adviser, Land Titling Project's Technical Assistance Team (Ausaid/World Bank), Ministry of Finance, Vientiane, Lao PDR.

MEG O'DONOVAN is the proprietor of Soaring Eagle Education in the Nicola Valley, British Columbia, Canada.

SOUNETH PHOTHISANE is the director, Lao National Museum, Ministry of Information and Culture, Vientiane, Lao PDR.

MARTIN STUART-FOX is the Professor in History and head of the Department of History, University of Queensland, St. Lucia, Queensland, Australia.

TRAN VAN QUY is a professor of history at the University of Hanoi, Vietnam.

ON THE WRITING OF LAO HISTORY: CONTINUITIES AND DISCONTINUITIES

Martin Stuart-Fox

The writing of Lao history presents peculiar problems, not because of the quantity and quality of sources available (though these leave much to be desired for certain periods), but because of the difficulty in deciding what is meant by 'Lao history'. There is a problem in identifying the object of study. Is Lao history the history of those territories inhabited by ethnic Lao, or of the state of Laos as it has existed at various times under various names? The Lao have spread far beyond the geographical boundaries of present-day Laos: many more ethnic Lao live in Thailand than in Laos. Moreover, the Lao state ceased to exist as a unitary entity in the early eighteenth century. What was reconstructed by the French nearly two centuries later and what exists today is but a fragment composed of territories belonging to former principalities inhabited by diverse peoples, many of whom are not ethnic Lao.[1]

One way to approach the writing of Lao history is to accept the discontinuities for what they are, and to identify and emphasise the continuities that transcend them. Another is to seek the historical precedents of the reality that is the modern 'pluri-ethnic' Lao state.[2] The first focuses on geographical areas inhabited by ethnic Lao and the abiding political structures they developed; the second emphasises the continuity of ethnic interaction and cultural diversity. I shall say something about both and show how they suggest a periodisation of Lao history.

POLITICAL STRUCTURES AND THE TRADITIONAL LAO STATE

To take 1365 as the date of foundation of the kingdom of Lan Sang, and to take Lan Sang as the first Lao state, is to begin with a discontinuity which is itself misleading. Prior to Lan Sang, Müang Sawa was a principality in the region of Luang Prabang whose ruling house was Lao. Over a prolonged period, Lao Lum (inhabitants of the valleys) had come to an accommodation with the Lao Thoeng (inhabitants of the mountain slopes, mostly Khmu) who had earlier been in possession of the land (though never constituting a political entity) when the first Lao settlers pushed their way down the valley of the Ou River. Forms of Buddhism were known and practised. Farther south Müang Vientiane had succeeded in throwing off Khmer suzerainty, as probably had Müang Si Khottabong covering the region of present-day Nakhòn Phanom. Siang Khwang covering the Plain of Jars was almost certainly never under Khmer domination. Only in the far south did Champasak still fall within the contracting *mandala*[3] of the Angkorian Empire. These were the major elements fused by Fa Ngum into his empire of Lan Sang.

The *mandala* system is perfectly suited to the rapid rise of empires constructed of constituent parts. Its founder is a *cakkavartin*, or universal Buddhist ruler, a conqueror whose conquests are ideally conducted without bloodshed, since his power alone should be sufficient to convince lesser rulers to acknowledge his superior merit and swear allegiance. The might of armies, retinue and symbols of Buddhist truth (*dhamma*) are recognised as outer manifestations of the inner merit accumulated by the *cakkavartin* over countless earlier incarnations, merit which might have achieved the inner goal of Buddhahood had it not been directed at the almost equally commendable outer goal of creating the universal Buddhist realm essential to the pursuit of *dhamma* by all sentient beings. The allegiance of lesser rulers was recognition of that superior merit. It could always be withdrawn from a king whose merit failed to sustain the central power of the *mandala*. This was most likely on the peripheries where alternative foci of power were available making possibly less onerous tributary demands. *Mandalas* tended therefore to expand and contract as a function of the power status of the centre.

The constituent parts of the *mandala*, known as *müang*, were political entities in their own right. Each such *müang* replicated the structure of the *mandala* of which it formed a tributary part. As larger *müang* might themselves incorporate several smaller *müang*, authority was exercised on a series of levels, each of which retained a degree of local autonomy. This political structure was characteristic of all the Tai peoples, who were thus remarkably free to conduct their own local affairs in return for allegiance, tribute and manpower in the event of war, contributions sustaining respectively the religio-symbolic, economic and military bases of the central power of the *mandala* of which they formed a part.

The whirlwind conquest of Fa Ngum—backed by Khmer arms and bolstered by Mongol designs though it may have been (Hoshino 1986)—built on an existing Lao population, already politically organised into traditional *müang*, a political structure already deeply imbued with, and thus reinforced by, Buddhist beliefs.[4] Lan Sang sprang not from a simple act of conquest, however, by one man whose individual merit was questionable enough for him to be actually deposed, but from pre-existing conditions created by the advantage taken by powerful regional Lao rulers of the decline of Khmer power to construct their own independent localised *müang*. Fa Ngum was the catalyst who forced these regional *müang* into a powerful *mandala*. From this derives his historical claim to hero status as the founder of the Lao kingdom.

The inherent weakness of the *mandala* he created derived from his failure to reinforce tributary allegiance through maintaining a permanent central presence in constituent *müang*. That was not the nature of the *mandala*. Spies there were, but no official representatives of central power in the *müang* in the form, for example, of the two Siamese commissioners (*khaluang*) appointed to the court of Luang Prabang in the late nineteenth century. Never were administrative mandarins appointed on the Chinese model. Tributary rulers betook themselves to the centre of power in costly and time-consuming attendance. The lack of central supervision allowed free rein to the personal ambitions of rulers of constituent *müang*, even

3

where there were governors appointed by and related to the king. The potential for disintegration was always present, an internal vulnerability particularly evident whenever a new potential *cakkavartin* appeared on the scene, providing the possibility of alternative allegiance.

For the Tai world, the alternative *cakkavartin* was usually Burmese, and the attraction particularly strong for northern Siamese *müang* such as Sukhothai and Phitsanulok (Wyatt 1984). Burmese invasions of the Siamese heartland never, however, succeeded in creating a single Buddhist empire in South-East Asia. The imperial *mandala* had a certain critical political extent, for political power, like centripetal attraction, appears to decrease proportionally to the square of distance from the centre. Centrifugal tendencies in the Tai world were always too great for the Burmese to overcome. So were they for King Setthathirat in his attempt to include Lan Na in the *mandala* of Lan Sang (Sila Viravong 1964: 55–7), or for the Siamese to include Lan Sang and Lan Na until both were weakened through either invasion or disintegration.

For Lan Sang, outer *müang* were always in danger of being lost. For variable periods Sipsòng Panna, Sipsòng Chao Tai, Hua Phan, Siang Khwang, even Nan formed more or less loosely cohering parts of the Lao *mandala*. To what extent Lü, Phuan, Phu Tai, even Yuan *müang* should be included in a history of Laos is a matter for debate. Should their fortunes be followed during periods when they escaped the orbit of Lan Sang? Is there a formula whereby we can include Siang Khwang and exclude Chiang Saen? What then of Sipsòng Panna? For the Isan *müang* of the Khorat plateau, there is initially no such problem: they were unambiguously Lao. Only with the disintegration of the Lao *mandala* does their status become questionable.

Peripheral *müang* could be excluded as of peripheral historical interest, except at such times as they become important for the changing relationships between contiguous *mandalas*. In the early eighteenth century, for example, peripheral *müang* become crucial as the disintegration of the Lao *mandala* permitted the extension of Siamese influence to include the Lao *müang* of what is now northeastern Thailand. The pretensions of Luang Prabang, Vientiane, even Champasak to inherit the status of Lan Sang could not be realised in large part because of the growing influence of Siam. The coherence of internal ties constituting the Lao *mandala* gave way to a set of ties linking separate Lao *müang* with Bangkok (Breazeale 1975).

The three Lao kingdoms of the eighteenth century—Luang Prabang, Vientiane and Champasak—could not simply divide Lan Sang between them. The tributary power exercised by three regional centres could never add up to the power of a single centre because the very act of division created a new set of peripheral *müang*. Where these lay on the dividing line between the three Lao *müang*, their inclusion in any history of Laos presents no problems. Difficulties arise, however, with *müang* on the dividing line between weakened Lao principalities and neighbouring power centres—the Siamese *mandala*, but also the expanding empire of Vietnam. The relative power imbalance translated into a geographical shift in *müang* allegiances. Tribute was increasingly paid to Bangkok by the Isan *müang*. As they became embedded in the Siamese *mandala*, so they were no longer available as constituent elements cohering around a Lao centre of power. Similarly, Siang Khwang looked first to Hanoi, then to Hué (Archaimbault 1967).

With the defeat of Chao Anuwong in 1828, Lao political structures shattered into constituent *müang*. Chao Anuwong had recognised the need to recreate the Lao *mandala*, just as Fa Ngum had originally done.[5] Had he held the Siamese at Khorat and negotiated a settlement posing no threat to Bangkok, it is unlikely that Luang Prabang could have avoided being drawn into his expanding Lao *mandala*. As it was, Luang Prabang was spared destruction only by accepting the suzerainty of Bangkok. Nevertheless, it remained the only Lao *müang* with any pretension to regional power status. Lao political structures had thus become hopelessly splintered. At this point, the history of Laos has either been written as the history of Luang Prabang, ignoring the collection of central and southern *müang*, each with its separate conflicts and conspiracies, or as the history of expanding Siamese hegemony over the Lao territories.[6] Both approaches present problems. The history of Luang Prabang is no substitute for the history of Laos, for it represented such a reduced fraction of the Lao people so as not to be able to stand for the whole in any but a symbolic sense.

To write the history of Laos as an adjunct to the history of Thailand is, however, equally unsatisfactory. A balance needs therefore to be struck between the discontinuity of even regionally centralised Lao political structures throughout mostly Lao territories, and the continuity represented by the decentralised political organisation of the *müang* in these same areas. By focussing on shared political culture, the charge that while the Lao people have a history, Laos does not, can be avoided. Moreover such an approach gives due recognition to the fact that local *müang* never ceased to function as centres of specifically Lao political power, for reasons that will be discussed below.

COLONISATION AND INDEPENDENCE

In 1893 Lao territories east of the Mekong were ceded to France, which constituted them as a territorial entity, divided at first into Upper and Lower Laos, and subsequently into the protectorate of Luang Prabang, plus directly administered central and southern provinces. Laos existed again, but not yet as a political entity in its own right, for no independent centre of Lao political power existed. Laos was but a territorial entity within French Indochina. Just as the Lao *müang* had earlier depended on Bangkok (and the Isan *müang* continued to do), so French Lao territories depended on the Gouvernement Général of French Indochina based in Hanoi. It was there that all major decisions were made that affected Laos.

Official French exploration of Laos was firstly in order to discover 'a river road to China' (Osborne 1975); secondly to extend the 'hinterland' of Vietnam and gain control of the Mekong (Meyer 1931: 7, 62). It was not to re-establish a viable Lao state at the centre of mainland South-East Asia. Auguste Pavie may have hoped to reconstruct Lan Sang for the greater glory of France, but the French came to view Laos entirely from the perspective of Vietnam— French Vietnam[7]—throughout most of their stay in Indochina. Not until 1940 did the French actually begin to conceive of Laos as a

6

separate political entity (and then primarily to oppose the pan-Thaiism of the Phibun Songkhram government in Bangkok; see Rochet 1946). Between 1940 and 1954 French views changed: Laos in Indochina, became Laos in the French Union, and finally, Laos the independent state.

Not all Frenchmen saw Laos exclusively from the perspective of Vietnam, of course. Those like Pavie who actually served there, for the most part, did not (for example, Reinach 1911). But their voices counted for little in Hanoi, and the prevailing French attitude remained. From the beginning the Lao territories were for France important not in their own right, but as an extension of Vietnam. Vietnamese claims to exercise a tenuous suzerainty over some parts of Laos became the basis for French claims to exercise sovereignty on behalf of Vietnam.[8] Lao territories were needed to give Vietnam strategic depth, and because they happened to intervene between Vietnam and the Mekong, which the French thought might still be useful as an artery to direct trade towards Saigon (Guillot 1894).

The more ambitious French colonialists saw the acquisition of the Lao territories as means to the end of imposing French control over Siam,[9] even though, given the dominant position Britain enjoyed in the valley of the Chao Phraya River, this was never a realistic hope. What the French did achieve in the Anglo-French agreement of 1896 was British acceptance that the Mekong basin constituted a French sphere of influence. Britain wanted Siam to remain an independent buffer state between the British Indian empire (which included Burma by then) and French Indochina. For that purpose a Siam shorn of its peninsular possessions (recognised by the 1896 agreement as a British sphere of influence) and the Mekong basin (and Cambodian territories) would still suffice (Goldman 1972).

It was widely expected, therefore, that as the nineteenth century drew to a close France would discover some pretext to annex not only Saiyaburi and Champasak west of the Mekong which she eventually obtained in the Franco-Siamese treaty of 1904 ('Conventions et traités' 1988), but also the entire Khorat plateau. This was what Pavie had urged; this was also what French administrators in French Laos wanted, for they were all too aware of the anomaly of the

French position (Reinach 1911: 36). After all, the French were well aware by then of the historical reality of Lan Sang. They knew that the Isan region was Lao, not Siamese (Barthélemy 1898: 2). The opportunity was there of claiming all Lao-populated areas in the name of the protectorate of Luang Prabang, as their de facto capital following the Siamese destruction of Vientiane. And yet the opportunity was lost through a combination of determined Siamese moves to reinforce their administrative control over remaining Lao territories west of the Mekong, British disapproval of further French annexations and diminishing French interest as attention turned to events in Europe.

The failure of France to reconstitute the Lao territories into an extended political entity, a resurrected kingdom of Lan Sang, sealed the fate of Laos as a component of French Indochina, for it relegated Laos to the status of an impoverished backwater, incapable of standing on its own fiscal feet. (The budget for Laos always received a subsidy from the general budget for Indochina.) As such it could never be more than French authorities in Hanoi had always considered it to be: a hinterland to be exploited through investment of French capital and Vietnamese labour. The future of Laos was to be assured by building a railway and encouraging Vietnamese migration on the largest possible scale.[10] Special reserves would be set aside for the Lao in their own country, for in the French view the future of Laos was as an extension of Vietnam.[11]

For the historian this colonial interlude of sixty years was in a sense no more than a continuation of the previous period. The only Lao political entity that existed was the kingdom of Luang Prabang, protected by France instead of being tributary to Siam. For the rest, dependent *müang* became dependent provinces administered by French officials as part of Indochina. Lao political structures ceased to exist in anything but name, and that in only half the country.

It took a combination of defeat in Europe, the stationing of Japanese troops in Indochina and the pan-Thai ambitions of the Phibun Songkhram government in Bangkok to force the French to rethink. The west-bank territories of Saiyaburi and Champasak were lost in 1941 (under the terms of the Japanese-brokered Treaty of

Tokyo, on 9 May 1941). What remained of Laos would have to stand on its own. But only for the duration of the war. Thereafter it was to be returned to the new French fold, a small contribution to refurbished French glory.

It was the Lao who decided otherwise. Six months of Japanese occupation resulted in the proclamation of Lao independence and unification of all Laos as a single political entity. The re-creation of an independent Lao state came not in 1893 but in 1945.[12] The struggle for its birth was drawn out until 1953 and owed even more to Vietnam than Burmese independence owed to India. In the process, a new, specifically Lao, political culture developed which proved sufficiently durable to provide a degree of historical continuity over the subsequent transition from kingdom to people's republic in 1975.

CULTURE AND CONTINUITY

The historical discontinuities in political structure thus briefly sketched point up the difficulties involved in writing a narrative history of Laos as a continuing political entity, and the need to take account of further dimensions that are both cultural and ethnic.

At no time has territory designated as 'Lao' been ethnically or culturally homogeneous. Ethnic Lao settled among previous populations: predominantly Lao Thoeng, Mon and Khmer. From the beginning, economic and political relationships took account of their presence. The Lao recognised the Khmu of northern Laos as 'elder brothers' who had an essential role to play in annually ensuring the continued prosperity of the kingdom (Aijmer 1979). Theravada Buddhism provided for subject populations both the possibility of conversion and an explanation of their position at the bottom of the merit-ranked social order. To be reborn in a non-Buddhist society was to be handicapped, but not insuperably so in terms of future, more desirable, incarnations. After all, a number of Jataka stories recount how the Buddha-to-be took the form of an animal. To complicate matters further, many of the upland Tai inhabiting the Sipsòng Chao Tai—the mythical birth-region of the greater Tai race—remain animists, yet are recognised as standing in an ancestral relationship to the ethnic Lao.

As for Mon and Khmer, it seems certain that as the former élite, many intermarried with Lao families, bringing with them important elements of their culture, not the least of which was a commitment to Theravada Buddhism.[13] Ethnically or culturally, therefore, it would be difficult to claim some kind of Lao purity of race. There has been continuous interaction and intermarriage. In fact the very diversity of the ethnic mix has been a continuous feature of Lao history. This is not, however, a sufficiently strong thread. To discover that, we need to take account of the durability of Lao culture in all its dimensions—ideological, economic, and socio-political—at the village level.

By ideological, I mean the religio-mythical synthesis that comprises the Lao world-view and that orders both the disposal of economic surplus and political interaction. At the village level, the cultural focus is the village monastery, just as at the level of the *mandala* the centre is the royal palace and royal monastery—where the symbolic ceremonial is enacted that underpins the office of ruler as the keystone holding the whole political edifice together (Archaimbault 1973 and Condominas 1968). At the level of the *müang*, as we have noted, the political structure of the *mandala* is replicated—ruler, *uparat, ratsawong, ratsabut* (which were the four topmost positions, in descending order of status and power)—because it conforms to the ideology of merit. Political office rests on social status which itself is determined by religious merit. And this is repeated throughout every social unit.

The village is the *müang* in miniature. Here is the basis for the continuity that carries through during those periods when central political structures disappeared. When Vientiane was destroyed, it gave way to a multiplicity of replicas, *müang* grouping a handful of villages, in each of which the political institutions of the *mandala* were reflected, and from each of which, conditions permitting, a new centre might arise. When a new centre was established (symbolically the royal capital of Luang Prabang, politically Vientiane) in 1945, it was accepted throughout what is present-day

Laos because the continuity of Lao political culture had maintained the necessary preconditions. The discontinuity of central political structures was overcome by the continuity of political culture based firmly at the village level, anchored in the socio-religious Lao world-view.

It was this cultural continuity which permitted the country to ride out the radical replacement of political structures that occurred in 1975. Then the discontinuity was not temporal—there was no hiatus in time between one political structure and the next—but rather ideological. On the face of it, the transition was dramatically abrupt. In fact it was moderated by providing official positions for the most symbolically powerful figures in the former regime. The king became supreme adviser to the president; the crown prince was given a seat in the Supreme People's Assembly; Souvanna Phouma, prime minister in the last coalition government, became adviser to the new government. These continuities were important in providing legitimacy for the new regime (Stuart-Fox 1983). Even more important was the position of Souphanouvong, scion of the cadet line of the ruling family of Luang Prabang, half-brother of Souvanna Phouma and clearly a man of merit.

Nevertheless the transition was not easily achieved. Strictures against Buddhism struck at the heart of Lao culture and threatened a deeper discontinuity (Stuart-Fox and Bucknell 1982). Mass imprisonment in re-education camps and mindless repression motivated by a desire for vengeance and power caused tens of thousands to flee. The fabric of Lao society was torn as severely as it had been after 1828. The effect of communist policy was de facto a depopulation as devastating as that of the Siamese. What carried the country through the period 1975 to 1979 (the 'hard-line' period immediately following seizure of power by the Pathet Lao, before the liberalisation ushered in by the Seventh Resolution; see Stuart-Fox 1981) was what carried it through the period 1828 to 1945: the resilience of Lao culture.

After the initial shock of the Pathet Lao seizure of power, cultural continuities began to reassert themselves. Buddhism stealthily, steadily, generated its own revival. Within ten years members of the Politburo were attending major Buddhist ceremonies. The Lao

People's Revolutionary Party surrendered any commitment it may have had to Marxism, as Marxism itself failed the ultimate economic test for a political economy in the Soviet Union. In Laos, Marxism ultimately became irrelevant. In the one area the party might have had a beneficial impact—on the morality of civic culture—it failed dismally. Social (read party) status and power remain inextricably linked to the benefit of personal gain, which in the political arena constitutes corruption. A resurgence of regional and more particularly family and clan interests reflected the party's failure to create a national commitment even among its own cadres (Stuart-Fox 1986b). Regionalism in particular remains a problem. Sadly one must conclude that the re-creation of the Lao state after 1945 has yet to overcome the historical legacy of the previous two and a half centuries of division and can only be achieved through development of a genuinely Lao nationalism.

ETHNICITY AND NATIONALISM

Let us return to the matter of ethnicity. The covenant between Khmu and Lao previously annually re-enacted in Luang Prabang dates from a time when the ethnic Lao were intruders, in all probability outnumbered by an indigenous population (Archaimbault 1973). The Khmu could not be ignored: they were too numerous, too important economically for the welfare of Müang Sawa in their role as gatherers and traders of valuable forest products. Progressively, however, as the Lao Lum population expanded on the riverine rice plains, the relative importance of the Lao Thoeng declined, in both the north and the south. Wisun, Setthathirat and Suriyawongsa ruled an extensive kingdom whose wealth, like that of neighbouring states, rested primarily on taxation of a rice-growing peasantry and royal monopoly of luxury trade. (Only as sea-borne trade promoted by the arrival of Europeans increased in value did the inland kingdoms of Lan Na and Lan Sang suffer a relative decline in comparison with Burma, Siam and Vietnam.) In time, the Lao Thoeng may have constituted as little as 10 percent of the total population—as they would today if the Isan Lao were included in the population of Laos.[14] Lao political culture in the kingdom of Lan Sang was the political culture of the ethnic Lao.

The Laos that gained political independence after 1945 was only superficially the linear descendant of Lan Sang. Most significantly, the balance of population had changed. Migration of Lao Sung (inhabitants of the mountaintops) since around 1840 and loss of the Isan territories meant that the ethnic Lao population amounted to not much more than half the total population of Laos. The division of territory between the royal Lao government and the Pathet Lao had a double effect. For the royal Lao government it obviated the need to develop and carry through 'ethnic policy', since in areas under government control the Lao Thoeng constituted a negligible minority. As for the Lao Sung, they gained their own de facto autonomy.[15] Thus for the royal Lao government the modern kingdom could be conceived as the traditional *mandala* reborn: politics in Laos could be equated with Lao political culture, and little needed changing.[16] For the Pathet Lao, by contrast, their ethnic Lao supporters constituted a minority. New political structures were essential to incorporate the majority comprising Lao Thoeng and Lao Sung—not in the form of autonomous regions, but to enable minority participation in a national political culture. Pathet Lao commitment to this end during the 'thirty-year struggle' was as commendable as it was necessary—not only for the Pathet Lao movement and its victory, but in laying the foundation for a new 'pluri-ethnic' nationalism (Christie 1979).

The creation of the Lao People's Democratic Republic (Lao PDR) in 1975 extended countrywide political techniques which had already proved remarkably successful in mobilising support for the liberation struggle. It also, however, transferred most seats of power (national and provincial) to the ethnic-Lao-dominated areas where Lao Lum cultural superiority is more or less taken for granted. The danger therefore was that what had been gained in terms of creating a Lao national political culture to replace ethnically specific forms, would be undermined by ethnic Lao cultural chauvinism. Until the present, only the Lao People's Revolutionary Party (LPRP) has recruited among the minorities on a platform of interest to them. No political party in the former royal Lao regime ever did so. Yet the central organs of the party are dominated by Lao Lum. Paradoxically, where minority cadres, either Lao Thoeng or Lao Sung, hold real political power at the province level, they do so through traditional Lao political structures (Stuart-Fox 1986a).

Provincial administrations today are the modern *müang*—enjoying considerable independence from the centre, in return for the payment of tribute (tax) which is often withheld. Where provincial administrations are run by minority cadres, they function as separate local power bases. Province administration provides for political participation by ethnic minorities, but at the expense of national consciousness. *Müang* to province is a continuity that is understandable, but inappropriate in a modern state. This does not occur to anything like the same extent in a more politically centralised state like Thailand.

It is clearly essential for Laos today to reinforce steps already taken towards creating a national political culture encouraging Lao nationalism in place of Lao Lum exclusivism. The Pathet Lao seized the nationalist initiative from the royal Lao government by creating institutions encouraging just such a development. Encouragement of Lao nationalism remains a priority, alone capable of countering Lao Lum exclusivism and nepotism. The contemporary historian can only be dismayed at signs since 1975 that the commitment of the party—in practice rather than theory—may be wavering. When finance was short, schools and clinics in minority regions have been closed first, and positive discrimination, despite some commendable attempts, has gone nowhere near far enough. If the Pathet Lao movement had anything positive to offer the country, it was a universal Lao nationalism, certainly not Marxism. If the present regime fails to carry this commitment over from insurgency to government, it will stand condemned, for its social and economic policies (effective depopulation, nationalisation, co-operativisation) have generally proved to be failures.

PERIODISATION OF LAO HISTORY

The continuities and discontinuities of Lao history impinge on historical narrative in the form of periodisation. How should the story of Laos be divided up for its telling? General histories of Laos are short on the ground. Sila Viravong (1964) stops before the arrival of the French. Le Boulanger (1931) virtually ends with the French in place at the turn of the century. Manich Jumsai (1971) takes events up to the 1960s in a cursory way, after devoting close on a hundred pages to Franco-Siamese relations from 1885 to 1904. Paul Lévy (1974) goes as far as the Second Indochina War in giving a more balanced treatment.

For the classical kingdom of Lan Sang, its creation by Fa Ngum in the mid-fourteenth century and its break-up early in the eighteenth century are pivotal points marking before and after: (1) origins, (2) Lan Sang and (3) division into the principalities of Luang Prabang, Vientiane and Champasak. It is with the division of Lan Sang that problems of periodisation begin. Sila Viravong dates the loss of Lao independence at 1779, the date of the conquest of all three principalities by King Taksin of Siam. He covers the period 1707 to 1779 in Chapter 6 and 1779 to 1893 in Chapter 7. French activities receive no mention except for the brief announcement that 'the territories on the left side of the Mekong River which constitute the present Kingdom of Laos became a French Protectorate' (Sila Viravong 1964: 143). Le Boulanger takes the separate histories of Vientiane and Luang Prabang up to the death of Chao Anuwong (1829) and the accession of Sukkasoem (1836), respectively. Chapters follow on the Siamese expansion and French intervention.[17] Lévy (1974) combines the period from the death of Suriyawongsa (1695) to the French Mekong expedition of 1866 in a single brief chapter entitled 'The Decline', which ignores its last forty years. Separate chapters are devoted to French intervention and French administration.

For Sila Viravong the key consideration has to do with continuation of Laos as an independent political entity. The turning points were the loss of independence and the destruction of Vientiane— two stages in a single downward trajectory. He ends the history of

Vientiane in 1828, after which the history of Laos is the history of Luang Prabang and Champasak, separated by a geographical space that lacks any history at all, since it lacked either ruler or political structure. The same lacuna is to be found in Manich Jumsai, though after 1828 he regards all Laos as incorporated into the Siamese state, administered by three commissioners from Bangkok: one stationed 'at Champasak for the eastern provinces, one at Nongkhai for the northeastern provinces, and one at Luang Prabang' for the north, including the Sipsòng Panna, Sipsòng Chao Tai and Hua Phan (Manich Jumsai 1971). The chapter is illustrated with pictures of the Siamese army and King Chulalongkorn. The same discontinuity is found in Lévy, and in Le Boulanger who also ignores Champasak.

All these authors identify Laos with state structures. Where these are discontinuous, so are their histories. But in that case, can we really write a history of 'Laos' at all? Does not the history of Laos break up into a collection of histories—a history of Lan Sang until 1707, separate histories of Luang Prabang, Vientiane, Siang Khwang and Champasak (each of different duration), a history of French Laos, another of independent Laos—but no history of Laos *tout court*. This is inherently unsatisfactory, for what gets left out is the continuity that links all these histories into one account of the same descent groups—Lao Lum, Lao Thoeng and more recently Lao Sung—inhabiting the same territory, combining to organise themselves, or to resist or adapt to the organisation of others, in a variety of political entities that themselves reflect at various levels one continuing model of political organisation—that of the *müang*. That story must be told, for it is central to the history of Laos.

I have argued that the rebirth of Laos as a political entity dates not from 1893 but from 1945. The French made no attempt to resuscitate the kingdom of Vientiane, or even that of Champasak. Still less did they attempt to resurrect Lan Sang. Only Luang Prabang was restored to something of its previous extent—less any rights over the Haut Mékong (Upper Mekong Province), the fragment of the Sipsòng Panna attached to French Laos and most of the Sipsòng Chao Tai (assigned to Tonkin), though all of Hua Phan was eventually restored to Laos (Gay 1989). Under France, the Lao territories remained divided in a curious legal no-man's land, part protectorate, part colony, neither enjoying the rights of either status (Iché 1935). However, the French period is sufficiently precise—Pavie at Luang Prabang in 1887 to the Japanese *coup de force* of 1945—to constitute a chapter of its own: the prologue to reconstitution of a Lao state.

After 1945, periodisation has tended to take the two Geneva agreements of 1954 and 1962 as the key points. Lévy (1974) does this. So does Hugh Toye (1968). Dommen (1971) focuses on the first and second coalition governments, which at least has the advantage from the point of view of Lao history of stressing internal developments over external conferences. Brown and Zasloff (1986), writing the history of the Pathet Lao movement, also take 1954 and 1962 as crucial turning points. They date the advent of armed struggle from 1959, and give no special significance in terms of periodisation to 1960, the year that Kong Le's coup d'état split the non-communist forces and opened up new opportunities for the Pathet Lao. The third volume of the official history produced by the Committee for Social Science Research of the Ministry of Education of the Lao PDR and published with party approval also takes 1954 and 1962 as major turning points and passes over 1960.[18] Jean Deuve (1985) makes much greater play of 1960, though he also accords significance to 1954 and 1962. For Deuve, however, two other dates are important—1953 and 1957, respectively, when Laos obtained independence from France and when the first coalition government was formed.

If we look at Lao history in terms of continuity and discontinuity, and of unity and division, the period after 1945 saw a struggle to achieve the unity proclaimed by the Lao Issara. A proclamation was not enough. Many Lao supported a continuing French presence. The French hung on for as long as they could, but their hold on Laos was always dependent on their hold on Vietnam. After 1949 the independence forces were divided between those agitating within the existing legal framework and those fighting outside it, a situation which continued even after full and final independence was achieved in 1953. The 1954 Geneva Agreements divided the country between areas controlled by the royal Lao government and by the Pathet Lao. The negotiations leading to formation of the first coalition in 1957 aimed both to heal the split in the Lao Issara going back to 1949, and to restore the unity of the country proclaimed in 1945. Formation of the first coalition for a few brief months finally reconstituted the political and geographical unity of Laos, and in this crucial respect is far more significant than 1954—which is a key date in Vietnamese, rather than Lao, history.

Already, however, Laos was being drawn into the Second Indochina War. International pressures were simply too great to withstand. The United States was adamantly opposed to the inclusion of communists in government, and strongly disliked neutrality in international relations. At the height of the Cold War one had to be either for 'the Free World' or against it. A neutral Laos, in the American view, would necessarily be against it. The collapse of the first coalition was largely due to American machinations. It signalled the failure of Laos to take the path of Cambodia. Sihanouk was able to keep his country out of the war until he was overthrown in 1970. Souvanna would have liked to do the same.[19]

Laos was drawn into the Second Indochina War after 1958 as insurgency was gaining momentum in southern Vietnam. The coup d'état of 1960 and return of Souvanna only plunged the country into further civil conflict and did nothing to extricate Laos from the gathering war. The American change of heart in 1962 to support an internationally guaranteed central government came too late. The damage had been done, the moment lost. Any neutrality for Laos would, like that of Cambodia, have had to be of the kind that turned a blind eye to the transit of Vietnamese forces and supplies through Lao territory down the Ho Chi Minh trail. But this was not the kind of neutrality the United States was prepared to countenance. For Washington, Lao neutrality was a device to prevent that flow, not to pretend it did not exist. The Geneva Agreements of 1962 no more constituted a turning point in Lao history than had the agreements of 1954. The second coalition never re-established either the political or the geographical unity of the country, for Laos was already too far down the path of war and revolution.

That the Lao revolution was aided at every step by the Democratic Republic of Vietnam should not be taken to imply that it was any the less Lao. The radical wing of the Lao Issara that chose to ally itself with the Viet Minh did so with exactly the same goals as those moderates who returned to take part in the political process: namely, to establish the independence and unity of the country, albeit as a communist state (Brown and Zasloff 1986). The advantage the Pathet Lao enjoyed lay not in external support from Vietnam—the right always received far more, first from France then massively from the United States—but in the form of nationalism to which the movement was committed. Both the nationalism and the commitment were crucial. As I have already argued, circumstances made it imperative for the Pathet Lao to embrace a Lao nationalism that transcended ethnic Lao cultural chauvinism to include the entire population. In successfully doing so, the Pathet Lao undermined the nationalist pretensions of the political right whose own claims had been hopelessly compromised by American financial largesse.

The third coalition government formed in 1973 reflected both the changing internal balance of power and the altered geopolitical balance of forces consequent upon American withdrawal from Indochina. The right and left shared the spoils of office. Only Souvanna remained neutral. Souvanna's neutrality, like Sihanouk's, was not ideologically rigid but flexible in form, leading him (again like Sihanouk) to shape policy in response to superior forces in an attempt to maintain a balance, rather than to hew a political line. He had hoped the third coalition would re-establish the gains of the first—the unity of the state and a unified national political culture—but by 1973 this was a forlorn hope. The third coalition merely papered over the division of the country into two separate administrative zones. National unity was no more than a pretence.

The year 1975 did constitute a turning point, but the Pathet Lao victory came at a terrible price. An opportunity did exist to maintain the third coalition government in form at least, with the intractable right excluded. Had it been maintained, 1973 would have marked the crucial turn, not 1975. By destroying the third coalition and replacing it by a government of the Pathet Lao, the victors in the 'seventeen-year struggle'[20] (1958–75) re-established the unity of the state but deliberately withheld the compromises necessary to extend the national political culture that as a movement

19

they had promised. The exclusivity of the party had an effect similar to the exclusivity of ethnic Lao chauvinism, for it effectively denied political participation to a substantial portion of the population. No integration occurred. The result might have been foreseen. The flood of refugees into Thailand, from the narrow perspective of the party, may have reinforced the party's hold on power by eliminating the Lao Lum bourgeoisie, but that meant eliminating 90 percent of the educated class. The depopulation policy of the Pathet Lao proved just as disastrous as any pursued by the Siamese[21] and was something that Laos, of all countries, could ill afford.

Abdication of the king and declaration of a republic was not the really destructive act. The king of Laos never attained the symbolic status of the king of Thailand. Opportunities for this were lost in 1945–6 and again in 1953 when the king should have moved to Vientiane. As it was, the king remained identified with Luang Prabang, a northerner to those of the south. He never became a national monarch. It was termination of the third coalition that destroyed any chance of building a unified political culture after 1975 to include those who had fought on both sides. The Pathet Lao could easily have exercised political control of the government, for the right had been thoroughly discredited and was without external support. The coalition government provided a symbol of political unity: its abolition served notice that unity was to be imposed, not negotiated. It also proved that the new leaders could not be trusted, a conclusion reinforced for those who fled by official prevarication over re-education.[22]

The Lao People's Revolutionary Party (LPRP), by its creation of a single party state, condemned itself to creating a new, unified, national political culture, not on the basis of Lao society as it existed, but by excluding those it did not want. The royal Lao regime had done the same, by excluding both the Pathet Lao and ethnic minorities. Exclusivity continues to be built into the dominant political culture in Laos, and exclusion of some can all too easily be extended to others. The exclusivity of the LPRP in determining to retain a monopoly of political power, even though it goes out of its way to include all ethnic groups in the political life of both party and state, actually creates the preconditions for a recrudescence of the exclusivity of ethnic Lao chauvinism—something that regrettably is already evident in the government's failure to fulfil its promises to the upland minorities (Ireson and Ireson 1991). Both aid and investment in the Lao PDR, as in the Kingdom of Laos, is overwhelmingly concentrated in Lao Lum areas. The minorities have little to show as yet for supporting the revolution.

IN CONCLUSION

I have tried to identify both the discontinuities that so evidently mark Lao history, and the continuities that nevertheless enable a historian to write the history of Laos. While the discontinuities are marked by changes in extent of political control, continuities are ethnic and cultural, descent groups inhabiting geographic territories, sharing a political culture expressed through locally constituted hierarchically organised socio-political structures: the *müang*. These formed the basis for a re-creation of political unity that only came to fruition with the declaration of Lao independence in 1945 and its substantive achievement eight years later. Between 1945 and 1953, however, new divisions arose which were only overcome through formation of the first coalition government in 1957. The struggle for independence and unity, and their political expression through evolution of a genuinely national Lao political culture, constitute dominant themes for the history of Laos post-1945. These form the proper basis for the periodisation of modern and contemporary Lao history, in preference to events provoked by external intervention, for they constitute the priorities for the future on which the continued existence of the Lao state will depend.

NOTES

1. The government of the Lao People's Democratic Republic at first claimed there are sixty-eight different ethnic groups in Laos, though no list was ever published. More recently the number has been reduced to thirty-eight. These are divided into three broad groups: The Lao Lum, or Lao of the valleys, comprise not only ethnic Lao but also upland Tai and account for about 65 percent of the population. The Lao Thoeng, or Lao of the mountain slopes, speaking Mon-Khmer languages, account for around 25 percent. The Lao Sung, or Lao of the mountaintops, speaking Tibeto-Burman languages account for perhaps 10 percent. The terms Lao Lum, Lao Thoeng and Lao Sung will be used to refer to these groups in this paper.

2. This is the term used in the Lao constitution.

3. The classical definition of *mandala* comes from Wolters (1982: 16–7): 'the *mandala* represented a particular and often unstable political situation in a vaguely definable geographical area without fixed boundaries and where smaller centres tended to look in all directions for security. *Mandalas* would expand and contract in concertina-like fashion. Each one contained several tributary rulers, some of whom would repudiate their vassal status when the opportunity arose and try to build up their own networks of vassals.' This concept is especially applicable to the Theravada Buddhist polities of mainland South-East Asia, including early Laos.

4. The interrelationship between traditional Tai-Lao and Buddhist concepts has been examined by Charles Archaimbault (1973). See also Goran Aijmer (1979).

5. The definitive studies of Chao Anuwong are by Mayoury and Pheuiphanh Ngaosyvathn (1988 and 1998).

6. Kennon Breazeale has already made a notable contribution to the history of this period. See, in addition to his thesis cited above, his paper 'Thai Provincial Minority Elites'. Referring to the Isan region, Breazeale notes (1979: 1,669) that 'Lao administration tended in exactly the opposite direction from unification. The ruling families failed to coalesce into hierarchies (as they did in central Thailand) centred around powerful individuals. Rather than combining to consolidate wealth and control over several towns, the ruling families remained independent of one another.'

7. This is well illustrated in the use of Vietnamese civil servants in the French administration of both Laos and Cambodia.

8. Unpublished French archival report, 'Exposé des droits historiques de l'Annam sur le Laos central,' Dépôt des Archives d'Outre-Mer, Aix-en-Provence, Fonds des Amiraux, 14488.

9. Grossin (1933: 38) refers to the debate over whether to *faire le Siam* or *faire le Tonkin.*

10. It was taken for granted until the late 1930s that a railway would be built (Meyer 1931: 55). Plans to encourage migration of Vietnamese into Laos were still being drawn up in the early 1940s (Pietrantoni 1957: 243).

11. For the suggestion that the Lao could be concentrated on reserves, see Aymonier (1895: 64).

12. The driving figure was Prince Phetsarath, buoyed up by the Lao Issara. We still await a detailed study of the events surrounding Phetsarath's proclamation of Lao independence, but see Gunn (1988: 139–47), in which, however, there are some minor inaccuracies.

13. Archaeological evidence for Mon presence in Vientiane and as far north as Luang Prabang is now overwhelming; see Gagneux (1972).

14. Accurate figures for the Tai-Lao population in Thailand are not available, but the combined Lao Thoeng and Lao Sung population of Laos accounts for only about one-third of the total population of Laos.

15. American support for the Hmong commander of military region two, General Vang Pao, during the 'secret war' in northern Laos created a virtually autonomous administration for the Hmong.

16. Apart from the cosmetic addition of Hmong leader Touby Lyfong to the cabinet, nothing was done to bring tribal minorities into the administration.

17. Despite entitling his work *Histoire du Laos français* ('A History of French Laos'), Le Boulanger (1931) has virtually nothing to say about the history of French Laos from 1904 to 1930.

18. Thongsa et al. (1989). Part 1 of this official history covers the period 1893 to 1954; part 2 covers 1954 to 1975; and part 3 runs from 1975 to 1988. Chapter 7 in part 2 covers 1954 to 1962, while chapter 8 runs from 1954 to 1973.

19. No detailed study of Souvanna's crucial role in modern Lao history has yet been undertaken. Deuve, Toye and Dommen are the best sources. On American policy towards Laos, see Stevensen (1977) and Goldstein (1973).

20. This is in contrast to the 'thirty-year struggle' from 1945 to 1975 to bring about the 'national democratic revolution', which presupposes a Marxist theory of history. The 'seventeen-year struggle' might have led to reintegration of opposing political forces in a single national political culture. That it did not in no way invalidates an alternative theoretical perspective.

21. Siamese policy was to depopulate Laos east of the Mekong by forcibly resettling people on the Khorat plateau, or even farther west. Major resettlement of Phuan from Siang Khwang took place as late as 1876–8 (Smuckarn and Breazeale 1988: 53–8).

22. The Party consistently lied to those with relatives undergoing re-education. It thereby destroyed precisely that trust in the regime which had led so many to undertake re-education voluntarily in the first place.

2

WEN DAN AND ITS NEIGHBOURS:
THE CENTRAL MEKONG VALLEY IN THE SEVENTH AND EIGHTH CENTURIES

TATSUO HOSHINO

This chapter discusses the important political entities in the interior of mainland South-East Asia that were known to the Chinese during the seventh and eighth centuries. At the turn of the twentieth century, these and other South-East Asian historical sites were scarcely known to Western scholars, who were beginning to rediscover the toponyms buried in the Chinese annals of the Tang period (AD 618–907). Paul Pelliot, in his monumental 1904 article, repeatedly expressed hesitation as he tried to identify such place-names, and a careful reading of his work shows that he did not expect his conclusions to be definitive. Successive Western scholars, however, have simply accepted works such as those of George Coedès, which depended on the provisional conclusions of earlier twentieth-century sinologists such as Pelliot. Instead of doing so, scholars would have done better to review and reassess the tentative geographical identifications, perhaps once every few decades, in the light of new archaeological findings and ethno-linguistic research. In this regard, it can also be useful to re-examine abandoned theories.

The discussion below scrutinizes the vague but tantalizing geographical references in Chinese texts written more than a millenium ago and attempts to place them side by side with the archaeological discoveries of the past half century. In addition to

This chapter is dedicated to Michel Ferlus.

textual analysis, the study ventures into the realm of linguistic analysis which, although highly speculative, may reveal valuable living links with the distant past and with long forgotten cultures.

TANG SOURCES AND TOPONYMS IN THE TEXTS

Numerous Chinese works of the Tang period have been preserved and contain valuable information for the study of mainland South-East Asia. Among them are the two major annals of that period, *Jiu Tang Shu* ('Old Tang Annals') and *Xin Tang Shu* ('New Tang Annals'); the geographies *Tai Ping Huan Yu Ji* (a geography of the Taiping reign period) and *Yuan He Jun Xian Tu Zhi* (a descriptive geography of the Yuanhe period, with details of prefectures and districts); the historical encyclopaedias *Tai Ping Yu Lan* (an encyclopaedia of the Taiping reign period), *Ce Fu Yuan Gui* (a basic source on pre-Sung government and political history) and *Tang Hui Yao* (a Tang dynasty reference source); and the hagiographies *Da Tang Xi Yu Qiu Fa Gong Song Zhuan* (biographies of Yi Jing and other monks) and Xuan Zhuang's *Da Tang Xi Yu Ji* (a diary of his journey to western lands during the Great Tang period). Additional sources for this period include the Vietnamese annals: *Dai Viet Su Ky Toan Thu* (the complete annals of the Dai Viet) and *Viet Su Luoc* (an abridged history of the Viet). Each of these works provides brief but precious details about South-East Asia—occasionally only a few sentences and sometimes nothing more than place-names.

The long references to the 'southern barbarians' (*Nan Man*) in the new Tang annals first speak about Huan Wang (which was in present-day central Vietnam), Pan Pan (in present-day southern Thailand)[1] and Fu Nan, which was overcome by Zhen La, its former vassal state. The references to Nan Man can be classified by section and occupy the third part (part C) of volume (*juan*) 222 of the new Tang annals (*Xin Tang Shu*, cited hereafter as XTS 222C). The second half of the Zhen La section—which deals with Land Zhen La (*Lu Zhen La*), also known to the Chinese as Wen Dan—is of immense interest to us. South of Zhen La was the intriguing country of He Ling, which was known also by the names She Po and Du Po.

Next the new Tang annals mention the well-known Duo He Luo (Dvaravati, also known as Du He Luo). On its west, Duo He Luo was bounded by the sea, and its neighbours were Zhen La to the east, Jia Luo She Fu to the north and Pan Pan to the south. The inhabitants of southern China may have played an intermediary rôle in reporting local names to the authorities in the capital of Tang China. There were many Chinese, Vietic and Daic dialects, and we can never be sure which groups were involved in sending such reports. Moreover, Tang Chinese officials must have differed somewhat from the indigenous South-East Asian peoples in their pronunciation of South-East Asian toponyms. Despite the millenium that separates us from them, it is still possible to attempt some comparisons, because Chinese historical linguists maintain that modern Cantonese has preserved the Tang-era pronunciation of Chinese.

The three Chinese characters for Dvaravati, for example, are transliterated from Mandarin (using the pinyin system of romanisation) as Duo He Luo. Transliterated from Cantonese, the same three characters can also be romanised as Doh Woh Loh or Duk Woh Loh. (Cantonese transliterations in this study are based on Wong's 1954 syllabary, with slight modifications.) In either Mandarin or Cantonese, we see that the Chinese tend to replace the South-East Asian r with an l, just as the Lao and Shan still do today.

In Cantonese, Hokkien and other dialects, there is another outstanding variation in which l is often interchanged with n.[2] The original pronunciation of Jia Luo She Fu, which is the name of the country to the north of Duo He Luo, could therefore be Jia Nuo She Fu (or some equivalent) in Mandarin. The Cantonese equivalents would be Goh Loh Fat or Ga Loh Fat.

Jia Luo She Fu (Śrī Canāśapūra)

In the same reference dealing with the central part of mainland South-East Asia, Jia Luo She Fu north of Dvaravati reappears and is further explained, but the Chinese authors wrote the name in a slightly different way: Ge Luo She Fen. This state had a common border with Dvaravati, on both its east and its south, which shows that Dvaravati's territory was large enough to wrap around two sides of Jia Luo She Fu, while also reaching the Gulf of Thailand to the west.

The fourth character in the name of Ge Luo She Fen is also found in the name of Xiu Luo Fen. The latter country, like Dvaravati, had Zhen La as a neighbour to its east. The final Chinese character in the names of these two countries (*fen* in Chinese, *bun* in Sino-Japanese) provides a clue to the original name that the South-East Asians adopted from Sanskrit. This character seems to correspond to the variants of the Sanskritic term *pūra* (meaning 'town' or 'city') that are used as suffixes to many South-East Asian town names. The variants *buri* and *bun*, for example, can still be discerned in modern town and province names such as Phetburi, Chanthaburi and Phetchabun, as well as in historical terms such as Si Khottabun, which is a Sanskritic name of the Lao kingdom. Given these considerations, the Chinese name Ge Luo She Fen must derive from a Sanskritic name, and a likely candidate is Śrī Canāśapūra.

An inscription dated AD 937 was found in Ayutthaya and published in a 1944 article by George Coedès. The inscription is written in both the Sanskrit and the Khmer scripts and lists the kings who ruled Śrī Canāśapūra. Another text (known as the Bo Ika inscription) was discovered in the extreme south-west corner of the Mekong basin at the site of Sima, west of modern Nakhòn Ratchasima. It describes a donation by a Śrī Canāśapūra king to a Buddhist monastery, and Coedès (*Inscriptions* 1954 vi: 83–5) thought it was written in the seventh century.

Dvaravati

The XTS account of Dvaravati (Duo He Luo) is poorly composed. The country's geographical position is described in terms of adjacent countries and of the five-month journey necessary to reach it from Guangzhou. The new Tang annals provide a detailed description of its two vassal states but none of Duo He Luo itself. The section next describes Duo Po Deng, which is mentioned in the previous section on He Ling together with Duo He Luo. The entries for He Ling and Duo He Luo should perhaps be regarded as a separate section, following the one on Zhen La. After the Duo Po Deng section, there is a long and detailed description of Tou He, a country with a name similiar to Duo He Luo and whose king's name was Tou He Luo (the character *luo* very likely being identical to the *dvara* element in Dvaravati). The new Tang annals provide a full account of major countries. Duo He Luo is mentioned several times before and after this account of Tou He, and it is treated as a major country with vassal states.

Zhan Bo

The Chinese writers list the countries in a specific geographical order, beginning with those closest to China and proceeding to each successive, contiguous country in its turn. A few sentences that perplexed Pelliot are inserted in the annals between the account of Tou He and the accounts of Ge Luo She Fen, Xiu Luo Fen and Gan Bi, which were contiguous with Champa. Pelliot thought that the geographical position assigned to these sentences in the text was an editorial mistake and that they ought to appear in the section about India rather than the section about South-East Asia. The passage lists two different names—Zhan Bo[3] and Zhan Po—for a country that had a river called the 'Ganges' and was noted for the abundance of its wild elephants. The passage also provides information about various places in this area.

Significance of the Ganges

The new Tang annals place Zhan Bo (or Zhan Po) south of the Jiang Jiahe (Ging Gahoh in Cantonese), which is the Chinese name for the River Ganges in India. The description, however, does not correspond to the geography of India. On the other hand, the people who lived along the Mekong had, for centuries, received Indian legends through their Hindu and Buddhist religious activities. The toponym Champa Nakhòn, for example, has always been found in Lao literature, and this literature (in the Lao version of the Ramayana, for example) compares the Mekong with the Ganges. More convincing evidence for this argument could be provided by South-East Asian stone carvings depicting Indian myths. It is possible that, during the Tang era, the name 'Ganges' was used in reference to the Mekong—the biggest river in the heartland of South-East Asia—especially by Indians and by the most knowledgeable indigenous people.

Zhan Bo Tribute Mission in 656–61

Zhan Bo, which was south of the Mekong, sent tribute to the Chinese court during the Xian Qing reign (656–61) of Emperor Gao Zong. Tribute was sent also during this period by four other countries: (1) Po An (Poh Ngohn), (2) Qian Zhi Fu or Gan Zhi Fu (Tsin or Gohn Dzi Fat), (3) She Ba Ruo (Sae Bat Jae or Sae But Jae, although another Cantonese rendering of the character for *jae* is *joek*) and (4) Mo La (Moh Lap). The text conveys the impression that these five countries were confederated politically and economically and that they differed culturally from the coastal region dominated by Dvaravati.

The new Tang annals have more to say about Qian/Gan Zhi Fu (which probably had one of the South-East Asian toponyms with a *pura* or *buri* suffix, reflected in the Chinese character *fu*). This city was once a south Indian colony, and it was also known as Ban Zhi Ba (meaning 'Five Hills'). Pelliot hesitatingly identified the place as Kancipura (Conjeveram) in South India, which has a mountain with five peaks.

According to the Tang annals, the country north of Qian/Gan Zhi Fu was called Duo Mo Chang (Doh Moh Dzoeng), and it could be traversed in one month from east to west or twenty-five days from south to north. The ruler of this country had an army of 20,000 men, equipped with various kinds of weapons but no horses. East of Duo Mo Chang was Po Feng (Poh Fung); to the west was Duo Long (Doh Lung); and to the north was He Ling (Hoh Ling). From Duo Mo Chang, travellers could reach Jiaozhou (Gau Dzau), the Tang provincial capital in the Red River delta, by passing through Sa Lu (Sat Lou), Du He Lu (Dou Hoh Lou), Jun Na Lu (Gwan Na Lou) and Lin Yi (Lam Jap). Lin Yi is usually identified as the forerunner of Champa in modern-day central Vietnam.

He Ling: One Name Applied to Two Sites

Anyone attempting to identify these Tang Chinese place names has to accept that some of them designate more than one place. Among the limited examples of such usage are He Ling (Hoh Ling) and Du Po (Dou Poh), which some past historians supposed were Kalinga and the island of Java, respectively. Another point, as we have seen above, is that Tang Chinese records tend to write the name of a single place in different ways, using different characters or shortened forms. One typical example is Dvaravati, for which the new Tang annals use four combinations of characters (1) Duo He Luo, (2) Du He Luo, (3) Tou He and (4) Duo Luo Bo Di.[4]

If the first-mentioned He Ling (south of Zhen La) is the same as the second-mentioned one (north of Duo Mo Chang), then Qian/Gan Zhi Fu must have been far away, at the southernmost extremity of Asia known to the Chinese at that time, because Dou Mo Chang was to the north of it. And it had to be one of four countries that looked north towards a 'Champa' that was south of a 'Ganges' when they sent tribute to China.

We cannot find a river large enough to be comparable with the Ganges in the islands of South-East Asia. Australia was not only unknown at that time but also unquestionably not Indianised. This point needs emphasis. Pelliot, Coedès and other distinguished scholars thought that the first-mentioned (southern) He Ling was on the island of Java, because Java was south of Zhen La and also because the Chinese were likely to use another name, Du Po, when they transcribed the name Java. Given that Java is south of Cambodia, then to fit the location described in the new Tang annals, 'Champa' (with the 'Ganges' River north of it) must have been in Australia! Obviously, such a line of reasoning leads to no conclusion.

He Ling: The Upper Mekong State

The first-mentioned (southern) He Ling must either have been Zhen La's immediate southern neighbour or a little farther south —although certainly not so far south as the archipelago beyond the South China Sea. (Its exact boundaries are not known, but it must have encompassed present-day southern Cambodia, extending as far west as Chanthaburi and east to Vietnam's Phu Quoc Island or probably even as far east as the lower Dong-nai River valley.) Given the relative geographical positions described in the annals, a second (northern) He Ling must have existed, probably in the northern part of the Mekong valley, in the area later known as Sipsòng Panna. Evidence for this view exists in the text of the new Tang annals itself.

Strangely enough, Pelliot mentions the evidence in his 1904 article. In his exhaustive search, he discovered another reference to He Ling in a biography of Wei Gao—a Tang Chinese hero who was an official in Yunnan and who, in alliance with the Tibetans, defeated the army of Nan Zhao. In 793 two of Wei's generals attacked and occupied a dozen enemy towns; as a result, eight chieftains of the West Mountain tribes came before Wei to pledge their allegiance. Each of the eight tribal lands is listed in the biography as a 'country' (*guo*), and the second one in the list was called He Ling. (The Chinese characters for this name are identical to those for the He Ling that was south of Zhen La.) This He Ling must be the one that was north of the broad territory known as Duo Mo Chang, which in turn was north of Qian/Gan Zhi Fu.

Qian/Gan Zhi Fu (Śrī Canāśapūra)

Qian/Gan Zhi Fu, as stated earlier, was formerly a city of south Indians. It was no longer an Indian colony, however, by the time that reports about it were sent to Tang-period China and by the time that its ruler (together with the rulers of the inland Champa and other countries) sent tribute to the Tang capital. Moreover, the description of Jia Luo She Fu (identified above as Śrī Canāśapūra) matches the new Tang annals account of Qian/Gan Zhi Fu in the notices concerning Dvaravati and the region that surrounded it.

ARCHAEOLOGICAL SITES ACROSS THE MAINLAND

At this point, it would be useful to review some of the archaeological sites of mainland South-East Asia, to show how the Chinese toponyms of the Tang-period texts might fit into the archaeological map and to consider what the texts may reveal to historians. The Chinese names for Dvaravati (such as Duo He Luo) in the new Tang annals and in other Tang records (such as the hagiography *Da Tang Xi Yu Ji*) seem to designate an area encompassing the Bang Pakong river valley, south-east of present-day Bangkok. Lopburi could have been within its sphere at one time, probably during the middle and late Tang period (see fig. 1 for the coastline of the Gulf at that time).

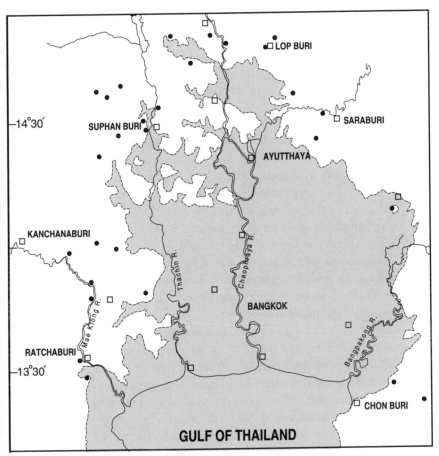

Fig. 1. Gulf Coastline of the Dvaravati Period, Seventh Century
Source: Compiled by Thiva Supajanya, 1987

Śrī Canāśapūra

The evidence indicates that Śrī Canāśapūra was an inland country
and had neither a port nor access to the seacoast.[5] One of the two
reports on this state places it to the north of Dvaravati, whereas the
other report specifies that its eastern boundary was continguous with
Dvaravati. We do not know when this territorial change took place,
but a comparison of the Chinese descriptions reveals that, at some
time between the dates of the two reports, Dvaravati expanded

towards the north-east, and it gained control of the area of modern-day Nakhòn Ratchasima and Chaiyaphum. As a result of Dvaravati's expansion, Śrī Canāśapūra relinquished control of the Nakhòn Ratchasima area, and its territory receded to the original core in the northern half of the Chao Phraya plain and the Sak River valley.

Qian/Gan Zhi Fu

Qian/Gan Zhi Fu must have been a settlement of south Indians in an inland place that was contiguous with the north-east region (Isan) of present-day Thailand, adjacent parts of the Mekong valley and Vietnam. Two very probable candidates are Lopburi and Sri Thep (Śrī Deva in the Sanskrit form). Qian/Gan Zhi Fu must initially have had strong ties with the home country in southern India, but at some point the ties were discontinued. It may be presumed that Dvaravati and Śrī Canāśapūra played a greater rôle in the process of making this settlement more South-East Asian in character than did the Khmer, who began their expansion in this direction in the tenth century. The inscription with the list of Śrī Canāśapūra kings is dated in the first half of the same century and contains Khmer vocabulary. Since the last entry in the new Tang annals is dated 907, the process must have taken place during the eighth and ninth centuries. Given the material evidence—the sacred hills at Sri Thep, the fact that the earliest Sanskrit inscriptions were written there, and the fine sculptures found in the vicinity of the town—Qian/Gan Zhi Fu could be a pre-Angkorian appellation for Sri Thep rather than for Lopburi. The name could have been used as an alternate in later centuries by descendants of coastal sailing Chinese or Malay seamen.[6]

Zhan Bo

Zhan Bo was in the middle Mekong basin and was apparently an important place. It is mentioned as the foremost among five states in this area, another of which was Qian/Gan Zhi Fu. It is also listed as one of the seventeen vassal states of Piao (the empire of the Pyu kings in present-day Burma) in the Piao section of the same volume of the annal. Zhan Bo was geographically between the two super-powers of the region and was therefore obliged to pay tribute to both.

In the same section of the annal, after the entry for Zhan Bo, there is a second toponym of interest to this study: Du Po. (The Chinese characters for this Du Po are identical to those for the Du Po identified as Java, but in this case the reference is to another of Piao's vassals.) Zhan Bo and Du Po were probably contiguous, because the two names appear one after the other in the list of the seventeen vassals. Moreover, they are listed in a separate entry, at the end of the list of Piao's vassals, as though Piao had no close relations with them. They were certainly separated from Piao by mountain ranges, and perhaps they sent tribute to Piao only on an irregular basis.

The state called Du Po was in contact with Chinese who probably resided in Yunnan, and the Chinese officials even knew that Piao was called Tu Li Zhuo (Tou Lei/Nei Dzyt) in the Du Po language. The new Tang annals also say that Piao was formerly known as Zhu Bo (Dzy Boh). One is tempted to say that the latter rendering of the name sounds more like 'Java' than Du Po does. Contrary to earlier theories, these 'Javas' were unquestionably not in the archipelago that constitutes modern Indonesia.

Drawing upon the discussion of the middle Mekong presented thus far, it would be helpful to identify possible sites of Zhan Bo and to determine the period of the Tang dynasty in which its rulers either were displaced from or abandoned their capital. The center of Zhan Bo was somewhere to the south of the Mekong. It may have been in the plain that extends along the Mekong from Loei to Nakhòn Phanom—the area that supported the much earlier Ban Chiang culture. Or possibly it was slightly to the south and lay on the other side of the Phu Phan range of mountains, in present-day central Isan.[7]

Zhan Bo's embassy to the Tang court, recorded in the new Tang annals during the 656–61 Xian Qing reign, coincided with an embassy in 655 from Ju Lou Mi (Koey Lau Mat), which is likewise recorded in the new Tang annals and also in *Tang Hui Yao* (THY 100). Ju Lou Mi was in the Champasak area. Six days to its northwest was Wen Dan.[8] The encyclopaedic dictionary (*Tang Hui Yao*) contains very valuable information, because its compilers preserved details that are not mentioned by the annalists. Pelliot used this source often in his study, but he surprisingly dismissed the record of this particular embassy from Ju Lou Mi. He thought that Wen Dan did not yet exist in that year, although he did not explain how he reached that conclusion. He wrote: 'the reading "Wen-tan" ['Wen Dan' in the modern pinyin system] is surely a faulty one, and it should be read "Tan-tan".' According to his theory, the state that was six days from Wen Dan had to be in the Indonesian archipelago. Since he knew that such a location was impossible, his only recourse was to change the Tang text to suit his theory.

The two embassies, which are recorded in two different Tang sources, are the key to the generations-old problem of Wen Dan. Scholars who have considered this problem include Bastian (1866–71), Schlegel, Pelliot (1904), Lefèvre-Pontalis (1914), Maspero (1918), Seidenfaden (1922), Dupont (1943) and Sugimoto (1956).

United Zhen La and Dvaravati

As mentioned earlier, the description in the Zhen La section of the new Tang annals is of supreme interest, and it will be useful here to summarise the first part of this section. Zhen La was known by another name: Ji Mie (Gat Mit in Cantonese). At an earlier time, it was a vassal state of Fu Nan. Its western neighbours were vassals of Piao, or at least they sent tribute to Piao's rulers. On its north it was contiguous with Dao Ming (Dou Ming), and on its north-east it extended as far as the territory of Huanzhou (in the present day Vinh and Ha-tinh area of Vietnam). The people were on good terms with (and went often to) Piao and Can Ban (Sam Bun or Tsam Bun). The king of Zhen La, who possessed 5,000 war elephants, attacked and was attacked by Huan Wang (Champa)[9] and a second state: Qian Tuo Huan. The name of this second state corresponds exactly to the Tuo Huan (Nou Tuo Huan)[10] described in the new Tang annals as one of the vassal states of Dvaravati: pre-Khmer Lopburi.

According to the new Tang annals, many wars were fought between Zhen La and Lopburi during the Tang period. Some of these conflicts could have been connected with the wars between Lopburi and Hariphunchai, which are recorded in various Thai-language works, such as *Jinakalamalini*, *Munlasatsana* and *Cham-*

thewiwong. In Tang Chinese sources, Zhen La's wars with Huan Wang (the Champa that was in present-day central Vietnam) are mentioned first, and thus given more prominence than those with Qian Tuo Huan (Lopburi), which implies that the wars on Zhen La's eastern front were more frequent and graver than those on the western front. The invaders of the two states most probably used the Ai Lao (or Lao Bao) pass as an attack route. This fact is important for determining the exact location of Wen Dan in the seventh and eighth centuries.

Wen Dan could not have been in south Laos or in the southern part of Isan, especially in the latter half of the eighth century. An Angkorian inscription in Sanskrit, found at Baphuon and dated 790, says that Indrayudha (whose father was the Khmer king Jayavarman II) as a young man captured a king of Champa (Coedès, *Inscriptions du Cambodge* 1964 vii, Baphuon inscription, K. 583). But which Champa does this inscription refer to? Was it the Champa in central Vietnam (Huan Wang), the one in southern Laos (Ju Lou Mi, formerly known as south Lin Yi) or the one in Isan (Zhan Bo)? Given our present knowledge, no identification can be made.

I have been following Pelliot and have agreed with him in identifying inland Champa with the Chinese Zhan Bo. But is it realistic to suppose that two countries with identical names existed in the same area and at the same time? Such nomenclature would seem to be impractical. Then why was Zhan Bo, which was south of the Mekong, called 'Champa' by the Chinese during the Tang period? It is conceivable that the name migrated with the people and that the Chinese applied the original name when referring to a new area where the migrants from Champa settled. The Chinese may then have assigned a different name to the original territory (now in central Vietnam) that was formerly known as Champa. Similarly, the inhabitants of Zhen La must have had a name of their own (other than 'Champa') for Zhan Bo.

Does the name Zhan Bo really refer to Champa? Nothing is absolutely certain in the reconstruction of ancient history. The opinion expressed here could be rejected, since it is not founded on sure evidence. Anyone who compares a map of the middle Mekong basin with one of the lower Ganges will be struck by a similarity:

the shapes of the great southward bends in both rivers are very similar. Given that the original Champa in ancient India was southwest of the great curve of the Ganges, did some Indians from north India discover this curve in the Mekong and therefore name the surrounding territory 'Champa'? If this is the case, we cannot use the same argument to explain why the coastal territory in present-day central Vietnam was called by the same name.

Tai Migrants to the Mekong

One major problem should not be neglected. Is it plausible to argue that Tai-speaking people migrated into the area of present-day Isan by the eighth century? If they were concentrated in a new Champa—in the valleys and flat lands of the middle Mekong—might they have advanced farther west to the Chao Phraya basin? It is probable that an early group of south-west Tai—perhaps Chamberlain's (1972 and 1991) Ph/B group—migrated from the southern part of Chinese-dominated Vietnam (Thanh-hoa and Nghe-tinh Provinces) and settled in the middle Mekong area during the fifth and sixth centuries. Over the course of several subsequent centuries, they could have spread across Isan and down into the Chao Phraya basin. This argument is supported by two assumptions. First, the earliest possible date for the westward migration of these Tai, whose language was tonal when they left Chinese-controlled Vietnam, seems to be the third century (Haudricourt 1972). Second, the history of Champa, as reported in Chinese and Vietnamese records, is difficult to understand unless one assumes that its northern part was inhabited by Tai-speaking peoples.

As an example, assuming that Śrī Canāśapūra was already Tai-dominated in the eighth century, since the earliest evidence about this state came from the Nakhòn Ratchasima region according to Coedès (*Inscriptions* 1954 vi: 83–5, Bo Ika inscription, K. 400), we might interpret history in the following manner: the Tai wanted to gain access to the Gulf (called Da Hai or Dai Hohi in the Chinese sources) by way of the Bang Pakong River, but they were barred along this route—initially by the Mon of Dvaravati and later by the expanding Khmer empire. They therefore moved west and settled in the Sak River valley and other lands north of coastal Dvaravati (see fig. 1, which shows the approximate coastline of the Gulf during the Tang era).

Attention has already been drawn to the Duo He Luo section of the Chinese records, which attributes two different geographical positions to Jia Luo She Fu in relation to Duo He Luo. In one reference, Śrī Canāśapūra (Jia Luo She Fu) was in the southern part of Nan Hai (Nam Hohi), which this study identifies with the middle Mekong basin, in contrast to Xi Nan Hai (Sai Nam Hohi), which was in the Chao Phraya basin (where Qian/Gan Zhi Fu was located). This reference must have been drawn from an early Tang report that was collated with a later report saying that Ge Luo She Fen was west of Duo He Luo. The compilers of the Chinese annals were usually conscious of chronological differences between their sources, and they seem to have placed the oldest record of Dvara-vati's geographic position first in the text. Thus, when they provided a short history of events and the Chinese relationship with the country, the text would appear to be in perfect chronological order.

WEN DAN

Etymology of the Name

Another linguistic reason for supposing that Tai or early Daic speakers already inhabited Isan and the upper reaches of the Chao Phraya basin is the existence of toponyms such as Wen Dan, other 'Wen' (also transliterated as Mahn) and Can Ban.[11] These names provide very important clues concerning ethnicity. Wen Dan, once reconstructed in my experimental but not yet systematic way, is a simple Daic name: Man Sem (or Man Sham) meaning 'Siamese villages'.[12] The whole name that appears in the Chinese sources— Wen Dan *guo*—can therefore be translated literally as the 'land of Siamese villages'. Daic dialects that use the term *man* for 'village' are spread across an area in Yunnan and Burma that is a P dialect area, according to Chamberlain's (1972 and 1991) classification. But no P dialects are known today in the middle Mekong and Chao

Phraya plain, with the exception of the Müang (northern Thai) villages in north Laos. Is it not probable, given the textual and living evidence, that the middle Mekong was also a P area before receiving the Ph cultural-linguistic wave?

Wen Dan's Vassals: Dao Ming and Can Ban

Wen Dan had two vassals. The northern one was called Dao Ming by the Chinese. This name is possibly a Chinese rendering of the Tai term *thao müang*, which means a vassal prince or chief. According to the brief description that has survived, the inhabitants wore almost no clothing, went about nearly naked, lived by hunting, and had neither salt nor iron. Given our present knowledge of ancient salt and iron industries, this state must have been outside the Isan area. Dao Ming was in the northern part of the Mekong valley, straddling the watershed north of the Vientiane plain (which has a salt mine at Ban Bò). Although this scrap of information seems miniscule at first glance, it is very important. Salt and iron may have been important commodities produced in Wen Dan. The Chinese of every era of history had a great interest in identifying local products because of the commercial and political advantages that could be drawn from them. By advising officials to take no notice of Dao Ming, which had no products of value to the Chinese, the compilers of this report were probably drawing a comparison with Land Zhen La, whose trade was already known to be relatively valuable.

The north-western Wen Dan vassal was Can Ban.[13] Can Ban is explained twice in the context of its relationship to Zhen La. The early Chinese references indicate that this state had frequent contacts and was on good terms with united Zhen La. In 625 and again in 628, Can Ban apparently sent tribute, which arrived in China simultaneous with tribute from united Zhen La (see the encyclopaedia *Ce Fu Yuan Gui* 970: 5–6 and Song edition, pp. 3–4). Another thirty years passed, however, before the Tang court received the first tribute mission from Wen Dan. By the time of the later references, Can Ban had become a vassal of Land Zhen La—that is, Wen Dan.

What happened in the interim between the dates reflected in

these references? The new overlord was known to the Chinese as both Land Zhen La and Wen Dan. Its capital was known to the Chinese as Po Lou, which is apparently a Chinese rendering of the Sanskritic term *pura*, meaning 'city'. Po Lou's growth was rapid. During the years 705–7 it separated from the lower part of Zhen La and became an independent state. Was the embassy that it sent in the second half of the 650s an assertion of its independence? In any case, China responded favourably.

The site of Can Ban, which is described in the new Tang annals as north-west of Wen Dan, can be identified with some certainty. It is mentioned as one of two states that were the most friendly to, and made the most frequent contacts with, Zhen La throughout the Tang period, both before and after Zhen La split into at least two (and probably more) states around 705–7. Can Ban could not have been in the north of present-day Thailand, although Tai settlements may already have existed in these northern valleys in the eighth century. It must have been slightly to the south, in the central plain region. It must also have been friendly with Indianised, united Zhen La from the time of King Mahendravarman, who is known for his inscriptions north of the Dong Rak range and is cited in the annals of the Sui dynasty (581–618) as the first king of Zhen La.[14]

The second of the most friendly states was Piao. Piao was farther from Zhen La than was Can Ban. It was also powerful enough to force all of the states west of Zhen La to become its vassals or tribute-paying neighbours. The records mention Can Ban before they mention Piao. The order of the names in the records and the political relationships are understandable, if the following assumptions are made about Wen Dan. First, it was a landlocked state in present-day Isan. Second, it was an expanding power. And third, it was seeking access to a seaport, but was blocked because Dvaravati controlled the south-west corner of Isan—that is, the area of modern Nakhòn Ratchasima, which dominated the trails leading across the mountains and down to the rivers that flow into the Gulf.

Given all these assumptions and qualifications, the most likely site for Can Ban would appear to be Sri Thep. This site, however, is south-south-west of Fa Daet (the likely central-Isan site of Wen Dan's capital), whereas the records specify that Can Ban lay to the north-west.

Therefore, the administrative seat of Can Ban may have been a local communications hub, although not a place of great political or commercial importance, farther up in the Sak River valley.

The encyclopaedia *Ce Fu Yuan Gui* (957), which is dated 1013, indicates that Can Ban was more than 1,000 *li* (more than 500 kilometres) south-west of Land Zhen La. It was close to the Gulf, and the site of the town was swampy. If this record describes Can Ban in the ninth and tenth centuries, the administrative seat must have moved by this time to a new site, which most likely was Suphanburi.

FEDERATION OF TOWNS HEADED BY ZHAN BO, THEIR SITES AND EMBASSY TO CHINA

Sri Thep was friendly to, and perhaps an ally of, Zhan Bo, the state that led the embassy to Chang-an (modern Xian), the capital of China, during the 656–61 reign. This embassy was epoch-making because Qian/Gan Zhi Fu (the old Indianised state) and three other states were, by this time, politically federated with inland Zhan Bo. The whole group appears to have been a chain of new states. Their federation resembles the short-lived relationships of princes and chiefs in the chain of states mentioned more than 500 years later in the Ram Khamhaeng inscription, although the chain headed by Zhan Bo consisted of only five little states.

Could Qian/Gan Zhi Fu be Śrī Canāśapūra, whose territory extended as far as Nakhòn Ratchasima in the seventh century? An affirmative answer to this question is given by Dhida Saraya (1985).

Among the other three states of the federation, She Ba Ruo is mentioned in the encyclopaedia immediately after Qian/Gan Zhi Fu, which suggests that it was south of Sri Thep. Po An seems to have been geographically closest to Zhan Bo.[15] The name of the fifth state, Mo La, resembles the name Mloi, which was previously used by the Vietnamese in reference to the Cham. If the ancient name has been perpetuated in the name Mloi, then Mo La could have been a Cham seaport town that served the trade lanes of the South China Sea. If this theory is correct, the tribute-bearers from the five federated states could have boarded Austronesian ships at the Cham port and sailed north to the coast of China. They would then have proceeded inland to the Chinese capital, Chang-an, which is on a tributary of the Yellow River.

IDENTIFICATION OF SITES

Zhan Bo in Isan

Zhan Bo was most probably in the central part of Isan, south of the Phu Phan range. According to the description in the Chinese, Zhan Bo 'extended [the verb here is *ju*] towards the north for some distance up to the Ganges'. Since it is clear that Zhan Bo was not on the Mekong itself, why then was it also called Champa? Did it have an Indianised city name at all? One possible explanation has been offered by researchers at the Cham research center in Phan-rang. That is, the name Champa may have been adopted from the name of a flower beloved everywhere in South-East Asia: the plumeria (known in India as *frangipani*). In this and many other cases, the argument about the origin of the toponym has to be de-Indianised, except where city names with the suffix *pura* (and its South-East Asian equivalents) are concerned.

Ju Lou Mi in the Region of Ubon and Stung Treng

The toponym Ju Lou Mi poses one such problem that can be solved with ease if it is de-Indianised. At the end of the long and important section on Huan Wang (Champa) in the new Tang annals, it is said that Ju Lou Mi (Koey Lau Mat) was in the south-eastern part of Nan Hai. It was therefore in the middle-Mekong area that roughly encompasses present-day Ubon, Champasak and Stung Treng, and perhaps as far down-river as Kracheh. From Huan Wang, this state could be reached by water routes within a month.[16]

According to the Tang-period Chinese geography, an additional six-day journey in a north-west direction was required to go from Ju Lou Mi to Wen Dan—or more precisely, to the administrative centre of Wen Dan.[17] We do not know the site of Ju Lou Mi's administrative centre or the extent of its territory. But, given that it

43

straddled the Mekong, above and below the confluent of the Mun, we can imagine a journey of six days beginning along this stretch of the Mekong—a journey that would terminate somewhere in the present-day provinces of Ròi Et, Maha Sarakham or Kalasin. In the area where the boundaries of these three provinces meet, three important archaeological sites have been investigated: Fa Daet, Kanthara Wichai and Nakhòn Champa Sri.

I have visited these sites several times, in an effort to determine whether they correspond to the Chinese toponyms. A clue to the identification of exact sites is provided in the Chinese observation that Land Zhen La had two capitals: an outer city and an inner city.

A system of two capitals is not a rarity in the early Tai or even the later Lao and Thai kingdoms. Luang Prabang, for example, was known by an old double name: Siang Dong and Siang Thòng. The Sukhothai kingdom had a second capital at Sri Satchanalai. In the Lan Na kingdom, King Mangrai lived in Wiang Khumkan (a village between Chiang Mai and Lamphun), even after he built his large, fortified and moated capital at Chiang Mai. Vientiane, another fortified and moated capital, was similarly paired with a tiny village: Wiang Kham on the Ngum River. Lopburi and Ayutthaya likewise were paired capitals.

Chinese sources provide evidence of this dual-capital system as early as the seventh century. The historical encyclopaedia *Ce Fu Yuan Gui* states that in 657 'Zhan *guo* Bo *guo*' sent a tribute mission to China (CFYG 970: 15 and Song edition, p. 9). At a later time, Zhan Bo was regarded as a single entity, but this reference clearly means two places: Zhan and Bo. The way this name is written in the Chinese encyclopaedia—with *guo* in each instance meaning a 'state' or 'kingdom'—is probably not a printing mistake. Instead, it probably refers to two different administrative centres. This record reflects the dual-capital system that evolved into a group of royal cities in an area governed by a single ruling family. Wen Dan seems to be an early example of this tradition. Given these considerations, a tentative match can be made between the textual and the archaeological evidence.

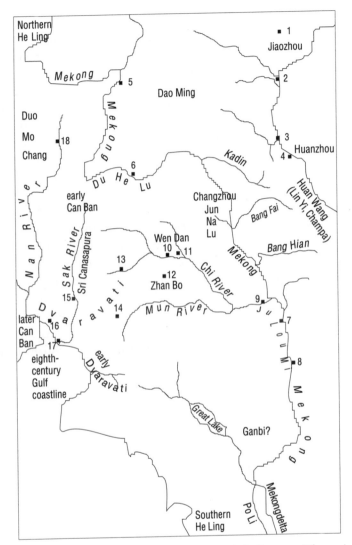

Fig. 2. The Central Mekong Basin in the Eighth Century: Theoretical Political Divisions

Key to Present-Day Sites: 1. Hanoi, 2. Thanh Hoa, 3. Vinh, 4. Ha Tinh, 5. Luang Prabang, 6. Vientiane, 7. Champasak, 8. Stung Treng, 9. Ubon, 10. Kanthara Wichai, 11. Fa Daet, 12. Nakhòn Champa Sri, 13. Chaiya-phum, 14. Nakhòn Ratchasima, 15. Sri Thep, 16. Lop Buri, 17. Saraburi, 18. Nan

Wen Dan and Zhan Bo

Most likely, Wen Dan had an outer capital (known as Wai Cheng to the Chinese) at the site of modern Fa Daet. The inner capital (called Nei Cheng in the new Tang annals), where the king of Wen Dan resided, was at the site of modern Kanthara Wichai (see fig. 2).[18] If this identification is correct, Zhan Bo must therefore have been at the site of Nakhòn Champa Sri, in present-day Na Dun Subdistrict of Maha Sarakham Province. The memory of the state's ancient name, Champa, has thus been preserved to the present day. Although these conclusions concerning these three sites are only tentative, they seem consistent with the textual evidence preserved by the Chinese.

Excavations in 1991 at Fa Daet revealed prehistoric graves on a large mound or hill, known as Dòn Müang Kao (literally the 'mound of the old town'). The base of the Buddhist stupa, known as That Yakhu (and popularly as That Yai, the 'great stupa'), may date from the early Dvaravati period. Stucco figures found at the site might be from a slightly later period. Although some Dvaravati-style artifacts have been found at Nakhòn Champa Sri, it is obvious to the trained eye that this site is more Khmer (Angkorian) than Mon (Dvaravati), although some of the moat could belong to the Dvaravati period.

Gan Bi

In the middle Mekong area, there was another state called Gan Bi by the Tang-period Chinese, and it could mobilise 5,000 soldiers.[19] Gan Bi's territory, as described in the new Tang annals, extended eastward for some distance and was contiguous with the territory of Huan Wang (modern central Vietnam). The site of Gan Bi was therefore north of Ju Lou Mi—the 'down-river' (krom) Khmer kingdom—and it was probably in the vicinity of present-day Savannakhet.

TRIBUTE MISSIONS TO CHINA

An entry in a Tang-period dictionary (Tang Hui Yao 100) states that Ju Lou Mi sent tribute to the Tang court in the year 655. Ju

Lou Mi was six days to the south-east of Wen Dan, and it has been identified as the Champasak region, in the vicinity of the confluent of the Mun and Mekong Rivers. During the Xian Qing reign (656–61), a number of other missions from the central Mekong arrived in the Chinese capital bearing tribute. After the first mission from Ju Lou Mi was received in 655, the Tang court welcomed a second, and larger, one from the same area. A mission arrived in 657 from Zhan Bo, the site of which is identified above as Nakhòn Champa Sri. It led a group of others from Po An (possibly modern Phon), Qian/Gan Zhi Fu (modern Sri Thep) and She Ba Ruo (modern Suphanburi). The last delegation in this group was from Mo La, which could have been either a Malay or a Mon town. In receiving this group of envoys, the Tang rulers must have acknow-ledged the leadership of Zhan Bo, which had two chiefs who must have been connected by some family tie.

Wen Dan was a late-comer to the tribute system, in comparison with other tribute-sending states in South-East Asia, which had the advantage of being as much as several hundred kilometres closer to the seacoast. (Only one state—He Ling, also called Du Po—entered the system after Wen Dan did.) The first mission was sent from the Wen Dan/Zhan Bo region during the Xian Qing reign—that is, sometime between 656 and 661. By the time of the second mission in 717, Wen Dan was definitely no longer linked to the formerly united Zhen La. According to the encyclopaedia *Ce Fu Yuan Gui* (CFYG 971: 2 and Song edition, p. 1), Zhen La's tribute in 717 was received simultaneously with, but separately from, Wen Dan's.

In the second half of the eighth century, Wen Dan sent three or four tribute missions to the Tang court. Tribute may have been sent in the 750s to commemorate the first mission to China, which had arrived a century earlier. Both of these missions brought rhino-ceroses to the Chinese court. A striking parallel is found in the records concerning Zhen La, which likewise sent two missions, roughly a century apart, each bearing rhinoceroses along with other items of tribute. According to the new Tang annals, tribute was received in 657 from Zhan Bo and the four countries to its west. Another source (CFYG 970: 15 and Song edition, p. 9) specifies that the envoys from 'Zhan *guo* Bo *guo*' presented elephants and rhinoceroses to the emperor in the same year of the Xian Qing reign (656–661). Nearly a century later, in 750, a tribute mission (probably from Zhen La) is recorded in the historical encyclopaedia *Ce Fu Yuan Gui*, and it, too, brought one or two rhinoceroses.[20]

The independence movement in upper Zhen La is mentioned above because, a half-century after the 656–661 tribute missions took place, Zhen La (which conquered Fu Nan in 627–634) split into at least two states, known as Land (*lu*) Zhen La and Water (*shui*) Zhen La. The original state may even have disintegrated into many small autonomous states. There would seem to be more reasons behind the rush of tribute-bearing missions during 656–661 than just a movement inside the old Zhen La state.

On the other hand, permanent large-scale 'united Zhen La' sites are not well confirmed in the southern part of Isan, not even in the places where small stone inscriptions, carved lintels and other sculptures have been discovered. The rulers of the northern Zhen La area may have pledged their allegiance to a king of united Zhen La, while simultaneously sending tribute to China independently, perhaps simply for commercial gain. Such an allegiance was a personal promise made by one ruler to his suzerain. Once the suzerain died, however, the ruler who made the promise was under no obligation to extend the promise automatically to the suzerain's successor.

A CHINESE PREFECTURE ON THE MEKONG: CHANGZHOU (TANGZHOU)

At this point, it would be useful to take another approach and examine the middle Mekong from the viewpoint of Huanzhou (Fun Dzau in Cantonese, Hoan-chau in Vietnamese). Pelliot (1904) thought that this place was in Ha-tinh, but Chinese scholars have subsequently identified it with Vinh (Tan 1982, vol. 5, pp. 72–73; Jing 1985).[21] For the purpose of the present study, it will suffice to suppose that Huanzhou was in either Vinh or Ha-tinh.

In the Tang-period Chinese administrative system, a prefecture was called a *zhou*. Chang (or Tang) Prefecture (Changzhou or

Tangzhou, depending on the Chinese character used by the writer)[22] was one of the Chinese administrative centres in the Mekong valley during the Tang period. One of its districts (*xian*) was Ri Luo, and Tang records show that this prefecture had a special status in the administrative system. In the seventh and eighth centuries, it seems that it was not dependent on Huanzhou, the larger prefecture that was immediately to its east. Instead, it was a prefecture under the direct control of the provincial government (*du hu fu*) at Jiaozhou (present-day Hanoi). As late as 791, Huanzhou became the provincial government that was in charge of the minor prefectures and districts inhabited primarily by non-Chinese (XTS 222C). Only after this date would Chang (or Tang) Prefecture have been given the status of a minor prefecture under Huanzhou. This date is of interest because, seven years later, Wen Dan sent its last tribute on record to the Tang court, and the prefectural name never again appears in the historical records. In fact, it is not known when Chang (or Tang) Prefecture was established under the Chinese prefectural system or when it ceased to be a prefecture.[23]

Chang (or Tang) Prefecture had only two districts—an arrangement that was not uncommon in Tang-period Vietnam. The journey from the first district to the second one (Wen Yang, or Mahn Joeng in Cantonese) took only three days. The name of the second district, when compared with the name 'Chang' (or 'Tang'), has a very Daic ring to it. Three place names are recorded along the route to the second district. To reach Wen Yang, a traveller went along Lou Lun River[24] and across the mountain Shi Mi of Gu Lang Dong. The river in question must be a tributary of the Mekong and must flow down from the cordillera. Gu Lang Dong is almost certainly the name of a Tai state, but the elements of the name have been arranged in Sinitic order. The names given by the Chinese to states in Vietnam and China likewise end with the term *dong*, which is used in many languages across the region in the sense of a 'country'.[25]

In the seventh and eighth centuries, the inhabitants of Chang (or Tang) Prefecture on the Mekong must have included many Tang Chinese officials, as well as their clients who were recent immigrants from Chinese-controlled Vietnam. These clients could have been ethnically identical to the people of Śrī Canāśapūra and Gan Bi, whose language they must have spoken. They may also have had friends and relatives in the chain of towns to the west and to the east, which would have enabled them to co-operate in many ways with the Chinese.

Modern Chinese scholars attempt to place Changzhou (or Tangzhou), the seat of the prefecture, in the area between modern Kham Koet and Pak San. Contrary to their opinion, the prefectural centre was either on the Mekong (in the vicinity of modern Tha Khaek and Nakhòn Phanom) or at Sakon Nakhòn—a site that had a Chinese-type city plan. Wen Yang District was on the Mekong and could have been in the vicinity of present-day Tha Khaek. Such a site, across the river from Nakhòn Phanom, is plausible because in ancient times the seat of the Nakhòn Phanom administration was on the left bank—a fact that is still remembered by the older generation in Laos. The old Si Khotthabun stupa in Tha Khaek provides additional evidence to support this theory.[26] Further confirmation is needed, however, and it can possibly be provided by future archaeological research along this stretch of the Mekong.

ROUTES ACROSS THE CENTRAL MEKONG BASIN

Lopburi is at the western end of a route that leads across the middle Mekong region and continues beyond the mountains to the South China Sea. This route was apparently preferred by some, if not the majority of, travellers who traversed the region between Lopburi and the eastern terminus of the route. The importance of the route can be inferred from the great number of archaeological sites and artifacts discovered along it in modern-day Isan. This evidence indicates that people were travelling and moving in various directions across this region, from prehistoric times to Tang times, and certainly between the seventh century and the beginning of the tenth century.

Trans-Cordillera Trail

Towards the end of the seven-volume geography, the new Tang annals (43C) provide a description of the route leading through Laos to the Wen Dan capitals. This is the best extant description of the route that crossed the cordillera. Unfortunately, the original Tang geography, which was used by the editors of the new Tang annals, has been lost.

According to the new Tang annals, a traveller setting out from Huanzhou went three days in a south-westerly direction, before crossing a mountain called Wu Wen (Mou Wan in Cantonese and Vu On in Vietnamese).[27] Two days farther along the route, he arrived at Ri Luo (Jat Lohk or Jat Lai in Cantonese, Nhat Lac in Vietnamese). The text gives no indication that the traveller had to change the general direction of his journey before reaching his destination. The overall direction and the distances travelled match the three historical sites in the centre of Isan that have been discussed above.

A Tang-period traveller, leaving the vicinity of present-day Vinh and going south-west, had a choice of several trails that crossed the cordillera. The northernmost is the Kaeo Nüa pass, which leads to Na Pae, immediately west of the watershed line. A traveller leaving Ha-tinh and going in the same direction towards some point in the central part of Isan had to cross the pass known as Muya (Mugia in French orthography). In the case of Muya, the direction of the journey from Ha-tinh is not south-west but south-south-west. This slight detour to the south to reach the Muya pass did not matter very much to early travellers, because the trail from the pass down to the Mekong runs almost due west. Chinese descriptions of such a route, however, did have to be precise. The directions for the initial part of a long journey are usually exact in a geographical description of the type contained in the Tang records. For this reason, it seems probable that the route began in Vinh rather than Ha-tinh.

From Huanzhou, it took about eight days to reach a Tai town on the right bank of the Mekong, probably near the site of modern Nakhòn Phanom. The traveller following the itinerary described in the new Tang annals most probably took boats along stretches of several rivers: the Nam Theun, the Nam Hinbun (with its tributary, the Nam Hai) and the Mekong, passing by an area lined with limestone formations. The Chinese writers described these lime-stone hills, which they called Shi Mi Shan, meaning 'rock-packed mountains'. The traveller then proceeded along the Mekong as far as a landing known as Man Yang. This was the main route towards Wen Dan.

Either the same route, or a slightly modified one, could have been used by the rulers and high officials of Wen Dan, who carried costly goods as tribute when travelling east across the cordillera. They also brought many tame elephants, and for these animals in particular, the route would have been different, since elephants could not have been carried in river boats. The waterways, which offered leisurely and rapid down-river transport, would probably have been skirted when travelling in the opposite direction with large animals such as elephants. The itinerary of a tribute mission setting out for China would, therefore, have been slightly more time-consuming than the route that travellers took when going from the cordillera down to the Mekong.

Trail from the Mekong to Wen Dan

To go from the Mekong to the capital of Wen Dan, travellers landed on the right bank of the Mekong and proceeded south-west towards the Phu Phan mountain range, following the course of a river known to the Chinese as Li Li Jiang.[28] The boat trip down the Mekong was rapid and refreshing, but during the segment of the journey from Wen Yang (on the bank of the Mekong) to the capital of Wen Dan (in central Isan), travellers experienced a complete change of conditions. The overland part of the journey was hot and tiring, even during the cool season. For this reason, they most likely crossed the forested Phu Phan mountains in a single day and then took the shortest route to a district (*xian*) known to the Chinese as Suan Tai,[29] which was in Wen Dan's territory.

This segment of the journey took four days. The first three were spent crossing the flat plain in the area south-west of the marsh known today as Nòng Han Luang, which lies along the eastern approach to the Phu Phan range. The fourth day was spent crossing the mountain itself, before enjoying the more pleasant continuation by river to present-day Khao Wong Subdistrict, north of Kutchi Narai District.[30]

The three days reported in the Chinese geography for the next segment of the journey, ending at Wen Dan, are precisely the time required to go from Khao Wong to Fa Daet. Anyone who had to present himself on official business at Kanthara Wichai (the ruler's residence) needed only one additional day to go there from Fa Daet. Thus the details of the itinerary, which have been preserved in the new Tang annals and in the geography *Tai Ping Huan Yu Ji*, coincide perfectly with a journey on foot and by boat from Vinh to Fa Daet and Kanthara Wichai.

Trans-Mekong Trade

Trade routes in the middle Mekong date from prehistoric times, and trans-Mekong commercial traffic was by no means new in the seventh century. The volume of trade seems to have increased dramatically during the Tang era, as the identifications in this study of Tang place-names suggest or confirm. The trade that flowed along the trans-Mekong route, from the seacoasts at both ends of the route, must have enriched a place that occupied a position not only along the route but also at the crossroads of other routes. There is not yet enough evidence to show when the trade along this route became active enough to give rise to a commercial hub such as Wen Dan. It could have become important during the Tang era, or it may already have been flourishing during a previous dynasty.

WEN DAN'S TAI POPULACE, WARRIORS AND RÔLE IN THE NAN ZHAO CAMPAIGN

Thus far, this study has established some basic geographical limits to the Wen Dan region and has pinpointed three historic sites as major settlements in Wen Dan's territory. Tang sources tell us more about Wen Dan and about other towns on the Mekong.

The Chinese text includes both a Chinese rendering of the title of Wen Dan's king and a royal title that sounds entirely Tai. This evidence tends to support the hypothesis that Tai-speaking people inhabited the area and were migrating across it during the Tang era. In the 'down-river' Khmer kingdom, which was in the territory that became the modern kingdom of Champasak, the majority of the people were probably not yet Tai at this time. But Gan Bi, with its military organization, could have been a Tai-dominated state—like Śrī Canāśapūra (in the Sak River basin) and Xiu Luo Fen (a state west of Zhen La), each of which had 20,000 warriors. The new Tang annals group these three political entities in a single category and indicate that the customs of each resembled those of the others. For example, they all had fortifications. Fa Daet was the largest fortified site of its kind. It was surrounded by an extensive flat plain that could be irrigated, and consequently it had the agricultural potential to support a relatively large population of rice-growing farmers.

Such farmers were typical Tai men, enjoyed a respected position in society and served as soldiers whenever needed. The laws of King Mangrai, which date from the thirteenth century in Lan Na, affirm that a state (or a town within a state) could not be sustained without a corps of such men. As the text reveals, moreover, what the Chinese of the Tang period wanted most from Wen Dan in the second half of the eighth century was no longer commodities such as rare birds and animals. Instead, China needed soldiers to fight in Yunnan against the Nan Zhao kingdom.

Tai Involvement in Mon-Khmer Relations

Sino-Tai relations in the eighth century can be better understood by scrutinising some additional Chinese texts. The lengthy Pelliot (1904) study pointed out that Can Ban (identified in the present study as north of Sri Thep) is mentioned in the annals of the Sui dynasty, which immediately preceded the Tang period. Tuo Huan also is mentioned in this source and is now well known as Qian Tou Huan (ancient Lavo or Lopburi). The Sui dynasty lasted only four decades, from 581 to 618, but the Chinese government at the time was as well informed about South-East Asia as its Tang successors. The Sui annals (*Sui Shu*) say that, during the Sui era, Zhen La was very friendly with Can Ban (in the upper central plain of modern Thailand) and with a country known as Zhu Jiang (possibly an old name for the Pyu empire)[31] but that it was constantly at war with Lin Yi (Champa) and Tuo Huan (Lavo). Since Zhen La's ally in the Sak River valley was separated from Lavo by a bare 100 kilometres, this Mon-Khmer rivalry was possibly supported by the Tai of Sri Thep and may have continued well into the Tang era.

Tai Military Organisation

With these facts in mind, it would be useful to consider both the Khmer and the Mon needs for military recruits. The Tai, whose language was tonal, were comparatively new to the area and perhaps could take sides with any patron who was willing to reward them. They were a migrating and expanding minority population during these centuries, assimilating various features of the new cultures that they encountered while searching for better, flatter agricultural land with a plentiful water supply. Their migration provoked conflicts and wars with others, which in turn moulded Tai social organisation around a core of trained fighting units. The new Tang annals, which praise the 40,000 fighting men who inhabited Śrī Canāśapūra (Sri Thep) and Xiu Luo Fen (a state west of Zhen La), say that they were excellent warriors.

Wen Dan's Rôle in the 751–4 Nan Zhao Campaign

In 753, a prince of Wen Dan led the embassy to China. He was a son of the Wen Dan king, and the emperor received him in an audience, together with his twenty-six officers. The title Brave Military Commanders (*guo yi du wei*) was bestowed on them, because the prince and his men had arrived on a mission to assist the Chinese in the war against Nan Zhao in Yunnan (CFYG 971: 19 and Song edition, p. 12; CFYG 975: 22 and Song edition, p. 14; XTS 222C).

From the viewpoint of the Chinese court, the assistance of skilled warriors, even from a distant southern land, must have been especially welcome during this troubled period. Although the long reign of Xuan Zong (712–56) marked a high point of prosperity in the Tang dynasty, the government suffered a series of defeats in the final years of the reign. During the 750s, conflicts arose not only on the south-west frontier (the Nan Zhao campaign) but also in the north-east and west of the empire. And in 756, the year after the Wen Dan forces returned home, rebels captured the imperial capital, Chang-an, and forced the court to flee. Given these circumstances, it should not be surprising that the tribute mission and the contingent of warriors from Wen Dan were so well received.

It seems likely that the previous Wen Dan envoy, who led the mission with the rhinoceroses three years earlier, returned home bearing the news about China's conflict with Nan Zhao and a Chinese demand for soldiers to reinforce the Chinese army. The king of Wen Dan responded promptly, almost as if he had been waiting for such a chance, and he sent soldiers to join the forces of He Lu Guang, who was the Chinese governor in Jiaozhou (present-day Hanoi).

Wen Dan's readiness to enter a war seems surprising. Wen Dan acted in a friendly manner, as though it were a close ally of Tang China—even as though it were a part of the empire (comparable with an extension of the provincial government of Jiaozhou)—and thus obedient to any order from the Tang court. Wen Dan must have possessed a courageous fighting force with skilled commanders. This military expedition was an episode in its history that accords with the success of later Tai kingdoms, which had rice farmers who could instantly be transformed into soldiers once an order was given. At the same time, the prince and his commanders served as a team of able diplomats. They were received in audience by the most powerful man on earth, who bestowed honorary titles on them before they went to war.

The military campaign under the general command of the Jiaozhou governor began in 751. The Wen Dan contingent remained in China during a lull in the campaign and joined the fighting when the campaign resumed in 754. They were then allowed to return home. The Wen Dan soldiers were sent as volunteers, to whom the Chinese authorities had to give titles and gifts. There seems to be no other instance of South-East Asians joining Chinese forces in a military action of this kind during the Tang era, and perhaps there is no similar case in any other era.

Wen Dan, 771

One episode in Wen Dan's short-lived relationship with China is especially noteworthy. In 771, the Wen Dan embassy—led by the heir apparent, Po Mi[32]—brought eleven trained elephants to present to the emperor. The envoy was entertained at a state dinner in the emperor's palace, together with a party of twenty-five other people from his kingdom (CFYG 965: 7; CFYG 976: 4 and Song edition,

p. 4; XTS 222C). The dinner took place on the *yi you* day in the eleventh month—that is, 13 December 771. The emperor himself gave an honourable Chinese personal name to the viceroy and bestowed high status on him with the title Special Supreme Regional Commander (*kaifu yitongsansi*). CFYG, however, refers to Po Mi only as the 'king' (*wang*) of Wen Dan.

According to a Song-era text on Yunnan, *Ji Gu Dian Shuo Yuan Ji*, this title was once bestowed on a pro-Chinese king of Nan Zhao, Pi Luo Ge, apparently in 735. It conferred a status higher than that of any minister in the Tang capital. It was on a level that had formerly been attained by only six chief ministers in China during the Tang dynasty, and it was equal in status to the second-generation imperial princes, who were only one level lower than the emperor's sons (Pelliot 1903: 667–668). This position was the second of the thirty tiers of the Chinese bureaucratic hierarchy. By comparison, most regional governors were ranked at only the fourth, sixth or seventh tier. For this reason, Po Mi had a higher position and a greater stipend than the Chinese governors of Jiaozhou, Guangzhou or any other provinces in China (Tsukiyama 1961). How he gained this status with such an income is a mystery. It may have been a reward for the valuable military services rendered in the 750s, but this intriguing question remains open to future scholarly investigation.

STATUS OF WOMEN

The status of women in the heartland of South-East Asia thirteen centuries ago merits further consideration in the light of the records about the 771 embassy. Another extraordinary feature of Po Mi's mission is the fact that he was accompanied by his wife. This instance of a consort being allowed to travel with a tribute mission and to visit the Tang court is unique.

The consort who accompanied Po Mi could have been the real ruler of his homeland, because a matriarchal family system existed in this region before the arrival of the earliest Tai migrants. As late as the thirteenth century, Lavo sent tribute to China jointly with a place called the 'Land of Women' (Nu Ren *guo*). The official history of Yunnan Province—*Yunnan Zhi*, also called the *Man Shu* and available in an English translation (*Man Shu* 1961)—states that there was a land of women in the Mekong valley, too. The *Yunnan Zhi* record dates from the ninth century and was written in Chinese-controlled Vietnam.

Under the system that has been perpetuated until the present day in the Mekong region, the youngest married daughter inherits her parent's home—whether a small hut or palacial residence—together with adjacent land and some paddy fields. The daughter's husband becomes the temporal managing male in the next generation, but in his old age, the same pattern recurs in the inheritance of the family home. His sons will have to live elsewhere, because his youngest daughter will inherit the house and land.

In former times, the king, heir apparent, princes and military commanders may have been active but temporary figures *managing* the country, whereas the women may have been the heirs and *possessors* of the land. As the well-known Minangkabau culture in Indonesia illustrates, the men of a matriarchal society tend to migrate away from and later back to the ancestral lands of their women, and this tendency to migrate temporarily seems to hold true especially if the land is difficult to till. Other factors may have prompted or accelerated such movements by the men. For example, rulers who became deprived of their revenues from trade or who were suffering from declining political fortunes might well move away and take their peasants with them, to found a new town elsewhere. Or they could simply seize and occupy someone else's territory, if they had well-trained soldier-farmers to fight for them. In either case, the migration then became permanent.

CHANGE IN CHINESE POLICY AND FINAL WEN DAN TRIBUTE MISSION

By the decade of the 790s, China's policy towards its valuable province in the middle-Mekong region had changed. In 791 Changzhou (or Tangzhou)—the Chinese prefecture on the

Mekong—seems to have passed under the control of Huanzhou—the major prefectural center on the coast of the South China Sea. Thereafter, Huanzhou assumed responsibility for overseeing the affairs of the outlying non-Chinese peoples in this region. It is also possible that Changzhou was simply abandoned as a Chinese administrative centre. Unfortunately, the documentation on Changzhou is sparse, and there are no clues to its fate. In Yunnan Province, the Chinese were victorious in a military campaign against Nan Zhao in 793. Those battles are well documented in the annals, but there is no record of any assistance rendered by Wen Dan at that time. The ruler of Wen Dan did not repeat the military aid rendered so successfully only forty years earlier.

The last tribute mission from Wen Dan arrived in 798 at Chang-an (CFYG 976: 6–7 and Song edition, p. 4; XTS 222C). This occasion seems to have been Wen Dan's final gesture to maintain a favoured position. The Wen Dan envoy's name is recorded in Chinese style using three characters: Li Tou Ji (Lei Tau Kap). On this occasion he was given a title that meant Guardian (or Defender) of the Imperial Palace (*zhong lang jiang*) in its original Han-period Chinese context. The application of this title had slowly changed over the centuries since the Han era, however, from Chinese regional commanders to non-Chinese. In the context of late-eighth-century Wen Dan, it denoted a general of the army or a regional chief who had the privilege of residing in or possessing his own palace or residence.

It is tempting to suppose that the king of Wen Dan, when planning his diplomatic strategy in 798, chose as his envoy a member of the Li clan, who could also have been a descendant of the pro-Chinese house of Po Mi. The clan name Li was common among the Tai-speaking peoples, and the Li were prominent in Guangxi Province and elsewhere in south China.[33] As a Li, the envoy could have conversed with senior Tang officials on the subject of his clan name and his clan's supposed origins among the Tang imperial princes of the same name. His given name, Tau Kap, sounds like the name of a Lao king or prince in Luang Prabang, during the period when the Lao kingdom was called Siang Dong and Siang Thòng. Indeed, a king whose title is similar to this name is listed among the later rulers of this kingdom.

PRECURSORS OF VIENTIANE AND LUANG PRABANG

Do the Tang-period records contain any toponyms that refer to sites in or near modern Vientiane and Luang Prabang? Although the research for the present study has unearthed insufficient information to provide a definitive answer to this question, it can be addressed very tentatively. Some likely candidates have already been mentioned above.

South of the upper-Mekong He Ling (which was in the area of modern Sipsòng Panna) was an important state called Duo Mo Chang. According to the Chinese records, travel through Duo Mo Chang territory was more difficult in an east-west direction than in a north-south one. It is reasonable to conclude, therefore that this state encompassed two or three valleys with navigable rivers bounded by mountain ranges, all of which ran from north to south, thereby making east-west travel relatively difficult. This description fits the geographic features of Lan Na (modern northern Thailand). Duo Mo Chang probably encompassed the Yom and Nan Rivers, together with some tributaries of the Mekong across the watershed.

A traveller setting out from Jiaozhou (present-day Hanoi) could go by way of Lin Yi (Champa, the coastal state in central Vietnam) and eventually reach Duo Mo Chang. Along the way between Lin Yi and Duo Mo Chang, this westward journey took the traveller successively through three states: (1) Jun Na Lu, (2) Du He Lu and (3) Sa Lu. One clue to the sites of these three states is provided by the final Chinese character of the names, which is identical in all three. In modern Mandarin, *lu* sounds almost exactly like the Daic term *lü*, which refers to the upper reaches of the Mekong. This character may have been appended to the names to indicate that they were up-river states—that is, they were in the Mekong valley above China's Changzhou prefectural centre.[34] Taking into consideration the geographical features of the region, the following tentative reconstructions can be suggested, to help in the identification of the Tai names represented by the Chinese characters for these three little states.

The first name, Jun Na Lu, is rendered Gwan Na Lou in Cantonese. The elements *na lou* could well mean literally 'Lao paddy-fields' (*na lao* in modern Tai). The *gwan* element could have any of three or more meanings. It could mean a 'sovereign' or at least a local ruler with some independence. (The thirteenth-century Tai equivalent, *khun*, is mentioned above.) Or, the *gwan* element in the name could have the same simple meaning as the modern Tai for a 'province' or 'area' (*khwaen*). Given the position of the name of this state in the Chinese list—which implies that it was up-river from and also the closest of the three to the prefectural seat—a likely site is the area of Sakon Nakhòn Province. If this interpretation is correct, the *gwan* element might refer to the large marsh in the province, which may once have been a natural lake (*kwan* in Tai).

The second place name, Du He Lu, is rendered Dou Hoh Lou in Cantonese. It could originally have been a river landing with a name such as Tha Hua Lü, meaning 'up-river landing'. It may have been in the vicinity of modern Tha Bò and Wiang Khuk, opposite the sites of the future Sai Fòng and Vientiane.[35]

The third place name, Sa Lu, is rendered Sat Lou in Cantonese. It could have been in the Luang Prabang area or possibly in the area of the ancient trade route that linked Phrae (in the upper Chao Phraya basin) to Chiang Khan (on the Mekong). The final *t* in the Cantonese pronunciation is a minor problem, since many examples of the disappearance of this final consonant are known in Tang-period sources. The resulting name, Sa Lou, could refer to indigenous tribal groups, known generically in recent centuries as the Kha.[36] Thus, the name Sa Lou could have been a Chinese attempt to pronounce the name of the Khamu kingdom of Sawa—the elusive northern 'Java' that appears in later Khmer and Thai inscriptions.[37] This may have been the kingdom that eventually came to be known by a Lao name—Siang Dong and Siang Thòng—and was the precursor of the Lao kingdom of Luang Prabang.

THRESHOLD OF A NEW ERA

A new era ran concurrently with the final years of Wen Dan and then diachronically followed the disappearance of Wen Dan. This was the era of Du Po ('Java'). Two states known as 'Java' existed in the Mekong basin: one in the upper reaches of the river and the other in the lower part of the basin. Definitely neither was located in Indonesia, contrary to the suppositions of past historians. Pelliot was aware of this problem when he wrote that 'the name Java seems to have existed on the upper Mekong, and M. Finot found it in a Cham inscription' (Pelliot 1904: 320). Furthermore, the southern He Ling had another name—Du Po—according to the new Tang annals

Even today, villages and towns with identical names exist not just in a single country but even in the same province or district. There is no reason to deny that two or more places—including He Ling, Pan Pan and Champa—were once called 'Java', because different adjectives could have been added to the names to distinguish between them when necessary. A Chinese monk-traveller, for example, reported that one such place was known as Maha Champa, presumably to distinguish it from the other Champa.

Pelliot and his followers did not perceive that the toponyms recorded in Tang-period Chinese records could be identified with sites in the Mekong basin, perhaps because they were not in touch with ordinary Lao villagers and thus had no opportunity to learn from living in the Lao milieu. They also did not have the present-day advantage of the wealth of archaeological data that has come to light in the course of the twentieth century.

Wen Dan vanished from the Chinese historical records at the end of the eighth century. In the present reinterpretation of the sources, however, Wen Dan's successors were standing at the threshold of a new era for the Tai-speaking peoples of South-East Asia.

LIST OF CHINESE CHARACTERS FOR NAMES CITED IN THE TEXT

跋	Ba
半支跋	Ban Zhi Ba
參半	Can Ban
冊府元龜	Ce Fu Yuan Gui
長	Chang
長安	Chang An
長/裳州	Chang Zhou
乘悟	Cheng Wu
大海	Da Hai
大唐西域求法高僧傳	Da Tang Xiyi Qiufa Gaosong Zhuan
大唐西域記	Da Tang Xiyi Ji
大越史記全書	Dai Viet Suky Toanthu
道明	Dao Ming
都督府	Dudu Fu
都訶盧	Du He Lu
獨和羅	Du He Luo
都護府	Duhu Fu
闍婆	Du/She Po
堕和羅	Duo He Luo
堕和羅鉢底	Duo He Luo Ba Di
多降	Duo Long
多摩萇	Duo Mo Chang
堕婆登	Duo Po Deng
扶南	Fu Nan

甘畢	Gan Bi
干支弗	Gan Zhi Fu
臘	Ge/La
哥羅舍分	Ge Luo She Fen
古郎洞	Gu Lang Dong
訶陵	He Ling
環王	Huan Wang
驩州	Huan Zhou
吉蔑	Ji Mie
迦羅舍分	Jia Luo She Fu
交州	Jiao Zhou
兢迦河	Jing Jia He
舊唐書	Jiu Tangshu
拘婁蜜	Ju Lou Mi
君那盧	Jun Na Lu
林邑	Lin Yi
陸眞臘	Lu Zhen La
馬留	Ma Liu
摩臘	Mo La
南海	Nanhai
南蠻	Nanman
南詔	Nan Zhao
內城	Neicheng
耨陀亘	Nou Tuo Huan/Xuan
盤盤	Pan Pan
驃	Piao

婆岸	Po An
婆鳳	Po Feng
婆利	Po Li
婆鏤	Po Lou
婆羅提跋	Po Luo Ti Ba
乾陀亘	Qian Tuo Huan/Xuan
千支弗	Qian Zhi Fu
日落	Riluo
薩盧	Sa Lu
舍跋若	She Ba Ruo
社婆	She Po
石密	Shimi
太平寰宇記	Taiping Huanyu Ji
太平御覽	Taiping Yulan
唐	Tang
唐會要	Tang Huiyao
棠州	Tang Zhou
投和	Tou He
投和羅	Tou He Luo
徒里拙	Tu Li Zhuo
越史略	Viet Su Luoc
外城	Waicheng
韋皋	Wei Gao
文單	Wen Dan
文陽	Wen Yang
霧溫	Wu Wen

西南海	Xi Nanhai
縣	Xian
新唐書	Xin Tangshu
修羅分	Xiu Luo Fen
玄宗	Xuan Zong
元和郡縣圖志	Yuanhe Junxian Tuzhi
占	Zhan
瞻博	Zhan Bo
瞻婆	Zhan Po
旃陀越摩	Shan Tuo Yue Mo
眞臘	Zhen La
眞臈	Zhen Ge/La
眞里富	Zhen Li Fu
質多斯那	Zhiduosina
朱波	Zhu Bo
朱江	Zhu Jiang

NOTES

1. The Chinese may also have used the name Pan Pan in reference to a site in the Mekong delta, although the latter identification is not yet certain.

2. My interest in the Tang-period Chinese records concerning Wen Dan originated in a discussion with Lao friends one evening in Vientiane during the 1960s. The central question under discussion was why some Chinese people use the sounds of the letters *l* and *n* interchangeably. We reached no conclusion, but the question intrigued me. I postulated that the southern Chinese might have had the same habit in their pronunciation a millenium and more ago. Some results of this line of reasoning are incorporated in the arguments given in this study.

3. In Cantonese, Zhan Bo becomes Dzim Bohk. The character *zhan* is definitely a variant (if not an earlier form) of the character *zhan* used for Champa. For example, *Da Tang Xi Yu Qiu Fa Gao Song Zhuan* uses a name with the same Chinese characters (*zhan bo* or *zhan bo fu*) for the country (Champa) that was south of Jiaozhou (the Tang-era province with its capital at present-day Hanoi). The seventh-century Buddhist monk Cheng Wu died in Zhan Bo on his way back to Jiaozhou, after residing in He Ling and other places farther south.

4. All these combinations seem to be shortened and variant forms of the original, complete name: hypothetically Duo He Luo Ba Di, although such a combination is never encountered in the section of the annals on Dvaravati.

5. According to the new Tang annals, Śrī Canāśapūra was south of Nan Hai. The name Nan Hai does not mean 'southern seas' (*les mers du Sud*), as the French incorrectly translated it, but rather the portion of mainland South-East Asia that lies to the south of the Red River basin (in northern Vietnam) and Nan Zhao (in China's Yunnan Province).

6. Perhaps also belonging to this tradition is the Zhen Li Fu that appears in Chinese records of the Sung dynasty (960–1275).

7. The Chinese name for Zhan Bo—also rendered as 'inland Champa'—resembles that of well-known coastal Champa. But its inhabitants were apparently either a different branch of Cham or perhaps not ethnically Cham at all.

8. Wen Dan was known as Man Dahn or Man Sim or Man Sin in Cantonese, and also as Bun Tan or Bun Sen in Sino-Japanese.

9. Huan Wang is the Tang Chinese name for Champa, which once encompassed much of the central part of modern Vietnam. From the early

centuries of the Christian era until modern times apparently, the Cham were generally called 'Mloi'. The new Tang annals (XTS 222C) record that the people of Huan Wang called themselves Ma Liu (Ma Lau). Rhodes (1651) identified the Mloi as the people of the Cham kingdom. The initial *m* has disappeared from modern Vietnamese pronunciation, and the Vietnamese today call them 'Loi'. The original name is a cognate of *malayu* (for 'Malay'). Lao Nyôi (Nhôi) and Nyo (Nho) could be other cognates.

10. An early appearance of the name 'Lavo' can be discerned in the Chinese character *nou*, which is pronounced *nau* in Cantonese. Thus if we attempt to reconstruct a full name for Tang-era Lopburi, it might have been Lavo Chandahan or something similar. The Cantonese pronunciation of Qian Tuo Huan is Goh Toh Wun (or Kin Toh Wun), which is possibly a rendering of an Indianised name such as 'Candapura' or 'Kandapura'. (In this case, the element *pura* could also be rendered in one of its alternate forms: *buri* or *bun*.) But the problem of the use of the Chinese term *huan* (rather than *fen*) for the South and South-East Asian suffix *pura* is not resolved here.

11. In fact, the characters *dan* and *can* can be rendered in other ways. The character *dan* can also be pronounced *shan* or *chan* in Mandarin. The character *can* can be pronounced *shen* or *cen*. Note that *dan* can be pronounced *sin* or *sim* or *dahn* in Cantonese.

12. Man Sem might also be rendered as Man Sham, although I acknowledge other possibilities such as Man Sim.

13. In Cantonese, this name is pronounced Sam Bun, and possibly it was a smaller Tai state whose capital city bore the suffix *bun* in Tai or *pura* in Sanskrit. Once again, the character for *can* could be pronounced *sem* or *sham*. A reference in the new Tang annals says that Can Ban was north-west of Wen Dan.

14. According to Mahendravarman's Sanskrit inscriptions, he was known as Chitrasena prior to coming to the throne. In the Sui annals, he is called Zhiduoxianna, which is the Chinese rendering of the name Chitrasena. It should be noted that the toponyms Zhen La and Can Ban are likewise Chinese renderings of local toponyms and appear only in Chinese sources. No inscription has been found that records the name used by Can Ban's inhabitants for their state.

15. It is tempting to think that the toponymn known as Po An to the Chinese still survives in the name Phon, which is a district in modern Khòn Kaen Province and perpetuates the name of the old provincial town in that area. The Cantonese pronunciation of the name is Ngohn but does not present any problem in this regard, since the *ng* in the Cantonese could

have disappeared. The name could be derived from a Sanskritic word adopted into Tai.

16. A journey of ten days, starting in Ju Lou Mi and going towards the south, brought a traveller to Po Li (Poh Lei), which has long been misidentified as a site in modern Indonesia. Pelliot (1904) thought Po Li was the island of Bali in the Indonesian archipelago, because the records specify that it was east of the southern He Ling. His reasoning was based on his assumption that the southern He Ling was the island of Java. In this identification, Coedès followed Pelliot, and all others followed Coedès. Given the evidence available today, their conclusions are obviously untenable.

An important clue to the site of Po Li—and, by association, the site of southern He Ling—is provided by the name Po Li itself. This name can be linked to the Lü (Tai Lü or Dai) people, who live along the uppermost stretches of the Mekong, in the region known as Sipsòng Panna. The term *lü* means 'upper reaches'. (It could be a cognate of *ulu, hulu* and other terms in Austronesian languages, and thus a remnant of an archaic Austric vocabulary.) Tai has another word with the opposite meaning: *khòm*, which refers to 'lower reaches'. The latter term corresponds to the Khmer term *krom*. One group of people in Isan are known as Khmer *lü* ('upper Khmer'), and they refer to the Khmer of Cambodia as the Khmer *krom* ('lower Khmer'). The Khmer of Phnom Penh, in their turn, refer to the Khmer who live in Vietnamese territory as Khmer *krom*, because the latter live farther down in the lower reaches of the Mekong. In the Tang period, the Chinese used three characters to write the name of the southernmost people of the middle Mekong basin. Given these considerations, the site of the southern He Ling (Hoh Ling) state becomes obvious: it was in present-day southern Cambodia and must have been south of Phnom Penh.

The letter *p* in Po Li can be voiced as a *b* and could have survived in the latter form to the present day. The *l* in the name could originally have been a southern *r* sound. Hence Po Li (in Cantonese, Poh Lei), if rendered in a South-East Asian language, might have been pronounced *bo rei*, which is identical to a modern Cambodian place-name element (*borey* in the French romanisation).

17. XTS (222C) and CFYG (957: 7) state that the king of Water (*Shui*) Zhen La resided in a city named Po Lou Ti Ba (or Dai Bat), from which one might venture to reconstruct a Sanskritic hybrid: Pura Thep. This hypothetical name, like Krung Thep (the Sanskritic-Thai name for Bangkok), literally means 'City of Celestial Beings'.

18. In 1976 I proposed (Hoshino 1976) to identify Wen Dan with the

Isan site known today as Fa Daet. The great boundary (*sema*) stones at this site, erected to mark the sacred precincts of a Buddhist monastery, provide evidence of a flourishing Buddhist society.

19. The name of Gan Bi's king is recorded in the new Tang annals as Zhan Tuo Yue Mo. (The Chinese character *yue* could be corrupt, however, and this syllable may have been pronounced *ba* instead.) Based on the sounds of this name, one way of Indianising it is 'Candabima'. The last two characters (*yue mo*) could be a Chinese rendering of the familiar element *var man*, which suffixed the names of great Khmer kings such as Suriyavarman and Jayavarman. Hence an alternative Indianised form would be 'Candravarman'.

20. The 750 reference in the historical encyclopaedia records the name of this state as 'Zhen Ge'. This record is apparently a writing or printing mistake for 'Zhen La'. Pelliot (1904) suggested the name might be derived from Land Zhen La and Wen Dan. He gave no clear reason for this hypothesis but merely observed that the historical encyclopaedia *Tang Hui Yao* does not treat the two Zhen La states separately.

21. These scholars adopt the view of some late-nineteenth-century European orientalists, however, and identify Wen Dan with Vientiane.

22. The character for Tang is replaced by the character for Chang in some texts, such as *Tai Ping Huan Yu Ji* (vo. 171). This Changzhou is identifiable with another Changzhou, mentioned immediately after it in the same volume but with a different character for the *chang* element. These two *chang* probably are Chinese transcriptions of the Daic word for 'elephant'. The modern Lao is *sang*, as in the name Lan Sang.

23. The Tang Ming kingdom of the Wu era (AD 222–80) was one of three countries that Chinese officials visited. (The other two were the better known Lin Yi and Fu Nan.) 'Tang' could be derived from an early Austro-Asian word for a 'big river'. It is also plausible that the indigenous name was something like T'meng and that the meaning of the word was 'lower basin'. The latter hypothetical reconstruction sounds similar to the final two syllables of Si Khotthabòng, which is another rendering of the name Si Khotthabun by which the Lao kingdom was known in legendary times.

24. Lou Lun has been explained in terms of the Kui vocabulary in my detailed Tai history in Japanese (Hoshino 1990). The explanation could also have been made with a So or Thavung dictionary, if either were available.

25. Some examples are Mendong and Mengdong, in the Indonesian *wayang* stories, and Magelang, Malang and Minang, as well as the Daic term *müang*. *Dong* is an ancient Tai word meaning a canal or a natural

waterway (the modern *khlòng*), referring in this instance to the Mekong. The same term is *gohng* in Cantonese, *jiang* in Mandarin, *stung* in Khmer and either *thong* or *song* in Vietnamese. A similar progression of related words for 'mountain' can likewise be demonstrated: *loi, doi, nui* and so on. By drawing attention to vocabulary that is obviously related across languages, South-East Asian history can be analysed from a more organic perspective.

26. It is not known when the sacred stupa, the That Phanom, was originally constructed on the riverbank near present-day Nakhòn Phanom. According to art historian Jean Boisselier (1965), the monument was rebuilt at the end of the ninth century or the beginning of the tenth century. The present account, however, is concerned with a much earlier period: the seventh and eighth centuries.

27. The various renderings of the name for the mountain (*wu, mou* and *vu*) correspond closely to the Tai term *phu* meaning 'mountain'. The continuation of the description of the itinerary is full of Tai words.

28. The name Li Li, which may have been recorded somewhat inaccurately by the Chinese, sounds like the simple Tai expression *di di*, meaning 'very fine' or excellent'.

29. In modern Tai dialects, *suan tai* means 'Tai gardens and orchards'. If this was the eighth-century meaning of this toponym, it would be the earliest known appearance of the word 'Tai' in the historical records of the middle Mekong basin. The same name could, however, have been in use in Vietnam or in China before the seventh or eighth centuries.

30. Evidence of a link between Wen Dan and Kutchi Narai is provided by the numerous boundary (*sema*) stones discovered in Kutchi Narai, which are similar to the great boundary stones found in Fa Daet, Wen Dan's outer capital.

31. The character for *jiang* in Zhu Jiang (Dzy Gohng in Cantonese) may be corrupt. It means 'river', and its left-hand radical is identical to that of *bo*, which means 'wave'. This toponym may in fact refer to Zhu Bo, an old name for the Pyu empire. The Ping and Wang River valleys seem to have been under its control from time to time. During the Tang era, Zhu Bo (or Zhu Zhang) was renamed Piao (Pyu).

32. The viceroy's name as recorded by the Chinese was Po Mi, which sounds like a simple Tai name. (*Mi* literally means 'to have' or 'to be wealthy'.) This name seems to be prefixed by the Daic term *pò*, which literally means 'father' but is used also in reference to a married man. Thus the name recorded by the Chinese may in fact be a kind of title plus a personal name. The *pò* element may, over the course of several centuries,

have evolved into the now-familiar, but still simple, Tai term for a king or independent ruler found in thirteenth-century inscriptions: *phò khun*.

33. Schafer (1970), in a book on Hainan Island during the Tang era, even went as far as asserting that Vietnam's imperial family, the Le dynasty (981–1009), was ethnically Daic.

34. On the other hand, the Cantonese pronunciation (*lou*) could have been a Chinese rendering of the names of the important ethnic groups in the upper Mekong basin, all of which sound similar: Lwa, Lawa and Lao.

35. If this supposition is correct, the origin of the modern name Tha Bò can possibly be found in the term *bo*, which appears as a toponym in various parts of Yunnan and Vietnam. Both *bo* (a pre-Tai word) and *tha* (a Tai word in current usage) mean a 'river landing' or 'port'. The change in usage of such words—and their juxtaposition—is illustrated by the modern name for the Si River in central Isan. The river is known in Lao and Thai as the Mae Nam Si. All three elements of this name have identical meanings (i.e., 'river'), although they come from three different sources: *mae* (Thai), *nam* (Lao) and *si* (Austronesian, called Hesperonesian by some linguists). The early Tai-speaking people might similarly have adopted the new term *tha* in conjunction with, and later in place of, the older term *bo*.

36. It should be remembered that all Tai-related ethnic groups in China refer to the Han Chinese by names such as Kha, Ka and Xa, meaning a powerful outsider or overlord. In ancient South-East Asia, the term applied to Austro-Asiatic overlords. In modern Vietnamese, the term is written *xa* (referring to indigenous tribes). In the dialect of the Lü (the Tai or Dai of Sipsòng Panna) it is *hò* or *sò* (referring to the Chinese).

37. The link between Sawa (also pronounced Sua) and Java is obvious to anyone who reads Tai scripts and also knows that the Tai letters *s* and *w* correspond, respectively, to the Sanskrit letters *j* and *v*. Hence the word that is pronounced *sawa* in Tai can also be romanised (in the Sanskritic form) as *java*.

3

EVOLUTION OF THE CHRONICLE OF LUANG PRABANG:
A COMPARISON OF SIXTEEN VERSIONS

SOUNETH PHOTHISANE

The theme of continuity and discontinuity in Lao history is examined in detail by Martin Stuart-Fox in a separate chapter of this book. As he indicates, the territory that forms present-day Laos became divided among several independent kingdoms at various times in modern history. Each of these kingdoms had its own chroniclers. But only one—the kingdom of Luang Prabang—had any pretensions to a continuous history extending back to the very origins of the Lao people. The chronicle of Luang Prabang is thus the only primary source for the study of Lao history that offers an uninterrupted record, at least for the northern part of Laos, from legendary times until the present century.

This study describes in chronological order all of the known compilations of this chronicle, both published and unpublished. The earliest known version is dated 1512 and evolved over a period of more than four centuries. The study also examines some of the substantive variations between manuscripts, to illustrate how comparisons of extant manuscripts can help to clarify some poorly understood events of past centuries and to avoid the pitfalls created by the editorial licence of successive generations of chroniclers.

The subjects treated in the chronicle can be divided into three periods. The first period encompasses Lao pre-history, leading to the founding of the Thaeng kingdom in AD 757 by Khun Bòrom. All accounts of the Lao during that period are legendary. The second is the transition period which extends from 757 to 1316. This period begins and ends, respectively, during the lifetimes of two famous kings: Khun Bòrom and Phaya Lang (Suwanna Kham Phong). It consists only of a bare sketch of the succession of monarchs, without mentioning any dates. The third period is the historical one. It begins with the birth in 1316 of the heroic King Fa Ngum and provides a record of the successive rulers of Luang Prabang from the early fourteenth century to the twentieth century. All months and days are recorded according to the lunar calendar that was used by all Buddhist countries of South-East Asia, and years are recorded in the Lesser Era (Chula Sakkarat, abbreviated CS).

A hurried and superficial reading of the first part of the work gives the impression that it consists merely of legends and that these stories are recounted at random and in a disorganised way. Some readers might therefore conclude that the chronicle is a work of pure fiction and has no genuine historical content. When attempting to interpret Lao history, however, it would be unwise to accept only the third period and to dismiss the earlier two as irrelevant to historical research, because the material presented for each period epitomises the spirit of the Lao people during that respective era. For example, the accounts of the legendary period contain valuable clues about and insights into the characteristics of early Lao society.

The various versions of the chronicle of Luang Prabang are known collectively in Lao as the *Phün khun bòrom. Phün* is an old Lao word meaning 'a history', and it was in use long before the term *pawatsat* was coined in the twentieth century. Thus, this popular Lao title indicates that the work was intended to tell the continuous story of the Lao people, beginning in the eighth century with the most famous of the legendary kings, Khun Bòrom. A careful analysis of the chronicle reveals that it is a document of fundamental importance to the Lao people. In comparison, other historical works can be considered secondary sources, because the events recorded in the Luang Prabang chronicle reflect concepts and memories that have been embedded in the psyche of the Lao since early in the history of the nation.

An understanding of any people can be reached only by bringing together many facets of historical analysis, including factual records, legends, various forms of art, ways of life and ritual observances. All of the peoples of China, Burma and Vietnam have their own legends, which have been handed down from generation to generation, and which have influenced them in various ways up to the present day. These ancient stories merit close consideration and analysis. The Khun Bòrom chronicle does not present much difficulty when compared with some other ancient texts of South-East Asia. A scientific approach for investigating its contents is facilitated, moreover, by the fact that its contents are clearly delineated into three discrete periods.

Some historical events of the legendary period, no matter how limited, may be documented in the chronicle. Its account of the origin of the Lao and neighbouring peoples, for example, appears superficially to be without foundation, since the creation myth traces the origin of humanity to a gourd and asserts that 'people rushed out from the gourd, two ethnic groups first and three afterward'. On close examination, however, this assertion seems to record a collective memory, perpetuated across dozens of generations, that the Lao were one of five distinct ethnic groups living in close proximity a millenium ago. The myth also recounts that the 'Phaya Thaen [gods] gave buffaloes [to enable the people] to grow rice'. This statement demonstrates the antiquity of the Lao term for rice cultivation (*het na*) and also attests to the existence of paddy fields very early in Lao history. Such examples illustrate the potential value of minute details contained in this document. The process of analysing it is similar to panning for gold on the sand-banks of a river and laboriously separating the tiny specks of gold from the enormous bulk of the sand. In the same way, it can be worthwhile to scrutinise every passage of the chronicle, to extract details that may contribute to our knowledge of the history of the Lao people and the world that surrounded them.

During the one and three-quarters centuries that the Lao were under foreign rule, efforts were made at various times, by both domestic and foreigner writers, to compile Lao history and legends. During the first period of colonial rule, from the 1770s to 1893, while Laos was under Thai domination, many Lao documents were carried off to Bangkok, and many unique records of Lao history were either destroyed or lost. At least seven attempts were made to compile histories of the Luang Prabang kingdom alone, based on whatever historical materials survived and were available to the writers of this period. During the second period of colonial rule, when Laos was under French control (1893–1954), the Khun Bòrom chronicle attracted the attention of French scholars. Despite the fact that the chronicle was not constructed in a manner that appeared logical to Western historians, French researchers studied it with care, because they believed that it was used by the Lao elders to teach succeeding generations about the collective personality of their society. In this respect, it had a functional social purpose, similar to the Christian Bible in the West, and it served to legitimise and perpetuate an established social order in the same way that the *Rāmayana* and *Mahabharata* did in India.

The chronicle has been handed down from generation to generation in the form of copies reproduced by hand on locally manufactured writing materials. The most durable of these materials is palm leaf, and many palm-leaf manuscripts have survived. They are written either in the Pali script of the Buddhist monasteries or in an old form of the Lao script. Sixteen different versions have been identified, including the published versions and all the unpublished manuscripts that have been discovered thus far.[1]

The earliest known version of the chronicle was compiled in CS 874 (AD 1512) by two high-ranking monks in Luang Prabang. The following statement appears at the end of their manuscript:

> This traditional history (*tamnan*) of Khun Bòrom has been compiled by Pha Maha Thep Luang, who is the Senior Ecclesiastical Councillor (*thamma sena ton phi ton nòng*) residing at Wisun Monastery, and by Maha Mongkhun Sitthi, who is the Lesser Ecclesiastical Councillor (*thamma sena ton nòng*), together with the king and the entire Royal Council (*sena*), so that others can add to it for the full 5,000 years.

An internal inspection of the text and the final entries recorded in it reveal that this document was written in the time of King Wisun (r. 1501–20),[2] during whose reign the text ends, that it was an official history and that the compilation was supported by the king himself. This version was edited by Sila Viravong and Nuan

Uthensakda and was published in a 110-page edition in 1967 under the title *Nithan khun bòrom rasathirat*—literally 'Legends of King Bòrom the Great' (Thep Luang and Mongkhun Sitthi 1967).

The second version of the chronicle bears the date CS 934 (AD 1572) and was written not in Luang Prabang but in the second capital of the kingdom, Vientiane, which around 1563 became the principal residence of King Setthathirat (r. 1548–71). The author is unknown, but the final sentences of the text give some indication of the cirumstances under which it was compiled:

> One year ago [in AD 1571, when King Setthathirat died] the majority of the people invited Phaya Saen Surin to take charge of the land. Phaya Chan was opposed [to these proceedings] and was killed by Phaya Saen Surin, who then became king. The texts of the chronicle of Khun Bòrom the Great and Meritorious have been compiled from generation to generation, and in the future, if any scholar wishes to supplement or develop them, they shall do so according to what their ears have heard and what their eyes have witnessed, for this land has no other chronicle.

The text is clearly intended to legitimise the exercise of power by Saen Surin—a high official and army commander, who was not a member of the royal family—as regent for the infant son of the deceased king. His rule was short-lived, however, because the Burmese invaded, installed an uncle of the infant king as ruler, and took the regent and infant king to Burma in 1575.

The third version of the chronicle was written in CS 962 (AD 1600) during the time of King Wòrawongsa (also known as King Thammikarat, r. 1596–1622). This version does not differ significantly in content from the previous one. It does, however, provide for the first time a full and accurate account of the intrigues of a woman who was the effective ruler of Laos from 1428 to 1438 and who has been depicted by successive Lao chroniclers as a blood-thirsty queen.

The story of this queen is important, not only because of political history but for what it reveals about the status of women five centuries ago and about the ability of a woman—who had many brothers, each a potential claimant to the throne—to gain and hold power in her own right. Her given name was Kaeo Phimpha, but she is usually known as Maha Thewi—a title (from the Sanskrit *mahādevī*) that was used by a senior royal consort. There are three theories about her position in the royal family and her relationship to King Sam Saen Thai (r. 1373–1416). (1) The oldest theory, recorded in the time of King Saiya Chakkaphat (who reigned at Luang Prabang from 1442 to about 1480), implies that Maha Thewi was a sister of King Sam Saen Thai.[3] The modern historian, Sila Viravong, shares this view in his *History of Laos* (1964: 41). (2) The 1512 manuscript of Maha Thep Luang maintains that Maha Thewi was the king's senior consort. (3) The version composed in 1600 during the reign of King Wòrawongsa identifies her as a daughter of the king. Unfortunately, her exact official position cannot be inferred from internal evidence in the text, because the honorific term *nang* that preceeds her given name and her title in the written records (where she is called Nang Kaeo Phimpha or Nang Maha Thewi) can refer equally to a queen or a princess.

The third theory seems to be the most reliable one for several reasons. First, at the time of King Sam Saen Thai's death in 1416, five of his six sons were still alive, and each of them had a legitimate claim to the succession. (1) Lan Kham Daeng was the eldest surviving son, and he succeeded his father on the throne of Luang Prabang. (2) Thao Kham Temsa was the governor of Pak Huai Luang and is known as Phaya Pak. (3) Thao Lü Sai was the governor of Kabòng and was called Phaya Mün Sai. (4) Thao Kòn Kaeo was the governor of Siang Sa and was known also as Phaya Chik Kham. (5) Thao Wang Buri was the governor of Vientiane and was called Phaya Khwa Pa Sak. With most of her brothers far away, Maha Thewi wielded much power and even rivalled the only brother still in the capital: King Lan Kham Daeng. With the death of this brother in 1428, she was in a position to exercise absolute power in the capital, while striving to ensure that her remaining brothers and other potential contenders stayed where they were.

If Maha Thewi was a sister (or a consort) of King Sam Saen Thai, she must have been in her sixties and possibly in her seventies while she exercised power from 1428 to 1438. (Her approximate age in this case can be inferred from our knowledge of King Sam Saen

Thai, who was born in 1356, succeeded his father in 1373 and died in 1416 at about the age of sixty.) Given the rivalry among King Sam Saen Thai's sons and grandsons over the succession, it seems unlikely that anyone at such an advanced age could exercise power so effectively for ten years. If she was a royal consort, however, it is possible that she was far younger than the king and therefore still in her prime in the 1430s.

The Wòrawongsa version of the chronicle records that Maha Thewi married a man named Wiang Pha and that, despite opposition from all of her relatives, she attempted to transfer her powers to her commoner-husband. Her amorous behaviour in the 1430s suggests that she was perhaps between 30 and 50 years old and therefore that she must have been a daughter (or a young consort) of King Sam Saen Thai. But, once again, it is possible that she was much older than this when she embarked on her love affair with Wiang Pha. Although no definitive conclusion can be drawn, these considerations suggest that she was most likely a daughter of King Sam Saen Thai, as indicated in the Wòrawongsa version of the chronicle.

The last sentence of the third version gives the following account of the accession of the next ruler, King Wòrawongsa, who is also known as King Thammikarat:

> Pha Wòraphita entrusted to his son Wòrawongsa the kingdom together with the elders, elephants and horses and a royal consort, Nang Kaen. Wòrawongsa then took up residence in Müang Kun in the year *kot chai* [second in the CS decade, year of the rat], the year 962 of the [Lesser] Era [AD 1600].

This version of the chronicle ends with the year 1600 but provides no information about the early period of Wòrawongsa's rule (during the 1596–1600 regency, until he came of age),[4] other than his unexplained move to a new residence outside the capital.

The fourth version of the chronicle was written in CS 989 (AD 1627), the first year in the reign of King Kaeng (also known as Mòm Kaeo). It is also known as the 'Phuan kingdom' version because of the emphasis it places on events in Siang Khwang, the Phuan capital in the plateau region of northern Laos. The last sentences of this document records that

The majority of the people selected Pha Maha Nam [also known by the title Phaya Nakhòn] as the successor and gave him the regnal name Phothisarat in the year *tao set* [fourth in the decade, year of the dog (CS 984, AD 1622)]. He reigned five years and died in the year *sawai yi* [eighth in the decade, year of the tiger], the year 988 of the [Lesser] Era [AD 1626]. The majority of the people then chose Mòm Kaeo, his brother, to succeed him as king of Lan Sang in the year *moeng mao* [ninth in the decade, year of the hare], the year 989 of the [Lesser] Era [AD 1627].

This version was published in 1967 by the Literary Committee of the Kingdom of Laos with the title *Nangsü khun bòrom rasathirat* ('The Book of King Bòrom the Great'), with a subtitle indicating that it is 'The True Ancient Version' of the chronicle. The text of the chronicle itself is only 65 pages in this edition, but the volume editor (Chum Chitamet) added a further 147 pages to this edition by appending to it the traditional Lao law code.

The fifth version of the chronicle is known as the version of the 'Hua Phan Müang Bun'. It is dated CS 1009 (AD 1647) and thus ends early in the reign of King Suriyawongsa Thammikarat, who ruled from 1638 until 1695. The last sentence says

In the year 1009 of the [Lesser] Era, the year *moeng khai* [ninth in the decade, year of the pig], on the second day of the waxing moon of the second month [27 December 1647], the Hua Phan Müang Bun at the Müang Phet Sai landing had this work written, to provide knowledge [of the events recorded in the chronicle] to all people.

Nothing is known about the compiler of this version of the chronicle. The official title of the man who sponsored the compilation is given only as the Hua Phan Müang Bun. *Hua phan* is a rank in the official hierarchy; Bun could be either the name of his home province or simply an official title. The reference to a river landing suggests that he may have been responsible for certain affairs on the Mekong, such as collecting taxes, supervising the movements of boats and overseeing the activities of traders.

One of the most important milestones of Lao history is marked by the compilation of the sixth version of the chronicle in CS 1070 (AD 1708). The date of this manuscript is also an important juncture of renewed discontinuity in Lao history, because it is the first compilation after the 1707 division of the united Lao kingdom into two separate states under two independent monarchs, one ruling in Luang Prabang and the other in Vientiane.

The period following the long reign of King Suriyawongsa was a troubled one. The king was succeeded by two men (a son-in-law and another man related to the royal family), neither of whom had a rightful claim to the throne. The king's nephew—Sai Ong We (also known by his regnal title, Setthathirat II, r. 1698–1735)—then became king in Vientiane. One of the grandsons of King Suriyawongsa, however, declared himself king at Luang Prabang, broke away from the united Lao kingdom, declared the independence of Luang Prabang in 1707 and left the nephew, Sai Ong We, to rule from Vientiane over only the lower part of the formerly united kingdom.

The last entry in the new chronicle, compiled the year following the partition of the kingdom, describes a religious occurrence at Luang Prabang and an important ceremonial act of the new king:

> In the seventieth year of the Era [CS 1070], on the fourth day of the waxing moon of the ninth month [5 August 1708], during the *kong ngai* period [between 7.30 and 9 o'clock in the morning], Pha Kêsa That Chao [the Sacred Hair Relic (Pali *kesadhātu*)] came to honour Phia Si Suttha Sinalongkan in his shoulder bag.[5] He placed the bag above the bed from which he was guarding the Prabang image at Pa Sak Luang Monastery. Phia Si Suttha was preparing to use this money to buy a golden bowl and to ordain a novice as a monk.

The sacred Prabang image was the palladium of the kingdom. To keep vigil over it at night, the official in charge (Si Suttha Sinalongkan) had a bed in the building where the image was kept. He was unaware that the Sacred Hair Relic had miraculously come to reside temporarily in his bag, and he placed the bag above the bed. The Lao text implies that he became aware of its presence only when he looked in his bag, apparently intending to count the money that was inside. The text continues as follows:

> He saw the Sacred Hair Relic and had it kept overnight for two nights with the Prabang image. He then presented it to the Royal Ecclesiastical Scholar who is the patriarch of Chan Monastery. After two nights, the Royal Ecclesiastical Scholar and Phia Si Suttha Sinalongkan presented it to the king, who gave orders for it to be placed with the Prabang image. The king gathered together [offerings of] eight *bat*-weight [120 grammes (4 troy ounces)] of gold and a *makbia*-coin, which were used to make an ornament for the head of the image.

The detailed record of this miraculous event and the royal offerings to the sacred image suggests that the immediate purpose of this text was to legitimise the position of King Kitsarat, who reigned in Luang Prabang from 1707 to 1713 and established the branch of the Lao royal family that ruled over this part of Laos until the twentieth century.

The date of the seventh version of the chronicle is not stated in the text, but the manuscript may have been completed about 1791, which is the last date recorded in it. This manuscript, known as the Phraya Pracha version, is a copy of a Lao manuscript obtained by a senior official of the Thai government, Phraya Pracha Kitchakòrachak (Chaem Bunnag). This version is more widely known than earlier ones, because it was transliterated into Thai script (retaining the old Lao idiom of Lan Sang) and has been published in several editions. It was first published in Thai script in the journal *Wachirayan* and was included in the first volume of the Thai-language history series (*Prachum phongsawadan*), which began in 1914.

The text is in two parts. The first relates events prior to the accession of Khun Lò (a son of Khun Bòrom) and provides a detailed account of Maha Thewi's reign. The second part is similar to previous manuscripts. The account of Lao history in this version was extended by the compilers through the period of the Lao loss of independence to the Thai kingdom in the late 1770s. The last date recorded in the work is the year in which King Suriyawong (r. 1771–91) died.

The eighth version was probably written about 1820, since the last event that it mentions is the consecration of King Mantha Thurat on the last day of the preceding year. The body of the text does not differ in substance from earlier versions, but this version does extend the record of historic events to the date of the compilation. It ends with the following statement, which requires some explanation:

> King Mantha Thurat, the eldest son of King Anurut, succeeded to the throne of Lan Sang in the year 154 [sic] of the Era, the year *kat mao* [sic], on the fifteenth day of the waxing moon of the second month.

King Anurut abdicated in old age in 1817, handed the reins of state to his eldest son and died two years later. The date in the text refers to the death of the old king at the age of eighty-two. The year of his death is recorded in two different styles: the Lesser Era (CS 154) and the Lao style (*kat mao*, fourth in the decade, year of the hare). It is common practice to abbreviate CS years, and 154 is automatically read as 1154. But that CS year is obviously wrong: it is not only too early (AD 1792/3) but also a year of the rat. Obviously the chronicler or a later copyist has retained the correct Lao year but has copied (or inserted) the CS year incorrectly. (It should be 181, or CS 1181, corresponding to 1819/20.) Thus the date in the text corresponds to 31 December 1819, the day on which King Anurut died. Meanwhile, King Mantha Thurat exercised effective power as king from the time of the abdication, and his reign is therefore usually given as 1817–36.

The ninth version of the chronicle is commonly known by the title *Tamnan luang prabang* ('A Traditional History of Luang Prabang'). It is called the Great Council of State (*khana senabòdi*) edition, since it was compiled under the chairmanship of a royal councillor who is known only by his title: Phaya Müang Chan. The last phrase of the text, which apparently refers to some auspicious moment in time, asserts that it was the *thae kaeo thiang* hour [the period from 9 A.M. to 10.30 A.M.] when Phaya Müang Chan completed this traditional history of Luang Prabang.

The text is dated CS 1200 (AD 1838) and begins with stories about the dynasties of mythical giants (*yaksa*), of Phaya Ngu Lüam (the 'Python Lord'), of Chantha Phanit and of Khun Sawa. All of these dynasties ruled over the kingdom of Sawa, which was the precursor of Luang Prabang. The document goes on to recount Khun Bòrom's arrival from Thaeng (the town known in Vietnamese as Dien Bien Phu) to rule over the kingdom of the Sipsòng Chao Tai ('Twelve Tai Lords') and the accession of his son, Khun Lò, as king of Lan Sang.

The tenth version of the chronicle was compiled in CS 1229 (AD 1867) under the supervision of King Chantha Kuman (r. 1851–70). Since a copy in Thai was addressed to the Thai interior minister at the Ministers' Pavilion (*sala luk khun*) in Bangkok, the manuscript is known as the Ministers' Pavilion Version of the Luang Prabang chronicle (*Phongsawadan müang luang phrabang chabap sala luk khun*). It makes a brief refererence to Khun Lò and then skips to the time of King Suwanna Kham Phong (r. 1316 to ca. 1344), at which point the continuous chronicle begins.

The eleventh version of the chronicle is the Thai-language copy of the manuscript compiled in 1867, and it is nearly identical to the tenth (Lao-language) version. It ends with an extract from an official despatch dated 11 October 1867. The manuscript was preserved in the interior ministry in Bangkok and was published in 1917 with the title *Phongsawadan müang luang phrabang tam chabap thi mi yu nai sala luk khun* ('Chronicle of Luang Prabang, According to the Manuscript in the Ministers' Pavilion'), together with several other documents in Part 5 of the Thai-language history series.

The eleventh version is known by two names, either as the Ministers' Pavilion (Thai-language) version or as the King Mongkut version, since the compilation was initiated at the request of the Thai monarch, King Mongkut (r. 1851–68). It begins, like the tenth version, with the reign of Phaya Suwanna Kham Phong. The final passages are concerned with the sacred Prabang image, which was taken from Luang Prabang in the latter part of the eighteenth century, when the Thai extended their control over the Lao kingdoms. The image was returned to Luang Prabang at the request of the Lao Heir Apparent, Prince Un Kham, who succeeded after his father died in 1870. This version of the chronicle ends with a lengthy description of the procession and ceremonies surrounding the re-entry of the image into the city in September 1867.

The twelfth version of the chronicle is well known and has long been in print in the Thai language. An unknown Thai author rewrote the late-eighteenth-century Lao-idiom manuscript of Phraya Pracha in central Thai idiom for King Chulalongkorn (r. 1868–1910), expanded the text and attempted (somewhat unsuccessfully) to extend the chronology up to the death of King Chantha Kuman in August 1870. This version was published as Part 11 of the Thai-language history series and has been reprinted several times. It is arguable that the eleventh and twelfth versions ought to be excluded from the list of chronicles examined in this study, since both were written explicitly for non-Lao readers and both bear the marks of foreign editorship. They are included here because they perpetuate, in form if not entirely in content, the tradition of compiling the Khun Bòrom chronicle.

Few versions of the chronicles have been published in any language other than Lao or Thai. For a long time, the only translations available were selections published by August Pavie (1898).[6] No translation was available in which the original Lao text could be compared, prior to the publication of a manuscript preserved in the library of the Ecole française d'Extrême-orient in Paris. This publication (Phinith 1987) includes not only a facsimile of the 59-page Lao manuscript but also a translation in French with voluminous explanatory notes.

This manuscript is counted in the present comparative study as the thirteenth version, although it records only one event subsequent to the year in which the 1867 versions were compiled. The copy preserved in Paris was made in 1900, but the last date recorded in the manuscript is 1874—the year in which King Un Kham formally ascended the throne. (King Chantha Kuman died in 1870; the ensuing interval of three years represents the period leading to his cremation and then to the ceremonial accession of King Un Kham.) Even the single event of 1874, which appears in the final lines of the manuscript, could be an entry added long after the chronicle itself was compiled. The main body of the chronicle follows the text of the Thai-language 1867 version very closely until the late eighteenth century, at which point the entries in the two texts begin to deviate significantly.

A brief comparison of the tenth, eleventh and thirteenth versions, all of which were probably compiled about the same time, provides some insights into the ways that historical records were rewritten to suit the times and the patrons of the compilers. The tenth (Lao) version contains some information that does not appear in earlier versions. For example, it states that:

> Formerly Luang Prabang was called Si Sattanakhanahut [its Pali name] Lan Sang Rom Khao [the kingdom of 'a million elephants and the white royal parasol']. It was an independent country. The land was ruled by a succession of its monarchs from the time of Khun Lò, who was a son of Khun Bòrom the Great.

This passage reflects the wording of a proclamation written in the 1850s by the Thai monarch, King Mongkut (Mongkut 1924: 82, proclamation 309), which discusses relations among the South-East Asian countries in previous centuries

> . . . in the days when Luang Prabang was still a fully independent state, or when Lan Sang (that is, Vientiane) was another fully independent state.

By contrast, the eleventh (Thai) version of the chronicle renders the same passage (*Phongsawadan müang luang prabang* 1963: 317) with a subtle difference:

> Formerly Luang Prabang was called Si Sattanakhanahut Lan Sang Rom Khao. It was a vassal state under Beijing. The land was ruled by a succession of its monarchs. Once every five years, they had to send tribute for presentation [to the Chinese emperor].

Even a superficial comparison of these two passages reveals that a certain amount of editing was performed on the text, to 'correct' and supplement it in the Thai version. In the passages quoted, the independent Lao kingdom of many past centuries (in the Lao version) is made to appear (in the Thai version) like a vassal state with inferior status and a much shorter history than it really had. Chronicle entries often make the interpretation of history difficult. Another example is the treatment of the Lao independence movement at the end of the reign of King Anuwong (r. 1804–28) of Vientiane. Both the Thai transliteration of the 1867 version and the Lao text of the 1874 version (Phinith 1987: 150–1, 404) assert that King Mantha Thurat (r. 1817–36) of Luang Prabang dissociated himself from and opposed King Anuwong in 1827, which implies that King Mantha Thurat resisted the cause for Lao independence espoused by King Anuwong. In contrast, the earlier Lao manuscript (version ten) does not contain this implication. It is possible, given the sequence of compilations outlined in this study, that this part of the eleventh version was written purposely to support the Thai version of these events and that this Thai editorial influence was perpetuated in the 1874 Lao version. When comparing different versions of the chronicle, therefore, scholars must be wary of the historiographical background to each compilation, to avoid the pitfalls of such editorial licence and its misleading implications.

The fourteenth version is called *Phongsawadan müang lan sang* ('Chronicle of Lan Sang'). It was compiled in 1898 and extends the account of Lao history to the middle of the reign of King Kham Suk (also known as Sakkarin, r. 1894–1904). It states categorically that Maha Thewi 'was Nang Kaeo Phimpha, a daughter of Phaya Sam Saen Thai'. This account is similar to the one in the version of 1600. There are some differences between this version and the eleventh and twelfth versions—not all of which are the fault of the copyists—and thus these versions merit close comparison by historians.

The fifteenth version of the chronicle is called *Phongsawadan müang luang prabang* ('Chronicle of Luang Prabang'). It was published in a 212-page edition by the National Library of Laos in 1969. The date of compilation is not known precisely, but the last events that it records, as illustrated in the following passage, suggest that it was written around the turn of the present century, by which time the French colonial authorities had imposed many important changes on Lao administration:

> In the year 1255 of the [Lesser] Era [AD 1893], the king of Siam, in a conflict with the French, was forced to relinquish the territory of Lan Sang to France. Since that time, France has introduced a new tax system, has forbidden the officials of the kingdom from using the people as servants, has prohibited the owning of slaves (who have thus been liberated), has levied a capitation tax of 2,000 *bia* [cowries] and has required the able men to perform forced labour for twenty days each year.

This version provides some interesting insights, not found in earlier manuscripts, into the power struggle that took place in mid-fourteenth-century Luang Prabang and the period of exile spent by the future king (Fa Ngum, r. 1353–73) and his father at the court of the Khmer king in Angkor.

An abbreviated chronicle is appended to the 1969 edition. There are ten versions of these abbreviated chronicles (known as *Chotmai-het yò wiang chan*), all written after 1560 when Vientiane became the capital. They contain very brief statements about major events and are useful for comparative purposes, when historians want to clarify or reconcile points on which the detailed chronicles are unclear or different.

The sixteenth version of the chronicle was written in 1926, during the reign of King Sisawangwong (r. 1904–59), and reproduced in manuscript form.[7] It was reprinted in 1967 by the Education Ministry in a 55-page edition titled *Phongsawadan haeng pathet lao khü luang phrabang wiang chan müang phuan lae champasak* ('Chronicles of Laos: Luang Prabang, Vientiane, the Phuan Kingdom and Champasak). Athough this text is the most recent of all the versions examined in this study, and has some characteristics of the transition to a modern style of historical writing, the compiler perpetuated the chronicler's tradition of writing in an archaic form of the Lao language. In this respect, the style adheres to that of earlier versions, and the text is presented, for the most part, according to the same pattern found in earlier versions. Near the end of this version, however, the author attempts to adopt a Western approach in presenting his material, and he divides his history into the formerly separate political entities that existed in the territory of modern-day Laos: the Luang Prabang, Vientiane, Phuan and Champasak kingdoms.

Among the early modern attempts to compile a history of Laos, the most widely known authors are Paul Le Boulanger (1931) and Sila Viravong (1957, 1964). Two additional works by Thai authors should also be cited. Phraya Pramuan Wichaphun published his interpretation of Lao history in 1939 with the title *Phongsawadan müang lan chang* ('Chronicle of Lan Sang'). He based this compilation on some of the earlier versions of the Lao chronicles, and he attempted to give his work a wider perspective by consulting additional chronicles about the northern, north-eastern and central provinces of the Thai kingdom. The calendrical system that he used reflects the changes made in the official calendar of the Thai kingdom, the discontinuation of the Lesser Era and the adoption of the Buddhist Era as the basis for the official Thai calendar. The author has, accordingly, converted all dates from the Lesser Era to the Buddhist Era. He has also attempted to draw parallels between the accomplishments of the Lao and those of surrounding kingdoms, by inserting materials from the discoveries of archaeologists and other modern scholars, as shown in the following passage (Pramuan 1939: 6):

> Lan Sang extended along both sides of the Mekong River and was independent for many centuries. It possessed important monuments dating from the time of the great [Indian] Emperor Asoka [who was ruling] in BE 236 [297 BC]. For example, the sacred Phanom stupa is older than the stone sanctuary towers of the Khmer [of the Angkor period], and the town of Nakhòn Phanom was once the capital of the Lao or Lawa country in the kingdom of Si Khottabun, which was called Fu Nan by the Chinese.

This version credits the Lao rulers of the kingdom of Si Khottabun with building monuments that are older than those of Angkor,

89

the capital of the ancient Cambodian empire. This assertion is similar to the claim made in the Ulangkha That ('Sacred Breast-Bone Relic') chronicle (Pruess 1976) that the Lao were the builders of the sacred stupa on the central Mekong. Other than these differences, the contents of this chronicle are similar to those of earlier texts—beginning with the story of Khun Bòrom and recounting the line of succession up to King Sisawangwong's accession to the throne of Luang Prabang in 1904.

The sixteen primary sources reviewed in this study are the only versions of the *Phün khun bòrom* genre that are available at present to scholars interested in Lao history.[8] It is likely, however, that other versions exist. If additional texts are discovered, they will probably be fragile, handwritten copies that have been preserved in the monasteries of the Lao countryside. Some unique manuscripts could contain the sole surviving records of important historical events. Searching for and copying such texts are difficult tasks, but this work must be carried out in the near future if these materials are to be saved for posterity. The discovery of some long-forgotten manuscript could provide historians with more complete and more accurate details that could resolve some of the mysteries of Lao history.

CHRONOLOGICAL LIST OF LAO CHRONICLES CITED

The chronicles are listed in order of the date of compilation or last date recorded in the text. Copies of the unpublished chronicles are available, mostly in typewritten form, in the library of the Committee for Educational Research, Ministry of Education, Vientiane. The typewritten versions were copied by Kham Champakéomani in 1980.

1512 Thep Luang, Maha, and Maha Mongkhun Sitthi, compilers. *Nithan khun bòrom rasathirat* [Tales of King Bòrom the Great]. Edited by Sila Viravong and Nuan Uthensakda. Vientiane: Saeng Panya Kanphim, 1967.

1572 Unpublished manuscript.

1600 Unpublished manuscript.

1627 *Nangsü khun bòrom rasathirat* [The Book of Khun Bòrom the Great: The True Ancient Version]. Edited by Chum Chitamet. Vientiane: Literary Committee of the Kingdom of Laos, 1967.

1647 Unpublished manuscript.

1708 Unpublished manuscript.

1791 Pracha Kitchakòrachak manuscript. *Phongsawadan lan sang tam thòi kham nai chabap doem* [Chronicle of Lan Sang, According to the Original Lao-Idiom Text]. In *Prachum phongsawadan* [History Series] Part 1 (Bangkok: Khurusapha Press, 1963), ii: 134–85. In Lao (printed in Thai script).

1820 Unpublished manuscript.

1838 Unpublished manuscript.

1867 Unpublished manuscript.

1867 Ministers' Pavilion (*sala luk khun*) version. *Phongsawadan müang luang phrabang tam chabap thi mi yu nai sala luk khun* [Chronicle of Luang Prabang, According to the Manuscript in the Ministers' Pavilion]. In *Prachum phongsawadan* [History Series] Part 5 (Bangkok: Khurusapha Press, 1963), iv: 315–69.

1870 *Phongsawadan müang luang phrabang* [Chronicle of Luang Prabang]. In *Prachum phongsawadan* [History Series] Part 11 (Bangkok: Khurusapha Press, 1964), x: 135–236. In Thai.

1874 EFEO manuscript. *Lamdap nithan müa pha phuthachao dai khao ma yiap nai din müang luang lan sang* [Sucession of Tales from the Time When the Lord Buddha Trod the Ground of Müang Luang Lan Sang]. Published in *Contribution à l'histoire du royame de Luang Prabang*. Translated and edited by Saveng Phinith. Paris: Ecole française d'Extrême-orient, 1987. In Lao and French.

1898 Unpublished manuscript.

ca. 1900 *Phongsawadan müang luang phabang* [Chronicle of Luang Prabang]. Vientiane: National Library, 1969.

1926 Unpublished manuscript.

NOTES

1. References are cited in the text for all the published versions of the chronicles. The unpublished versions are listed in the notes above.

2. Some authors give later dates for the beginning of this reign. The year 1501 is implied by an entry in the Hua Phan Müang Bun version of the chronicles, which records that after Wisun ruled for five years, his son was born in CS 868 (AD 1506/7).

3. A work known as *Lam phün khun bòrom* was probably written by Paj Hua Kham during the reign of Saiya Chakkaphat (r. 1442–80). The extant version consists of two bundles of palm leaves (34 leaves, for a total of 67 pages) written in the Buddhist Tham script. Although it is apparently the oldest record, it has not been included in the list of chronicles surveyed in this paper, because it has not yet been transcribed into modern Lao script.

4. Pha Wòraphita was the husband of Nang Kham Khai, the youngest sister of King Setthathirat. In 1591, Setthathirat's son, Pha Nò Müang (also known as Nò Kaeo Kuman), was sent back to Laos from Burma, and he ruled at Vientiane until his death in 1596. Pha Wòrawongsa succeeded and was known also as King Thammikarat (r. 1596–1622). Since he was only fourteen years old in 1596, the Burmese appointed his father, Wòraphita, to serve as regent. Burmese power receded during this regency, with the collapse of the empire and the sack of the Burmese capital at Pegu.

5. The Lao term is *thòng paeng*, a cloth bag with a shoulder strap, especially the type carried in the past by a bhikkhu or former bhikkhu.

6. See note 7 and the annotation in the list of references concerning the mysterious *Les annales du Laos* (1926), which is cited by some modern authors.

7. This handwritten edition may be the one cited in Le Boulanger (1931: 363) with the title *Les annales du Laos: Luang Prabang, Vientiane, Tran-Ninh et Bassac* (Hanoi, 1926). The National Library in Vientiane does not have a copy of the 1926 Hanoi edition, and despite the title cited by Le Boulanger, the work apparently was not translated into French.

8. There are, of course, many other important records. For example, a 1627 chronicle (*Phün müang phuan*) cited by Lorrillard (1995: 17) is similar to the works surveyed here. It is not included in this study because it focusses on the Phuan kingdom in the plateau region of northern Laos.

EARLY EUROPEAN
IMPRESSIONS OF THE LAO

MAYOURY AND PHEUIPHANH
NGAOSRIVATHANA

The lands inhabited by the Lao people extend across the heart of
the South-East Asian peninsula, from the frontiers of China on the
north to the borders of Cambodia on the south. This vast hinterland
is isolated from the coastal states of the region, and early European
visitors rarely penetrated far enough into the interior to gather even
the meagerest of information about it. Prior to the second half of
the nineteenth century, it was almost a *terra incognita* to Western
mapmakers, charted mainly by 'cartographic imagination'.[1]

THE EARLY EXPLORERS

Possibly the first Europeans to venture into Laos were a group of
Portuguese, who are thought to have accompanied a Burmese envoy
on a mission about 1545 from Pegu to Luang Prabang and back.
Long after this journey took place, Fernão Mendes Pinto reported
that he was one of nine Portuguese prisoner-servants in the envoy's
entourage. He probably had no means of keeping notes or a journal,
and therefore it is not surprising that his subsequent recollections of
geographical details, toponyms and titles of officials appear confused
and unintelligible. He published a description of a kingdom he
called Calaminham (Pinto 1989: 352–64). This entire section of
his book was long thought to be either a figment of his imagination
or an amalgam of random recollections from his extensive travels

elsewhere in Asia. Doubtless, it bears the embellishments of a good story-teller, who wrote down these observations in the 1570s, more than a quarter of a century after he visited the upper Mekong. He used neither the term 'Lao' nor any toponyms that gave readers an obvious clue to the places he was describing.

Reseach in the present century (Campos 1940: 20) has shown, however, that some of his toponyms, while appearing to bear no relation to any known Lao names, could be Portuguese corruptions of names that he learned from the Burmese and Mon members of the embassy—who in turn did not render the Lao pronunciation of names with any precision in their own languages. In a new English translation published by Chicago University Press (Pinto 1989: 564, 606–7), R. D. Catz has drawn upon modern scholarly works in an attempt to identify places and terms that appear in the chapter on Luang Prabang. Despite the length of his description of Laos, Pinto's record of his visit has always been regarded as part fact mixed with many fanciful tales. His book first appeared in print in 1614 and has been translated and republished many times in various European languages. But unfortunately he made no contribution to contemporary Europeans' knowledge of Laos.

The earliest recorded European exploration of the central Mekong took place in 1596, when two adventurers—a Portuguese (Diogo Veloso) and a Spaniard (Blas Ruiz de Hernán Gonzáles)—travelled from the coast of central Vietnam across the cordillera and then went up the Mekong to visit Vientiane briefly. Veloso and Ruiz reported their visit to Spanish colonial officials in Manila, and the brief summary that was published in 1609 (Morga 1971: 124–5) provided first-hand impressions by Europeans of the country, its people and topography.

A small group of Dutch merchants led by Geebaerd van Wusthof investigated the potential for trade in the central Mekong in 1641, but likewise went up-river only as far as Vientiane. In 1642, while some of the Dutchmen were still there, two Catholic priests arrived in Vientiane (Wusthof 1986: 196). One of them—an Italian Jesuit, Giovanni Maria Leria—worked in Laos until 1648.[2] The information that he collected was published in Italian in 1663 by another priest, Giovanni Filippo di Marini, and in a French translation three years later. This work provided European readers with their first detailed description of Laos and its people. It was soon followed by the Dutchmen's journals of their commercial mission, which was published in Dutch in 1669 (Lejosne 1986). For the next two centuries, Europeans made no attempts to explore the deep interior of the South-East Asian peninsula. Or, to be more precise, if any Europeans did venture into Lao territory, no record of them has been found. British merchants and officials ventured into the interior from the coast of Burma in the late 1820s and the 1830s, but they explored what eventually came to be called 'Burmese Laos' (i.e., the Tai-speaking Shan States and Sipsòng Panna) and 'Western Laos' (the Tai-speaking kingdom of Lan Na, with its main power centre at Chiang Mai). After Leria, two centuries passed before another European explorer, Henri Mouhot, ventured into the upper Mekong (or 'East Laos' as he called it) and bequeathed to European readers a published description of the Lao and the city of Luang Prabang, where he succumbed to malarial fever in 1861.

As Mouhot planned his explorations, he was unable to glean useful details from European publications. He was reflecting not the state of geographical knowledge in his day but merely the lack of information in Western languages when he complained:

> To consult any existing maps of Indochina for my guidance in the interior of Laos would have been a folly, no [European] traveller, at least to my knowledge, having penetrated into East Laos, or published any authentic information respecting it. To question the natives about places more than a degree distant would have been useless. (*Siam Repository* 1869: 95)

Mouhot obviously had no means of learning anything from the people who did indeed have extensive knowledge of the hinterland, its trade routes and its geography: that is, local officials throughout the upper Mekong region (who frequently visited the coastal areas where Mouhot began his overland journey) and traders of many ethnic groups, who regularly criss-crossed the region. Moreover, Mouhot may have imagined that he was the first European to travel in the Mekong valley north of Cambodia. He may have been unaware of Marini's and Veloso's accounts of the central Mekong. The report by van Wusthof was available only in Dutch, and no one yet suspected that Pinto had visited the upper Mekong.

LAOS IN EARLY EUROPEAN MAPS

Although European mapmakers knew very little about the upper Mekong valley until the second half of the nineteenth century, Western scholars even in ancient times knew the name of a place that may be an antecedent of the Lao kingdom. The earliest extant reference is Ptolemy's map *Indiam extra Gangem* (The Indies beyond the Ganges), compiled about AD 160, which mentions a country called Daona. Gerini (1909) suggested that Daona's territory encompassed the upper Mekong and Chao Phraya basins and that its inhabitants included 'one of the original ten families of the Ai Lao, mentioned from before the Christian era'. These ten families are recorded in legend as the ancestors of the modern Lao (Luce 1960 and Gogoi 1968: 32–57). Like other writers of his time, Gerini imitated the Thai habit of making no distinction among the major Tai-speaking ethnic groups who lived in the Mekong valley and the upper reaches of the Chao Phraya basin. Well into the twentieth century, Europeans followed the Thai practice of using the term 'Lao' indiscriminately when referring not only to the Lao of the Mekong valley but also to the Shan of north-east Burma, the Tai-dialect speakers of Chiang Mai and Sipsòng Panna, the Phuan of northern Laos, and others. Writings of early travellers should be treated with caution, partly for this reason and partly because toponyms were so poorly understood.

European travellers naturally attempted to transliterate toponyms according to the contemporary spellings of the sounds in their own languages, whether Portuguese, Italian, Spanish, Dutch, French, English or even (among priests) Latin. In addition, two people who speak the same language may perceive the sounds of a name differently and therefore spell the name in different ways. This problem is compounded by the fact that the travellers' informants and guides themselves spoke different languages (Burmese, Khmer, and Mon, for example) and had other versions of the same toponyms in their own languages. It is not surprising, therefore, that different names for even a widely known city often seem to have no relationship. Yet another difficulty arises in transcription by European typesetters and cartographers, who may simply have misread unfamiliar names in a handwritten document.

The problem of identifying places in the interior of South-East Asia is further complicated by an absence of knowledge about the political structure. The Lao of the Mekong basin called their kingdom Lan Sang. Its capital was originally at Luang Prabang but moved in the 1560s to Vientiane. Variations in spelling reflect early European attempts to transliterate the word Lan Sang—literally, the 'Land of a Million Elephants'—which was the name of the Lao kingdom on the upper Mekong from at least the fourteenth century.

The northern part of the Chao Phraya basin and some adjacent territory in the Mekong valley was known locally as the kingdom of Lan Na. Its capital was called Chiang Mai by its inhabitants, but the Burmese called it Zin-mè and the Mon had yet another variant of the pronunciation. Since Europeans first learned this name from the coastal peoples, it is not surprising to find a bewildering variety of European spellings of it. The spellings that derive from the local name, Chiang Mai, include one by Tomé Pires, who spelled it 'Jangoma' in 1517 and mistakenly thought that it was 'bounded by Burma and by Cambodia' (Pires 1944: 111). The same spelling was used by de Barros in 1563 and Boccaro in the 1630s. Among the other variants of this name are Jangumaa (Pinto 1614) and Jangama (Saintbury 1617, cited in Petithuguenin 1949: 204). Yet others include Janguma, Jangoman, Jagoman and Jagama. Among the variants apparently derived from the Burmese Zin-mè are Zangomay, Zimmay and Zimmé. Some variants even appear to be hybrids of the two names, such as Jamahay, Jamahey and Jangamay.

The earliest known map on which one of these names appears is dated 1505 and, at first glance, appears to use the spelling 'Fangoma' (Hoshino 1986: 224–5). A comparison of other maps of the period suggests, however, that this reading is related to the old fonts and scripts and that the cartographer or typesetter used not an *F* but an ornamental upper-case *I* (which in those days was used instead of the modern *J*). Thus the correct reading of this name may simply be Iangoma, which is another variant of Jangoma. In the 1571 map by Ortelis, for example, the *I* of Iangoma has been printed with a broken font, and the name could, therefore, easily be misread as 'Fangoma' or even 'Tangoma'. Alternatively, the typesetter may have used a defective font, or set the word with the wrong letter entirely.

Maps dating from 1590 to 1595 sometimes use the spellings 'Langoma' and 'Laugoma', which illustrates a likely misreading of handwritten material by the cartographer himself when setting the type. It is very common even today to misread a handwritten *n* for a *u*, or vice-versa, especially in a word that is unfamiliar. Both of these spellings appear in one Dutch atlas published in 1636 (Mercator 1636: folios 415–6 and 419-20), although on different maps. The published account of Ralph Fitch's 1587 visit to Chiang Mai uses the spellings Tamakey and Tangomes, which appear to be similar misreadings by early typesetters of the handwritten Jamahey (Chiang Mai) and Langomes (Jangomes, people of Jangoma, meaning Chiang Mai). In the 1590–5 maps, the city of Langoma is placed at some distance, however, from the true site of Chiang Mai (Hoshino 1986: 233).

The compilers of the 1759 *Universal History*, reprinted in the present book, note that mapmakers did not always leave enough room in the interior to represent all the kingdoms that were known from travellers' accounts. This tendency is evident in the Portuguese maps compared by Manguin (1972), to illustrate the early evolution of European cartographic knowledge about the coastline of Vietnam. These maps also show the early evolution of knowledge about the interior and the representation of the Mekong River and cordillera. Details of the interior do not appear on any of the maps until one dated ca. 1592–4 by Bartolomeu Lasso. This map shows the Mekong flowing from deep in the interior, and a city called Iangoma directly west of the well-known seaport of Sinoa, near Hué. At first glance, this map seems to show the city of Vientiane, although it is placed on the wrong side of the river. In fact, it seems likely that the cartographer knew the name Iangoma (the capital of an interior kingdom), and also knew that there was a Lao capital (Vientiane) on the Mekong at the latitude of Sinoa. Thus he appears to have marked the city of Vientiane in roughly its correct position in the map, but has labelled it Iangoma (Chiang Mai, the capital of Lan Na), partly by mistaken assumptions and partly because the map has little space for Chiang Mai in its true position.

A later Dutch map uses a name that is closer to the Lao pronunciation of Lan Sang. A Dutch trader at Ayutthaya named De Groote published a map in 1636 with the title *Me-nam of te Moeder der Wateren* ('The Menam, or the Mother of Waters'), which shows the name Müang (meaning 'land of') Land Yangh (a Dutch spelling of 'Lan Sang') at approximately the site of modern-day Vientiane on the Mekong (Kennedy 1970: 320). It is not surprising that at this juncture, finally, the map begins to show the Lao capital, because the Dutch company sponsored a major trading mission to Vientiane only five years later.

European writers were using the name 'Laos' (albeit spelled in slightly different ways) at least by the 1560s (Barros 1563, Galvano 1563, Camões 1572). The earliest map in which Laos is identified is dated 1613. It is in the Portuguese manuscript of Eredia's description of South-East Asia (but not in the 1930 English translation). Born in Melaka in 1563, Eredia must have known about Laos at an early age, and his map gives it a prominent position among the countries east of the Bay of Bengal (see fig. 3).

Father Alexandre de Rhodes's 1651 book on the Vietnamese empire was accompanied by a map (reproduced in Tâm 1989: 58) that attempted to outline the adjacent territory. Rhodes used a Latin caption, *Laorum Pars*, which means literally that the territory of only a 'part of the Lao peoples' is shown on the map. Rhodes also used the French term 'les Layes' in reference to 'the Lao people', probably copying the spelling 'les Laïs', which appeared a few years earlier in a French account by a Portuguese Jesuit, António Francisco Cardim (1646: 180). Laos is given even greater prominence in the maps of Father Martino Martini, a Jesuit who arrived in China in 1643, published in his *Novus Atlas Sinensis* in 1655. In this geographical study, based on Chinese knowledge of the region's geography, 'Laos' is shown to occupy the entire centre of the interior territory south

Fig. 3. The Earliest European Map Showing Laos
Source: Manoel Godinho de Eredia, *Declaração de Malacca*. Manuscript in Portuguese dated 1613 in the Bibliothèque Royale Albert 1er, Brussels (catalogue number BR 7264)

of China. Laos is represented on the Martini map by the Latin caption *Reg. Laos*—an abbreviation of *Regnum Laos* (the 'Laos Kingdom'). The Martini map also gives a romanised version of the Chinese name: *Lao guo*, likewise meaning 'Lao Kingdom'. A map published in Paris by Nicolas Sanson (1669) represents the area by the caption Layes ('the Lao people'), obviously following the spelling used by priests such as Cardim and Rhodes. A map published in Nuremberg by Johann Mathias Hase (1744) uses the caption 'Laotshova' (possibly a Yiddish compound) for the country, under which the name 'Laos' (again meaning 'the Lao people') appears as the name of the inhabitants. In the nineteenth century, some French writers (Cortembert and Rosny 1862: 268–72 and Rosny 1872: 16–21) were still using the name Lao (*le Lao*) for the country and were still calling the people 'the Laos' (*les Laos*). These differences reflect attempts by Europeans to distinguish, in their own languages, between the singular and plural forms of the name of the ethno-linguistic group and the name of the kingdom. Eventually, the French, who were by far the most interested in the upper Mekong valley, settled on the modern terminology: the land was Laos (*le Laos*) and its inhabitants were the Lao (*les laotiens*).

PORTUGUESE WORKS: THE EARLIEST PUBLICATIONS IN EUROPE ABOUT LAOS

The earliest published descriptions of Laos appeared in Portuguese. None of the writers visited Laos, and their information was drawn from a variety of people, including ship captains, merchants, priests and adventurers who frequented Goa (the seat of the Portuguese viceroyalty in India), Melaka (the Portuguese stronghold in the Malay peninsula) and the other major seaports of the region. An epic account of Portuguese exploits in Asia was compiled by João de Barros in the 1550s. The third volume of this work appeared in Lisbon in 1563 and was the first European publication in which the modern term 'Lao' (spelled 'Lau' in his Portuguese romanisation) was used to describe three kingdoms in the interior of mainland South-East Asia:

The first is called Jangama, whose chief city is called Chiamai [Chiang Mai], from whence many have reason to call the kingdom Chiamai; the second Chancrai Chancran; and the third Lancha [Lan Sang], which is below these and borders on the kingdom of Cacho or Cauchinchina [Cochinchina],[3] as we call it; the Lao of which [three kingdoms] have their own language. There are two more kingdoms, one bordering the other, both maritime: the first is called Como [Champa], and the second Camboja [Cambodia], each of which has a different language. (Barros 1946: 79)[4]

In describing the mountains of the interior, Barros wrote that they were

> as rough as the Alps, wherein dwell certain folk called Gueos who fight on horseback, with whom the King of Siam is at war perpetually. They are his neighbours only to the North. And among them are the Laos who surround all this Kingdom of Siam as well as to the north as to the east along the River Mecon [Mekong], and who march with [i.e., whose lands adjoin] the great region of China. . . . And these Laos who surround the Kingdom of Siam to the north and east being lords of lands so great that they contain three Kingdoms, are yet subject to the King of Siam, although ofttimes they rise up against him. And if they yield any obedience whatsoever it is because he protects them against these Gueos. . . . [The Gueos] dwell in high and rough mountains where none may enter, they come down from these rugged abodes to the open lands of the Laos and do great mischief there; and were it not for the might of the King of Siam, who wages war against them with hosts of horsemen and footmen and war-elephants, the Laos had ere now been destroyed, and even the lands of Siam taken by them. (Dames quoting Barros in Barbosa 1921: 167, note 1)

Some of Barros's details were gleaned from a report by a Portuguese soldier-adventurer who lived for a time in Ayutthaya. The description is in large part inaccurate, although it does seem to reflect some real events that were described to the informant. One assertion—that Lan Sang was a dependency of the Thai kingdom and depended on the Thai for military protection—is obviously false. The Thai had no claim at that time to any territory along the upper Mekong River.

The assertion by Barros that there were three Lao kingdoms in the deep interior, between the coastal states and Chinese territory, requires some explanation. In fact, several kingdoms were called 'Lao' kingdoms by coastal peoples: Lan Sang (the Lao kingdom of the central Mekong valley), Lan Na (a kingdom of the upper Chao Phraya basin), Khemmarat (the Shan kingdom of Chiang Tung or Kengtung, in the upper Mekong valley), and Sipsòng Panna (the Lü kingdom, even farther north, bordering on China). The Chinese, likewise, used the name 'Lao' when referring to any of the Lao and other Tai-speaking peoples in the interior (Schafer 1967: 48–9).

The habit of using the name 'Lao' indiscriminately was adopted by Europeans, as illustrated by a young French missionary and future bishop, Jean-Baptiste Pallegoix, who arrived in Bangkok in 1830. Pallegoix set himself the task of learning everything that he could about the vast and mysterious interior of mainland South-East Asia, which he knew only as 'Laos', and he questioned Lao villagers who lived in the river valleys above Bangkok. His informants generally thought that there were seven Lao kingdoms altogether, but Pallegoix could identify only the main ones, such as Chiang Mai, Nan and Vientiane.

Henry Yule examined the question from the viewpoint of Burma, borrowing the similarly generic term 'Shan' from the Burmese to refer to all the Lao and other Tai-speaking peoples east of Burma. He ascertained that, although Europeans used the term 'Lao' for the entire region, it was used locally only in reference to the people of the Mekong valley who lived in the formerly united Lan Sang kingdom:

Among the Shan themselves [i.e., all the Tai-speaking peoples of the interior], the people of the States of Wintchian [Vientiane] and Lantchian [Luang Prabang] (otherwise called [respectively] Chandaporee, and Muang-Luang-Phaban), on the Mekhong, only are known as Lau. I do not know from which side our geographers got the appellation of Laos; but probably it is only an European plural of the last-named word, which has been applied to the whole Shan [i.e., Tai-speaking] country. (Yule 1857: 91)

This generic use of the terms 'Lao' and 'Laos' was abandoned only in the twentieth century, and it has caused much confusion in the past for historians.

An attempt to define Laos geographically was made by Gaspar da Cruz, the first Portuguese Dominican to proselytise in Cambodia. But in the 1550s Cruz was able to do little more than list the names of the surrounding coastal states and other places that he had heard about:

> Beyond this kingdom of the Cauchins-chinas [Southern Vietnamese] lieth another very great kingdom, which runneth within [i.e., is contiguous with] the land along China, which some do call Laos, and others *Siões maōs*. This by the other side towards India, doth confine with [i.e., border on] the kingdom of Camboja, and with the great kingdom of Siam, and with the very rich kingdom of Peguu, with all the which kingdoms it hath traffic [trade]; in sort that there remaineth to this kingdom towards the sea of India, all the coast from Peguu unto the ends of the kingdom of Champa, which doth confine with Cauchim-china [Cochinchina]. So on the side of these Laos towards the Indian Sea, there lie the great kingdom of Peguu, and that of Tanaçarim [Tenasserim]. . . . (Cruz 1953: 73–8)

Cruz continued by relating news that he must have heard in Cambodia, concerning recent political events far up the Mekong:

> This kingdom of the Laos, or *Siões maōs*, was subdued by the Bramas [Burmese] . . . in the year of fifty-six [1556]; and among some [of the people] which they brought captive to Peguu they brought some Chinas [Chinese] which the Laos held captives, as one Jorge de Mello, who went for Captain of the voyage to Peguu, affirmed unto me. . . commonly there be no wars between these Laos and the Chinas, because of the great mountains that are between them, on the which the Chinas have good strongholds on that side in the province of Camsi [Guangxi]. . . .

King Bayin-naung, the Burmese conqueror who made Pegu his capital, took control of Lan Na in the mid 1550s, but there seems to be no evidence of a Burmese incursion into Lao territory in 1556—at least, not as far down-river as Luang Prabang. Cruz was unable to distinguish Lan Na from Lan Sang, and he therefore called both of them 'Laos'. The 1556 conflict that he reports therefore seems to refer to the Burmese capture of Lan Na and subsequent action against the Lao ruler, King Setthathirat, whose temporary residence at the time was Chiang Saen. Under threat of a Burmese invasion, Setthathirat withdrew from Chiang Saen and established his new capital at Vientiane, which was much farther from Burmese-held territory and therefore more secure than the old capital at Luang Prabang.

After mentioning the political conflict, Cruz turned to the subject of trade. He observed some Lao merchants and boat operators on the Mekong in Cambodia, and also added some notes about the appearance and dress of the Lao:

Before these Laos were subdued by the Bramas, they carried to Siam, and to Camboja [Cambodia], and to Peguu some very good musk and gold, whereof is affirmed to be great store [supplies] in that country.... [This musk] is the ware which they brought to the above said kingdoms, carrying in return cotton-cloths and other things they had need of.

This people [the Lao] is not very brown; they wear their hair all cut round underneath, and all the rest above ruffled, raising it many times upwards with their hands, that it remaineth to them like a cap, and serveth instead of one, for they wear nothing on their heads. They go naked from the middle upward; and from the thighs downwards they wear certain cotton-cloths girt about them and all white. The women go covered from the breasts to the half leg; they have their faces somewhat like the Chinas; they have the same heathenish ceremonies as do the Peguus [Mon], the Sioes [Siamese] and the Cambojas [Cambodians]; the priests of their idols do wear yellow clothes girt about as the rest of the people, with certain folds and seams in which they hold their superstitious charms. I saw many of this people in Camboja, who had remained there from the year before by the way of traffic [i.e., trade]; and that year that I was there, they came not because of the wars wherein (as I said) they were subdued by the Bramas.

These Laos came to Camboja down a river many days' journey, the which is very large and they say has its origin in China, as do many others which run into the sea of India.... When these Laos do return to their country, it takes them three months, as they go against the stream. ...

In 1595 Jan Huyghen Van Linschoten, a Dutchman, published a lot of commercial information that he had compiled about South-East Asia, while serving in the Portuguese colony of Goa in India. Knowing little about Laos, except for its approximate geographical position, he wrote:

Upwards in the land behind Cambaia [Cambodia] and Sian [Siam] are many nations, [such] as [the] Laos, which are great and mightie, others named Avas [Avanese] and Bramas [Burmese].... (Linschoten 1885: 121–2)

The editor of the 1885 edition, Arthur Burnell, observed that this description was obviously inspired by the writings of the great Portuguese poet, Luis Vas de Camões. Camões was in the Portuguese colonial service in Goa during the 1550s and 1560s and was shipwrecked at the mouths of the Mekong on his way back from Macau in 1570. In his 1572 *Os Lusíadas*, an epic masterpiece depicting Portuguese overseas exploits in verse, he described the interior of mainland South-East Asia, as he must have imagined it from first-hand accounts that were related to him. The following passage attempts to convey in verse the poetical character of his work, in which he described the region east of India through the voice of a nymph:

In that huge tract you see a countless throng
Of tribes whose names a man can scarcely tell,
The Laos in their lands and numbers strong,
And on vast hills Burmese and Avas dwell. (Camões 1950: 380)

The translator's poetic licence unfortunately obscures or omits details that are of interest to historians, as the following prose translation reveals:

> And here now is a vast territory, dotted as you can see, with the names of a thousand nations you have never even heard of: the Laos, powerful in extent and numbers, the Ava and Bramas, who have their homes in great mountain-ranges. . . . (Camões 1973: 243)

Not long after Camões published this work, Portugal ceased to compete independently for trade advantages in the region. With the Portuguese and Spanish crowns under a single monarch beginning in 1580, the initiative in Laos passed temporarily to the Spanish, and the first European mission to the Lao capital at Vientiane was reported to (although not sent by) the Spanish colonial government in Manila.

SPANISH OVERTURES

Antonio de Morga, who became lieutenant governor of the Philippines in 1593, preserved unique accounts and letters of eye-witnesses to events in Laos and Cambodia in the mid-1590s. His book *Sucesos de Las Islas Filipinas* ('Events in the Philippine Islands') was first published in Mexico in 1609 and has appeared several times in English translation. It contains numerous references to Laos, beginning with the arrival in Manila of some survivors of the invasion and sack of the Cambodian capital (Morga 1971: 80):

> In the year 1594 when don Luis [Perez Dasmariñas] was Governor, there came to the Philippines a large junk with some Cambodians and Siamese, several Chinese and three Spaniards, one, a Castilian named Blas Ruyz [Ruiz] de Hernan Gonzalez. . . . While they were in the city of Chordemuco [Phnom Penh] in Cambodia, with the king, Prauncar Langara [Sattha I of Cambodia], the king of Siam [Naresuan] attacked him with many troops and elephants, seizing all the land and the king's house and treasure, so he fled inland to the kingdom of Laos with his wife, mother, sister, and a daughter and two sons. . . .

Morga continued with an account of a Portuguese named Diogo Veloso,[5] who was taken prisoner during the 1594 Thai attack on Cambodia, remained in Siam for some time and later made his way to the Philippines. Blas Ruiz and Veloso returned to Cambodia early in 1596, where they discovered that the invaders had withdrawn and that a senior Cambodian official had seized the throne. Following a conflict among the Spanish, the Chinese and the Cambodians, Captain Juan Juárez Gallinato, who was in command of the Spanish fleet, arrived in Cambodia. Morga recorded that while Gallinato was negotiating with the Cambodians, Veloso and Blas Ruiz

> offered to go overland to the kingdom of Laos, where king Langara of Cambodia was, in order to bring him back to his kingdom. (Morga 1971: 85)

Gallinato took Blas Ruiz and Veloso aboard his ship, sailed up the coast and put them ashore with instructions to try to reach Laos:

> These two went to the king of Sinua [Thuân-hoà, the main port near Hué],[6] the son of the ruler of Tonking [Tonkin], and they asked him to assist them on their way. He gave them all they needed and they were well treated and served until they reached the city of Alanchan [Lan Sang (i.e., Vientiane)], the capital of the kingdom of Laos, where they were warmly welcomed by the king there. (Morga 1971: 86)

Sinua (more commonly spelled Sinoa) was a logical starting point for the journey inland. Europeans believed that this town was at the same latitude as the Lao capital—as illustrated by a 1634 map (Humphreys 1989: 133)—although in fact it is slightly south of Vientiane. The two men most likely crossed the cordillera at the Ai Lao pass, in the mountains west of modern Quang-tri and Hué, before descending the valley of the Bang Hian River and proceeding up the Mekong to Vientiane.

Morga provided little information about the mission to Vientiane, and he did not indicate the exact period of time that it encompassed. The context of his account shows, however, that the

first Europeans to reach Vientiane must have travelled west across
the cordillera in 1596 (maybe late in the rainy season, which began
about June) and must have returned to the coast in late 1596 or
early 1597. In his account, Morga included a letter written to him
from Cambodia in July 1598 by Blas Ruiz, providing greater details
of the Spanish mission. The following extracts from this letter begin
with the journey into Laos (Morga 1971: 124):

> The king of Sinua, a province of Cochinchina [the southern
> Vietnamese kingdom], fitted us out for the journey to Laos with
> good equipment, giving us an embassy to that country and giving us
> persons to accompany us on our journey. Thus all along the way we
> were well provided for, everywhere respected, honoured and looked
> up to, for this was something unheard of before in those countries.
> We were all sick on the road, but were greatly helped in our woes by
> the affection of the people who warmly welcomed us everywhere.
>
> So we reached Lanchan [Lan Sang, meaning the city of Vientiane],
> the capital and royal seat. It is a large kingdom, thinly populated
> however, because it has been frequently laid waste by Pegu. It
> contains mines of gold, silver, copper, iron, brass, and tin; and it also
> yields silk, benzoin [gum benjamin, an aromatic gum], lac, brasil
> [aloes wood], wax, ivory and has rhinoceroses, and many elephants
> and horses, larger than those found in China. Laos is bounded on the
> eastern side by Cochinchina, on the north and north-east by China
> and Tartary, from which places it gets the sheep and asses that I saw
> when I was there. A great deal of its merchandise is exported by
> means of these. To the west and south-west lie Pegu and Siam, and
> on the south and south-east side there is Cambodia and Champan
> [Champa]. It is a rich country and everything imported there is
> expensive.

One purpose of the Spanish mission was to try to assist the
rightful ruler of Cambodia, King Sattha I, to regain his throne—an
accomplishment that would ensure a privileged position for Spanish
traders in Cambodia and might facilitate trade with the Lao. By the
time the mission reached Vientiane, however, the old king had died.
His son and heir, moreover, was a mere youth, whose mother and

grandmother resisted the Spanish proposal to take him back to Cambodia. At that juncture, however, news reached Vientiane that the Cambodian usurper had died, and an agreement was reached that the Spanish fleet would assist the young prince to regain his throne and that the Lao would send forces to Cambodia. In the account of his departure from Vientiane, Blas Ruiz recorded the Lao king's friendly gestures towards the Spanish:

> The king of Laos sent another embassy begging for friendship and urging that the fleet should return to Cambodia; adding that should Gallinato [the Spanish commander] not wish to return, he would help us with large forces which he would entrust to the heir himself [Baromreachea V, the son of the deceased King Sattha I of Cambodia]. With this we left for Cochinchina. (Morga 1971: 125)

Blas Ruiz then described his return to Cambodia. In the interim, the deceased usurper's son had taken the throne, but he, like his father, was very unpopular. He and his brother were ultimately driven out of the capital by the senior Cambodian officials, who then

> ordered a fleet of rowing-boats to go to Laos to welcome the new king [of Cambodia] who was said to be already coming from there. They sent Ocuña de Chu [Okya Decho, a Cambodian minister . . . who] set off on the road [waterway] to Laos, but since he did not meet his king, nor was there any news of him, he resolved to go to Lanchan [Lan Sang] and to ask for him there. He continued on his way but suffered from shortage of supplies because he had set out from the kingdom unprepared for such a long journey. On account of this, some of his men deserted him, but at last he arrived at Lanchan with ten armed praus [river boats], and his coming caused alarm throughout the entire kingdom, for it was thought he had come to make war. Many left their towns and property, fleeing into the mountains until at last they realized his aim was peace, at which they grew calm again. (Morga 1971: 128)

Meanwhile, Blas Ruiz and Veloso were crossing the cordillera again, on their return to central Vientam. The Nguyen lord at Hué once again assisted them, and Blas Ruiz ended his references to Laos with the arrival of the Cambodian minister in Vientiane.

> When he [the minister] arrived there, we were already on the way to Cochinchina, and, on account of his coming, the king [of Hué] sent us back immediately to Lanchan. The king [of Laos], aware of what was happening in Cambodia, despatched a large fleet there by sea and also troops overland; and he sent the king [the young Baromreachea V (r. 1597–9)] to Cambodia and me to Cochinchina to give them news of events and take the ships to Cambodia.

Blas Ruiz continued by describing the return of the heir to the Cambodian throne and events up to July 1598, when he wrote this letter.

The documents preserved by Morga are a unique record of the first European diplomatic mission to Vientiane. Unfortunately, the Spanish records provide relatively few details about internal affairs in Laos. By contrast, the Spanish gathered extensive information about personalities and domestic politics in Cambodia, because Spanish interests at that time were primarily concentrated on Cambodia, which was easily accessible from the sea. Even so, these records provide valuable clues for further investigations in Lao history.

INTERNATIONAL TRADE IN LAO COMMODITIES

Laos as a source of certain tropical commodities came to the attention of Europeans in the sixteenth century, and this trade has been documented by Europeans ever since. For most of this time, however, Europeans knew very little about the land and people themselves. Many products from Laos formed part of the international trade in luxury goods. Although small in volume, this trade was great in value by contemporary standards. Not unexpectedly, some writers made wild exaggerations about the wealth of the interior, based on what they learned at second or third hand from coastal peoples. An example is provided by Alexander Hamilton, a ship captain who spent more than thirty years sailing between southern Africa and Japan. In an account of his travels, published in 1727, he reported a tour he made in 1720 to ports along the coast east of the Malay peninsula, and in the midst of his description of Cambodia, he inserted the following observations about Laos:

> The kingdom of Laos borders on Siam, Cambodia, Couchin-china [Cochinchina, the southern Vietnamese kingdom] and Tonquin [Tonkin, the northern Vietnamese kingdom]. It produces gold, raw silk, and elephants teeth [tusks] are so plentiful, that they stake their fields and gardens about with them, to keep out wild hogs and cattle from destroying their fruit and corn [grain (i.e., rice)]. They are all Pagans in religion.
>
> The natives of Laos are whiter in complexion than their circumjacent neighbours. I saw some of them at Siam, of both sexes. Their women were little inferior to Portuguese or Spanish ladies. (Hamilton 1811: 480)

One reason why the extensive trade in Lao products and their export from the interior of the South-East Asian peninsula have been virtually overlooked is that the local people who engaged in this trade left no records of their activities. Unlike the representatives of the great Dutch and English merchant companies, the Lao and other local traders had no one to chronicle their accomplishments. They sought out, gathered and processed local products, carried them by pack animals across the mountains, sold them to middle-men in or near the coastal areas, and purchased imported goods to carry back to Laos. As noted by Tran Van Quy in his chapter of this volume, petty officials at the borders regularly helped themselves to some of the goods from every pack caravan. But the common man and woman perpetuated this trade, in spite of obstacles thrown in their way. European merchants and travellers quickly grasped the importance of this trade, and their accounts provide rare glimpses of what it included and how it operated.

Peter Williamson Floris, a Dutchman in the employ of the English East India Company (chartered in 1600), was sent to investigate the trading opportunities on the mainland of South-East

Asia and to observe the current operations of the company's Dutch counterpart. Trading prospects, however, were very poor at the time of his arrival, because of the troubled political situation and a glut of imported cloth. He had predicted brisk sales of the cloth and red yarn that he brought from India. But contrary to expectations, local merchants were not buying such goods for shipment to Vientiane and other places in the interior. Floris (1934: 57–8) lamented:

> Butt wee are juste those that hitte on this badd tyme, the mooste or greateste halfe of our cargason [cargo] imployed in goods serving for that place, as being the mooste famous place of all the Indies; for wheras the mooste India cloth and red threed [yarn] were wonte to bee vented [i.e., were usually sold] in Camboja, Lanjangh Lau [Lan Sang], Jagoma [Chiang Mai], and those places, I lette others judge what there is to bee looked for att this tyme in trading.

The Portuguese did not publish accounts of their trade in the Mekong valley. They were individuals, each trading on his own account, and probably did not keep records. Three Portuguese traders went up the Mekong at some time in the early seventeenth century: Father Cardim, writing in 1642, mentioned them but did not record their names or the year of their visits. The following information about the Lao kingdom was probably obtained from Portuguese compatriots whom he met while he was in Macau, Vietnam and Siam in the 1620s and 1630s:

> This kingdom has no seaport, and consequently there is not much trade with the Portuguese. Also, from the beginning, only three [Portuguese traders][7] are known to have been there, and to accomplish this they had to travel for a period of eight months on the Cambodian river. The cause of such a long journey is the strong current of the river, and in one place there is a waterfall so great that there is no means of crossing it by boat. To go farther on, the boats have to be taken out of the river and carried a distance to another place, where the river is navigable, which takes a lot of time. One of these three Portuguese observed the characteristics of the kingdom, which he says is rather rich and fertile. The people are brown in colour. Their

clothing is like that of the Siamese, and each wears his hair long at the front of the head, gathering it back against the ears, on which he wears earrings. (Cardim 1646: 181)

Among the European merchants, the Spanish and Portuguese had a near monopoly of the trade that flowed by way of the Mekong through Cambodia at that time, in spite of efforts by the English and the Dutch East India Company to gain access to the interior. Nonetheless, in 1641 some Lao merchants, who had come down-river to Cambodia, managed to travel on a Dutch company ship to Batavia, where they sold their cargo of gum benjamin and insect lac (from which shellac and and varnishes were made). They asked the Dutch governor to send a mission to their country—an idea suggested to them by the head of the Dutch trading post in Cambodia (Lejosne 1986: 21). In response, van Wusthof, a company employee who was already in Cambodia, was sent on an exploratory mission to Laos.

Two aims of the van Wusthof mission were to break the Spanish and Portuguese monopoly of trade in the lower Mekong basin and to gain direct access to the export products that came down-river from the interior. Van Wusthof travelled up the Mekong River from Cambodia to Vientiane in 1641. He was accompanied by five other Dutchmen, a Malay interpreter from Patani (named Intse Lanangh Patanees) and a Lao merchant-boat captain (named Kwan Monthip).

In his report at the end of the journey, van Wusthof enthusiasti-cally endorsed a scheme to establish trade with Laos, but his pro-posal failed for at least two important reasons. First, an early ex-ample of cost-benefit analysis showed that, to use the Mekong as a trade route, at least two years would be required for each commer-cial venture with the Lao. Such a trading pattern would tie up Dutch capital for too long. Perhaps more serious, the lower Mekong, which provided access to Laos, was dominated by the Spanish and Portu-guese. They made every effort to prevent the Dutch from gaining a foothold in Cambodia (Népote 1986: 20–1) and soon managed to eliminate the Dutch as trade rivals in Cambodia. Thus the Lao at-tempt to enlist the Dutch as trade partners, thereby gaining a direct link to the international trade network, did not succeed. It was not until 1866, more than two centuries later, that the French expedition led by Ernest Doudart de Lagrée renewed the efforts to explore the central and upper Mekong systematically. The French, however, did not plan expressly to trade with the Lao. Instead, their mission was designed to investigate the central and upper Mekong as a potential trade route with south-west China.

The trade interests of the Spanish and Portuguese are illustrated in the writings of Domingo Fernandez de Navarette, a Spanish Dominican who left his country in 1646 for Mexico. In 1648, he arrived in the Philippines, lived there for nine years and then went to China. Between December 1669 and February 1770 he sailed from Guangzhou to Melaka, before returning to Europe by way of India. His account of Laos, which he never visited, was probably based on information that he obtained from traders in the Philippines and perhaps fellow travellers on board in 1669–70, because it stressed the importance of the trade in Lao commodities:

> Above it [Cambodia] it is the large Kingdom of the Laos, a Country abounding in Musk, Civit, Frankinsense, [gum] Benjamin and Storax, which Commodities they carry to Manila, and thence they are sent into New Spain [Mexico]. The Country swarms with People; on the West it borders upon Siam, on the North it draws near to the Kingdom of Tibet; North-west of it is Bengala, and then it stretches a little up to the Mogol's Dominions [Mughal India]; lower [farther south] is Narsingha [in southern India], but at a considerable distance. (Navarette 1962: 383)

Navarette obviously had a vague grasp of geography and attempted to place the vast interior of South-East Asia in a broad geographical context, by listing the names of major countries that he knew. Southern India was mentioned perhaps because the kingdom of Vijayanagara (known to the Portuguese as Narsingha, with its capital near modern Hyderabad) was well known to the Portuguese and was an important trading partner.

References to Lao products such as these—however brief—help to place Laos in the context of the international trade network of past centuries. The same sources, as shown below, also provide a wider perspective on the foreign relations of the Lao kingdom than is found in indigenous Lao records.

INSIGHTS INTO LAO POLITICS AND FOREIGN POLICY

Pieter Floris, in the account of his voyage from England to the Gulf and back during the years 1611–5, mentioned a political imbroglio involving Laos and its western neighbours. He prefaced his remarks with a note concerning the fate of Pegu, the capital of the Burmese kingdom, which became the regional superpower in the middle of the previous century. By the end of the century, as observed by Floris, the mighty empire had begun to disintegrate, and the balance of power had changed:

> This in briefe is the destruction of Pegu, whereby Siam is come upp agayne, which, because of the domination of Pegu, was somewhat decayed, bringing under his [the king of Siam's] subjection the kingdomes of Camboja [Cambodia], Laniangh [Lan Sang], Jagomai [Chiang Mai], Lugor [Nakhòn Sithammarat], Patania [Patani], Tenesserin [Tenasserim], and dyvers other places and kingdomes, till *anno* 1605, whenas the Blacke King [Naresuan, r. 1590–1605] deceased withoute any issue [children]. . . . (Floris 1934: 55)

One event recorded by Floris provides evidence of Lao military power in the early seventeenth century. He was aware of the potential for trade with the inland kingdoms of Lan Sang and Lan Na, but he did not have a clear understanding of their respective relationships with Ayutthaya. Contrary to his assertion, Lan Sang never submitted to any of its powerful neighbours, and there is no historic basis for mentioning Lan Sang in the list of Ayutthaya's dependency states. Floris himself visited Patani, but no other mainland towns, and his reference to Lan Sang is based on inaccurate second-hand information that he and his associates gathered from local informants. Lan Na fell temporarily under Thai rule in the 1590s, but Ayutthaya lost control of it two decades later. His confusion about the two inland kingdoms is further illustrated in a later assertion that the Burmese were waging war against Lan Sang in 1614, when in fact the Burmese were fighting for control of Lan Na (Floris 1934: 91, note 1).

Floris recounted the fate of Naresuan's successors: his brother (who executed his own son), an attempt at usurpation and the accession of a young nephew, who soon faced a mutiny of Japanese palace guards. Floris continued with an account of this and other armed confrontations in 1612:

> Uppon the newes of this mischaunce happened to this young King [Song Tham, r. 1611–28], the kingdomes of Camboja and Laniangh [Lan Sang] rebelled, as also one Bangade Laa [Banya Dala, governor of Martaban], a Peguer; and the King of Laniangh [King Wòrawongsa of Vientiane] came the laste yeare into Siam within 3 dayes journey of the towne of Ondya [Ayutthaya], hoping to fynde the countrye yett entangled with the troubles of those slaves of Japan; butt they [the Japanese] being departed, the King of Siam came foorth to meete him, butt the King of Laniangh, being afrayde to abyde him, retyred backe again. . . . (Floris 1934: 57)

Floris's colleagues arrived in Ayutthaya more than four months after these events took place. A more detailed account of King Wòrawongsa's military expedition is provided in a letter (Vajiranana 1915 i: 6–7) written less than a month after the withdrawal of the Lao forces, by a Dutch merchant who was in Ayutthaya when the Lao armies arrived. This letter reveals that the Lao forces were camped for four months, from about January to mid-April 1612, only one day's march north of the Thai capital, and that they apparently intended to remain permanently, because they were accompanied by wives and children. The Dutch, who were obliged to assist in the Thai battle preparations, thought that the Lao had intervened, on the mistaken assumption that Japanese rebels had killed the Thai king. The Dutch also thought that the Lao sought to overcome the rebels and take control. After several weeks of increasing tension, the Lao departed on 15 April (Gregorian calendar). No battle took place, but many Lao soldiers lost their lives as a result of Thai strikes against their rear column.

The second half of the seventeenth century witnessed a flowering of interest about Laos in the burgeoning French literature on South-East Asia. French diplomats, military officers and priests flocked to this region in hopes of securing a strong French presence, and their extensive references to Laos supplement Dutch records. French writers such as Chaumont (1686), Tachard (1686), Choisy (1687) and La Loubère (1691) provide unique insights into the tangled relations between the Lao and the Thai. The Lao are shown to be enterprising in their endeavours, and they did not hesitate to take sides even with the Thai heir apparent and intervene in the internal politics of Ayutthaya. The French writers also reported some of the news that reached Ayutthaya concerning affairs in Laos. Their increased knowledge of the interior enabled the French to make important advances in cartography during this period, including cartographic work relating to Laos (Gagneux 1980).

Among the items of political reconnaissance recorded by the French, a tragic episode at the Lao court was documented in a letter written to a French priest:

> The King of Lahos [Laos] has a son and a daughter by different wives. Last February [1686] it was discovered that they were cohabiting in secret with the consent of their respective mothers. The King gave orders for the decapitation of the young people and their mothers, and sent out to arrest all their friends and dependents. They came to take refuge here [in Ayutthaya] to the number of six hundred. (Hutchinson 1940: 77)

This event took place near the end of the reign of King Suriya-wongsa (r. 1638–95), and it proved to be a great tragedy for Lan Sang. Forty-five years earlier, when the king was in his twenties, he did not yet have any children (Wusthof 1986: 136, 166). When he died, his only direct heirs were two grandsons—mere boys who were too young to rule. A court official ruled briefly and was succeeded by one of Suriyawongsa's relations, who ruled only two years. The grandsons became locked in a dispute over the succession with a nephew, whose father (an elder brother of Suriyawongsa) had been sent into exile and was excluded from the throne. About a decade after the old king's death, the succession struggle ended in the division of Lan Sang into two kingdoms, with the grandsons forming their power base in Luang Prabang and the nephew retaining control of Vientiane. Even more tragic, the reduced territory ruled by Vientiane soon shrank further, when the governor of Champasak threw off his allegiance and established a separate kingdom of his own in southern Laos. Thus the fragmentation of Lan Sang, and even the destinies of its weakened successor states, can be attributed in part to the human drama played out at the court in 1686.

The long and relatively stable reign enjoyed by King Suriya-wongsa is often depicted as a golden age in Lao history. The fate of the king's heir was recorded by the Lao annalists (Phinith 1987: 60). But another, darker side of history was not explained in the annals. Contemporary European witnesses provide a unique view of the development of hostile relations between the Lao and Thai kingdoms during the half century prior to the investigations of the French in the 1680s.

The Dutchman Jeremias van Vliet was a contemporary of van Wusthof and was likewise a representative of the Dutch trading company. He lived in Ayutthaya during the 1630s, and one of his accounts, written in 1640, helps to place Lao political and commercial relations in a wider regional perspective. His observations about King Prasat Thòng of Ayutthaya (r. 1629–56) set the tone for the trade friction that was still evident to French writers later in the century.

. . . in the year 1636 he [King Prasat Thòng] sent ambassadors to Malacca [Portuguese Melaka] and [Spanish] Manila in order to renew the treaties of friendship with the Governors of those places, and in order to offer them peace, which, however, was only concluded in the year 1639, by the intervention of a Chinese ambassador of Macau. He sent also, at the beginning of his reign, ambassadors to the Kings of Ava, Pegu, and Langhianch [Lan Sang]. By means of all embassies and by the treaties that he thereby concluded, he assured peace with his neighbours and the repose of his Kingdom. The jealousy of these Kings of Pegu and of Linghiangh [Lan Sang] is so great that they live in a state of continual distrust, and hold themselves on their guard, for fear of being attacked and surprised by the King of Siam. As a matter of fact there is little ground for such fear since the King of Siam, being anxious to secure the Crown for his family and for that purpose to gain the good will of his subjects, tries to ensure their living in peace and to enrich them by trade. (Vliet 1938: 150)

Prasat Thòng may, as van Vliet believed, have been anxious to ensure that the merchants of Ayutthaya enjoyed the benefits of trade. But these benefits were definitely not extended to merchants who came from neighbouring states. Further evidence of the trade conflict between the Lao and Thai is provided in van Vliet's observations about the relations between the two courts in the mid-1630s.

> . . . the princes[8] of Langsiangh [Lan Sang] have sent an ambassador to the Siamese Court with presents in 1633. These presents were made more or less with selfish reasons. For the ambassador brought with him many products from the highlands, such as gold, [gum] benjamin and Melaka gum with a view to exchanging these for cloth, for which there was great want in Langsiangh at that time. Many private merchants accompanied the ambassador in order to be able to sell their goods with less trouble in the name of the ambassador. But the ambassador and all the people with him had to stop about two miles above the town and was not allowed to enter the town before the day that His Majesty gave audience to him and the day the ambassador took leave. They were also so annoyed in their trade by all kind of monopolies and ill treatment by the King's factors [officials in charge of trading affairs] that they never came back to Siam again. (Vliet 1910: 34–5)

Van Vliet's account implies that the subsequent tense relations between the two countries originated in the change of Thai trade policy and practice in the 1630s, as a result of the royal monopolies on many trade products passing through Ayutthaya. The Thai king realised that this policy was detrimental to his own interests, and made several attempts during the next few years to rectify the problem, as van Vliet added:

> The Siamese king, seeing afterwards that the absence of the highlanders [Lao] was a drawback for him and his country, ordered Oya Poucelouck [the governor of Phitsanulok] and Berckelangh [the Phra Khlang, the Minister of External Affairs and Maritime Trade] to send several ambassadors to Langsiangh to invite the people to come back and promising them better treatment and more freedom than on their last visit. But no highlanders appeared in Judia [Ayutthaya] (apparently kept away by distrust), some of them went as far as Poucelouck [Phitsanulok] with their goods. In December last [1637] the King sent an ambassador to Langsiangh to remove any objections and to ask the King of Lansiangh to send his subjects again to Siam as in former days promising his people many privileges and much freedom. Up to now it is uncertain what has been the result of this mission.

It is not known how long trade was disrupted. Records during the next decade show that the Lao were actively trying to restore overland trade early in the reign of their young king, Suriyawongsa, who came to the throne in 1638. Van Wusthof's journal at Vientiane documents a large group of Lao merchants, who left Vientiane prior to the rainy season in 1640, stayed in Ayutthaya for about a year and returned to the Lao capital in late 1641 with a caravan of about seventy oxcarts. Another one hundred carts were left at Ayutthaya to await the arrival of ships with imported cloth from India (Wusthof 1986: 147, 157). They reported that the Thai trading monopolies were still extremely troublesome and that every obstacle had been thrown in their paths, as van Wusthof observed:

> I was told by the Lao who returned recently from Siam that the treatment they received in Siam was a plague on their business dealings and that they were prevented from trading freely. As soon as they arrived there [at Ayutthaya] with their carts, they were obliged to take lodgings with their goods in a designated house, thronged with spies, so that they could not sell to anyone other than the

noblemen. In a totally arbitrary way, the [Thai] noblemen bought their best goods at cheap prices and gave them, as payment, some poor-quality garments at high prices, without their being able to make any protest. By comparison, Cambodia enjoys a good reputation, because of the freedom [of trade there]. The [Lao] witnesses say that they would not go back to Siam, except with reluctance. It took them nineteen months to make the trip to Siam and back. In the same space of time, they could have gone to Cambodia two times or more. (Wusthof 1986: 157)

While continuing to subject the Lao merchants to the new restrictions of the Thai trade regime, the Thai court pursued ostensibly friendly diplomatic relations with the Lao court through the exchange of envoys. One Lao envoy, for example, was sent to Ayutthaya in 1641. Meanwhile, a Thai envoy left Vientiane after the 1641 rainy season, and another Thai envoy arrived in Vientiane before the rains began the following year (Wusthof 1986: 137, 158, 192). A glimpse of these diplomatic exchanges was provided by the Dutch assistants who were still in Vientiane in July 1642. They reported that

we were informed by the interpreter, Insi Lanang, that the ambassador from Siam is forbidden to go out of doors and that the Siamese are watched by guards at all times. Nor do they have the right to buy anything whatever, and they must remain shut up in their lodgings throughout the day. They mistrust each other, although they are friends; if they go out of doors to bathe, they are constantly accompanied by men [guards]. If the [Lao] noblemen send for them, they can go to the noblemen's homes, but only under guard. The Lao are treated in the same way in Siam, and thus His Majesty [King Suriyawongsa] has not yet decided whether he will send an ambassador to Siam. In any case, if he sends one, [the delegation will consist of] two or three people, but certainly no more. (Wusthof 1986: 195)

Another factor that had to be taken into account by King Suriyawongsa, as he pondered the question of sending an envoy to Ayutthaya in 1642, was the competition faced by Lao merchants.

In recent years, both Thai and Muslim merchants had made attempts to dominate the overland trade, bringing their own oxcart caravans to the Lao commercial centre, which was not far down-river from Vientiane and on the opposite bank. Van Wusthof thought that this competition might divert Lao traders to Cambodia, where they could obtain imports of better quality and at more reasonable prices from the Dutch company:

> ... the Lao prefer to go to Cambodia [to trade] and, for the past two or three years, they have found the garments of the [Dutch East India] Company better than those in Siam. The Muslims try to bring [to Vientiane] the best [garments] themselves and to sell the poor-quality ones to the Lao traders in Siam. It is therefore evident that the Muslims and the Siamese reach understandings about coming [to Vientiane] every year with substantial supplies of delicate garments in keen demand, which ensures their profits. Thus, they are seeking to assert themselves here and have already begun to do so. (Wusthof 1986: 159)

Van Wusthof did not identify the Muslims who were involved in this trade, but his reference to cloth brought by their ships from India implies that they were South Asians. One of them may have been a cause of the break-down of diplomatic exchanges and the onset of openly hostile relations later in the reign of King Suriya-wongsa. Choisy, a French diplomat who was in Ayutthaya during 1685–6, explained in his discussion of trade with Laos that

> Formerly there was much trade between Siam and Laos. From Laos came gold, musk, benzoin [gum benjamin] and silk; in exchange were sent cloth, chintzes, plushes, etc. But the King of Siam has declared war on the King of Laos, because he [King Suriyawongsa] did not wish to hand over a Muhammadan merchant who had robbed him and who had retired to Lanchang [Vientiane], the capital of Laos. (Choisy 1993: 236)

Details of this sort in European records add greatly to the outlines of history left by contemporary court chroniclers—who perhaps dared not attribute an event as great as a war to the petty actions and jealousies of their sovereigns. The chroniclers provide only indirect evidence of economic activities such as these. European records show that the merchant cited by Choisy was not an isolated invididual. Indeed, as the van Wusthof mission revealed, many Muslim traders were established at Vientiane in the 1640s, and they carried on a flourishing overland trade in imported textiles that came from India. In his description of the Thai military campaign against Vientiane, Choisy unfortunately did not give any indication of the date of these events, but he showed clearly that the Lao kingdom had a reputation as an important military power:

> Laos is great and powerful; it has benzoin [gum benjamin], musk, and silk. Lanchang [Vientiane] is the capital city. There has been war for several years between Laos and the King of Siam. The late Barkalon [Phra Khlang, a senior Thai minister] invaded the country with a large army, and advanced to within two leagues of the capital. The King of Laos announced he would leave his city at the head of his army to go and fight him; but the Barkalon replied that he did not dare pitch his sword against that of His Majesty, and he was going to withdraw, content at having beaten his generals. This he did, and brought back to Siam 3,000 Laotian slaves, to whom land was given to cultivate. The King of Siam told him on his return that that would have been all right in the time when they still wiped their noses on their sleeves and ordered a few floggings for him for having missed such a good occasion. The first [Siamese] Ambassador[9] was on this expedition with his brother the Barkalon. Since that time there has always been war between Siam and Laos. Each watches over its frontier, makes some sallies, and takes a few slaves without killing them. (Choisy 1993: 219–20)

Choisy noted that Lao prisoners were captured in the war and forcibly resettled in Siam, and that more captives had subsequently been taken away and treated as slaves. Such treatment of captives in wartime was a very old practice among bitter enemies, and it plagued relations between the two kingdoms.

ENCYCLOPAEDIC WRITERS OF THE EIGHTEENTH AND EARLY NINETEENTH CENTURIES

Although many European writers from the mid–eighteenth to the mid–nineteenth centuries mention Laos, they added very little information to the basic facts compiled earlier. This characteristic is illustrated by the *Universal History*, an encyclopaedic work that appeared in London in 1759. Most of the knowledge about Laos available to its compilers was old. They devoted a relatively long section to Laos (reprinted in this volume), in an attempt to encapsulate all the facts available to them about this little-known country. They relied in large part on a missionary's impressions of Laos recorded in the 1666 French edition of the book by Marini. They also tended to repeat or paraphrase the information published by Engelbert Kaempfer (1727) and the Reverend Father Jean Baptiste Du Halde, a French geographer whose general history of China was an important source for many subsequent authors. Du Halde's information was incorporated into the *Universal History*, on the mistaken assumption that the kingdom of 'Lahos' (Du Halde 1736 i: 101–7) referred to the Lao kingdom of Lan Sang. But in fact Du Halde described the now well-known caravan route that winds from Yunnan Province in China through the Sipsòng Panna kingdom, the Shan States and other Tai-speaking areas such as Lan Na—all to the north and west of the Lao kingdom. At least the compilers of the *Universal History* tried to bring some order to the jumble of facts and contradictions published by travellers who had visited South-East Asia and others who had studied it.

Two decades later, a French secular priest (*abbé*), Jérôme Richard, published a two-volume work about the Lao and Vietnamese. Richard wrote books on a variety of subjects, including the natural sciences, and the following passage from his 1778 study of Laos reflects the encyclopaedic range of his intellectual interests, which included natural products, trade, politics, local customs and beliefs:

Laos, which signifies thousands of elephants [i.e., the literal meaning of the name Lan Sang], has [gets] its name from the number of those animals, which fill the forests of that country. The climate is so temperate, and the air so pure, that it is said that men of a hundred, and even a hundred and twenty years old, retain the freshness and vigour of their prime. Bountiful nature spreads her flores [plant life] over the plains and valleys, and even on the mountains. The canals [waterways], which receive the torrents precipitated from elevated places, distribute them with economy over the lands, and there are neither marshes, nor stagnant waters. The two banks of the river have different qualities: the eastern side is much more fertile, and produces larger and stronger animals, the trees are more lofty, and of an incorruptible quality. The best rice of India [i.e., southern Asia] grows there. The lands where it has been sowed, after it is gathered in, becomes covered with a kind of froth, which hardened in the sun becomes solid salt. The best [gum] benjamin and lacker [insect lac], from which they make Spanish wax [shellac], comes from thence: it is a kind of earth, with which the ants cover their dwellings and magazines [storage places].

Though their ivory is of an excellent quality, they prefer the horn of the rhinoceros. Superstition has attributed to it the virtue of fixing fortune. The great, as they become elevated, part with the one they possess, and purchase one of more efficacy. There is no treasure so carefully preserved. The flowers, which enamel [dot] the plains, support numerous swarms of bees, which furnish wax and honey. The mines of tin, iron and lead are very productive. Gold and silver rolls in the rivers, from whence they take it in wire nets. Musk, in which they trade considerably, is not a produce of the country,[10] but they have a composition of ambergris, and a juice which they extract from the body of a cat [the civet], which spreads an agreeable odour. There are many wild animals in the forests. They cultivate the earth with buffaloes and oxen. The rivers breed such enormous fish, that two men can scarcely carry one.[11] The poor people feed on salted herrings [dried fish] and rice. Though there is no salt water in the whole country, it produces beautiful rubies; but doubtless that scum which covers the earth after the rice harvest, supplies the want of it, in forming that precious stone in the bosom of the earth. (Richard 1811: 764–5)

Richard's references to salt and rubies are not unconnected. His information about salt in the rice fields may refer to the unusual soils north of the Mun River and immediately west of the Mekong, where salt rose by capillary action as the fields dried, creating a white frosting on the surface. According to European scientific belief in Richard's time, salt water was the origin of rubies. He therefore concluded that the surface deposits of salt caused rubies to form deep in the earth.

Richard continued his discussion with a reference to the trade between China and Laos prior to the overthrow of China's Ming dynasty by the Manchus (Tartars) in 1644:

> The Chinese, before the eruption of the Tartars, carried on a considerable commerce with this country; they brought velvets, silk stuffs, camlets, carpets, horse-hair, cottons, gold, silver, and porcelain, which they exchanged for ivory, opium, and medicinal herbs.
>
> In the province of Laos, which gives its name to the kingdom, is a deep pit, from whence they obtain rubies, and particularly emeralds, one of which, in the possession of the King, is as large as a common orange. The trade that might be carried on in this country would furnish a certain advantage, because they are the most upright people in business, and the most faithful to their engagements of any in India [i.e., southern Asia]. Not but what they are tempted to obtain whatever they see uncommon in the hands of a stranger; but they prefer obtaining it by importunity rather than by violence. The most flattering praise they can receive is to hear themselves extolled as keeping their promises inviolable. Theft or murder on their highways are seldom heard of: the police prevents all such disorders. The towns and villages in whose territory the traveller has been insulted, are obliged to make good his losses.
>
> Their virtues however are not without a mixture of vices. Buried in eternal gluttony, they only work to supply the indispensable wants of nature. All fatigue disheartens them: enemies to perseverance they cannot fix long to one object, and they never see below the surface. Boundless in their inclination for women, they seem to live only to multiply their kind. Sorcery and magic are the sources of many crimes and superstitions; but it is a disorder of the mind, which is

most inveterate throughout the East, where nothing important is undertaken, without consulting and liberally paying those accredited impostors [i.e., astrologers and practitioners of the magic arts].

The purity of the air prolongs life, and though the country is not very extensive, they can raise five hundred thousand combatants, and it would be easy to form an army of centenaries, all healthy and vigorous. They are not so abstemious as in other countries of India; they have four meals a day; rice, fish, and buffalo's flesh is their common food; they seldom eat veal, beef, or poultry; they roast the birds in their feathers, which gives the flesh a disagreeable taste.

The magistrates and ministers generally take but one wife; but that is less an effect of their moderation than of their avarice. They would wish it to be understood, that too much occupied by their public duties, they cannot bestow that time on their pleasures which they consecrate to business: but the great number of their concubines makes amends for confining themselves to one wife. Marriages are engagements for life, but divorces are so common, that they seem to be only transient and capricious unions. When a woman is convicted of adultery, the husband may inflict what punishment he pleases.

Their funerals are rather festivals than scenes of grief. The priests are paid and sumptuously feasted, who cry and sing funeral hymns, to instruct the dead on the road to heaven. They put sums of money, in proportion to his fortune, in his tomb. It may be presumed that the priests, who are the guardians of these tombs, cause those treasures to circulate in society, which imbecility would bury in the earth.

It may be observed that the commerce of this kingdom has experienced different revolutions: formerly its productions were brought to Siam: but since the irruption of the Bramas [Burmese], they have passed to Pegu. The animosities that continual wars maintain between the two nations, has transferred the trade to Camboya [Cambodia], where the Laos have a ready and easy sale for their benjamin, lacker, and other articles.

Richard ended his commentary on Laos with observations about religious beliefs and practices:

This ignorant people boasts of having taught the Siamese the art of writing on the leaves of the palm-tree. The language and characters are the same: but the Laos cannot pronounce the letter *l*, and *r*. It is said that in their earliest times, their worship, more purified than that of other nations, was free from superstitions. They had no temples, and adored a God the creator, who watched over the welfare of the world, and whom they could only please by the practice of virtue, and not by sacrifices or ceremonies. They believed that after a certain revolution of ages, the universe would be renewed, and this system of the great periodical year has been adopted, by almost all the nations of antiquity. Their commerce with the Chinese changed these simple notions. They had priests who erected themselves to legislators, and who, that they might not be refuted, produced books written in foreign characters. Their doctrine not being understood appeared the more mysterious, and was respected. It was easy for those artful impostors to bestow on it a divine origin.

Although a few of Richard's assertions are inaccurate or pure fantasy—for instance, the notion of Lao soldiers aged one hundred or more—his study of Laos from the European texts and reports available to him reflects the intellectual trends of the age in which he lived. Like some of his contemporaries, he attempted to distill all available knowledge about a little-known country and people into a single comprehensive work. Yet, like the compilers of the *Universal History*, most of his information was old and copied primarily from Marini (1666).

John Pinkerton, a Scot, was another writer who drew upon the works of Kaempfer and Du Halde. The entry for Laos in his *Modern Geography* summarises the views of these two authors and points out that European knowledge of the interior of South-East Asia had barely improved during the century since their work was published:

Laos. According to Kaempfer this was a powerful state, surrounded with forests and deserts [uninhabited territory]; and difficult to access by water, because the river is full of rocks and cataracts. But by the newly discovered river of Anan the passage from Siam may perhaps be expedited. The soil is represented as fertile in rice; and Laos furnished the merchants of Cambodia with the best benjoin and lacca [gum benjamin and insect lac]. Exquisite musk is also brought from Laos, with some gold and rubies; and the rivers boast of the fresh water mya [sic], which yields pearls. The religion and manners resemble those of Siam; but in personal appearance the people of Laos resemble the southern Chinese. The chief towns were, in Kaempfer's time, Landjam [Lan Sang] and Tsiamaja [Chiang Mai]. The former is also styled Lantchang [Lan Sang]; and Sandepora is added in modern maps: from the former the people are called Lanjanese [Lan Sang-ese, or people of Lan Sang]. (Pinkerton 1802: 227–8)

This description illustrates the absence of any new knowledge in Europe about the main towns and rivers in the interior. In the late eighteenth and early nineteenth centuries, Europeans believed that part of the waters of the upper Mekong flowed south into the Thai kingdom. As this account illustrates, European cartographers may have got this idea from the Chinese as well as from informants in South-East Asia. The map of the *East India Isles* in an atlas published by John Pinkerton (1815) shows a river named Anan, linking the Mekong (at a point some distance up-river from Vientiane) to the Chao Phraya (at a point immediately below Phichit). Although no such river exists, the line along which the river is drawn on the 1815 map was a well-travelled route, along which passed much of the trade between the upper Mekong and upper Chao Phraya basins. It is easy to understand why European cartographers imagined this river link, especially if they received reports about the use of river transport along this route. In fact, the traders did make use of small rivers on both sides of the watershed line. The name Anan may be derived from the Nan River, because one of its tributaries served as the trade route on the western side of the mountains. Another small river on the eastern side led down to the eastern terminus of the overland route at Paklay on the Mekong, up-river from Vientiane.

Pinkerton's attempt to include 'Sandepora' in his description illustrates how Europeans were still struggling to identify toponyms. This name is merely a variant spelling of *Candra Pura* (City of the Moon), which is a Sanskrit name for Vientiane. He continued by attempting to identify Laos in relation to nearby countries that were already well marked on European maps:

This kingdom, from its inland situation, is less known than any other state of further India [i.e., South-East Asia], and scarcely any recent materials can be indicated. It remains an object of curious investigation to future travellers. Du Halde has however published a route from China to Siam by land, in which some account is given of Lahos or Laos. In the language of the country Mohang [*müang*] signifies a town; and the capital is styled Mohang Leng [possibly Müang Luang, capital of Sipsòng Panna] by the Chinese. It is of considerable extent, but only inclosed with a palisade: on the west are large forests and several rivers. This city stands on both sides of a river called Meinam Tai, which by the Chinese accounts joins the river of Siam, so that perhaps the Anan is to the south of the capital. Fish is rare, but buffalo and venison are common in the markets. About five days journey to the north of Mohang Leng are mines of gold, silver and copper; and one of rubies near the city: emeralds are also found of great size. Tin, red sulphur (perhaps cinnabar), cotton, tea, sapan or brasil wood [sapan wood], are also exported. Laos [i.e., Sipsòng Panna] was then tributary to Ava: but the chief trade was with the Chinese. Du Halde's account is not a little confused; and though he gives the names of many provinces and towns, it would be impossible to construct a sketch of a map from his description. The chief river is styled Meinam Kong [Mekong], which afterwards passes through Cambodia. It would seem that branches of the same river are distinguished by different names. In Mr. Dalrymple's valuable map of exterior India this grand stream is called Kiou Long, or Maykaung [Mekong]; and Mr. Arrowsmith [an English cartographer] derives it from the Tibetan alps, where it is styled the Satchou, and afterwards by d'Anville the Lan-tsan Kiang; which seems to identify it as implying the river of Lantsang, or Leng, the capital of Laos.

Pinkerton knew various names for the Mekong, but he was unable to explain them. His Kiou Long (Jiulong in *pinyin*) is another Chinese name for the Mekong and literally means 'Nine Dragons'. Similarly, his Lan-tsan Kiang is today the usual Chinese name for the Mekong, now romanised Lancang Jiang (in *pinyin*), meaning the 'Lan Sang River'. Long after Pinkerton's time, the great river that flowed out of the heart of South-East Asia continued to be a mystery, in both name and topography. Europeans still most often called it the river of Cambodia—even in the delta region, which had been controlled by Cambodia when Europeans first explored it but which became predominantly Vietnamese in the course of the seventeenth and eighteenth centuries.

European cartographers of the early nineteenth century still drew the Mekong valley on their maps as a narrow tract of land bounded to the east and west by long chains of mountains. These maps, like those two centuries earlier, gave the impression that Laos should be relatively easy to reach from either Vietnam or Cambodia. This possibility naturally caught the attention of Catholic missionaries, almost as soon as they began arriving on the coast. Various efforts were made to establish a mission in Cambodia in the 1590s (Briggs 1950, Groslier 1958). All these ventures were unsuccessful, and the priests made no attempt at that time to ascend the Mekong into Laos. Plans for a mission in Laos were conceived not long after, however, by the Jesuits who had successfully established themselves on the Vietnamese coast.

EARLY CATHOLIC REPRESENTATIONS OF THE LAO: SEVENTEENTH AND EIGHTEENTH CENTURIES

The Catholic missionaries in the northern part of Vietnam belonged to the Tonkin Mission, which was established about 1627. The mission extended south to the port of Vinh, from which several overland routes led into the Mekong basin. Various proposals were made in the 1630s to send priests to Laos, and eventually at least four missionaries reached Lao territory, one of whom provided a valuable report on the central Mekong region.[12]

Raimundo de Gouveia, a Portuguese priest in Tonkin, was planning to go to Laos in 1638 (Blair and Robertson 1905 xxix: 37–8), but he abandoned his plan and returned to Macau. About the same time, an envoy of King Suriyawongsa was sent from Vientiane to Tonkin. The envoy was converted to Christianity (or so the priests claimed), returned to Vientiane and reported to the king about this previously unknown religion. According to mission reports, the king sent a message to the Jesuits in Tonkin, inviting them to visit his kingdom. Another Portuguese missionary, António Francisco Cardim recounted the unhappy ending of the first attempt to reach Vientiane, made by an Italian Jesuit:

> We had no information about this kingdom, but as soon as we had some, the Father Superior of Macau at once sent Father Giovanni Baptista Bonelli, of the Milan diocese, to work in this new vineyard. He had already travelled two months for this purpose, when he reached the end of his career and died. (Cardim 1646: 181–2)

A label on a seventeenth-century French map (Lejosne 1986: 368) indicates that 'Jean-Baptiste Bonel' (the French spelling of Bonelli's name) died in the *déserts* of Laos—meaning the uninhabited and forested areas on the west side of the cordillera. Nothing further is known about him, but the efforts of another Jesuit are better documented. Cardim, writing in 1642, added that

> When the news of his [Bonelli's] death became known, Father Giovanni Maria Leria was sent there [to Laos]. He is still on his journey at present, and we hope that he will arrive [in Vientiane] soon. We are awaiting good news from there, so that we can go there to help in his work. The inhabitants are by nature gentle and good. And already, the envoy from the king of the Lao to the king of Tonkin has converted [to Catholicism] and is called Thomas. On his return [to Vientiane] he spoke so powerfully to his master [King Suriyawongsa, who came to the throne in 1638], about our holy Faith and about our fathers who preach it, that his master wrote to them in Tonkin and invited them to his kingdom. That is why Father Giovanni Maria, when he arrives there, will no doubt find the harvest [of souls] well prepared, so that he can gather it in and place it in the granaries of the Church.

Leria was an Italian who had worked in central Vietnam during the 1630s but was expelled with the other missionaries in 1639. Many of the Jesuits took refuge in the Portuguese port of Macau, but Leria went south across the border into Champa—the remnant of an independent state between southern Vietnamese territory (modern central Vietnam) and Cambodian territory in the Mekong delta region. His exact route into Laos is not known, but most likely he stayed for some time in Cambodia, perhaps to learn the Lao language from the Lao boatmen and traders who regularly brought cargoes down-river as far as Phnom Penh. One of these Lao merchants took Leria and another priest, Mateo Cebrián, up the Mekong, and they reached Vientiane in July 1642 (Wusthof 1986: 196). Another Italian priest, Jacinto Uranda, arrived in Vientiane at the end of 1645, with a letter from the Father Superior in Tonkin, remained for nearly two years but died in the forests in October 1647, while exploring a route across the cordillera (Bressan 1998: xxvii), apparently intending to find a passage from Laos to Hué, the southern Vietnamese capital.

Leria travelled widely but did not proselytise successfully in this part of Asia. He stayed in Laos until 1648, primarily in Vientiane, where he became involved in heated debates with the Buddhist monks. He did not publish an account of his experiences. But after he returned to the Tonkin mission, the information that he obtained about Laos was published in Italian in 1663 by another Jesuit, Giovanni Filippo de Marini, and appeared in a French translation in 1666. The rich detail of his work is illustrated in the following impressions of the city and royal palace:

> The main city, where the king ordinarily resides, is in the middle of the kingdom, at 18 degrees north latitude. It is called Langione [an Italian pronunciation of Lan Sang]. To defend itself from enemy action, the city has good moats and extremely high walls on one side and has the great river on the other.
>
> The royal palace, whose structure and symmetry are admirable, can be seen from a great distance. Truly it is stupendous in scale and so large that it would seem to be a city, in terms of both its size and the innumerable people who live inside. The king's apartment, which has a superb and magnificent facade, and a number of beautiful rooms, along with a great hall, are all of incorruptible wood and decorated inside and out with excellent bas-reliefs, so delicately gilded that they appear to be covered with gold lamination rather than with gold leaf.

From there, when entering the courtyards, which are extremely spacious, one at first sees a large group of houses, all of brick and covered with tiles, where the second-rank wives usually live, and beyond them a row of other houses, which have been built at the side with the same symmetry for the chief officials. I could fill an entire volume if I tried to provide an exact description of all the other parts of the palace, its riches, its sub-divisions, its gardens and many other things of that sort. (Marini 1666: 341–2)

As a priest occupied with numbers of souls to be saved, Leria collected data that is useful for historical demography in his estimations of the population:

Because of the kingdom's fertility and the abundance of the necessities of life, it is so populous that a census not long ago enumerated five hundred thousand men who are capable of serving the king in war and carrying arms. The census did not include the elderly men, who are so numerous and so robust that even those who are aged one hundred could form, in case of need, a very sizable army for the defence of the kingdom. (Marini 1666: 343)

Leria's sharp-minded observations, perhaps due to his Jesuit training, provided a detailed and entertaining description of the people he called 'Lanjans'—that is, the 'Lan Sang-ese' or Lao people. He made lengthy observations about religious beliefs and practices that he observed. Despite his contemptuous remarks about the religion of the Lao, Leria left behind thoughtful impressions of a land of faith, in contrast to the Dutchman van Wusthof, whose primary concern, as a merchant, was the material wealth of the country.

By the time of Leria, permanent Catholic missions were being established in the accessible coastal regions of mainland South-East Asia. The priests who worked in the coastal areas of the Gulf and the South China Sea dreamed of founding a mission in Laos, but no effective efforts were made to establish such a mission in the interior until the 1880s. The clergy, nonetheless, did write about Laos from time to time. French interest in Laos was renewed in 1773, for example, when the Holy See gave jurisdiction over religious affairs in Laos to the French bishop in West Tonkin, who had proposed to establish a mission in the interior of the peninsula. The bishop died before the project could be carried out, however, and during the next century only a few priests and converts ventured in the direction of Laos.

NINETEENTH CENTURY CATHOLIC MISSIONS

From the sixteenth to the eighteenth centuries, the adventurous Catholic missionaries were important sources of new information about the geography and peoples of little-known lands such as Laos. During the late eighteenth and early nineteenth centuries, the flow of new knowledge from this source dried up almost completely. The disruptions of the French Revolution and the Napoleonic wars in Europe greatly reduced the number of missionaries in mainland South-East Asia, and plans for proselytising among the Lao were not revived until the 1820s. During the next several decades, numerous ideas for making contact with the Lao were proposed by missionaries in northern and central Vietnam, in Cambodia, Siam and Burma, and even in southern China.[13] Each mission acted independently, however, and none of their schemes succeeded. The most important factors were the small number of priests available in the coastal areas, the chronic lack of money available to the bishops and the extreme difficulties of travelling in the interior.

In 1826 the aged Bishop Joseph Florens in Bangkok expressed a desire to extend his mission's efforts into Laos, but he had no missionary to send. Indeed, his mission was too impoverished to support such an endeavour. During the 1830s, several of his priests worked among Lao villages in the central plain, which could be reached from Bangkok by boat, but none of them crossed the mountains into the Mekong valley.

Two young French priests joined the mission in 1830. One of them, Father Deschavannes, set out almost immediately to evangelise among the Lao who lived in the narrow Sak River basin, north-east of Bangkok. Unwisely roaming the countryside during the rainy season, he soon contracted malaria and died.[14] His companion, Jean-Baptiste Pallegoix, followed in his footsteps, spent some time in the same Lao villages and learned as much as he could about Laos from the villagers, to supplement the information that he gathered in the capital. In 1834 Pallegoix composed a formal proposal for mission work in Laos, but he himself never went farther than the foothills of the mountains that lead from the Chao Phraya basin across into the Mekong valley. He, too, contracted malaria, and his health and subsequent ecclesiastical duties (he was consecrated as a bishop in 1838) prevented him from pursuing his plans, which would have required a long sojourn deep in the interior. He published an article about the Lao (Pallegoix 1836 and Langlois 1836), based on the information that he gathered, but he made no attempts to extend the mission's work into the Mekong valley.

Meanwhile, the French missions in Vietnam were formulating their own plans for proselytising among the Lao. Sometime between 1828 and 1830, several brief excursions were made into Lao territory by Vietnamese priests from Tonkin. In 1830 Bishop Joseph-Marie Havard of West Tonkin was thinking about training Vietnamese priests and sending some of them to Laos. One of his missionaries, Father Masson, was responsible for the Nghe-anh area, which had the advantage of the relatively easy overland routes to the Mekong, by way of both the Na Pae pass and the Trim Treo trail (described in the chapter by Tran). In early 1832 Masson sent a Vietnamese priest to reconnoitre and report on conditions for missionising, but the priest and his catechists disappeared and apparently died in Laos. Masson survived the persecutions of Christians, which began the next year in Vietnam, but he did not revive the plan for Laos after the decimated mission began to recover. In early 1846, Bishop Pierre-André Retord of West Tonkin and another missionary ventured into the mountains bordering on Laos but went no farther than the montagnard villages.

At that time, the headquarters of the Cochinchina Mission was still in central Vietnam. The bishop who headed the mission, Jean-Louis Taberd, was responsible not only for central and southern Vietnam but also for Cambodia and nominally for Laos. In 1832 he was planning to send a mission up the Mekong by way of Cambodia, but his plan had to be abandoned because of internal events. At the beginning of 1833, a persecution of Christians began in Vietnam. And even if the missionaries had not been forced to leave the country temporarily, efforts to proselytise in the interior would have been forestalled by the war that erupted the same year on the lower Mekong—a protracted conflict that badly affected many Lao towns of the middle Mekong valley for many years to come.

Taberd did, however, make an important contribution to the study of Laos. In 1837 he published a map with the Latin title *Tabula Geographica Imperii Anamitici* (Map of the Vietnamese Empire). Up to that time, European cartographers had no data on the course of the Mekong River and no concept of the true size of the Mekong valley from east to west. European maps in Taberd's day showed the Mekong flowing in a nearly straight line from north-west to south-east, through a uniformly narrow valley bounded to the east and west by chains of mountains. As the bishop explained, his map was the first one drawn by a European to show the true course of the river:

> One of the most essential alterations and which I had the greatest hesitation in adopting, was—what do you think?—to change the course of one of the finest and largest rivers in Asia. The present map is altogether different in this respect from the ancient [i.e., previous] ones. In all the European maps, this great river of Laos is represented throughout the whole of its course as straight as an arrow until it reaches Cochinchina. I think it a decided mistake; I will give you my reason for thinking so. I was always persuaded that in regard to a geographical map, the same rule holds as for a geographical dictionary: one copies the map of another and enlarges it more or less, and adds a few more names, and it is lucky if in thus copying the errors are not augmented.
>
> ...I have given to the river which flows through Laos a course quite different from that in all the other maps, because the two maps I had with me drawn by engineers of the country gave it this direction. They know the country, they visit it every day and have measured all the windings of the river of Laos which is also called Meykon or

Mecon [Mekong]. To lay down the interior of Camboge [Cambodia],
Laos and a part of Thon-king [Tonkin], I have used an ancient and
a modern map of the country designed by his majesty's engineers.
(Tabert 1837: 319)[15]

This advance in western cartography drew upon the knowledge
and skills displayed during the reigns of Emperors Gia Long
(1802–20) and Minh Mang (1820–41) by Vietnamese cartographers—who doubtless obtained their topographical knowledge from
a variety of Lao sources, including exchanges of envoys between the
royal courts and merchant-informants who regularly travelled between the two countries. The new map also revealed the true dimensions of the territory in the interior. Laos was a much bigger
land than anyone had previously imagined.

The vision of reaching Laos, both overland across the cordillera
and up the Mekong, was revived during the next decade by Jean-
Claude Miche (1852, 1854), a French priest who arrived in South-
East Asia in 1836. He was assigned to the central and southern
Vietnam mission, with responsibility for evangelising among the
Cambodians, and he attempted several times to make contact with
the Lao and the montagnard peoples of the lower cordillera. He set
out from central Vietnam with a fellow priest in early 1842 and
travelled up the valley of the Ba River, proceeding along one of its
tributaries that flows down from the massive Darlac plateau region.
The two priests managed to go only as far as the first montagnard
villages, when they were arrested by a contingent of Vietnamese
soldiers. They were subsequently imprisoned in Hué, under
sentence of death, but allowed to leave Vietnam aboard a French
naval vessel the next year.

Miche later went to Cambodia and took up residence near
Phnom Penh. He became a bishop in 1848, with renewed responsibility for evangelisation in Cambodia and also, if possible, in Laos.
He made an excursion up the Mekong in early 1849, but his boat
could not go up-river farther than the Cambodian village of
Sambok. In July 1853 he finally reached the southern fringes of Lao
settlement. This time, he travelled in the rainy season, when the
floodwaters were high above the rocks that had blocked his way four

years earlier. His second journey up-river was undertaken to inspect the work of French priests who had been sent the previous year to investigate conditions at Stung Treng and learn to speak Lao. His account of his first and apparently only venture into areas that had Lao inhabitants unfortunately tells us nothing about the Lao, except to observe that they seemed even less likely than the Cambodians to convert to Christianity.

In 1850, the Cambodia Mission was separated from the southernmost Vietnam mission, and it was given nominal charge of evangelising in Laos. The responsibilities that fell upon Miche in subsequent years proved to be too great, and the hopes of the Cambodian Mission to extend its work into the southern Lao towns never materialised. Nonetheless, two missionaries from southern Vietnam settled in 1850 among the montagnards in the plateau region, near the trijuncture of the modern boundaries of Laos, Cambodia and Vietnam, thus setting in motion at least part of the work that Miche first attempted eight years earlier.

Independent proposals were made for yet more attempts to reach Laos from three additional directions. In 1840 Father Abbono of the Burma Mission formulated a plan to evangelise among the peoples of Laos. He was encouraged by promises of elephants and other transport assistance, offered to the Italian priests at Moulmein by visiting Lao traders. The 'Lao' he mentions may have been Lan Na people from Chiang Mai or perhaps Shan traders from even farther north or perhaps Lao traders from Luang Prabang. It is possible that the Italian archives of the Oblates of Turin contain an account of this venture—if indeed he did undertake the journey into Laos from the west.

A northern route was attempted by Jean-Baptiste Vachal, who was a French missionary initially assigned to Bangkok. He succeeded in reaching Chiang Mai in 1844, but contracted malaria and was sent to the colder and more healthful climate of Yunnan. Having long been intrigued by the mystery of Laos and the possibilities of evangelising in the upper Mekong valley, he set out in 1850 on a journey from Yunnanfu (modern Kunming) to spread the Gospel among the frontier peoples of Tonkin, Laos and Burma. He got only as far as a Chinese town near the Tonkin border, however, where he was arrested and died in prison.

The evangelical encirclement of Laos was completed in the mid-1860s by the bishop of Southern Tonkin, who spent several years planning the evangelisation of the Siang Khwang plateau region. Fathers Colombet and Taillandier, did reach this area but did not succeed in establishing a mission among the Phuan. Both priests contracted malaria and died.

Each of the missions in South-East Asia was aware of the efforts of the other missions to reach Laos, but no concerted effort was envisioned until the 1850s. Miche had long been anxious to find some means of making contact with the Lao, but his Cambodia Mission lacked the necessary resources. In 1854 he suggested that a conference be held in Bangkok, for the purpose of joint action to evangelise in Laos. But his efforts were soon diverted by the effects of the French and Spanish military intervention of 1858 in Vietnam, the cession of the southern Vietnamese provinces to France and the establishment of the French colony of Cochinchina. During this period, Miche's Christian community in Cambodia was threatened with extinction, because of civil war in Cambodia, and was then overpowered by a flood of Christian refugees from Vietnam, who sought Miche's protection. More demands were made on Miche to assist with negotiations for the 1863 treaty that established the French protectorate in eastern Cambodia. Then, in January 1865, he was suddenly called to Saigon, to assume the title and duties of the incumbent bishop of southern Vietnam, whose health was failing. For many years thereafter, Miche remained nominally responsible for Cambodia, but no bishop was appointed to replace him. Despite Miche's early personal commitment and determination, a quarter century passed between his proposal for a conference on Laos and the laying of concrete foundations for a Lao Mission.

In 1880, Bishop Jean-Louis Vey in Bangkok sought the Thai government's permission for some of his priests to reside in the southern Lao towns. Fathers Prudhomme and Mathurin-Marie Guégo went out and founded the first permanent mission post among the Lao in 1881. By this time, the missionaries had become aware of an overland route that was long overlooked by Europeans.

This route, described by Father Dabin (1885) when he made the journey, was very difficult but still practicable even by oxcart in the dry season—all the way from Battambang in western Cambodia by way of Ubon to the Mekong. Within a decade, four Christian communities sprang up near the banks of the Mekong (Smuckarn and Breazeale 1988: 85). Meanwhile, French missionaries crossed the cordillera from Vietnam and began work farther north on the east bank of the Mekong River. Finally, in 1898 the Holy See created the vast new diocese of Laos, which encompassed the entire central Mekong valley. It extended from the boundary of Cambodia north to the boundary of China, thereby unifying, under a single bishop, the Catholic mission that had been barely more than a dream for a quarter of a millenium.

Many efforts were made by all the mission bases surrounding Laos, to launch the Catholic assault into the heartland of the old Lao kingdom during the middle of the nineteenth century. Although missionaries constantly spoke of Laos and took a deep interest in the Lao people—to a far greater extent than any other Europeans did—unfortunately they bequeathed to us few eye-witness accounts of Laos during this period.

PROTESTANT MISSIONS

Not long after the French bishop in Bangkok first expressed an interest in Laos, the Protestants began to arrive in his vicariat. As they extended their work in South-East Asia in the 1820s, they too took an interest in the Lao whom they encountered in the coastal areas. Karl Friedrich Gutzlaff was one of the first two Protestant missionaries who arrived in Bangkok in 1828, and he wrote extensively about this part of Asia. Gutzlaff made two long visits to Bangkok, which extended over a period of nearly three years. During this time, assisted by his fellow missionary, Jacob Tomlin, he translated some portions of the Christian Bible into Lao, Cambodian and Thai, although no copies of his translations are known to have survived.[16] Much later, he published at least one article about the Lao (Gutzlaff 1849). He never visited Laos, however, and had contact only with Lao villagers and war captives who were forcibly resettled near the Gulf after the destruction of Vientiane in 1828.

A flurry of publications appeared in the United States, at the end of the nineteenth and beginning of the twentieth centuries, penned largely by the American missionaries of the Protestant Laos Mission.[17] They also publicised the work of their mission in the *Laos News*. This newspaper was published from 1904 to 1916, but the name was changed to *North Siam News* in 1917, to reflect its actual geographical coverage. The Protestants were most active in the upper Chao Phraya basin (the so-called 'Western Laos'), and these works therefore are not much concerned with the Lao of the Mekong valley.

By the time the Protestants became firmly established near northern Lao territory, the colonial era boundaries had been drawn around northern Laos. At the turn of the twentieth century, Protestants were working to the north of Laos (in Yunnan Province), to the west (in the Shan States of Burma) and to the south-west (in Thai territory). A request was made to the French authorities to allow American Protestants to evangelise in northern Laos, and at least one European Protestant (the Swiss missionary Comtesse) sought permission to work in Laos also. The French did not refuse, but were unco-operative, and no Protestant mission emerged.

CONCLUDING REMARKS

Laos first came to the attention of Europeans during the century between the mid-1500s and the mid-1600s, when the major seafaring nations of western Europe were exploring the potential for commercial gain in many parts of Asia. During this period, a few Portuguese, Spanish and Dutch traders and at least four Catholic priests ventured inland as far as Vientiane, to observe and gather information on the spot. By contrast, English, French and other traders relied on accounts obtained at second hand from coastal peoples. Much additional information about Laos was compiled and published by Jesuit missionaries. As illustrated in this study, some details of the early European descriptions are inaccurate or misleading, although in some cases indigenous records can be used to identify the grains of truth that they contain.

Early European sources are valuable for the study of Lao history, because they provide unique descriptions of the marketable natural resources of the interior of South-East Asia, the export-import trade in which the Lao were engaged, the political relations between the Lao and their neighbours, and many aspects of Lao customs and everyday life. In this regard, European records differ profoundly from the historical records maintained by the Lao themselves. The Lao annals tend to record only the major political and religious events, and pay attention almost exclusively to the concerns of the ruling élite. When analysed and interpreted together, these two very different types of documentation can be used in complementary ways. Further comparisons between local records and the early European writings about Laos can help to unravel some of the mysteries of Lao history and fill some of the gaps left by the annalists. Western sources are also a rare source of details about the lives and activities of ordinary people who lived in a relatively isolated world that has long since vanished.

NOTES

1. Hafner, Halpern and Kerewsky-Halpern (1983: 1). For assessments of early cartographic work on the Indochinese peninsula, see Maitre (1909), Brébion (1910), Fraisse (1948), Manguin (1972) and Fell (1988).

2. Leria's companion, Mateo Cebrián, stayed in Laos only a year and then left. An Italian priest, Jacinto Urando, arrived in Vientiane at the end of 1645 but died in the forest between Laos and Cochinchina in October 1647 while trying to find a new route between the two kingdoms (Bressan 1998: xxvii).

3. Up to the middle of the nineteenth century, Europeans used the name Cochinchina in reference to central Vietnam, with its capital at Hué, which owed allegiance to the Lê emperors in Hanoi but was governed independently by the Nguyen lords. After the Vietnamese gained control of the Mekong delta and Saigon, that area was often called 'Lower Cochinchina', to distinguish it from central Vietnam. The name Cochinchina was applied specifically to the southern provinces of Vietnam only after the French colony of Cochinchina was established in the mid-nineteenth century.

4. The authors are grateful to Dr. Michael W. Charney of the University of London (SOAS) for providing a translation of this passage.

5. Diogo Veloso is the Portuguese spelling. Spanish writers, however, spell his name in Spanish style: Diego Belloso. Some modern writers use the old spelling, Ruyz, instead of the modern Ruiz.

6. This king was Nguyen Hoang, the first of the Nguyen lords who were to rule Southern Vietnam (Cochinchina) independently from the Trinh lords of Hanoi until the 1770s.

7. Cardim obviously did not know about Blas Ruiz or Diogo Veloso, who was killed about mid-1599 in Cambodia. Cardim indicates above that the Mekong was, in his day, the major route into Laos and was the route taken by the three Portuguese known to him. Cardim seems to refer to a single journey by three Portuguese merchants, who went up and back down the Mekong together. He gives no clue to their identity. It is possible that he met or heard about them in Macau in the early 1620s or in Ayutthaya during 1626–9. It seems likely that these merchants and other traders were one source of information about the Lao (the other was the envoy sent by King Suriyawongsa to Hanoi), which led the Jesuits to send a mission to Laos immediately, as Cardim states. Assuming Cardim's manuscript was completed in 1642 or 1643, these merchants may have gone up the Mekong any time during the 1630s or earlier.

8. Who were these princes? In the context of 1633, he may have been referring to the family of the future King Suriyawongsa, who at that time had two elder brothers and at least two male cousins (plus one or more uncles) still living. The envoys who led this trade mission may therefore have been in charge simultaneously of a joint trade venture sponsored by one or more of these princely relatives.

9. Choisy was referring to Kosa Pan, the chief among the three Thai envoys who visited the French court at Versailles in 1686 and 1687.

10. True musk was produced only in south-west China, but the Lao produced and exported a similar product from the civet cat.

11. Richard was obviously copying from Leria's observation in the 1640s about some of the fish he saw in Laos: 'Such heavy ones are found there, that two fishermen, no matter how strong they may be, cannot carry one without considerable difficulty' (Marini 1666: 341). This description is not a traveller's tall tale. It is probably the earliest European reference to the *pa bük*, the renown giant catfish of the Mekong.

12. For further notes on Catholic mission activities and the biographies of Leria and Marini, see Bressan (1998).

13. Most of the discussion concerning nineteenth-century Catholic missions is a condensed summary of notes provided by Kennon Breazeale, based on contemporary sources, particularly the *Annales de la propagation de la foi* (Annals of the Propagation of the Faith), which began publication in 1822 as the journal of the French missionary society (the Missions Etrangères de Paris).

14. Henri Mouhot (1966: 126) referred to Deschavannes, without naming him, when he wrote that 'During the last twenty-five years, only one man, as far as I know, a French priest, has penetrated to the heart of Laos, and he only returned to die in the arms of the good and venerable prelate, Mgr. Pallegoix.' This passage illustrates how vague the meaning of 'Laos' was to Europeans, even in the early 1860s. Deschavannes worked in the lower and middle Sak (Pasak) River valley during 1830 and 1831, but never crossed the mountains into the Mekong valley.

15. For appraisals of this map and its importance, see Folliot (1889) and Tâm (1989: 47–9). One commentator in the late 1880s understood the potential political importance of the Taberd map and advocated that it be used to strengthen French colonial claims over the entire Mekong valley. He wrote that the 'map drawn by Bishop Taberd constitutes a document that France and Annam would have to put forward the day we have to settle differences that could be raised about some provinces in the Mekong valley. It is a claim to be carefully preserved.' (Sylvestre 1889: 8)

16. Samples of the Lao alphabet and Lao writing first appeared in published form in works by Marsden in the 1820s and James Low in the 1830s. Pallegoix compiled a French-Lao dictionary, although he never published it. A sample of the Lao alphabet appeared in the *Bulletin de l' Athénée Orientale* (Paris) in 1868–9, together with notes by Charles de Labarthe (cited in Léon de Rosny 1886: 191, note 1).

17. See for example Curtis (1903), Freeman (1910), McGilvary (1912), and *Siam and Laos as Seen by Our American Missionaries* (1883). For a study of the Protestant Laos Mission between 1867 (when the first missionaries arrived in northern Siam) and 1913 (when the name 'Laos' was abandoned), see Swanson (1984).

THE UNIVERSAL HISTORY:
AN EARLY EUROPEAN
ACCOUNT OF THE LAO

Meg O'Donovan

The Modern Part of an Universal History, published in England in 1759, is a valuable compilation for the study of historical interaction between Europe and mainland South-East Asia. Published in the English language, it synthesized a variety of earlier European travelogues and reports previously available only in French, Italian, and Portuguese. The *Universal History* is also a useful complement to indigenous accounts of social conditions and economic activities in the Lao kingdoms prior to European colonialism. Commenting on the merits of early European contributions to the historiography of mainland South-East Asia, Donald Lach explained that the

> European sources, while admittedly meager, are nevertheless important because the native annals on the period before 1600 are sparse, non-existent, unreliable or written so long after the event as to be suspect. (Lach 1968: 562)

This chapter provides an introduction to the section on Laos in the *Universal History*. It seems helpful to begin with a rough chronology of the earliest European reports on the Lao. Although many of the same sources are mentioned in the *Universal History*, there is little regard for establishing a historical sequence. Next, a few interesting topics are discussed, to serve as a guide for reading the text of the *Universal History*. Appended notes provide a brief glossary of uncommon terms, which may facilitate the reading of the *Universal History*'s descriptions.

THE SOURCES

Southeast Asia's ports and coasts were a familiar sight to Arab merchants, whose maritime trade took them along Asia's coastlines before the arrival of Marco Polo, the most famous of European explorers in Asia. Polo, the first European to document his overland journey to the East, likely never travelled south to the territories of the Lao during his extended thirteenth-century journeys through China. Thus his accounts provided little useful information on peninsular South-East Asia, as the British writer, Hugh Clifford, noted at the beginning of the twentieth century:

> And once again the fate, which we have noted as dooming the Indo-Chinese peninsula to obscurity, causes this portion of Marco Polo's narrative to be more tangled and more destitute of detail than almost any other chapters in his book. (Clifford 1904: 24)

An English translation by Sir Henry Yule of Marco Polo's adventures described (from hearsay) a land lying to the east of Burma, known as Caugigu or Cangigu, and reported to have its own king and language, as well as an abundance of gold, elephants and spices. Its people were known for their body tattooes (Yule cited in Le May 1926: 41–2). Later writers speculated that Marco Polo's description fit the location of Müang Yòng (also spelled Mong Yawng), which is between Chiang Saen and Chiang Rung (Siang Hung).

A crucial portent for East-West relations occurred in 1497 when Vasco da Gama sailed around the African continent via the Cape of Good Hope. Soon Portuguese adventurers enjoyed the status of being among the first Europeans to describe the inland regions and inhabitants of the South-East Asian peninsula and the first to meddle in regional conflicts. (Portugese military advisers and instructors, for example, were used by the Thai after 1518; see Lach 1968: 521.)

Fernão Mendes Pinto's commentary on Chiang Mai and the Lao is the first European account of the Lao mentioned in the *Universal History*. Although he had journeyed through the Malay peninsula, touched the shores of the kingdom of Champa and lived in Ayutthaya, Pinto's travel accounts described many areas of the interior that he apparently never had the opportunity to visit. Thus, his accounts as reported in the *Universal History* are as confusing as the reports by a Portuguese compatriot, Antonio de Faria, who gained the dubious reputation of 'envoy, pirate and private merchant' (Le May 1926: 48)

Despite never having visited the Lao, Faria portrayed them as good-natured and honest, as well as brutal and uncivilized. Relaying on hearsay accounts, generalisations and contradictions is a weakness to which even contemporary commentators on the Lao still succumb, given the dearth of direct observation.

Gaspar da Cruz, a Portuguese Dominican who resided in Cambodia during 1555–6 (Lach 1968: 562), had plenty of direct contact with Lao merchants who traveled down the Mekong River to sell musk and other commodities each year at the Cambodian capital, Lovek. As a lower-Mekong trading center, Lovek was a gateway to information about Laos:

> Because of Lovek's connection on the upper Mekong with Laos, we know through the European merchants and missionaries a relatively large amount about the Laotian kingdom and its people. (Lach 1968: 570)

In the wake of the Burmese attacks in the upper Mekong in 1556, the visiting Lao merchants delayed their return home, so Cruz seized an opportunity to question them about their homeland, customs and compatriots. Cruz's findings, however, are scarcely mentioned in the *Universal History*.

Ralph Fitch, an English merchant who journeyed from Pegu to Chiang Mai in approximately 1587 (Lach 1968: 536) described that city as large and populous with stone houses and wide streets. Fitch admired the people of Chiang Mai for having strong physiques and fair women. He also noted the male tradition of wearing 'bells in their privy members'. Such sexual topics were given short shrift in the *Universal History*, except in reference to polygamy and the 'loose' moral education given Lao children.

An English sea captain, William Eaton, noted the trading potential of Chiang Mai in 1617. He believed that the Lao territories could export gold and gemstones as well as other commodities such as gum benjamin, insect lac and deer skins to the ports of India, and in turn provide an export market for goods carried by English traders, such as Indian-made fabrics and clothing. Eaton's observations that merchants from Lan Sang delivered to Ayutthaya a 'great store of merchandise' (Le May 1926: 44–5) confirmed that the Lao were already experienced long-distance traders.

Despite Eaton's optimistic narrative, the land-locked Lao territories remained a treasure chest, guarded by the dangers posed by malaria, rugged tropical terrain and local wars. Another Englishman, Thomas Samuel, who was sent on company business to explore the trade prospects of Chiang Mai in 1618, was reported to have died shortly thereafter, the hapless victim of a Burmese war party (Clifford 1904: 113).

Most of the *Universal History*'s descriptions of the Lao kingdoms and customs is attributed by the compilers to Giovanni Filippo de Marini, an Italian Jesuit whom the text identified as 'the almost sole author who treats expressly of Lao'. Marini was reported to have published at least five books in Italian—including a work on Tonkin and the Lao territories that was translated into French in 1666. The source of Marini's information about the Lao was another Italian Jesuit, Giovanni Maria Leria, who visited the land of the Lao and lived there from 1642 to 1648 (Bressan 1998). The Chinese sources, alluded to but not identified in the *Universal History*, were published by Du Halde (1736 i: 101–7).

Although numerous books were published in French as a result of the French embassies to Siam in the 1680s, the French did not travel north into Lao territory until much later.[1] As shown in the chapter by the Ngaosrivathanas, missionaries proposed from time to time to go to Laos, but did not succeed for more than 200 years after Leria's departure.

Also notably absent from the *Universal History* are valuable

Dutch sources, such as the account by van Wusthof (1669) who documented his 1641–2 boat trip up the Mekong, which the Dutch called 'the River of Laos', from the Dutch trading post at Lovek. As an agent of the Dutch East India Company on official business from the Governor of the Dutch East Indies, van Wusthof's purpose was to establish friendly relations with the Lao king, Suriyawongsa, and scope out the trading potential of Vientiane. During his journey, the Dutch trader confirmed that Siamese, Peguans, Tonkinese and South Asian Muslim traders were already buying and selling in Laos, and that a trading route linked the middle Mekong with Vinh on the Vietnamese coast.[2]

After several months in Vientiane, van Wusthof sold his wares and bought a cargo of gum benjamin, a musk-like essence and insect lac to transport south. The value of the economic intelligence contained in his log was not recognized until 1669 when his valuable observations were published in a work on Cambodia (Wusthof 1669). During the expansion of French colonial power in mainland South-East Asia, the Mekong River became a vital economic concern, as the English and French vied with each other to find a 'back door' access to trade (and profits) in China. Thus the story of van Wusthof's expedition was later resurrected by Francis Garnier, the famous French colonial explorer, who had the Dutch merchant's account translated into French and published with some of his own notes in 1871 (Wusthof 1871).

To prime the reader's curiosity, the following topics discussed in the *Universal History* will be introduced: (1) definition of geographic boundaries, (2) clarification of the errors of early geographers and travellers, (3) portrayal of the society and customs of the Lao, and (4) description of trade and economic activities.

GEOGRAPHIC BOUNDARIES

The fixing of geographic boundaries was a difficult task for the early Europeans for two reasons. First, their limited travel arrangements led to much speculation and broad assumptions. Secondly, the shifting politics of the peninsula, with Siam, Burma and Vietnam vying for dominance over the Lao kingdoms, made international borders problematic (Lach 1968: 561). To avoid confusion, the *Universal History* does

> not pretend to divide this country into its particular kingdoms or provinces, but content ourselves with dividing it into two great parts only; one called the northern or proper Lao; the other the southern Lao, or kingdom of Lanjang [Lan Sang].

Although the editors of the *Universal History* described the kingdom of Chiang Mai as under the jurisdiction of Lan Sang, they nevertheless distinguished it in a separate chapter.

Kingdom of Jangomay (Chiang Mai)

Citing a lack of detailed information, the writers were vague in defining the kingdom of Chiang Mai as 'originally, or by conquest, a part' of a Lao kingdom. Chiang Mai was described as lying directly north of Siam, flanked by the territories of Laos on the east and the kingdom of Ava on the west. The Chiang Mai kingdom was said to be bounded on the north by the country of the Tai Yai (Shan states known to the Chinese as Ko-sang-pyi) which lay to the west of the northern Lao.

Land of the Northern Lao

The territory of the northern Lao was reported to be bounded on the west by Ava and Siam, on the north by Yunnan, on the east by Tonkin and on the south by Cambodia. The area's coordinates given in the *Universal History* were between 15 and 22 degrees north latitude and between 119 and 122 degrees east longitude. It was said to run 483 English miles from north to south, and 203 of the same from west to east. On another page, it was said to be bordered on the south by the kingdom of Lan Sang, covering about three degrees or 210 English miles from north to south and sharing the same breadth as Lan Sang.

The southernmost province or district reported by the Chinese was Chiang Saen, which was stated to be north of Chiang Rai and south of Kemarat (the Pali name of a Shan capital, known as

Kengtung or Chiang Tung). Also north of Kemarat was Müang Leng (also spelled Lang),[3] which itself was bounded on the west by Ko-sang-pyi, the land of the Tai Yai (other Shan areas). The ruler of Müang Leng, the capital of Lahos, was said to pay tribute to Ava. On the basis of the Chinese sources there was also mention of the province or district of Le, thought to be situated north-east of Leng towards China, and a provincial capital called Meng, rich with cities and metals, including copper, silver, tin and iron mines.

Kingdom of Lan Sang

The compilers of the *Universal History* were apparently unable to decide precisely the coordinates of the southern Lao kingdom of Lan Sang. Since Chiang Saen was mentioned to belong to the northern kingdom already described above, it was assumed that the frontier lay at approximately 19 degrees north latitude and stretched south almost four degrees.

The breadth of the southern kingdom was said to be at least equal to that of the northern Lao kingdom, and augmented by another hundred miles or so if Chiang Mai was included. Based on these assumptions, the text stated that the area of Lan Sang was nearly twice as large as that of the northern Lao (Laos). Lan Sang merited a glowing tribute to its healthy climate, centenarian elders, fertile soil, high-quality rice and tall, straight trees.

GEOGRAPHIC ERRORS

The *Universal History* text demonstrates the limits of European knowledge of mainland South-East Asia in the pre-colonial period. The compilers were candid about the ambiguous basis of geographical information and attempted to identify some of the earlier writers' misconceptions about the geography of the Lao territories.

For example, the *Universal History* casts doubt on the credibility of Pinto's tales of a mighty Lao empire called Kalaminham. He was criticized for extrapolating its existence from other reports of a people called the Siões Maõs (mentioned by Cruz 1953: 73) and 'out of his own fertile imagination', with the result of overestimating the Lao territories. There is a reference to 'his fictitious journey to the court of the Kalaminhan', an early warning that European explorers were not always reliable sources, especially when they relied so heavily on hearsay information.

Examples of the difficulty in charting distances and locations are given. The *Universal History* reckoned that La Loubère's estimation of the distance between Chiang Mai and the Siamese frontier was too great, and that the city's correct location was not more than 20 degrees 30 minutes north latitude (it is actually 18 degrees 40 minutes).

There is also the question of a lake, which Pinto called Kunabetec and also Singapamor, which he believed to be the source of the river that flowed through Chiang Mai and then south into Siam. According to the *Universal History*, the Siamese who attacked Chiang Mai in the seventeenth century knew nothing of the lake. Clifford (1904: 93–4) suggests the river was the Mekong and the lake was the Tonle Sap, the Great Lake of Cambodia.

The course of the Mekong greatly confused Europeans. Marini believed that, just beyond the territory of the Lao, the river divided into a western branch that emptied into the Bay of Bengal and an eastern branch that ran north to south through the Lao territories (as the Mekong actually does). The text cites Kaempfer (1727), who thought a branch of the Ganges ran through the kingdom of the Lao. To correct these errors, the *Universal History* claimed that the Jesuit maps of China fixed the source of the Mekong with 'great precision', rising on the north-west border of Yunnan.

The *Universal History* also noted authors' tendencies to shrink the lands of the Lao. The territories' dimensions are said to be a topic 'which the geographers seem to have been much mistaken in'. One reduced the northern Lao territory's width 'from east to west to a narrow gut of land'. Others relied on La Loubère's map of Siam and expanded Siam's domain northwards, varying from 20 to 23 degrees north latitude, to the point that in some cases Siam overlapped China's southern border. The *Universal History* refers to La Loubère's map with much skepticism, based on its unscientific methodology as well as the statement that 'the author declares himself, that he does not think it correct'.

PORTRAYAL OF THE SOCIETY AND CUSTOMS OF THE LAO

Despite vague treatment of the political organization of the Lao and contradictory descriptions of Lao society and religion, the *Universal History* presented plenty of information useful not only in its depiction of the Lao in the seventeenth century, but also for its representation of European perspectives on Asian society.

The text identified three dominant socio-political groups: kings, officials and monks. The country of the Lao was said to be 'divided among several kings', and royal power was based on both material wealth and religious prestige. The king of Lan Sang was represented as an absolute monarch with 'no superior either in temporal or spiritual affairs', who owned all land and property in the kingdom. According to Marini, there were no private or family inheritances:

> The offices, duties, honours and riches depend absolutely on the king, who promotes those who most please him to the highest offices of the kingdom; who creates stipends for them, and gives them fiefs . . . which he takes away from them sometimes even during their lifetimes, and always at their deaths. . . . The most that he leaves to the orphaned children consists of movable possessions; but the houses, property, fiefs, gold and silver revert to the crown, which benefits greatly from them. (Marini 1666: 358)

The king was also said to exercise some monopoly rights on foreign trade, by requiring that any imported valuables be sold to him, 'the duties arising from which are of great advantage to his revenue'.

Royal will was said to be the fount of legal decisions, because there were few laws. Nonetheless, there were judges for civil cases, who referred to precedents and, lacking written legal commentary, decided cases according to their own opinions, with no recourse of appeal for the parties judged guilty.

The king of Lan Sang was described as a recluse, showing himself but twice a year to his subjects. He could be seen visiting Buddhist temples in his capacity as the 'grand master' of the religion in the kingdom. His temporal power was reported to parallel his religious responsibilities:

> He appoints the days for fasts and festivals; the ceremonies of which are regulated by him. He resolves all doubts and reconciles the different scriptures, explains the difficulties found in their book; and never suffers anything to be printed without his approbation . . . In a word, he is the sovereign judge of whatever relates to the conduct of the *Talapoy* [Buddhist monks], and punishes them for their offenses: but, as if there were something sacred in them, suffers none to vex them on any account.

The European commentators thought that there was no Lao nobility privileged by birth. The king relied instead upon appointed governors to administer, collect taxes and raise armies. A viceroy-general, identified as the intermediary between the provincial governors and the king, assisted the king in affairs of government and served as temporary regent on the occasion of the king's death. The text portrayed the provincial governors as power-hungry oppressors of the people, taking what they desired by force and sometimes by black magic. Yet these same 'chief officers of the state' were reported to be honored to serve the Buddhist monks, even by performing physical labor themselves, such as carrying wood to the monasteries, because it was 'the sure way to recommend them to the favor of the king'.

References to the Buddhist monks, called priests or *talapoy* in the text, are frequent and mostly negative. The tone of the European authors, discussing the religion and its hierarchy, was very critical and contradictory. The monks were derided as 'a lazy, slothful race, and the sworn enemies of industry' but also said to be learned in 'all sorts of trades, and work at them in their convents, which seem to be changed at present into so many shops of mechanics and merchants'. In addition to their labours, the monks were sometimes supported by people whom the king obliged 'to serve in their temples, in lieu of the tribute due to him. He sometimes gives up whole towns and villages to them'. Forest-dwelling monks also received unflattering descriptions.

While the early European authors vented their disdain for the Buddhist hierarchy, they often praised the lay people for their religious piety and devotion. The text noted that although Buddhism 'is spread over the farther peninsula [i.e., South-East and East Asia], it flourishes in no part of it so much as it does in Lao, or among the Lanjans [people of Lan Sang]'. The book begrudgingly recognized the good hearts and honesty of the Lao:

Nothing is more surprising than the piety and devotion of the Lanjans; who are so far from the thoughts of robbing temples, that they exhaust themselves with making presents, without desiring anything more than to have them acceptable to their false god. . . .

Despite the assertion that Lan Sang was very populous, there are only minor descriptions of the common people's physique, dress, diet, housing and customs, perhaps due to the urban bias of the observers. Early European traders and missionaries were attracted to the centres of economic and royal power located in the largest cities. Only when explorers such as Henri Mouhot (1864) began to trek through the Lao territories, did detailed descriptions begin to appear of the hinterlands, dotted with small villages and farming households.

DESCRIPTION OF TRADE AND ECONOMIC ACTIVITIES

A large portion of the *Universal History*'s commentary on the Lao territories is devoted to an inventory of their economic products and potential. The Lao lands were heralded as veritable paradises with abundant natural resources. Although the Lao people were said to be 'slothful and averse to business . . . [applying] themselves to nothing but agriculture and fishing', they were active participants in regional commerce. Regional politics was identified as a factor in trading patterns:

We are told by Da Cruz that musk and gold were carried to Sion (or Siam) before the Bramas (or rather Barmas [Burmese]) conquered Pegu; after which it was removed thither. The trade with Siam, in process of time, was restored: but the king of Siam having invaded the Laos, and taken a province from them . . . ruined the good understanding, which had subsisted between the two nations, and caused the trade to be removed to Kamboja. . . .

The *Universal History* cited Fitch's reports that the kingdom of Chiang Mai was rich with copper and gum benjamin, and received other precious metals, silks, musk and pepper from Chinese traders. Lan Sang was known for products such as gum benjamin, insect lac, ivory, rhinoceros horn, fish, honey, wax, cotton, gold, iron, lead, salt, silver, tin, timber, 'excellent rice', fruit, buffaloes and oxen. Among its trading partners, the area of Müang Leng was said to produce plenty of rice, fruit, livestock, copper, gemstones, gold, lead, silver, sulphur, tin, cotton (both raw and spun), tea, lacquer, medicinal roots and wood. Farther north, Müang Meng was known for fruit orchards, mines (copper, iron, silver, salt, tin) and musk.

The Chinese played a strong economic role in the Lao territories, as import-export caravan traders and as miners and managers at the silver mines in Leng, but the *Universal History* does not mention any Vietnamese merchants. The text is also silent on the destinations of the Lao traders themselves, despite evidence by Cruz, Marini, and van Wusthof in other books, who confirm that Lao merchants were experienced travellers to distant trading centres such as Ayutthaya, Batavia and Lovek.

CONCLUSION

The text has its weaknesses. Stylistically, it suffers from disorganization, repetition, inconsistent spellings and lack of graphics. The compilers relied on authors who themselves often used second-hand, incomplete and contradictory information. The chapters on the Lao are full of contradictory descriptions, inconsistent logic and embarassing flaws, such as the religious intolerance prevalent in descriptions of Lao religious beliefs and practices. Given the Protestant English bias of the book, much ink is wasted on scorning the Buddhist monks as well as bashing the Catholic missionaries who provided many of the earliest original reports on the Lao.

Despite many imperfections, the *Universal History* remains an interesting and informative collection of the earliest of European perspectives on the Lao. A glossary is included in the notes to this chapter, to assist the reader's intellectual journey to the historic lands of the Lao found in the pages of the *Universal History*.

GLOSSARY OF TERMS AND NAMES FOUND IN THE
UNIVERSAL HISTORY

algalia: This is the Italian, Portuguese and Spanish term for the civet cat—an animal found in Laos, from which 'counterfeit musk' was extracted.

Arrakan: Arakan, a kingdom encompassing the territory that is now Burma's west coast.

Ava: The old Burmese capital, adjacent to modern Mandalay. Also referred to as Pama-hang and Hawa.

benjamin: Gum benjamin or benzoin (*Styrax benzoin, Styraceae*), an ingredient used in ointments and perfumes.

callico, calico: A cotton cloth of white or bright colors.

camblets: Fabric of tightly woven hair.

civet: The civet cat, from which an extract similar to musk was produced for use in perfumes.

Gnay: Cited as a people on the borders of China, who traded in musk.

Gueo: According to a Portuguese informant in the first half of the sixteenth century, these people caused much turbulence on the northern frontier of the Ayutthaya kingdom. Numerous modern scholars have attempted to identify them. Campos (1983: 18) thought they were the Wa and Lawa, who live on the frontier between Burma and China, and that the Barros report of a Siamese army of 250,000 men waging war on the Gueo referred to a war between Ayutthaya and Chiang Mai. Gueo might be a Portuguese romanisation of the Thai term *ngiao*, which refers to the Shan east of the Salween. Or it might be the Thai terms *hò* or *kaeo*, which appear in Lan Na records and refer to various groups (including Chinese) from Yunnan Province.

Ishuren: The Hindu deity, Iśvāra (Śiva).

Jamahay, Jamahey, Chiamay: The city of Chiang Mai, Jangomay's capital.

Jangoma, Jangoman, Jagoman, Jangomay, Janguma, Zangomay: The kingdom of Lan Na, with its capital at Chiang Mai (known as Zin-mè in Burmese).

japan: Glossy black lacquer or varnish used for coating objects.

Jun-nan, Vinan, Yun-nan: Yunnan Province in southern China.

Kalaminham, Kalaminhan: An inland 'empire' described by Pinto, now presumed to be Lan Sang, with its original capital at Luang Prabang.

katis: A measurement for silver; the modern Chinese catty-weight is about 0.6 kg.

Kemarat: The Pali name of Chiang Tung (Kengtung in the Anglo-Burmese spelling).

Ko-sang-pi, Ko-sang-pyi: Described as 'a vast forest' and the country of the Tay-Yay (i.e., Shan).

Kochin-china: Cochinchina, the southern Vietnamese kingdom ruled by the Nguyen lords at Hué, comprising part of the central and southern coast of modern Vietnam.

kori shells: Cowries, a type of seashell used in place of small coins by the Lao and Thai.

kot-wha-bwa (Siamese), *tong-quey* (Chinese): A medicinal root.

kotso: Identified only as 'a kind of medicinal root'.

Kunabetec, Singapamor: Thought by Pinto and sixteenth-century cartographers to be a lake, deep in the interior and the source of two or more major rivers.

Kyang-hay, Kyay: Chiang Rai.

Kyang-kong: Chiang Khaeng, a Lü kingdom (known as Kyaing-hkaung in Burmese).

Kyang-seng: Chiang Saen, depicted in the *Universal History's* Chinese sources as a province or district; placed by the 1759 compilers in their so-called northern kingdom of Laos.

lac, lack, lakka, lakre: (1) Insect lac (sticklac) is an animal product, a reddish resin produced by the lac insect, and is processed into sealing wax and red dye. (2) Lac is black lacquer, a vegetable product processed into shellac, varnish and laquerwares.

Lahos, Lauhos, Lawhos: A country bounded by Ava and Siam on the west, Yunnan on the north, Tonkin on the east, and Cambodia on the south. Located between 15 or 16 and 22 degrees north latitude and 119–122 degrees east longitude; for further identification, see editor's note 3 below.

Lan-chang, Lanjan, Lanjang: Capital of Lan Sang lying at 18 degrees north latitude; originally at Luang Prabang, but in Marini's time at Vientiane.

Lanjans, Lanjens, Lanjeyannes, Lenjeyans: Inhabitants of the Lao kingdom of Lan Sang.

Le: Possibly the La River valley in Sipsòng Panna (a Lü kingdom, the present-day Dai Autonomous Prefecture of Yunnan Province).

Leng or Lang: A kingdom whose capital city is of the same name, north of Kemarat, east of Ko-fang-pyi.

maha ing, ingo: Described as 'a medicinal wood'; *maha hing* (*asa foetida*) is a medicinal gum resin formerly used as a prophylactic.

Meng: A provincial capital to the north of Laos, possibly in the area of modern Simao, immediately north-east of the Dai Autonomous Prefecture in Yunnan Province.

Moang, Mohang, Muhang: *Müang* is the Lao prefix that identifies a toponym as a political entity (a town, district, province or kingdom).

musk: The basis of fragrance which was derived from a variety of sources, including a scented secretion taken from the musk deer, an animal called *she chiang* by the Chinese (romanised *ye hiam* in the 1666 French translation of Marini). Musk was used to make perfumes and medicine. The Lao made a musk-like substance (called *algalia* in Italian) extracted from the civet cat, which appeared in Europe earlier than genuine musk.

Pahima Pan: The Lao term for the Himalayas, epitomized in Lao legend as a Shangrila on earth. The 'Himaphan Forest' refers to the forested slopes of the Himalayas and the homeland of the Lord Buddha.

Pegu: The Mon Kingdom (Ramanyadesa), with its capital at Pegu, in southern Burma, whose inhabitants were called Peguers. A century before Marini's time, it was conquered by the Burmese and became the Burmese capital.

popish: A disparaging term for Roman Catholic.

quicksilver: An amalgam of tin, used to back mirrors; also liquid mercury.

senes: A measure defined in the text as eight fathoms, thus about
14.6 meters.

Shaka: Sayka, a name of the Lord Buddha.

Sion (Sião): The Portuguese name for Siam.

Siones Mãons: A Portuguese name for the Lao people.

Sions: A Portuguese name for the Siamese.

Talapoy, talepoy: *Bhikkhus* (Buddhist monks).

Tangu: Toungoo, capital of a political division in lower Burma.

Tay-noe: The Siamese (literally 'Lesser Thai').

Tay-yay: The Shan (literally 'Great Thai').

Thiem: A kingdom inhabited by the 'Ke-moy', a people who had
'neither king nor religion', north-west of Cochinchina.

Tongking: Tonkin, the northern Vietnamese kingdom ruled by the
Trinh lords at Hanoi.

Wishtnu: The Hindu deity, Vishnu.

zhadam: Identified as 'an earth or medicinal paste'.

NOTES

1. Henri Mouhot, a French naturalist and explorer, made a courageous overland trek to Luang Prabang, where he died of malaria in 1861. The expedition of Ernest Doudart de Lagrée and Francis Garnier set out in 1866 on a journey that took them up the Mekong to Luang Prabang and eventually into China. For a survey of French and other writings about Laos prior to these first modern explorations, see the chapter by Mayoury and Pheuiphanh Ngaosrivathana.

2. Such reports are also attributed by Clifford (1904: 95) to Fernão Mendes Pinto.

3. Editor's note: The *Universal History* discusses Leng in the context of the so-called kingdom of Lahos, which was north of the kingdom of Luang Prabang. This information was published by Du Halde (1735), based on a Chinese description of the trade route from Yunnan Province to the kingdom of Lan Na and Chiang Mai. The caravan route is well documented in the nineteenth and early twentieth centuries. Lahos was not a Lao territory. It was the Lü kingdom of Sipsòng Panna, straddling the upper Mekong. The modern capital is on the Mekong at the site of present-day Siang Hung (pronounced Chiang Hung and Chiang Rung in other Tai dialects). When the Chinese description was compiled, the seat of government was at Leng, some distance to the west of the Mekong.

THE KINGDOM OF LAOS:
AN EDITED REPRINT OF THE 1759 *UNIVERSAL HISTORY*

The text reproduced here was first published in an encyclopaedic work titled *The Modern Part of an Universal History,
From the Earliest Account of Time. Compiled from Original
Writers. By the Authors of the Antient Part.* The text appeared
as chapter 7 (The Kingdom of Lawhos, or Laos) of book 11
(Description of the Countries Contained in the Farther Peninsula of India), in volume 7 (Modern History: Being a Continuation of the Universal History). This series of volumes
was published in London in 1759 for S. Richardson, T.
Osborne, C. Hitch, A. Millar, John Rivington, S. Crowder,
P. Davey, B. Law, T. Longman, and C. Ware.

THE BOUNDS, NAME, MOUNTAINS, RIVERS, PROVINCES, AND CITIES. ERRORS OF GEOGRAPHERS

Bounds and extent.[1] The country of Lawhos, Lao, or of the Laos, of
which Jangoma [Chiang Mai] was originally, or by conquest, a part;
taken in its largest sense, is bounded on the west by the dominions
of Ava and Siam; on the north, with the province of Yun-nan, or
Jun-nan, in China;[2] on the east, with Tong-king [Tonkin]; and on
the south, with Kamboja [Cambodia]. It is situated between the
15th or 16th and the 22d degrees[3] of latitude, and between the
119th and 122d degrees of longitude; so that the territories of the
Laos, taken all together, may extend in length from south to north

about 420 geographic miles, and in breadth from west to east about 180,[4] although most geographers make it scarce half so much. It is surrounded on all sides by mountains covered with forests,[5] which serve as ramparts to secure it, and break the force of rapid torrents which descend from thence into the plains.[6]

Name. The name generally given by travellers to this region is Lao, or the country of the Laos; by some, as Pinto, written Lauhos, or Lawhos.[7] Da Cruz says[8] the Laos are by some (but whom he nameth not) called Siones Maons;[9] and Marini says, that this country is more properly called the Kingdom of the Lanjens, than of Lao.[10] But we apprehend that this is giving to the whole, what belongs only to a part, which has for its capital Lanjan, or Lanjang [Lan Sang (Vientiane)]; as the northern part, or perhaps the whole, has for its metropolis Leng [Sipsòng Panna].[11] With regard to the name of Siones Maons it seems to be given to the Laos on account of the great Siams, called Tay-yay[12] [Great Tai, i.e., Shan] who possessed the country to the west of Lao, and of whom the Laos probably are the remains.

Mountains and rivers. The country of Lao, or of the Laos, seems to be for the general flat and to have scarce any hills or mountains but those which encompass it on all sides, and serve as barriers against the potent kingdoms with which it is inclosed. From these mountains descend infinite rivulets, which drain into one large river, that crosses the whole region from north to south.[13] The source of this river has been but little known to former geographers; but the Jesuits, of late, have fixed it with great precision. According to their map of China, it rises in the north-west borders of the province of Yun-nan.[14] Near its source it is called Lan-tsan Kyang [Chinese *pinyin* Lancang Jiang]; and where it enters the kingdom of Lao, within ten miles of the east border,[15] it bears the name of Ku-long Kyang.[16] The Laos call it Menan Kong [Mekong]; in its passage forthwards it washes the cities of Lê [La],[17] Kyang-kong [Chiang Khaeng], Kyang-seng [Chiang Saen], and Lan-chang[18] (or Lan-jang) [Lan Sang]; afterwards it enters the kingdom of Kamboja [Cambodia], which it crosses, and falls into the sea at Bonsak [the Bassac channel of the Mekong delta].[19]

The Me-nan Kong; strange effect. From Kyang-kong, downwards to its mouth, it carries large barks [barges and other river boats]; but from Lê, upwards, it bears none; so that one is obliged to travel from thence to Yun-nan by land.[20] Although such a number of streams fall into this river, yet we are told, that it never overflows, by reason of a caufey [dam or levee], fifteen or sixteen feet high, which runs along its banks, and prevents inundations, even in those years when the rains have fallen in the greatest abundance. As soon as this river enters Kamboja, its waters seem to change their qualities; so that the fish, which pass the frontiers, die immediately: in like manner, such as ascend the stream from Kamboja into Lao, feel the same effect; which surprising circumstance has given occasion to the proverb, 'Each in his own kingdom'. The rivers usually swell with the heavy rains, which begin to fall in May; and sometimes with the quantity of snow, when it melts on the mountains of Tibet, which are seen from Lao. This great increase of water continues commonly from September to January, yet without interrupting commerce, or the transportation of merchandizes. It is true, that they who are obliged to ascend the stream are extremely incommoded, not only on account of haling [towing or rowing] the bark along, but also from the rays of the sun, which cast a heat like that of a furnace.

Navigation dangerous. For all this, it is much safer to sail against the stream than with it, for the current is so rapid, that the bark seems to fly as swift as an arrow out of a bow; and, by the violence of motion, is often overset, or sunk downright, and all the goods lost. For this reason, when they arrive at the place which separates the two kingdoms [the Khon falls, between Laos and Cambodia], it is necessary to unload the bark, destroy one part of it, and make use of wagons to convey the commodities for the space of three miles over land; while the barge-men employ ten days in haling up the residue of the vessel through the falls by force of arms. A missioner[21] proposed to remedy this inconvenience by means of sluices; but the king would not consent to destroy what he deemed a strong barrier.

Errors about it. Travellers have fallen into errors, with regard to the course of this river, misled, doubtless, by the reports of the people in these parts. Marini says, that a few leagues beyond Lao it begins to carry boats, and divides into two great branches:[22] one, running west, passes through Pegu into the gulf of Bengal; the other, forcing through rocks, spreads in several channels through the kingdom of Lao, and divides it from north to south.[23] On the other hand, Kaempfer tells us, that a branch of the Ganges runs through this country, and falling into the river of Kamboja [the Mekong] renders it navigable.[24] But the map of the Jesuits, above-mentioned, discovers these informations to be false, no less than that of Mendez Pinto, who derives all the great rivers of this peninsula from a fictitious lake.

Provinces and cities. We meet with very little in authors touching either the cities or provinces of this kingdom. Marini indeed tells us, that it contains seven provinces;[25] but mentions not the name of one. As to cities, besides Jamahay, or Chiamay [Chiang Mai], the capital of Jangoma [Lan Na], we find the names of several others; with an account of some of them, and their distances one from another, in a journal of some Chinese merchants, of the road they took from Siam to China in the year 1652. Whether all the names of places are those used in the country, or by the Chinese only, we cannot resolve; but, as that journal contains nearly all which we have relating to the geography of this region, we shall give our readers some extracts from it.

Journey through Lao by some Chineses. These merchants set out on horseback from Kyang-hay[26] [Chiang Mai?], or Kyau, on the borders of Siam, and in seven days got to Kyang-seng [Chiang Saen]; in seven others they came to Kemerat [Chiang Tung]; and in eight more to Leng, capital of Laos [sic, actually Sipsòng Panna]. The way hitherto was full of woods, rivers, and settlements, for the most part impassable for wagons;[27] but free from either wild beasts or robbers. From Leng they were seven days going to Lê [La], and eleven more on the road to Meng [a Chinese town in Yunnan Province]; in all forty stages: here they turned northward to get into Yun-nan,[28] from whence, in a short time, they arrived in China.[29] Here then we have an account of a road almost through the whole extent of Lao,[30] from south to north. It is true, that this itinerary is defective, inasmuch as the situation neither of Kyang-hay nor Meng (the two terms of the journey) is fixed, by their distance being marked from some known places. For all that it is of considerable use, as the positions of the intermediate places are in good measure ascertained; the rather as we find two of them, Lê and Kyang-seng, are seated on the Menan Kong. To these may be added Kyang-kong [Chiang Khaeng], lying between those two cities and Lan-chang (or Lan-jang) [Lan Sang and its capital, Vientiane], standing lower down than Kyang-seng, upon the same river. More than this, we have the latitude of Lan-jang (if it may be depended on) to regulate the position of the whole. So that, by means of these materials, joined to the description which is given of the above-mentioned places, we may be said to know more of the inland parts of Lao,[31] than of any other country in the farther peninsula of India, Siam and Pegu excepted.

Lao wrongly exhibited in the map. But, before we proceed farther, it will be necessary to say something farther with respect to the situation and dimensions of Lao, which the geographers seem to have been much mistaken in. Mr. De L'Isle [1750], it is true, has given this country its due extent from south to north; but has reduced its bounds from east to west to a narrow gut of land. He has likewise placed Lanchang in twenty degrees of latitude;[32] in consequence of which situation Kyang-seng, Leng and other cities are placed too much northward; and the distance between Kyang-hay and Meng, which is forty days journey, is reduced to less than half that measure. This was owing to his relying too much on Loubiere's [La Loubère (1691)] map of Siam, which places the northern borders of that country in twenty-three degrees of latitude; and consequently near one degree imperfect and a half more northward than the southern bounds of China. Mr. Bellin, in his late map,[33] has given Siam the same extent; but, that the frontiers of the two kingdoms might not appear to break-in upon each other, he has taken care to make those of China give way, by removing them two or three degrees more eastward than they ought.

This procedure in Mr. Bellin is the more surprising, as he could not but know that the bounds of China had been determined both by measures and astronomical observations;[34] whereas it does not appear that those of Siam towards the north were at all regulated mathematically, or that the map, published by Loubere, was drawn with any accuracy; on the contrary, that author declares himself, that he does not think it correct. Methinks therefore Mr. Bellin ought to have taken the contrary course; and, instead of altering the bounds of China as laid down in the Jesuits map, have placed those of Siam three or four degrees more to the south. By this way only room can be made for inserting the places mentioned in the Chinese journal: and, in this case, Lan-chang must be removed lower. Which shews that the latitude of eighteen degrees, given to it by Marini, must be much nearer the truth than that assigned either by him or Mr. De L'Isle.

Accounts of travellers very defective. The country of Lao, considered at large, is commonly represented as subject to a single monarch; and Marini expressly affirms as much, informing us farther, that Lao contains seven provinces; that the royal seat was at Lanjan [Vientiane]; and that the proper name of Lao is Lanjans.[35] On the other hand, we find by the journal of the Chinese merchants, who travelled through the country much about the same time when the missionary was there,[36] that there were two kingdoms within the region of Lahos, or Laos, namely, Kemerat [Chiang Tung] and Leng [Sipsòng Panna]: which latter, they tell us, is more properly called Lahos; and that its chief city is the capital of Lahos: and a third author names a fourth kingdom, named Thiem, with a certain wild people called Ke-moy,[37] who have neither king nor religion; both bordering on Kâchinchina to the north-west.[38] To reconcile these different accounts, we must suppose the following things, viz. that Marini ascribes to the whole what only belongs to a part of the country: that the whole is divided into several distinct kingdoms or parts: that it is inhabited by several nations; different, at least, in name and interest: that the Lanjans are, in this sense, a distinct people from the Lahos; although originally they might have been all the same people, going under the name of Lahos, or Laos, till they came to be divided under different princes.

Marini is not the only traveller who has applied to the whole what only belongs to a part. Kaempfer, speaking of the Laos, informs us, that their two chief cities are Lanjang [Vientiane] and Chiamay [Chiang Mai].[39] But if Lao was here to be understood in its full extent, we should imagine Leng [Sipsòng Panna] would have been joined with Lanjang; and not Chiamay, which is a city of Jangomay, a province or part belonging to the jurisdiction of Lanjang. It is evident from hence, that Kaempfer knew nothing of the provinces of Lao, to the north of Lanjan; and although Marini extends the country of Lao as far as China, yet he supposes the whole to be under the jurisdiction of the king of Lanjan; and to be inhabited by Lanjans. At the same time both these authors acknowlege Lanjan to be inhabited by the Laos; only the latter says, that the name of Lanjans more properly belongs to them.[40]

Division of Lao. The defects of European travellers is in good measure supplied by the Chinese memoir: but although Lanchang, or Lanjang, is therein occasionally spoken of, it is not said to be the capital of a kingdom; nor is any mention made of the kingdom of Lanjang, because the author of it does not enter into the description of any place which he was not at;[41] and therefore, there may have been other kingdoms or states in Lahos, besides those two specified in the journal: for this reason we shall not pretend to divide this country into its particular kingdoms or provinces, but content ourselves with dividing it into two great parts only; one called the northern, or proper Lao; the other, the southern Lao or kingdom of Lanjang.

THE SOUTHERN LAO, OR KINGDOM OF LANJANG

The name. The kingdom of Lanjan, Lanjang, or Lanchang, as others pronounce it, would seem to most persons to derive its name from that of its capital city: but, we are told, it takes that denomination from the great numbers of elephants with which the country abounds; the word Lanjens, or Lanjans, signifying properly, thousands of elephants.[42]

Its dimensions. We cannot precisely determine the extent of this southern Lao, or Lau, from south to north, authors not having so much as mentioned any city subordinate to that of its capital; or indeed in the whole country, excepting Chiamay may be considered as one. However, upon a supposition that Kyang-seng [Chiang Saen], which is situated on the Menan Kong [Mekong], to the north of Lanjang, belongs to the northern province, and is not far from the frontiers of the southern; this latter will extend to near the nineteenth degree of latitude, and consequently, containing almost four degrees in extent from north to south, will have the larger half of Lao to its share; as its breadth from west to east will be equal to that of the other: but, in case we comprise Jangoma [Chiang Mai] within its limits, the breadth will be augmented perhaps a hundred miles, or more. Upon this footing, the province or kingdom of Lanjang will be near twice as large as the northern Lao.

Climate very healthy. The climate of this country is somewhat more temperate than that of Tongking, but exceedingly more healthful: so that one meets with old men, of a hundred and a hundred-and-twenty years of age, who are as robust and vigorous as if they were but fifty.

Soil and produce. Excellent rice. Plenty of salt. The soil is generally very good, being rendered fruitful by a great number of canals cut from the great river (Menan Kong [Mekong]); which serve both to water the lands on each side, and drain-off the streams, made either by the torrents descending from the hills, or the great rains which fall at stated times, so that they never make any marshes or stagnant pools in the country. It is remarkable, that the lands on the eastern side of the river are vastly better and more fertile than those on the western side: the very animals, such as elephants and unicorns,[43] are larger. The rice too is incomparable, and of a particular scent as well as flavour. The forest, and other trees are high, straight, and, for the general, incorruptible; qualities wanting in those on the western side, where they are ill-shaped, and the rice so hard that it is scarce fit for boiling. As soon as the rains begin to cease, certain southerly winds blow, and the lands, which had been sown with rice immediately after the harvest, produce a kind of scum, which, covering this champain [open countryside] like snow for several miles, is hardened with the sun, and becomes solid salt.[44] There is so great a quantity of it produced in this manner, that not only the whole kingdom is supplied with it, at a very trifling expence, but enough is left to serve strangers, who come every year and carry away as much as they think fit. Then the new rains, which succeed this second gathering, cleanse and meliorate the soil in such a manner as gives the rice that delicious taste above-mentioned, which the rice of other countries hath not.

The principal drugs found in this kingdom are benjamin and lakka.[45]

Benjamin. The benjamin [gum benjamin] is reckoned the best in the east, and is found in great abundance. The tree, from which it distils, grows mostly in the mountains. The leaves are like those of the chestnut tree, and the flower very beautiful, being white and odoriferous like those of orange trees. The fruit likewise is sweet-scented, of the shape and bigness of an acorn, but very ill-tasted, and degenerates when planted in foreign soils; yet, as the gum produces a great revenue to the king, the Lanjans are forbidden to sell the fruit to strangers.

Gum lakka. The lakka, or lakre [insect lac], which is used in making Spanish wax, is nothing but a certain kind of earth, found in forests round about the ant-hills, and with which those insects cover the surface of their little territories for the use of their magazines [storage places].

Ivory. There is not better ivory, nor greater plenty of it, in any country than this; and no wonder, since it has its name from the number of elephants found in it, as hath been already mentioned. But the unicorn's (or rather rhinoceros's) horn, is the thing most prized by the Lanjans; from a belief, that whoever is possessed of one may command fortune. And as some have more virtue than others, when a person is advanced to a new post, he sells the horn which he had before, and buys another, of a better kind, at the expence of several hundred crowns. His next care is to hide it so effectually that he shall be in no danger of having it stolen, and so deprived of all the good-luck which they think inseparable from it.[46]

Mines. As the forests are of great extent, and the plains enamelled [dotted] with a variety of flowers, they make abundance of honey, wax, and cotton. One meets also with several mines of iron, lead, and tin, in which they are at work. Gold and silver also are found here; but the inhabitants gather those metals out of certain places of the river, by means of iron nets. The utensils which are made with what they thus fish up, bring great advantages to the kingdom, but not so much as the king could wish. From the neighbouring countries they have red amber and musk, with which they drive a great trade. The amber comes from the kingdom of Ava, and is found in the forests at the roots of certain very old trees, which grow among the rocks and inaccessible places. The musk is brought from the kingdom of Gnay,[47] and taken from a bag joining to the navel of an animal, which the Chineses call *ye hyang*, or the musk stag.[48] The Lanjans make likewise a counterfeit musk, with ambergris, and the juice drawn from the body of a cat, which they call *algalia* [the civet cat]. This mixture yields a more agreeable and mild smell than the pure musk; and this kind of musk is what first appeared in Europe.[49]

Animals, fruits, fish. The Lanjans make great advantage of several other animals, particularly buffaloes and oxen; whose number is almost infinite, and which are employed in the service of the plains. Their garden fruit is likewise very profitable to them, as well as their excellent rice. Their rivers abound with fish of several kinds; some so large and heavy, that two men can hardly carry one of them.[50] The smaller sorts are caught in such plenty, that a hundred-weight of them may be had for the value of five-pence. They pickle them, as we do herrings, and the poor eat them with their rice; which is their ordinary food.[51] According to Kaempfer, Lao produces precious stones, especially rubies; also pearls, called by the Siamites, *muk*; which that author esteems the more strange, as the country does not lie near any salt sea:[52] but probably his surprise would have ceased, had he known of the above-mentioned saline quality of the land, which must needs be communicated to the flooding waters.

Provinces. The kingdom of Lanjans contains seven provinces, and several considerable cities; for what Marini ascribes to Lao in general,[53] we apply, for the reason already taken notice of, to Lanjan in particular. But this correction, if it be one, is of no great advantage to us, since that author neither describes, nor so much as mentions the name of any one of them all, excepting the capital Lanjan. On this occasion, we cannot forbear censuring the negligence of travellers, especially the missionaries, who have frequented this, and the neighbouring countries;[54] yet in their relations treat of them so superficially, that the reader is no way benefited by what they publish. Thus geography receives little or no improvement from the persons from whom only it can expect any; and is more obliged to the small journal of some Chinese merchants, so often mentioned, than the united informations of all the European missioners, who have spent several years in travelling over the country. It is this silence of Marini, the almost sole author who treats expressly of Lao,[55] which supports our division of that region into upper and lower, as well as our opinion, that his relation is to be confined to the latter only, although he would make it extend to the whole. For we impute his silence to his want of knowing the country; and, on his want of knowlege, we ground our diffence from him. However, if Marini has mentioned but one city, amongst a great number (for one author says, there are no fewer than thirty-eight cities[56] in the kingdom of Lanjang); other travellers have not done more; and what gives him the preference to all the rest, he is the only one we meet with who describes it.

City of Lanjan. King's palace. Lanjan, written also Lanjang, and Lan-chang, according to the Chinese pronunciation, is by Marini, Choisy and Kaempfer, reckoned the capital of the kingdom of Lao; which words we restrain however to the territories of the Lanjans, for the reasons already mentioned. It is the city where the king usually resides, in the latitude of eighteen degrees [Vientiane].[57] It is defended on one side by good ditches, and walls exceeding high; on the other by the great river.[58] The king's palace is of so vast extent that it may well pass for a city, both with respect to its magnitude, and the number of people who inhabit it. It appears to the view at a very great distance; and is admirable, as well for its structure, as the symmetry of the buildings which compose it. The royal apartment is adorned with a magnificent portal, and a great number of beautiful chambers, accompanied with a grand salon or hall: the whole, built with incorruptible wood, is adorned both on the inside and outside with excellent bas-reliefs, all so delicately gilded, that they seem to be covered rather with plates, than leaves, of gold.

From the king's apartment you enter into very spacious courts, where you behold a long series of houses, all of bricks, and covered with tiles, in which usually dwell his wives of the second class; and beyond them another range of buildings, equally neat and uniform, for the officers belonging to the court. It would require a volume, says Marini, to give an exact account of the riches, gardens, and other quarters, of this sumptuous mansion.

The houses. The houses of the grandees, and persons of condition, are very high and fair, well contrived and ornamented: but those of the inferior people are no better than huts. The priests alone have the privilege of building their houses and convents with brick or stone. People of fashion, instead of carpets and other furniture, make use of certain mats made of reeds, so very finely wrought, and adorned with figures of various kinds, that, in our author's opinion, nothing looks more beautiful or agreeable to the sight. With them they commonly hang the wall of their houses and their chambers, both within and without. Their apartments are exceeding neat; and they take more than ordinary care to keep them so.[59]

THE NORTHERN LAO, OR LAHO

Extent. We consider the territories within these limits as the proper country of the people call Lao, Lau, or Laho,[60] distinct from that of the Lanjans, which bounds it on the south.[61] Its extent, from south to north, is about three degrees, or 210 English miles; and its breadth the same with the whole country in general, already mentioned. The country, soil, and produce, are much of the same nature with those of Lanjang. However, every province seems to have something peculiar to it in those respects. The number of provinces, however, is not mentioned by authors, unless we suppose Marini's seven to be comprehended in both the northern and southern Lao. All the account we have, relating to them, is contained in the Chinese memoir or journal, so often before cited; and that only mentions two or three large provinces at most, each of which has under it several lesser provinces or districts, whereof we find the names with some light concerning their situations: the whole subject to Ava.

Kyang-seng province. The most southern of the provinces or districts mentioned in the Chinese journal, is Kyang-seng [Chiang Saen], seven days journey from Kyang-hay [Chiang Mai?], or Kyay, on the frontiers of Siam.[62] This is all we meet with relating to this province, excepting that, as to its situation, it lies north of the province or district of Kyang-hay, and south of that of Kemerat. The chief city of that name also stands on the river Menân Kong [Mekong], which from thence flows southward, into the kingdom of Lan-chang or Lanjan. The denomination of *Mohang* [*müang*] is prefixed to all the local names inserted in the journal, and signifies, as it is applied, either province, district, colony, or city:[63] but we have omitted it, to avoid a needless repetition.[64]

Kemerat province. The province of Kemerat [Chiang Tung] next occurs. It is bounded on the east by that of Lê, on the north by Lang,[65] on the south by Kyang-seng and Kyang-hay. After this account of its bounds there is subjoined another; for, we are told, Vay, Rong, Ngong, Lahi, Maa, and Laa, lie to the east; Hang, Kroa, Loey, Jang, and Pen, to the north. Possibly the first bounds respect the province of Kemerat in general, and the latter relates to the district of Kemerat in particular; for it is added, that these eleven cities or colonies are in the jurisdiction of Kemerat. We are farther informed, that it is one day's journey from the city Hang to Kroa; and the same from Loey to Jang. This province of Kemerat is said to be 400 *senes*[66] in compass, and eight days journey in length: its capital city, of the same name, seven days journey from Kyang-seng, is situated on the river Menân-tay, or Menân-lay, which falls into the Menân-kong towards the town of Bankiop; lying, as we judge, to the southeast from Kemerat, and between the cities of Kyang-kong [Chiang Khaeng] and Kyang-seng [Chiang Saen]. When the Chineses passed through it, a king resided there, named Prachyau Otang,[67] who was tributary to Hawa or Ava, and sent ambassadors thither every year with his acknowlegements, consisting of two small shrubs, one having its leaves and flowers of gold, and the other of silver.

The inhabitants use fire-arms. Trade with China. In this country they have the use of fire-arms, great and small cannon, muskets, *zagays* (or darts), and cross-bows.[68] While the Tartars [Manchus] were subduing China, in the last century, a great number of Chinese fugitives out of Yun-nan[69] fell upon, and reduced, the neighbouring territories, among which was Kemerat, whose inhabitants abandoned the city. Before the Chineses drove those people out, they went every year to trade with them, carrying velvets, and other silks, camblets, carpets, hair [ceremonial yak hair?], blue and black callico, musk, quicksilver [mercury], kori shells [cowries], and bonnets (or hats); kettles, and other utensils of copper; precious stones of a green coulour, emeralds, gold, silver, and china-ware. In exchange for these commodities they returned with cotton-thread, ivory, an earth or medicinal paste called *zhadam*; a sort of medicinal wood named *ingo* by the Portugueses, and *maha ing* [asa foetida, a prophylactic] by the Siameses; likewise opium; *kotso*, a kind of medicinal root so called; and white linen cloth. All these commodities were brought from Ava; and the Chineses repaired to Kemerat in the three first months, in order to carry them home in April.[70]

Leng kingdom. The kingdom of Leng [Sipsòng Panna], or more properly Lahos,[71] has on the south Kemerat; on the east Luan and Rong-faa; on the north Put, Pling, Ken, Kaam, Paa, Saa, Boönoy, Ningneha, Kaan, and Ghin-tay, cities all depending on it;[72] on the west it is bounded by Ko-sang-pyi, the country formerly possessed by the Tay-yay, or great Siams [Great Tai, i.e., Shan]; and farther west is the great forest of Pahima-pan [the fabled Himalayan 'Himaphan Forest' of Buddhist history]. They reckon eight cities or places in this kingdom, each containing a garrison of 1,000 men.

Soil and produce. Mines of gold, silver, rubies. The country of Leng produces rice in abundance; buffaloes, stags, and other animals, are common, and their flesh cheap; but fish is scarce. Five days journey north from Mohang Leng, there are mines of gold, silver, and copper; also a kind of red sulphur, which has a very stinging smell. Two hundred *senes* or cords from the city, on the same side, is a pit or mine of precious stones, full 100 *senes* deep, out of which they get rubies, some of them as big as a walnut; also emeralds, or green stones, of which the king of Lahos has one as large as an orange. There are stones likewise of other colours: and a brook, which runs through the mine, carries several down its stream, which sometimes weigh two or three *mas*, that is, a quarter or third part of an ounce. The king draws from the silver mine above 360 *katis* [about 216 kg] annually. They are Chineses who work in, and direct, it. The merchants of Kemerat, Lê, May, Teng Maa, Meng, Daa, and Pan, repair to this mine, which is inclosed by mountains, 300 *senes* in height, covered with grass, preserved continually fresh and green by the dew.

There is found here a medicinal root, called *tong-quey* by the Chineses, and by the Siameses *kot-wha-bwa*. Also a tree named *vendez-hang*, which bears flowers about the thickness of one's finger, of a very agreeable smell, and of various colours, as red, yellow, white, and black. The fruit, when come to perfection, has the shape of a duck; and the dew falls in greatest quantity in the parts where the trees most abound.

Trade and commodities. The inhabitants of Leng traffick with their neighbours, who come to fetch their commodities, consisting in precious stones, gold, silver, tin, lead, sulphur, both red and common; cotton spun and unspun, tea, lack [insect lac], japan [liquid black lacquer], or brazil wood [aloes wood], and the medicinal root above-mentioned. The merchants of Mohang[73] bring them elephants; the Chineses raw and manufactured silk, with white hair, as fine as silk, and civet. Of this hair, taken from a certain animal [the yak],[74] the great tufts are made which adorn the elephant's ears, on which the king of Siam rides, and hang down to the ground; also the tufts worn by the Chineses on their bonnets. The western merchants from Tay-yay and Pama-hang (or Ava), bring iron, yellow and red sanders [sandal wood], linen, chints [chintzes], or painted callicoes, venison, a kind of red medicinal paste, opium, and other commodities of Hindûstân [India]; which they exchange for gold, silver, precious stones, etc. Lastly, those of Kemerat and Kyang-hay [Chiang Mai?] bring cows and buffaloes, to barter for silver, tin, and sulphur.[75]

City of Leng. Tributary to Ava. The city of Leng, capital of the Lahos, is eight days journey from Kemerat, and situated on both sides of the river Menân Tay, or Menân Lay, which runs thence to Kemerat. It has neither walls nor fortress; being inclosed only with palisades; and in circuit about 400 *senes* or cords, each twenty Chinese fathoms. Rice is so plenty in this city, that one may have fifty or sixty pounds of it for a few halfpence. Fish indeed, is scarce; but, to make amends, the markets abound with the flesh of buffaloes, stags, and other animals. The months of May, June, and July, are the season for fruit, of which all sort may be had there, found in the kingdom of Siam, excepting the Thûrian, or Dúrian, and the Mangústan [mangosteen]. The king of Leng, or Laos, is tributary to Hawa [Ava], or Pama-hang; and an ambassador is sent annually from this capital to pay the tribute. This does not hinder the Lahos[76] from appointing a successor, when their king dies; but they are obliged to notify it to the king of Hawa, or Ava. The king of Lahos employs but one minister of state; and, for his revenue, besides 360 *katis*, which he receives yearly from the mine, to the north of Leng, he raised 860 more out of the rest of his territories.

Lê province. The Chinese memoir gives no account of Lê, and its province or district, farther than that the city is seven days journey distant from Leng, towards China, and situated on the Menân Kong

[Mekong].[77] According to our estimation it seems to lie north-eastward from Leng.

Meng province. The next place mentioned in the journal is Meng, eleven days journey from Lê. This, we are told, is the capital of a particular province,[78] which has on the west Pan and Kaa, on the south Tse, and on the east Chiong and Kû, both dependent on Vinan, or Yun-nan. It is seventeen days journey in length, from north to south, and about seven from east to west. The whole country is without the tropic; for the inhabitants never see the sun directly over their heads. A river crosses this province, which rises from a mountain in the north, and falls into the Menân Kong. They reckon in it eighteen cities, which depend on the capital.

Soil and produce. Musk animal. The soil of Meng produces all sorts of fruits which are found in Siam, excepting the Dûrian and Mangústan. There are mines of *kalin*, or tin, on the west side; of silver, copper, and iron, towards the north; and on the south side there is one of salt. The musk animal is found in this province, but chiefly about Pang, Chay-daw, and Kong, all three depending on Vinan. Many also are caught in the district of Tay-yay. It is as big as a young goat, with a purse under its belly, three or four inches thick; which, when cut, seems to be a piece of fat, or bacon. They dry it till it may be reduced to powder; and then sell it in the country for its weight in silver. The natives being prohibited from selling the true bags to strangers, they make counterfeit ones, which they fill with its blood, rotten wood, and other ingredients. The peasants bring great quantities of them to Meng, which they exchange for things of small value: but the buyers sell them again to foreigners at a pretty dear rate.

This is all which is contained in the Chinese memoir or journal relating to Lahos or Laos, except a few particulars touching Moang Chay, or Vinan, a district belonging to a province of China, and probably to Yun-nan; if it be not, according to the missioners, Yun-nan itself.[79]

INHABITANTS OF LAHOS, PARTICULARLY THE LANJANS, THEIR MANNERS AND CUSTOMS

Their persons. The Lanjans are well-shaped and robust, rather fat than lean, and of an olive-colour. They are good-natured, affable, courteous, and obliging.[80] The Laos resemble the Chineses in shape and mien, but are more tawny and slender, consequently of a much handsomer appearance[81] than the Siameses. They have long ear-laps, like the Peguers, and inhabitants of the sea-coast.[82] They are of a very sprightly genius, and sound understanding. They are fond of strangers, and value themselves on being sincere. They are free from deceit, and of great integrity; never breaking their promise or their trust. This character they are zealous to acquire; and the rather, as they are subject to covet what belongs to another. When they see any thing which pleases their fancy, they never cease importuning the owner till they get the whole, or some part of it. However, in case of refusal, they never offer to take it by force.

Their virtues. The Lanjans are extremely honest; so that there are no thieves to be met with throughout the whole kingdom. In case there is any report of a robbery or murder being commtted on the highway, all the enquiry imaginable is made after the criminal: because, if he be not found, the neighbouring towns or villages are obliged to indemnify the parties injured; and thus both the lives and goods of people are secured throughout the kingdom of Lao. But the cities are not altogether so free from these inconveniencies, which our author wisely ascribes to the power of sorcerers; who, by their art, can throw the people of any house into a dead sleep, and keep them in that condition till they have robbed it.[83]

Very numerous. As the kingdom of Lanjan enjoys a very wholesome air, and abounds with the necessaries of life, it is very populous, and the inhabitants live to a very great age. In a numberment which was made of them about the middle of the last century, there were reckoned above 500,000 able to bear arms, without taking in the old men; who are so numerous and robust, that even out of those aged 100 years, a very considerable army might be formed, for the defence of the king. For all this the Lanjans are not of a warlike disposition, nor expert in the use of arms: which may be owing to the advantageous situation of the country, inclosed with mountains and steep precipices; serving as so many natural fortifications, sufficient to defend them against the insults of the enemies: and should any such break through those ramparts, they have a way to get rid of them, by poisoning their rivers. It was thus that the king of Tong-king was obliged to retreat, after having lost a great number of his army, with which, about the year 1650, he proposed to annex this monarchy to his own. Before this, several petty kings joining their forces with the same design, against the inhabitants of Lao, lost so many of their men and beasts, by drinking the water of a river along which they encamped: that they were at last compelled to retreat, without daring to cross the stream and fight their enemies, who insulted them on the other side of it.[84]

Their vices. Men hunters. In effect, the Lanjans are very slothful, and averse to business. They apply themselves to nothing but agriculture and fishing. They quite neglect all arts and sciences: so that they lead an indolent life, without troubling themselves about matters which require any great attention of the mind. They are much addicted to women,[85] which is the bane of many. But their belief in witchcraft and magic is still more pernicious, especially as it prevails among people of rank. Some great men have a notion, that if the head of their elephant be rubbed with wine, in which a drop or two of human gall be put, the beast will become more robust, and themselves more courageous: so that ever after they may assure themselves of victory, either in war or on any other occasion. In this ridiculous conceit the governors sometimes, though but rarely, employ desperate fellows, who, for twenty-five or thirty crowns, will go into the forests to hunt men; and the first they meet with, of either sex, whether young or old, priest or layman, open his belly and stomach while alive; and, taking out the gall-bladder, cut off his head, to convince the more savage purchaser that he has not deceived him. In case the assassin does not perform his engagement in the limited time, he is obliged to kill either himself, his wife, or a child, that his employer may take out the gall of the unhappy victim.

The Lanjans would be an almost faultless people, and free from reproach, could this most horrid and cruel practice be once rooted out of the country: but although the king had used all means imaginable to effect it, he had not been able to succeed when our author wrote, because the most considerable people of his kingdom, and even the magistrates themselves, were addicted to that stupid, as well as execrable, superstition.

Their diet. The diet of the Lanjans consists in rice, fish, divers kinds of legumes, and the flesh of buffaloes. This is their usual meat; for they seldom eat any other sort, not even veal or poultry. They kill animals designed for food by knocking them on the head with sticks or clubs, and not by cutting their throats: for they hold it very barbarous and criminal to shed the blood of living creatures, and take away their lives in that manner. They make four meals a day; and roast their fowls, which they have in plenty, with all their feathers on; notwithstanding the insufferable stink arising from that kind of cookery.[86] They have, indeed, excellent stomachs; but much cannot be said in praise of their cleanliness: for the vessels they keep their water in, and even those they drink out of, are commonly hung up in their smoaky chimnies.[87]

Their dress. The Laos wear gowns close to their bodies. They go with their feet bare, and the head commonly uncovered. Their hair is clipped round, and short, like a lay-brother's; excepting one lock on the temples, which is left to grow, and run through holes made in the ears for that purpose.[88] One author says, their bodies are adorned with blue figures, made with hot irons, down to the knees:[89] another, that they paint their legs from the ancle [ankle] to the knee with flowers, and branches of trees, like the Siameses, as a badge of their religion and manhood.[90] The women wear pieces of gold in the holes of their ears, until they are married; after which they lay them aside: but the men wear none at all.[91]

Monogamy. Their marriages. The Lanjans approve of having only one wife; and say, that a man ought not to marry any more: but this they do rather from a principle of covetousness, to avoid charges, than of virtue. Accordingly they, in their songs, rally the magistrates, and officers of state, who are content with only one wife. Nor is this so great a piece of self-denial, since they make their she-slaves subservient to their pleasures, maintaining great numbers of them, according to their quality, as well for sake of indulging their passions as for grandeur. The king [Suriyawongsa] who reigned in 1658 had two hundred women; but there is only one of the number who is named the principal, as being the first with whom the man is contracted; and the rest are considered only as second wives. Their marriages are for life, and performed in this manner. They choose out the oldest married couple they can find, who have lived in perfect agreement together, and promise, before them, to do the same till death. But often these fair promises are not long binding; and the parties have recourse to very frivolous reasons to separate, and marry with others. This conduct is, in good measure, owing to the loose education given their children, whom they abandon to their own inclinations; permitting even the boys and girls to live together, and frequently visit one another, without considering the consequences which may arise from such familiarities. The most dangerous opportunities are the rendezvous's, which continue for a month in the house of a new lain-in woman, where all the family and relations meet, to divert themselves with dancing, and other kinds of merriment; in order to drive away the sorcerers, and prevent them from making the mother lose her milk, and the child from being bewitched by them, as they often are, says the sagacious Jesuit, to such a degree, that they die.[92] These revels are the more dangerous, as fornication is tolerated among the laity. But a woman convicted of adultery becomes a slave to her husband, who treats her in what manner he thinks fit; and may even oblige her to pay a sum of money.[93]

Their burials. When any of their relations die, they make a feast also, which holds for a month; and celebrate their funeral with great magnificence. The corpse is put in a coffin, daubed over with a kind of bitumen, to hinder any offensive smell from getting out. None are invited to wake the dead, but the *Talapoy* [Buddhist monks], or priests, who attend less to weep over the corpse, than for the sake of good cheer. However, they employ a great part of the time in repeating certain hymns, adapted to the occasion; by means of which the soul, as they say, is taught the way to heaven, to the end it might not stray in those unknown regions. When the month is expired, they raise a curious pyramid [cremation pyre], according to the quality of the defunct, set-off with an infinite number of ornaments, and elegant bas-reliefs. Then, after they have deposited the corpse therein, they set fire to, and reduce it to ashes. These ashes, being carefully gathered up, are carried into one of their temples, which is filled with very sumptuous monuments; in erecting which, wealthy persons spend several thousands of crowns.

State of the soul. After this ceremony is over, the relations think no more of the defunct, nor ever name him: because, according to the doctrine of the transmigration, which is received in the country, they believe the soul is gone to the place destined for it, and consequently belongs no longer to them. It is certain that they would willingly avoid those great expences, if they were not obliged to conform themselves to an ancient custom, and afraid to offend their *Talepoy*; who, to secure the gain arising from thence, have inserted it in their ceremonial, as an indispensible law, to be observed by all. And the people are the rather inclined to comply with this usage, as they are told that, by neglecting to render the last duties to their predecessors, their survivors may be induced to refuse paying the same honour to them.[94]

Their commerce. We have already taken notice of the trade and commodities, both exported and imported, of the particular Kingdoms or provinces into which the upper and lower Lahos or Laos are divided. It remains only to observe, in general, that the commerce of these countries has passed into different channels, according to the vicissitudes of affairs. We are told by Da Cruz, that musk and gold were carried to Sion (or Siam), before the Bramas (or rather Barmas) [Burmese], conquered Pegu;[95] after which it was removed thither. The trade with Siam, in process of time, was restored: but the king of Siam, having invaded the Laos, and taken a province from them, which yet he kept not long,[96] ruined the good understanding, which had subsisted between the two nations, and caused the trade to be removed to Kamboja; whither the Laos carried their benjamin and lak, which meets with a good vent [sale] there, because better than the kinds which grow in the country.[97]

Language and characters. The language of the Laos, or Lanjans, as well as their characters, are much the same with those of the Siameses; who, they say, have had the art of writing, and their sacred language, from them; but they cannot pronounce the letters *l* and *r*. They write on the leaves of trees [palm leaves], like the Peguers and Malabârs; and in the manner which the Siameses write their religious books. But matters relating to civil affairs are inscribed on a sort of coarse paper, with earthen pins [a kind of chalk pencil].[98]

RELIGION OF THE LANJANS

Primitive Religion, Providence, Origin of Things, &c. Their primitive religion. The religion of the Lanjans, and probably of all the Lahos or Laos, is the same at bottom with that which prevails in all the countries comprised in the farther peninsula of the Ganges [i.e., mainland South-East Asia]. They lived a long time in form of a republic, and observed the laws of nature, rather than those of the Chineses their neighbours, which they, in part, followed, before they had kings, and were subject to their empire. The worship of images was, in those times, unknown to them; uncorrupted as they were with the superstitions of other nations. The open sky was their temple; and they adored one being, whom they esteemed above all things, under the name of *commander*. They had some imperfect notions touching the origin of things; but held that this inferior world would be renewed; and that there were sixteen other worlds or kingdoms under heaven, one subordinate to the other.

Corrupted by Shaka. In this simple and uncorrupted state the Lanjans continued, till such time as the disciples of Shaka [the Buddha] began to spread their doctrines over the earth. Some will have it that they received this polluted religion from the Chineses;

but our author rather follows those who think they had it from Siam. However that be, the Jesuit speaks of it as a most impious and idolatrous religion; not considering, at the same time, that it is the very counterpart of his own. Presently after the disciples of Shaka arrived in this kingdom, the Lanjans saw themselves surrounded with temples consecrated to idols, and priests named *Talapoy* [Buddhist monks], destined to their service. These priests, soon getting the ascendant over the minds of the people, prescribed laws to them; and introduced books written in Indian characters, which the Lanjans did not understand; in order to render their doctrines the more mysterious and sacred, for appearing in their original dress, as coming from the hands of Shaka.[99]

Notion of Providence. However, this new religion could not so thoroughly root out the old, but that the Lanjans still preferred the first impressions which they had received, concerning the immortality of the soul; and a particular providence which continually directs affairs in this life; for they hold that the commanders, or intellectual beings, who are above all the sixteen worlds, direct and govern this lower world which we inhabit, as a part dependent on them. Yet these tenets, being mixed with opinions of the different sects, are much corrupted, and far from appearing in their original simplicity.

Their schools. The schools of those who pass for doctors, and heads of their religion, consist in three principal classes, which are filled with laymen, as well as clergy. The doctrines taught in the first class concern the origin of the world, of men, and the gods; mixed with a thousand fabulous and ridiculous circumstances, which extravagances are substituted in place of the ancient law. In the second class they treat of the religion of Shaka, which passes for the new law. In the third they are employed to reconcile the opposite principles, to solve doubtful passages, with the opinions of those who have written about them; and to square the ancient doctrine with the new.

The authors of this third class assume the title of *illuminated*; and their authority is revered by the name of *concord*, although nothing is farther from it than their writings; in which the sense of words is so strained and distorted, to make contradictory doctrines and opinions agree, that this third decretal is full of obscurity, confusion, and unintelligible explanations.[100]

Origin of the world and present earth. According to this new theology, the Lanjans believe that the heavens are from all eternity; and that, perpendicularly under them, lie sixteen terrestrial worlds, containing all the pleasures of life, which, in the highest, are in greatest perfection. They hold likewise that this earth, which we inhabit, is eternal; but that, after a certain revolution of years, fire will descend from heaven, and reduce the whole mass to water. Yet things are not to continue in this state; for they who dwell in the first heaven, and of whose care this earth is the peculiar object, will re-unite the scattered parts together, and establish it in the condition it was before. In effect, they hold that it hath already undergone a great many such revolutions.

With regard to the original of the present world or earth, which had its beginning 18,000 years before the age of Shaka, they say, that, having been reduced to water after the manner above related, a commander, or divinity,[101] descended from the first of the sixteen worlds, armed with a simitar [scimitar]; and perceiving a flower floating on the water, cut it in two. Immediately there springs out a beautiful maiden, with whom being enamoured, he longed to marry her, in order to get a brood of children, to people the earth; but the innocent maid preferring her chastity to the quality of a mother, rejected his courtship. Although he burnt with amorous flames, yet, judging it to be unbecoming a man of his condition, descended from the gods, to use force, he gave over the pursuit, and took another method to obtain children by her, to answer his design. To effect this, he placed himself at a certain distance from her, that they might reciprocally look at each other; insomuch that, by the intense glances from his eyes, she at length conceived, and became a mother, without losing her virginity.[102]

How peopled. By this contrivance they had soon a numerous issue: but as cares and uneasiness are the usual consequences of a great many children, the commander, though a god, found himself violently attacked by them. To free himself, therefore, from these disquietudes, he resolved to make use of his power, and supply his family with all the conveniences of life. In order to do this, he furnished the earth with mountains and vallies, spacious plains, and agreeable hills. He likewise created trees, bearing various kinds of fruits; and rivers, abounding with all sorts of fish. Nor were mines of precious stones and metals forgotten. In short, nothing was omitted, which might contribute to the benefit and delights of life. Yet for all he approved of what he had newly created, and had made this earth a most delicious mansion, of which he was the lord, he could not resolve to continue here: but panting after the etherial abodes which he had quitted, and were vastly preferable to this inferior world, he determined to return to heaven; without having foreseen, that he could not get thither with the same facility which he came from thence. In a word, he was obliged to remain without: where he suffered so severe a penance, that the other commanders, or sovereign divinities of heaven, were at length moved with compassion, and admitted him into their society, to enjoy with them the highest kind of beatitude.

Whence the blacks. The Lanjans have another opinion concerning the peopling of the earth. They say that the inhabitants of heaven, having divided themselves into two parties, on account of the women, began a furious war, and fought several bloody battles. At length one party becoming victorious, to punish their enemies, they banished them into the great desart island, which was the earth; and as it was, at the juncture, reduced to water, they dried it, so that it became firm land again. The worst of it was, there were no women to be found. To supply this want, they got upon the highest mountain in the island, and, from a tree of prodigious height, called out to their wives: who, to testify the affection which they bore to their husbands, came down from heaven to them. But as the number of women exceeded that of the males, each of these latter took several of the former; by which means their offspring, in a short space of time, multiplied to such a degree that, taking up arms, they went about to extirpate certain black men, who were demons, and had by force lain with several of those white women, whose children were as black as their fathers. Nay, those whom afterwards they had by their white husbands, were as sooty as those begotten by the demons. And thus the blackmoors became so numerous in several parts of the earth.[103]

Another opinion. Some account for the origin of black people another way. They say that the commanders (or divinities) of heaven, having shut themselves up in a great stone which was upon this isle, the angels and demons, who heard that there were men within it, were resolved to know if it was fact. Accordingly the demons made a great fire round the stone; that being softened by the heat, the angels might enter it with greater facility. On the first impressions of the fire, some of the commanders rushed out, but as black as charcoal: whilst others, who were not in such a hurry, escaped, without being incommoded by either the fire or the smoke. After this, falling in love with women, whom they had never conversed with before, the black commanders associated with black women, who were the wives of demons; and the whites with white women, whom the angels loved. To compass their design, after levying troops, they made war on the angels and demons, whom they drove out of the island; and obliged the women, who remained behind, to surrender at discretion.

A third tradition. The Lanjans have a third tradition for the origin of the white and black people, not more romantic than either of the two former. They tell us, that formerly a buffalo, one of the most deformed creatures which ever was seen, lame, ill-shaped, extremely fearful, weak, and apt to start, fell from heaven into the sea; where, by the mere strength of imagination, he conceived a monster, and soon after brought forth a gourd full of white and black men.

Government of the World. Reign of Shaka

This is the substance of the Lanjan belief concerning the origin of the world. With regard to the government of it they relate, that, 18,000 years before the renewal thereof, there were four gods; three of whom, after they had governed the space of fifty years, being weary of so great a trouble, retired into a very high and spacious pillar, situated towards the north, where they enjoy all the sweetness of life, which a man who loves his ease can desire. At present, they say, the god Shaka [the Buddha] governs the world, and is to reign 5000 years, of which 3000 are yet to come. That, after he had raised himself to a degree of perfection, greater than any person ever can attain, he resolved to pass to a still higher degree, never heard of before, which was to annihilate himself. But for fear this perfect state of nothingness, to which he was arrived, should be attended with any bad consequences, and the world suffer inconveniences by being deprived of his protection; he, before his annihilation, commanded temples to be erected in several kingdoms, and an infinite number of statues to be made[104] in brass and marble, with a design to honour them with his presence on solemn festivals, where-ever great numbers of people should be assembled; and, by blowing on them before all the congregation, communicate to them his divinity, which might supply his place, by assisting them who should pray to him in their necessities. For all this, says Marini, it is certain that the breath of Shaka has never animated those images; and that they are at present dumb, unless some demon makes them speak:[105] which is, in effect, to confess the fact which he denies.

His successor. After the 5000 years of Shaka's government are expired, the Lanjans expect another god, whom they name Fa-mit Tay [Maitreya, the future Buddha]. This deity, says our author, like an Antichrist against Shaka, will demolish all the temples which he finds standing, throw down and break in pieces the images, burn the books, persecute and prohibit the exercise of all religions, particularly that of Shaka: he will also prescribe new laws, opposite to those of his predecessor: promulgate other sacred books; choose other *Talapoy*; in one word, change and reform every thing a-new.

God of Christians removes to west. In a conference held with the Romish [Catholic] missioners, some *Talapoy* advanced an old kind of theology, possibly invented to mortify the Jesuits. They said that, 5000 years before the birth of Shaka, the world had been governed by the god of the missioners; who finding himself very old, when his successor appeared, and no longer able to discharge so many cares, began to think seriously of the course he had best take for his interest. As he could not dispense with obeying the orders of this new god, from whom he apprehended some violent treatment; and was desirous to avoid the reproaches due to his ill conduct, for having used some with too much lenity, and others with too much severity, he assumed the form of a very poor and despicable person, in order to move Shaka to compassion. In this abject condition he presented a petition, by which he begged leave to continue one year longer in discharging the functions of his office. Shaka, who was very benevolent and generous, signed the petition in a very obliging manner; but under this condition, that the missioners god should quit the rich and pompous kingdoms of the east, to retire into those of the west, which are miserable and barren. By this division of the empire and sovereign power, the jurisdiction of each god was much weakened, but that of Shaka infinitely surpassed the other in beauty and wealth.[107]

According to this agreement, the god of the missioners left the east, in a very poor habit [clothing], accompanied with only a small number of people, his followers being very few. He was so confounded on this occasion, that, from thenceforth, he began to perform such extraordinary things, as manifested his greatness: so that he entered his kingdom of the west with an equipage suitable to his merit; and appeared as rich as if he had found immense treasures, or opened mines of gold and silver. This great and sudden change in his condition, made the inhabitants of the east conclude him to be some notorious robber, who had acquired so much wealth by unjust means. To discover the truth of this, they hired some about him, as spies, to observe all his motions; till such time as having detected him in some theft, they should put him to death for his crimes. He was accordingly watched, and often caught in the very fact; but the moment they were about to arrest him, he vanished out of their sight. However, in revenge for this disappointment, they seized his only son, and put him to death on a cross, instead of his father, who had merited the same punishment, for withdrawing into heaven. Not withstanding all these disgraces, the occidentals cease not to render him worship; and acknowlege him for a god: because that, in voluntarily delivering himself up to death, although innocent, to expiate the transgressions of his father, he, by such great submission, shewed himself to be more than man, and that his father, as well as he, deserved to be adored as deities.

His law defective. It is thus the Lanjan priests treat the god of the Christians, as represented to them by the Romish missioners; and turn into ridicule the history of the birth and crucifixion of Christ. They add, that, after the coming of Shaka, the Christian law, which had prevailed over the east for 5000 years before, ceased to be practised: and that it is defective, because those who profess it can expect from it neither gold nor silver, nor prosperity, nor the enjoyment of pleasure, nor several women.[107] On the contrary, it seems to draw advantage from confusion and affronts; to consider poverty as real wealth, and death as the greatest of all goods. But because Shaka is an enemy to such rigours, and the course which he prescribes is very commodious, broad, and accompanied with all the delights of life; therefore his sectaries [adherents] have him in infinite esteem, and consider him as a more indulgent deity.[108]

State of the Soul, Hell, and Paradise

Ancient doctrine of souls. Although the *Talapoy* have had some knowlege of hell, yet they do not care to speak of it, for fear of disturbing the thoughts of their followers, immersed in sensuality, with the consideration of those dreadful and eternal pains. They who still adhere to the doctrines of the ancient law, and deny the transmigration of souls, say, that those of the wicked are annihilated at their death: but that the souls of good persons assume a body of air, as pure and simple as the light of the sun. After this, passing through the sixteen heavens, where they enjoy all the pleasures with which they abound, they return at length, very happy, to re-unite themselves with their bodies, and become men, in the same condition which they enjoyed before; but so replenished with goods of every kind, as, by their means, to obtain the rank of kings.

The present doctrine. Hell and paradises. Various transmigrations. On the contrary, the followers of the doctrine of Shaka, and the fabulous histories of the priests, hold that the souls of bad men have no retreat after this life but hell, where they must expiate their crimes by suffering inconceivable torments. Their hell is divided into six wards, where there are so many degrees of punishments; and is situated under that vast column of the sixteen worlds, which are the paradises of the blessed. They, who are condemned to go thither, languish in torments for the space of some ages; after which they return to this world. But before they re-animate a human body, they are obliged to enter those of animals, beginnning with the most contemptible, and gradually transmigrating into the more noble, till at length they assume a human shape, as before, but yet in the most deplorable circumstances; in hopes, however, of being raised to a more prosperous state, provided they give liberally to the *Talapoy*. In this case they come to die a second time, they shall obtain a pass to be admitted into one of the sixteen paradises, without being obliged to do any farther penance. From thence likewise, when tired with delights, they may return to this world; not indeed in the form of deified men, but infirm and imperfect like those who are here at present: however with these advantageous circumstances, that they shall be caressed and honoured on account of the riches they shall be possessed of both in this world and in heaven, which will shower down gold upon them in profusion, to answer the several occasions of life.[109]

Talapoy evasions. But whereas losses, disgraces, and other misfortunes, attend their most zealous devotees and benefactors, no less than others; to solve this difficulty, they pretend that such afflictions are the punishment of the crimes committed by them in a former life, although they have no remembrance thereof.[110] These impostors likewise promise a mansion in the sixteenth heaven to those who shall be charitable to them: on the other hand, they declare, that the evils which happen to those, who either cannot or will not bestow alms on them, as well as to infidels, are a just punishment for their avarice; and because they have preferred riches to the joys of heaven, therefore the idol begins to chastise them in this life: but let a man be ever so vicious, dishonest, or wicked, all is well, provided he is but charitable, and gives alms to the priests.

Souls retire into a corner. We must not omit another superstitious conceit of the Lanjans, which is, that the souls, after their separation from the body, retire into a corner of the house; and that the heirs are severely punished, in case they fail to render them the honours due to their quality, such as making a pompous feast, and performing other ceremonies, established by the antient [ancient] customs. On the contrary, they who acquit themselves punctually, with regard to these duties, shall receive great temporal rewards. As the Lanjans are very fond of life, and afraid to die, when they find themselves in the least out of order, they immediately implore the assistance of these souls, making them presents; and setting victuals of several kinds before them, they invite them to eat with them, and talk to them, as if they understood and saw every thing which is said or done. The entertainment is accompanied with music and singing, which continues day and night, till the sick person either recovers or dies. They do all this, in a belief that, by such means, the souls lodged in the house are appeased; and that, if they do them no good, they will at least do them no harm. The people of this persuasion believe nothing, says our author, either of hell or paradise, angels or devils; but live in the most dissolute manner imaginable.[111]

Polygamy a future reward. On a certain day several of the most understanding *Talapoy,* or priests, of different sects, meet in presence of one of the missioners, in order to reconcile so many varous opinions, and bring people to one way of thinking. After a long conference, they came to this decision: that there was, for certain, another life; that the reward to be expected in it was a plurality of wives, and the punishment to be feared consisted in not having any. The Jesuit hereupon asked them, if a charitable man was to be rewarded with several wives, how many husbands was the woman to have, who gave considerable alms? These learned doctors of the law, it seems, were so nonplus'd with this unforeseen question, that they went back to their convents, and turned over their books: but not meeting with any thing to the purpose, came to this resolution among themselves; that such a woman, for her reward, would be changed into a man; and that they who were covetous, would become the wives of devils, or of some *Talapoy,* black, filthy, old, and deformed; in short, more horrible than the devil himself.

Gain to the priests. These imposing priests promise those who are kind, and assist them in their necessities, that they shall have as many wives as all the alms which they had bestowed on them during their lives, were able to purchase: and that the particulars of their good actions, recorded in the book of life, should be made known, when it came to be opened. The Lanjans, charmed with doctrines so agreeable to their sensual inclinations, think they can never give their priests too much; and this infatuation so universally prevails, that the good missioners, who took a great deal of pains to open their eyes, could never dissuade any of them from squandering their money in such ill bestowed charities.

A shameful doctrine. For all the *Talapoy* have no conversation with women, from whom, by the rules of their profession, they are obliged to abstain; yet they affirm, that such of their order as observe continence in this life, will have the power to create, and produce from nothing, as many women as they have a mind, and dispose of them at pleasure: while they, who in this life are addicted to the sex, shall, after their death, be doomed to hell torments, and not have the disposal of any women. As if what is a vice on earth, could be a virtue in heaven; or that men could be rewarded there, for what they are punished here. When these things are objected to the priests, and they are asked how they can condemn, as a shameful practice in this world, that which is tolerated as a commendable action in the other, their answer is: that altho' the incontinence of a *Talapoy* be a crime in this life, and a sin against the divine precept, yet God dispenses with it in heaven; and that chastity, which is a meritorious action in this world, is, in the next, the punishment of the damned. A theology and doctrines which Epicurus himself would be ashamed to publish.[112]

Their Priests, Orders, Habits, Exercises

Priests: their name. Although the priests of Lao are called *Talapoy*, a name borrowed from Pegu, yet, in the language of the country, they are named *Fé* [*pha* in Lao]. This class of men are reckoned the most perfidious in all the kingdom, as well as the very dregs of the people. A lazy, slothful race, and the sworn enemies of industry. Their convents, says our author (but it is a priest of another religion, though not much different from theirs, who speaks), are so many seminaries of very profligate men, retreats of vagabonds and drones; in a word, schools of all sorts of wickedness and abominations. The baser their extraction, the more proud and insolent they become, when raised to that dignity. They are hard-hearted and inhuman beyond expression; more merciless and cruel than the wild beasts. But what can be expected from men, who sacrifice every-thing to their interests, and devote all their wit and vigour to debauchery.[113] This is the picture of the priests of Lao, painted by the Jesuits, exactly like that which the protestants draw for the priests of Rome.

The novices. The *Talapoy* begin to embrace a religious life in their most tender age, and inure themselves to the rigours of profession, during their noviciate, which continues till they are twenty-three. After this they are examined on the subjects of their theology, and ceremonies, by persons appointed by the community, who, on their report, receive the novice into their body, by majority of voices. The first thing the new *Talapoy* does, is to seek out some magistrate who is rich, and well related, to assist him in quality of godfather. Although this office is expensive, yet as it is reckoned an honour to be applied to on that account, nobody refuses it. On the contrary, the invitation is received with great complaisance; and the person who accepts it, always acquits himself with the greatest pomp, in order to gain the applause of the people, as well as the approbation of the *Talapoy*.

How become professed. In the first place, the magistrate, chosen godfather, presents the novice, who is going to be professed, with rich habits. Then, on the day appointed, he orders his best trained elephant to be pompously harnessed, and, with a little house [howdah] on his back, led to the convent: where the novice, bloated with vanity, mounts the animal, and issues forth, at the head of the principal lords of the city, richly drest [dressed], followed by several regiments of foot [infantry], and a multitude of people. In this order they march through the principal streets, to the temple, where the novice is to make his profession; the ceremony often lasting till night. After this, a feast is made in the temple, whose altars serve for tables, on which are served the costliest viands; and, for three days, nothing passes there but revelling. During this time, all distinction of persons is laid aside; and a man of quality makes no difficulty to eat off the same plate with a mechanic. This expence, though exceeding great, does not come up to that which the present costs, made by the magistrate to the new-professed.

May quit the convent and return. What is very singular on this occasion, the person, after making so solemn a profession, may, if he has a mind, return to a secular state; as many do who marry, and live with their wives, so long as the substance lasts which they gathered while *Talapoys*; and, when their stock is out, quit them, and retire again to their convents, where they are admitted without any opposition by the elders, who perhaps had experienced the same indulgence themselves. And this they do as often as they please.

Their habit. The *Talapoy* wear a short cassock of yellow linen, which reaches to their knees, and is girt about them with a red cloth. They shave their heads, even to their eyebrows, twice a month, on the first days of the new and full moon.[114]

Their convents and superiors. Their convents, where they live in community, are like those of the Chartreusians, and St. Romuald, among the Romish orders.[115] All the cells are separate, in which they have several little apartments, made with boards: whereas the superior's cell is built with bricks, and the chambers very magnificently furnished, as well as decorated with curious ornaments, finely gilded. His throne stands very high, and is set off on the sides with curtains of very costly silk. This officer is always chosen from among those *Talapoy* who are of an established reputation, and have devotees of both sexes; who cram them with necessaries, and never let them want for any-thing.

Their employments and meals. These religious rise at a certain hour; and, before the sun is high, walk out by two and two, very modestly, and with profound silence: then separate to beg alms in different parts of the city. This they do by signs; and, at their return, laying up the daintiest morsels for themselves, give the rest to their servants, or send it to the prisoners, after throwing a part to feed the poultry. When this distribution is over, they break silence, and each repairs to his cell, where he breakfasts. After this, they go to sleep for three hours; and then repair to the common refectory, where they find a table covered with all sorts of provisions, which are generally well dressed. As they live at the expence of others, they usually dine on small birds, fowl, and game. If the victuals which their friends send them do not please them, they break the plates; and have the insolence to threaten them, in very injurious language.

After dinner they sleep for an hour; then rise, and go to their respective exercises. The novices fall to study their ceremonies; the scholars to read and write. This they do in two languages: one the vulgar or common language of the country; the other peculiar to the *Talapoy,* and may be called the learned language, as Latin is in Europe. The rest apply themselves to other amusements. Some learn to sing; others pass their time in conversation, at the door of the convent, where they receive visits, and learn the news of the town. Towards evening they make a light supper, without candles; and, having said grace, repair all to the temple, none daring to be absent. There they sing certain prayers, which sometimes they contract, or hurry over, that they may go take the air after sun-set: because then they are at liberty to do what they please.[116]

Pride and arrogance. They exert as much authority over the people, as if they were their subjects. They always appear very serious; and affect a proud disdainful air, with a great deal of gravity. They behave very haughtily to those who are not liberal to them, scarce deigning to look at them. They are extremely ambitious of honour; and very desirous of having much respect paid them, without returning any. Their eyes are in perpetual motion; and their brows being shaved,[117] adds to the severity of their looks. When they want anything, they do not civilly ask, but imperiously demand, it: for with them the virtue of humility is reckoned meanness, and civility subjection. They pretend to lord it over others, and expect a blind submission to their opinions; considering the least objection as want of the respect due to them.

Instance of cruelty. In a word, they surpass other people in nothing but pride and wickedness. A young man being in great haste to finish some affair of importance to him, happened to pass un-awares before a *Talapoy*, without alighting, as is the custom; which so enraged the priest, that he sent persons to seize him, and had him so cruelly bastinado'd [beaten with a stick] in his presence, that he died of his wounds next day. What is more shocking, when this outrage was complained of, many had the insolence to take the part of the *Talapoy*, and engage the judge to determine the matter in their favour; praising the murder as a generous action, done by the priest in defence of his religion and order. Thus the more mischief they do to others, the more they are feared and respected.

How punished for crimes. The *Talapoy* who are in their convents are not suffered to commit any debauchery: but if any of them is convicted thereof, especially of having sollicited and attempted to force a woman, a strict enquiry is made into the affair, and the aggressor punished according to the nature of the offence. As all matters relating to this insolent rabble are brought before the king, the accused appears at his tribunal: and however positively the crime may be proved upon him, yet if he has any thing at all to say in his defence, the king readily acquits him, in order to engage those religious in his interests, as having so great an influence over the people. But in case the crime be so flagrant and notorious, as not to admit of any palliation, the offender is condemned for life to serve the elephants, which is the most infamous of all employments. Was his majesty to punish with equal severity all those who are caught in the fact, there would not, in a little time, be left one *Talapoy* among the Lanjans: but as he calls himself their protector, and bears the title of general of their order, he is not willing to destroy the jurisdiction, which he has over their sanctuary: besides, he is afraid, in case he should not be favourable to them, that they would raise a rebellion against him.[118]

Confession. Among other rules of *Talapoy,* they are obliged to go to confession fourteen days in every month. Their manner is like that observed in the Romish convents. They assemble in a great hall, where being seated, according to their rank, the oldest leave their places one after another, and going into the midst of the company, on their knees, declare aloud the faults which they have committed in the preceding month, with regard to eating, drinking, diversions, anger, doing injury to others, speaking untruths, or the like. Absolution immediately follows the confession, each of them having power to give it: but where the satisfaction is so easy,[120] they never scruple repeating the crimes.

Holy water. They likewise make a kind of holy water: but our author is at a loss to know how that usage came among them; unless from Ethiopia or India, by means of the disciples of St. Thomas.[121] They send it to the sick, as a sovereign remedy, and keep good store for the purpose; because, in return, they get so many bottles of good wine. But although the people receive no benefit from it, they have great faith in its virtue.[122]

Offerings to images; beads. The honour which they give to the idols or images, does not consist in sacrifices: they only offer flowers to them, accompanied with perfumes, and a little rice, which they lay upon the altars; where solely on such occasions they light up tapers. They carry in their hands certain bracelets, consisting of 100 beads strung together like rosaries: these they conn over [learning by repetition], standing before the image, and continually repeating their hymns.

Talapoys of the woods. What has been said relates to the *Talapoy* who reside in the towns: but there are others who lead a more solitary life, in caves made in the woods and forests; the horrors of which, according to our author, are proper to conceal the enormity of their crimes.[121] They retire to such places to pursue their debauched inclinations with more freedom: and, by degrees, the resort of women has become so great, that the solitude of these hermits is at present become a populous colony, and the desarts [unpopulated places] may be said to vie with the cities; with this difference, that, in the latter, the children know their parents, which is not the case of those who are born in these solitudes. These hermits receive more alms than the *Talapoy* of cities. They admit a fast of three months, to dispose them to celebrate their Easter. I would say, says our author, that they have three months of Easter [Buddhist Lent], with two feasts a day: one of flesh, which is eaten in private, and cooked in the house; the other of fish, which is sent by their friends, and eaten publicly.[123]

Lao an university. Our author passes over several other particularities, because they are either the same, or very little different from those mentioned in several relations, and in the history of the Bonzas [bonzes, Buddhist monks] of Japan; who, according to some authors, say they are the disciples of the *Talapoy* who were the followers of Shaka, and passed thither from Lao or Siam. However that be, at present they of Siam go to Lao, as into an university, there to learn the maxims of Shaka; which are at least more in reputation than the ancient doctrine, if they are not entirely conformable to it.

Talapoy knavery. To conclude, the number of these *Talapoy* is so greatly increased, that, fearing they shall in time fall short of necessaries, they learn all sorts of trades, and work at them in their convents, which seem to be changed at present into so many shops of mechanics and merchants, whom they even circumvent in their business. For if an artisan in the city has contrived any extraordinary piece of work, or invented some new fashion, they labour secretly to get the model and draught; and, having effected it, give themselves out for the inventors: so that when the author thinks to surprise the town with something new in its kind, they produce the model, to shew they were beforehand with him; and in case the true proprietor disputes the invention with them, the king is sure to ascribe it to the *Talapoy*.

The king's supremacy. The great credit which the *Talapoy* have acquired in Lao, is owing chiefly to two causes, their skill in magic, and the king's protection. His majesty, who is, as it were, the general or grand-master of their religion, loads them with honours, and, at the same time, takes care to govern them. He continually admonishes them to observe their rules, and sets before them the obligation of monthly confessions. He appoints the days for fasts and festivals; the ceremonies of which are regulated by him. He resolves all doubts, and reconciles the different scriptures; explains the difficulties found in their book; and never suffers any-thing to be printed,[124] without his approbation. He likewise corrects the faults of such pieces. In a word, he is the sovereign judge of whatever relates to the conduct of the *Talapoy*, and punishes them for their offences: but, as if there was something sacred in them, suffers none to vex them on any account.

Talapoys indulged. Whenever the king sees any of them, his majesty salutes him first, by raising the right hand, which is the usual mark of civility. He makes slaves of his vassals, and obliges them to serve in their temples, in lieu of the tribute due to him. He sometimes gives up whole towns and villages to them, obligeing the inhabitants to maintain the convents within their precincts; which they always submit to with reluctance, on account of the insatiableness and insolence of such masters: for they would choose to be slaves to others, rather than be dependent on them. However, the king, for the reasons above-mentioned, takes care to preserve their friendship, and over-looks many of their transgressions. In 1640 a *Talapoy* and his disciples, having been detected in coining and uttering abundance of false money, the informations were carried before the council: but the king caused the indictment to be quashed by an order, in which, after taxing the laity with avarice, he praised the piety of the *Talapoy*; who, for want of being relieved in their neccessities, and finding their temples to be quite deserted, had been obliged to invent a way of relieving themselves, by coining money, and, out of a little, making a great deal.[125]

Instance in an assassin who escapes punishment. But this piece of lenity was infinitely more excusable than that which he shewed on another occasion. A *Talapoy* having cast a covetous eye upon the gold bracelets which two young ladies, who were sisters, wore upon their arms: under some pretence got access to them, about nine or ten at night, and, thinking they were alone, murdered them both with a dagger. After this he fell to romage [rummage or search] the chamber: in doing which, to his surprize, he found a servant girl hidden in a corner; and, to prevent a discovery, aimed to dispach [kill] her also: but the maid, having made shift to avoid the blow, got out of the window into the street, and gave the alarm. The villain hereupon thought it time to withdraw: but was seen in his passage by three other servants, who, next morning, along with the girl, went to a magistrate, and gave evidence of the horrid fact. On this information the *Talapoy* was cited before the king, in the hall of audience: where, on protesting his innocence, and offering, in test of it, to undergo the ordeal trial, his majesty commanded, that he should remain seven days in the woods; and if, in that time, he received no hurt, either from the wild beasts or venomous serpents, he should be declared innocent. The assassin accordingly repaired to the woods; but took care to engage a company of slaves to attend him as his guard; so that he came off unhurt. Upon this the king, though convinced of his guilt, said, that the devil, in shape of a *Talapoy*, must have been the author of that execrable deed, in malice to those priests, that they might no longer be considered as fathers and masters. After this acquittal, the murderer, to be revenged on the poor girl who was his accuser, prosecuted her so violently, that she was condemned to lose her liberty: nor did the king interpose in her favour.[126]

Pretend to magic; abuse the credulous. As to magic and sorcery, the other means by which the *Talapoy* have gained authority and reputation, our author represents them as greatly skilled therein. He says they do things which seem miraculous; yet blames the credulity of the people, who, on that account, think them to be more than men: that they make use of their art to hurt people, and often merely to divert themselves: that they catch and tame wild elephants, by means of a plaister [plaster] or ointment put on the back and crupper of a female, whom they follow from the forests into the cities, without doing any harm; and that, as soon as the plaister is taken off, they grow wild again, till made tractable by management and confinement: that they do not scruple to exercise their sorcery on their benefactors, in order to obtain more by that means, than they could hope from their liberality; and frequently bewitch those who assist them, as well as those who do not, to oblige both parties to have recourse to them for relief: that when any person is seized with any distemper or sickness, the *Talapoy* is sent for, who cures him, only by taking off the charm. Our author is so weak as to believe all this stuff, and tells of a great man, no less silly than himself, who, after taking medicines for some disorder without effect, fancied himself bewitched, and applied to the *Talapoy*. Those magicians, it seems, recovered him: but, as he was extremely liberal to them, they laid the spell on him, from time to time, in order to make their farther advantage of him.

Impose on the sick. When a poor man is sick, they agree to cure him for his weight in rice; and then send him one of their cast-off habits to wear, as a sovereign remedy. As they believe there is something sacred in the very touch of a *Talapoy*, the patient often sends a new garment for the priests to sanctify, by putting it on his back: but, instead of returning it, the priest sends him one of his own old ones; assuring him, that there is no remedy comparable to their tattered gowns. And, as daily experience shews that those sorts of relicks do not work miracles; the *Talapoy*, to save their credit, ascribe the cause to the poor man's covetousness, and want of faith.[127]

Served by noblemen. Oftentimes the chief officers of state do not disdain to serve the *Talapoy* in the most servile offices. They go in winter into the woods, fell timber, carry it on their shoulders to the city, and through the streets, to the convents, in order to let the people see, that it is an honour to serve those religious men; and that the sure way to recommend them to the favour of the king, is to imitate their own example. During the great heats, these great men carry also to the *Talapoy* vessels full of medicinal waters; accompanied with simples [a medicament made of a single substance], and choice perfumes, for their use, when they go to bathe themselves.

Festival or jubilee. The principal revenue of the *Talapoy* arises from the offerings which are made in honour of Shaka, in April, which is the month of their jubilee, and plenary indulgence. On this occasion the idol Shaka is exposed to view upon an eminence, in a great court, accompanied with *Talapoy*; who receive the immense offerings which are made of gold, silver, rice, cloth, stuff, and all sorts of necessaries. Nor does our author doubt, but that the priests, who are appointed to guard the statue, purloin a large quantity of gold and silver, without being missed; the sums which they receive are so prodigious great. All these alms and offerings are hung up in the temple; so that when the inferior *Talapoy* come to sweep it, they take a good share, over and above what they find on the ground.

Shaka's statue. Our author learned from a Tong-king lord, who was ambassador at the court of Lanjang, in the time of this great solemnity, that he observed a tower in the middle of the temple, about 100 cubits [maybe 50 metres] high, pierced on all sides, and adorned with many large windows, for the better view of Shaka's statue; which is laced in the middle, and surrounded with numerous leaves of fine gold, like tinsel, which hang about it, and, with the gentle motion of the air, make such a sweet and agreeable harmony, that one would imagine it was a concert of several musical instruments: they were hung there to serve as so many little vails [veils], to hinder insects from getting to the idol. The ambassador informed Marini likewise, that the great altar was decorated with two pillars of solid gold, ten cubits high, and proportionably thick, which were always exposed to view, without danger of being stolen: although a missioner, from whom our author had a great deal of what he relates, never mentioned that particular.

Piety of the Lanjans. Nothing is more surprising than the piety and devotion of the Lanjans; who are so far from the thoughts of robbing temples, that they exhaust themselves with making presents, without desiring any-thing more than to have them acceptable to their false god, as they are assured by the *Talapoy*: whose words are as firmly believed as an oracle, or a revelation from heaven, out of a persuasion that it is impossible their priests should deceive them in an article of so great importance.[128] A persuasion which prevails no less among the Romanists; and almost every-where else.

Preaching and Commandments

Art of the Talapoys. They preach every day in the temple, during this month, to multitudes of people, and never change their text; which is to endeavour to persuade their auditors, that there is no time in the year so proper to render themselves worthy of the benefits both of this life and the next. In this hope they make every day a holiday: all business, as well public as private, is laid aside; and people mind nothing but to make presents, and visit the temples, which at that time, are always open. To render the visit more agreeable, and draw even those whom devotion could not move, the *Talapoy* provide all sorts of diversions in the courts and porches of the temple, which are finely adorned. There the people are entertained with comedians, who recite verses, and act very agreeable farces. Others expose to view several sorts of workmanship. And, in short, every one does what pleases him most: some sing; others dance, or play on instruments; all in view of Shaka, annihilated.

Way of preaching. To put an end to this feast with more pomp and magnificence, one of the most famous preachers among the *Talapoy* mounts the chair [an elevated platform for sermons]; where, having recapitulated all which had been advanced on the subject, during the whole month, he adds an elegant discourse. The way of preaching here, as well as in Tong-king is to stand up, motionless, like statues, the arms across the breast, held in that posture with great modesty,[129] and never once stirring them. On these occasions they endeavour to persuade their hearers to renounce the world, and take the *Talapoy* habit, in order to preserve religion in its splendor, and prevent its ever failing. It is incredible how many advantages they promise, as well as how much fervour and zeal[130] they express on this occasion, so far as to load, with grace and benedictions from

Shaka, the families which sacrifice their children, by devoting them to their convents. To excite them to this, they instance the example of their most ancient and pious *Talapoy*; who, when they have neither brothers nor nephews of the order, buy children of their nearest relations: that so their family may not want the imaginary blessings of Shaka, and may always boast of having one belonging to it in his service.

Commandments and dispensations. Towards the end of the sermon, the preacher exhorts his auditors to an exact observance of the law which consists in five negative precepts: 1. Not to kill any-thing which has life. 2. Not to commit adultery. 3. Not to lye (or deny the truth). 4. Not to steal. 5. Not to drink wine. But however obligatory these commandments may be, there is none who keeps them: and the *Talapoy*, who assume the power of giving dispensations, sell them at no small rate to such as sollicit them, in order to avoid the guilt and punishment of breaking the commands. But the crafty priests never grant them for more than one precept at once; and that only for a certain term:[131] so that when the time is expired, they are obliged to apply for a new licence to sin. These instruments, issued from this chancery, are written with an iron style, on palm-tree leaves, in characters which none, perhaps, can read, but he who traces them.

All reduced to charity. In one word, all the fruit of the *Talapoy*'s preachment turns to the profit of him and the convent; never to the advantage of the auditors: because reducing the five precepts to one, the infamous priest, says our author, returns to his first lesson, and insists on the necessity of doing alms, from which there can be no dispensation. To inforce this the more, these cheats are continually telling the people, that if they will not observe this single precept, which is so easy to be performed, it is a sure sign that they do not believe in Shaka: that it is indifferent to them whether their holy faith and religion be preserved in the kingdom, or whether there be any *Talapoy* there to teach it, and pray for them. So that the poor Lanjan laity, to avoid such reproachful imputations, as well as the wrath of Shaka, pay to the priests, under the title of alms, not only yearly, but every month, the tithe of all which they get by the sweat of their brows.

Arts of Talapoys; to force alms. The better to secure themselves, and augment such considerable revenues, they have introduced a custom, seemingly to do honour to their benefactors; but, in reality, the more effectually to pick their pockets, and suck the very blood of the people. The day before the full moon, from whence they begin their month, according to their rubriks, is always consecrated to offerings, which, pursuant to their infamous policy, they accompany with the following ceremonies: first, they require, that every one should carry his present on his head, so that all may see it; and, as the people assemble on that occasion, the *Talapoy* send persons to sound the trumpet, and play on several other instruments: in order, as they pretend, not so much to do honour to the people who make the offerings, as to sollicit the governors of heaven to receive them as alms given the *Talapoy*, in honour of Shaka. When they are going to offer them, they must raise them three times upon the head, to signify: 1. that both their mind and eyes are turned towards heaven: 2. that they implore aid from the ministers of its justice: and 3. that they pray to them not to refuse their protection, but to be kind to them in necessity. Lastly, they deliver the offering into the hands of the *Talapoy*; and then retire perfectly well satisfied.[132]

We have dwelt the longer on this subject, to give our reader as full an account as we could of the religion of Shaka, known, in the hither peninsula [India], by the name of Budda [Buddha]; in China by that of Fo, or She-kya; and in Tibet, whence it had its original, by the name of La. For although this religion is spread over the farther penisle [South-East Asia and China], it flourishes in no part of it so much as it does in Lao, or among the Lanjans; and our author Marini is the only one who has spoken of it in any detail, though neither so particularly, nor with such exactness, as could be wished. We shall therefore, before we quit it, add a few remarks more.

Religion of the Lamas; vastly extended. The Indians, that is, the original inhabitants of all the countries and islands eastward of Persia, as far as the oriental ocean, seem to be divided between two religions, each of very great extent. For distinction sake, we shall call one that of the Brâmmans; the other that of the Lamas. That of the Brâmmans prevails over Hindustan, and the hither penisle: where, although the Mogols [Mughal empire] are become almost wholly masters, yet it is computed that, in Hindustan itself, there are at least 100 idolaters, or image-worshippers, to one Mohammedan; consequently their numbers must be much greater in the peninsula, several countries of which are yet intirely [entirely] under the dominion of the Râjahs. On the other hand, the religion of the Lamas is the established religion of Tibet, of all that part of Great Tartary called Western Tartary, of the whole farther peninsula of India [i.e., South-East Asia and China], and of Japan. It has likewise spread over most of the oriental islands: and although it is not the established religion of China, yet it seems to be embraced by much the greater part of its inhabitants. So that the religion of the Lamas may be said to be extended over three or four times as much ground as that of the Brâmmans.

Differs from the Brâmman. These two religions, though agreeing in the moral precepts, the doctrine of the soul's transmigration, and the use of images,[133] yet differ in several essential points: as the distinction of people into tribes, eating of flesh, frequent washings, and the like; but especially in the article relating to the supreme being:[134] for the Lamas hold, that God himself assumed flesh, and actually dwells among them in a human shape; whereas the three incarnated deities of the Brâmmans are inferior and created beings. Not but the sects which hold Wishtnû [Vishnu] or Ishuren [Iśvāra (Śiva)] to be the supreme god, seem, in this point, to differ but little from the Lamas.

Origin from Tibet. We have already spoken of the original of the Brâmman religion, in our description of the hither India: as to that of the Lamas, it seems to have had its rise in Tibet, where it has, at present, its principal seat. For there, we are told, that God himself, as the head of this religion, reigns in a human shape; so that the inhabitants of Tibet may be said to live under a real theocracy, according to their own belief. This god, in human form, is, in Tibet, named La; in China She-kya, and also Fo; which name he assumed after his apotheosis, or deification: he is, in his own country, called Lama-Konjû (or Konchok), that is, the *eternal father*: he is also stiled Dalay Lama [Dalai Lama], or *the grand Lama*, that is, high priest, pope, or head, of the religion.[135]

Its several branches. From this fountain all the other gods, or founders of religion, in the several countries professing the same, seem to be derived: as the Budda, or Boutta, of the hither Indians; the Shaka of Laho, or Lao, and Japan; the She-kya of China; Thikka of Tong-king; and Sommona Kodom of Siam. Some of these gods, or legislators, seem to be acknowleged the same with him of Tibet, particularly She-kya, or Shaka: the account likewise which is given by authors, of their origin and doctrines, internal and external, is nearly the same. It is true, none of those nations seem to acknowlege him for their god, who is at present adored in Tibet; although they derive their gods from some part of India, west of China:[136] but rather consider him as coming from a distant country, and taking up his abode among them. Thus the Ho-shang, or priests of China, called, by Europeans, *Bonzas*, do not recognize the god of Tibet for the head of their religion; and bear a great enmity to the Lamas, whose footing in China they strenuously oppose. The worshippers, therefore, of She-kya, or Shaka, must look on the great Lama of Tibet as an impostor, and not as the real Shaka, whom they adore: for it does not appear, that, they hold him to be existing any-where on earth visibly, and in a human shape.

Budda; the same with Sommona Kodom. With regard to Budda, and Sommona Kodom, who seem to be the same, their votaries refer his original to the island of Seylan, or Ceylon; if they are not rather at a loss from what country to derive him. According to a Balli [Pali] book, cited by Loubere, the father of Sommona Kodom, called also Pouti Sat, that is, lord Pouti (Bouta, or Budda, as we conjecture), was a king of Seylan;[137] whence it may be presumed, Kodom himself was a native of that island: although the Chingalasses [Singhalese] of Seylan, who worship Buda, or Budda, as an inferior deity, say he was not born in that island, and that he died on the continent.[138]

Budda and Sommona Kodom seem to be the same, for two reasons: first, that the latter is, by the Siamese, called also Pouti Sat, or lord Pouti, which is doubtless the same with Budda: for, as Mr. La Croze well remarks, throughout the Indies his name is given to Wednesday; which, in the Samskret [Sanskrit] or Samskrotam language, is called *Boutta-varam*; in that of Seylan, *Bouda-dina*; in that of Siam, *Van Pouti*; and in the Malabaric, *Boudèn Kirûmei*.[139] The second argument (which we are surprised to find has escaped Mr. La Croze), is taken from the praenomen *Sommona*, which, in the Balli language, signifies a religious man of the woods;[140] and answers both in term and signification to Sammanîn, or Shammanîn, a sect formerly in Malabâr, and other parts of the hither peninsula [India], who dwelt in woods, and adored Boudda, or Budda.

His origin. From what has been said in the preceding paragraph, it may be inferred, that Sommona Kodom, is not only the same with Budda, of the western Indians, but that his worship was brought into Siam by the Sammanîns, possibly on their expulsion out of the hither peninsula, whence they were driven by the Brâmmans, about 500 years ago.[141]

Budda's antiquity. After all, our knowlege of the Indians, and their histories, is so very imperfect, that we cannot determine whether Budda be the very same person with Shaka, and the god of Tibet; or whether he was not a different person, pretending to the same divine extraction, who possibly came out of Tibet, and introduced the religion of that country among the western Indians. However, this is certain, that his origin is of great antiquity: probably long before the birth of Christ. For, not to mention what authors say from the tradition of these eastern countries, we find him spoken of by several of the ancient writers, particularly Clemens Alexandrinus; who calls him Boutta, or Butta, and says he was worshipped as a god by the Sarmanes.[142] St. Jerom, and others, writes Boudda, or Budda; and says he came into the world through the side of his mother, who still remained a virgin:[143] in the same manner as the Indians, at present, relate of him, of Shaka, and of Fo.

The Shammanes. That this Butta, or Budda, was not a person newly sprung up in the days of those primitive doctors, appears from hence; that, according to the first of them, he was worshipped as a god, on account of his holy life, by the Sarmanes, of whom he gives the following account:

> There are two kinds of Indian gymnosophists, or philosophers, one called Sarmanes, the other Brachmans [Brahmans]. Those of the Sarmanes, who are termed solitaries, neither dwell in cities, nor make use of houses; but cover themselves with the barks of trees, and feed on fruits. Water is their only liquor, which they drink out of their hand. They abstain from marriage, and live after the manner of the Encratites.[144] They obey the commandments of Butta, and honour him as a god, on account of his holy life.[145]

These Sarmanes are the same with the Germanes, mentioned by Strabo,[146] after Megasthenes, however the name came to be corrupted; for he speaks of them in nearly the same terms.

Their learning. This is a remarkable testimony of the antiquity, as well as eminency, of the sect of Sarmanes, in the hither India; and a confirmation of what the Indians of Malabâr relate concerning the Shammanes, or Shammanins, who, without dispute, are the same people. These Shammanes, according to the Malabâr authors, were the ancient inhabitants of India, and anterior to the Brâmmans [Brahmans] in the hither peninsula [the Indian subcontinent]. They were skilled in arts and sciences; which the Malabârs had from them. Several of their books, still remaining, are in great esteem; and quoted by the modern Indians, in the same manner as the Greek and Roman authors are with us.

Their sects; extirpated by the Brâmmans. The Shammanes were divided into two sects, Buddergueuls, that is, the adorers of Budda, and Shammanergueuls. They openly blasphemed the religion of Wishtnû [Vishnu] and Ishuren [Iśvāra (Śiva)]: they detested the sacred books of the Brâmmans; and compelled the Malabârs to embrace their doctrines.[147] This accusation, perhaps, is brought to justify the proceedings of Brâmmans against them. However that be, it is certain, that these latter, by degrees, gained over the Indians to their way of worship: and, as soon as they found themselves the stronger party, began to persecute the Shammanes, whom they at length drove beyond the Ganges, into the farther peninsula of the Indies [i.e., South-East Asia]. On this occasion, doubtless, it was, that the Brâmmans have invented the fable of Wishtnû's sixth incarnation, into the Brâmman Vegoud Dova Avataram, who, by means of twelve disciples, destroyed the two above-mentioned sects.[148] But we learn from another quarter, that this great revolution was brought about by the Brâmmans, who, in several kingdoms of India, stirred up the princes to make a horrible massacre of them.[149] Considering that the Malabârs have no regular cycle of years, and that their history is so blended with fables, it is hard to determine when this bloody tragedy happened: but, as it appears by the books of the Shammanes, that 500 years ago there were yet some remains of them, on the Choromandel [Coromandel] coast, it is probable that the idolatry of the Brâmmans hath not had the absolute dominion in that country above five centuries. However that be, we are told the religion of the Shammanes, at present, is to be found neither there, nor on the coast of Malabâr.[150]

Sommona Kodom. Although, from the name of Sommona Kodom, chief lawgiver and idol among the Siameses, we are inclinable to believe, that he was a Shamman, from the coast of Malabâr, or Choromandel; yet his arrival in Siam is not to be dated from the expulsion of Shammans, by the Brâmmans: for the Siameses place his death from whence their aera [era] is computed, about the year 544 before Christ.[151] Neither must we conclude, although he established the worship and law of Budda in Siam, and seems to bear the name of Budda in that of Pouti Sat, or lord Pouti, as hath been before observed, that he was really Budda himself: for Budda seems to have been worshipped in the hither India, many centuries antecedent to that aera; and his religion settled in that peninsula long before the Brâmmans entered the country. It must, therefore be thought, either that the name of Putî Sat was given to him, on account of having introduced the doctrine of Budda into

Siam; or that he pretended to be Budda, regenerated in the person of Sommona Kodom.

GOVERNMENT AND HISTORY OF LANJANG

Government of Lanjang

Chief officers. The country of Laos, as hath been already observed, is divided among several kings; concerning whom we meet with nothing more than what hath been related, excepting him of Lanjang.

The principal dignities and offices of this kingdom are eight. The first is that of viceroy-general, who manages one part of state affairs, and assists the king in all matters which concern the government. On the demise of his majesty, it is his business to assemble the council, convene the states, and, in short, take on him the quality of regent, until the successor is enthroned; all other officers or ministers being obliged to obey him. And, because the kingdom is divided into seven provinces, there are appointed seven other viceroys, with equal power, for the government of them: but they reside continually at court, as the king's companions in office, and his counsellors, where they enjoy the revenues, and other benefits, of their respective departments, which they commit to the care of their lieutenants, or deputy-governors. Besides the provinces, there are other lesser governments, which depend on the greater, in respect both to civil and military affairs.

Each province has its own militia, consisting of both horse and foot; whose officers depend on the viceroy or governor, he on the prime viceroy, and this last on the king. The troops subsist on revenues assigned them in each province, and are obliged to serve, on that consideration, on all occasions which the kingdom may require.[152]

Their state. The governors appear with large retinues, and often oppress the people, seizing by force whatever they take a fancy to, especially of foreign merchandize; nor dare any oppose such violence. However, the king does not countenance such acts of injustice; and they are punishable by the laws. His majesty, far from abusing his power in that manner, as soon as he is informed that a merchant has brought any curiosity into his kingdom, which he has a mind for, immediately orders him not to expose it to sale, and sends the full value of it, to prevent the ruin of commerce; the duties arising from which are of great advantage to his revenue.[153] What is still more barbarous in these governors, they often enter into measures to destroy particular men: for, being infatuated with the belief in magic and witchcraft, they hire assassins to hunt and kill men in the woods, in order to procure their gall, for making charms,[154] as hath been before related.

Laws few. With regard to laws, the Lanjans have very few; nor need they many, where they have the customs of the country for the guide and rule of their conduct. Besides, the will of the king stands in place of laws, where they are wanting: nor does he exert that authority to the detriment of his subjects. And, in matters of dispute between the people, the opinion of the judges in former cases is made use of, as precedents. There is one custom almost peculiar to this country; for, though tolerated in Siam, it is not established there: this is, a certain subjection and dependence which every family has on one person, as the chief or superior: so that all the Lanjans, excepting the *Talapoy*, who do not descend in a right line from the principal branch of any family (be their condition what it will, dignified or not, rich or poor), must depend thereon during their lives, without ever having it in their power to free themselves.

Subjection of families to their chief. When they, who issue directly from the main branch, come to marry, the family divides itself in such sort, that the male descendants follow the degree and branch of the father, the female race those of the mother. This dependence or subjection is very strict and incommodious. First, they are obliged, twice a year, to pay their acknowlegements, and make presents, to the head of the family: secondly, they are obliged to serve their chief in whatever he commands them, whether he wants to build a house, to celebrate an idol-feast, or take a journey, they are obliged to attend him at their own expence, to obey his orders, and contribute to the expence of the work. On the road some must serve him as soldiers, for his guard, and others as his domestics. This custom proves of great use to the king; who, in a short time, may raise a considerable army: for he has nothing to do but to gain over the chiefs of families. The worst of all is, that, by the same custom, if the chief happens to be convicted of any enormous crime, all those who, in the least degree of affinity, belong to him, are, at the same time, stripp'd of all their rights, and become more miserable than ever; for they are destined thenceforth to serve the king's elephants, to gather herbs for them every day, to keep them clean, and watch them in the night.

Justice: how administered. Justice is not altogether well administered; and, because crimes are very rarely committed here, many laws are not required: however, they have a few, which prove sufficient to preserve peace and union among them. The severity, for instance, with which not only blows, but angry words, are punished, is a great means of keeping people in awe. With regard to civil matters, justice is in a very languid state. They have no comments to explain their laws: so that they are all subject to the interpretation of the judges, who are not without their prejudices, and many, on the slightest grounds, condemn the parties; who cannot appeal from his sentence, but must suffer the penalty which custom has established.[153]

The king. The king of Lanjan is an absolute independant prince; and acknowleges no superior either in temporal or spiritual affairs. The property of lands lies wholly in him; who disposes at pleasure of the effects belonging to his subjects: nor can any family in the kingdom inherit or possess any thing left them by will.

No nobility. One here meets with no kind of nobility; nor is it to be acquired either by birth, riches, or virtuous actions. Employments, honours, and wealth, depend solely on the king, who confers those benefits on whom he pleaseth; and resumes them at their deaths. The most he does in favour of their children, is to leave them in possession of the moveable effects: as for houses and lands, money and arms, they all return into the exchequer. No man can say he is master of one foot of land; only the *Talapoys* can dispose of such spots as are inhabited: but for the rest, the king distributes them among the governors and commanders, to some more, to others less. These farm them out for three years only to persons, who agree to give one half of the third year's produce to the king.

Viceroys; their state. Every viceroy has a very numerous retinue: but the court of the king, whose splendor is vastly set off by the magnificence of these grandees, appears chiefly in the incredible number of pages who compose it. These are always at hand to sollicit for vacant places, to which they are promoted according to the years which they have served: but, generally speaking, they are advanced through favour, more than merit, as is the case in other countries. Besides the above-mentioned officers, there is an infinite number of others, who have their different occupations. The rank of all courtiers is distinguished by certain gold or silver boxes, which their pages carry after them where-ever they go. The prime viceroy has the privilege of riding upon an elephant richly harnessed, when-ever he goes abroad; but the rest are allowed only to be carried in little chairs, adorned with cloth of gold, and accompanied with several footmen in handsome liveries. The other officers, let their quality be what it will, are obliged to go on foot; and although they have their boxes also, yet they must not be carried after them exposed to public view.[156]

King of Lanjan. Whatever other monarchs may think of the king of Lanjan, he thinks them all his inferiors; nor will yield the superiority to the emperor of China himself. To inspire his subjects with the greater veneration for his person, he appears but seldom in public; and daily withdraws himself more and more from the eyes of his subjects, as if he was of a species something more than human. He is distinguished from others only by the holes made in the fleshy part of his ears, which are of an extraordinary size: they are made so wide by stretching the holes with pipes, putting in a larger every month, till at length the tips of his majesty's ears touch his shoulders. He wears no crown, but such as the ancient emperors used, which is a gold band or ribband, which serves also to bind his hair.

Seldom appears. His Lanjan majesty shews himself but twice a year to his subjects: who, in return for that honour done them, strive all they can to divert him, by means of elephants trained to do a thousand little tricks; and wild beasts, whom they set a fighting. They have also wrestlers and gladiators on this occasion, who exert their strength and utmost skill to please the king.

Visits temples. But the time to see the court in all its splendor, is when the king goes to visit some temple; on which occasion all the magnificence of the kingdom is display'd in the dress and equipage of the officers, as well as of his majesty himself, mounted on a lofty elephant most richly accoutred. The king is preceded by his chief officers, and followed by a multitude of horsemen, armed with muskets, and in good order. The cavalcade is closed with several beasts loaded with presents, which his majesty, in behalf of his people, is to make to the idol; whose temple, on that occasion, resembles an exchange, rather than a place of devotion. On this day the women are not permitted to stir out of their houses: but, when the king passes by, they appear at the windows, and sprinkle both him and his presents with the perfumed waters of Nasse; which wetting is very agreeable to him. His majesty is met at some distance from the temple by the *Talapoy,* drest [dressed] in their most pompous habits, who attend him through the ceremony, and, at the end, divide the most valuable offerings among themselves.

His audiences. The magnificence which appears in this festival exceeds that which is displayed at court, when an ambassador is to have his audience, or the petty kings, who are his tributaries, come to pay him homage. On this occasion he receives them in a great hall, sitting on a very high throne, and drest in his robes of ceremony. He returns their compliments by the mouth of his chancellor; and never speaks to them but by an interpreter.[157]

History of Lanjang

Ancient state. We meet with very little in authors concerning the history and affairs of the Lanjans. It has been already remarked, that they were, many centuries ago, in subjection to China; as were all the other countries of the farther Indian peninsula: but, after they had shaken off the yoke, and were powerful, they formed themselves into a kind of republic, which continued till the year of Christ 600, when their state became a monarchy.

Free and independent. For the country having become more populous by the great resort of Siameses, who, for that end, had leave to settle there; the Lanjans, to secure the power to themselves, elected a chief or commander, whom they invested with all the authority, and acknowleged for their sovereign. But factions arising among them, through the intrigues of the Siameses; these latter, having had a powerful party, procured one to be raised to the throne, who was of the family of the kings of Siam. From this prince the kings of Lao, or rather Lanjan, have been lineally descended, for above a thousand years; in so much that they still retain both the language and dress of their ancestors. From this time, likewise, they seem to have continued independent, although some authors report that they pay tribute to the king of Tong-king.[158] But that is a mistake, arising from a circumstance which they were not sufficiently acquainted with, and is as follows.

Subject to Ava. The governor of a province of Lao having usurped the sovereignty, the king of Tong-king, to whom that province formerly belonged, invaded and obliged him by force to pay him tribute. This he did for some time: but, towards the end of the sixteenth, or beginning of the seventeenth century, the king of Ava [Bayin-naung, r. 1551–81], after conquering Pegu and Siam, made himself master, not only of that province, but of all Lao (or Lanjan), whose inhabitants he carried to Pegu, in order to people that country. The Lanjans, who bore their captivity with the utmost impatience, at length formed a general conspiracy, to recover their liberty; and rising on a day appointed, put the Peguers to the sword, where-ever they met with them. Their enterprise was attended with so great success, that, had they pursued their good fortune, they might easily have reduced the whole kingdom under their subjection: but the desire they had to return to their own country made them hasten thither, from whence they quickly expelled their enemies, who had it in possession.[159] The news of this revolution coming to the ears of the natives, who had fled for shelter into the neighbouring mountains and forests, they presently returned, and re-peopled Lanjan, the capital of this kingdom, which soon recovered its former splendor, under its legitimate king [Wòrawongsa, r. 1596–1622].

Throw off the yoke; become independent. The king of Ava and Pegu [Tha-lun, r. 1629–48] not being able, at that juncture, to revenge the insult, dissembled his resentment; and the better to compass his design by fraud, pretended to relinquish his right to the kingdom, and make an alliance with the Lanjans; contenting himself with a very small acknowlegement on their side. Mean time he, underhand, made great preparations for war: but his death, which happened in the year 1647, frustrated his intentions. However, his successor [Pindale, r. 1648–61], pursuing the same scheme, sent ambassadors to the Lanjans, with rich presents, and very obliging letters; by which he demanded, but in very moderate terms, a yearly tribute of only one choice elephant, and a beautiful maiden. The king of Lao [Suriyawongsa, r. 1638–95], far from agreeing to the proposal, was so provoked, that he caused the ambassadors and their equipage to be seized as spies. At the same time he sent some of his best troops towards the frontiers of Pegu, where the king of Ava had his magazines filled with warlike stores, ready for his intended enterprise: but as he left them unguarded, in order to take off all suspicion, the Lanjans came on them by surprise, and burnt them to the ground. This unexpected blow ruined all the measures of that formidable monarch, who durst neither attack them, nor pursue their retreat, as well for want of ammunition, as for fear of a rebellion, knowing that his subjects hated him.[160]

This is all the account we are able to give of the affairs of Lanjan; as having received very little information from that country, since the middle of the last century, when the missioners found it impracticable to propagate their religion among the inhabitants, who were too much under the influence of their *Talapoy*, or priests.

NOTES

The body of the text has been transcribed with as little modification as possible. Glosses were printed in the margins of the 1759 edition; they have been moved to the first line of respective paragraphs and printed in italics. Names or terms that may be difficult to recognise or find in a dictionary are followed in square brackets with a modern equivalent or other identification. Everything that appears in square brackets has been added by the present editor. The original spellings and inconsistencies in usage have been retained as they appear in the original text. The only major modifications have been to omit the italics used in the original edition for many proper names, mostly of foreign origin, and to use italics for the titles of works cited in the notes.

The 1759 edition employed a system of two types of footnotes, distinguished by upper and lower case letters. The first type were references to published works. The second type were substantive comments by the compilers. To simplify the typesetting of the present edition, the two types have been combined into a single set of endnotes. (This arrangement unavoidably creates the impression of inconsistent use of the term ibid., which appears in the original only when the same source is cited more than once at the bottom of a single page.) The references cited in the footnotes are identified in square brackets and are included in the integrated references section of this volume.

All notes below (except those marked as the present editor's notes) appeared in the original 1759 edition.

1. Editor's note: The compilers struggle to define Laos as they comprehended it in 1759. European maps at that time still represented the central and northern Mekong valley as a somewhat narrow strip of territory, extending north in a nearly straight line and bounded to the east and west by parallel ranges of mountains. Very few toponyms were known to European cartographers. The compilers, in their definition, include not only the Lao kingdom of Lan Sang (in the central Mekong basin) but also four kingdoms that did not form part of Lan Sang: Lan Na and Nan (both in modern northern Thailand) and Chiang Khaeng and Sipsòng Panna (which were up-river from Luang Prabang).

2. Marini [1666] places on the west Pegu, on the north Ava, with the province named U [the U River area] and Lu [the Lü kingdoms of Chiang

Khaeng and Sipsòng Panna]; extending it still more north, to the borders of the people called Gnay [pronounced 'yai', apparently referring to a Chinese group in Yunnan].

3. Marini makes it extend from 14 degrees to 22 degrees 30 minutes, the space of 500 geographic miles from south to north. Marini *hist. de Tunq. et de Lao* [1666], p. 329.

4. That is 483 English miles one way, and 203 the other; its extent northward, along the borders of China, is marked in the Jesuits map at about one degree and a half.

5. Kaempfer [1727] says, it is separated from the neighbouring states by forests and deserts. *Voy. to Japan*, p. 26.

6. Marini *hist. Tunq. & Lao*, p. 331.

7. The Chineses call them Lau, and their country Lau Chwa [Lao Sawa], or the kingdom of Lau. Lao is the Portuguese pronunciation.

8. Ap. Purch. [*Purchas His Pilgrims*] vol. iii. p. 168 [see Cruz (1953) for a modern edition].

9. From this name, possibly, Pinto [1989] has made his Siamon and Mons, as before has been observed. Sion is the Portuguese way of pronouncing Siam.

10. Marini, ubi supr. p. 329.

11. Editor's note: Here, the compilers are trying to interpret fragments of information from informants who travelled separately in different parts of the interior, and a fundamental flaw in interpretation is the result. In Marini's time (the 1640s), Lan Sang was still a united kingdom. In or about 1707, it split into two kingdoms, with their capitals at Luang Prabang and Vientiane. Within another decade, Vientiane split into two kingdoms, with the establishment of independent Champasak in the south. The so-called northern Lao kingdom, which the compilers struggle to identify, was Sipsòng Panna, the kingdom of the Lü (another Tai-speaking group on the upper Mekong). Chinese caravans passed through Lü territory on their way south to the Shan kingdom of Chiang Tung and then farther south into Lan Na.

12. See before, p. 135. [Editor's note: This is a cross-reference by the compilers to the section of the *Universal History*, p. 135, on Jangoma (Chiang Mai), which is as follows:]

It hath been already observed, that Europeans know little or nothing of the dominions of the Avan empire, from its capital northwards, to the borders of China, either as to the different kingdoms and states it contains, or even the country and inhabitants. We only find, in general, from the journal of the four Chineses above-mentioned, that after they passed out of the provinces of Yun-nan they met with nothing but desarts [deserts, meaning unpopulated, forested territory] for five days together: but from thenceforward the country put on another aspect; and they found plantations along the river every day. Whether this be the condition of the country along the frontiers of the two empires of China and Ava, as far as the territories of the Laos, which bounds the latter eastward, we cannot determine, for want of sufficient information. We only know, in general, from the observations of the latitudes made at the capital of Ava, and along the borders of China, joined to the surveys of Tibet and Yun-nan, communicated by the Jesuits, that there must be a large space of country within the above-mentioned limits; and that, according to the tradition of the Siamites [Siamese], the Laos and the other neighbouring empires, it was formerly inhabited by a very powerful people, who had formed a dominion of vast extent.

These people were named Tay-yay ['Great Tai' meaning Shan], that is, the great freemen, or Franks; so they are called at present, both by the Chineses and Siameses. They were situated to the north of these latter; who acknowledging themselves to be descended from them, take the name of Tay-noe ['Lesser Tai' meaning the Thai to their south], or the little freemen. Their country is called by the Chineses, Ko-sang-pyi, and was, according to them, three months journey in length and governed by priests (Loubere [La Loubère 1693] *relat. Siam*, p. 7; Du Halde's *descr. China* [1736], vol. i. p. 62). These people were probably called by the Peguers, Sions or Siams [Siamese]; which, in their language, we are told signifies free: and from them, doubtless, the Portuguese took the name of Siam, for it is not known in the country itself. It is probable, likewise, that the Laos are descended from the same people; and hence they might have gotten the name of Sions, or Siams Maons; and the rather, as the Siamites are alleged to be derived from the Laos (Loubere, ubi sup.).

13. Much after the same manner that the Nile does Egypt, to which this country bears some resemblance, excepting that the Menan Kong [Mekong] does not overflow the neighbouring lands. Hence it is perhaps, that, as Kaempfer observes, the soil, being a fat clay, is so hard in summer that they thresh their rice on it.

14. Latitude 27 degrees 30 minutes Long. from Paris 96 degrees 40 minutes and 27 degrees 20 minutes west of Peking [Beijing].

15. Lat. 21 degrees 40 minutes Long. 99 degrees 5 minutes.

16. Editor's note: The Chinese spelling (in *pinyin*) is Jiulong Jiang, which means literally the 'River of Nine Dragons'. See Sila Viravong (1964: 7), who spells the name 'Kiu-lung' and equates it with nine Lao brothers and legendary origins of the Lao people.

17. Editor's note: Lê could refer to any of four places in the upper Mekong that were known to the Lao, Lü and Shan as La (or Müang La, see Phinith 1987: 244). The reference in the next paragraph to Lê as being situated near the uppermost navigable point on the Mekong (which was slightly above Chiang Saen), together with the subsequent statement that Lê was on the Mekong, suggests that the author is referring to the town of La on the La River, west of the Mekong and just south of the modern Burma-China boundary.

18. Afterwards, p. 64, a different river is said to pass by Kyang Kong and Lanjang. But the memoir, whence our account is taken, is not very exact.

19. Editor's note: Bonsak refers to the western channel of the Mekong delta, known as the Bassac channel. A town of the same name is mentioned frequently in Thai sources of the eighteenth and nineteenth century, at a site apparently mid-way along this channel, in the region of modern Cantho. This name should not be confused with the Lao town of Champasak, which was often shortened in spoken Lao to Pasak (spelled Bassac by the French).

20. Du Halde *descript. China*, vol. i. p. 63.

21. Editor's note: In the 1640s, Giovanni Maria Leria, an Italian Jesuit missionary, proposed that King Suriyawongsa construct a series of locks around the falls (Marini 1998: 4), to facilitate the movement of boats. The king rejected the plan for defensive reasons: the falls were a natural barrier to invasion by boat.

22. Mention is made of other rivers in Lao, as the Menan Tay, or Lay, which is full of rocks; it rises in a mountain near the city Kemarat [Chiang Tung], and falls into the Menan Kong [Mekong] near Bankiop. 2. The river of Siam, rises in mount Kyang-daw [Chiang Dao, north of Chiang Mai]. 3. The Kyang-hay [Chiang Mai?], or Lay, falls into the principal river of Siam, called Menan. Du Halde, *China* [1736], vol. i. p. 62.

23. Marini, ubi supr. p. 333, & seq.

24. Kaempfer, *hist. Japan*. p. 27.

25. Marini, p. 359.

26. In the journal, the word Meang [*müang*] is prefixed to the name of each place; but as it signifies no more than city, or colony, we have omitted it. This word is variously written by authors, Moang, Muang, Mong, Meuang, Mohang, Moan, and the like.

27. Kaempfer observes, p. 26, that the road from Siam to Lao is troublesome by land, on account of the high mountains; and by water, on account of the rocks and cataracts in the river Menan, which runs through Siam.

28. In the original Vi-nan, which, with the Vi reversed, makes Yun-nan.

29. Du Halde, ubi supr. p. 61.

30. Editor's note: The Thai used the term 'Lao' in reference to all the Tai-speaking peoples of the interior. This caravan route passed through Lan Na, Shan territory and Sipsòng Panna. All these are Tai-speaking areas, but this route was far to the west of the Lao kingdom of Lan Sang. The Chinese description was published by Du Halde (1736 i: 101–7).

31. Editor's note: Again, the authors are referring not to the Lao kingdom of Lan Sang but to the Tai-speaking kingdoms to the west and north of it. Luang Prabang is the only Lao town in this list.

32. Mr. [Jacques Nicolas] Bellin, in his map of *Siam, Tonquin, &c.* inserted in Mr. Prevost's *hist. gen. des voy.*[1747–80] tom. ix puts Lan-chang near half a degree higher.

33. Mentioned in the foregoing note.

34. As the map of the Jesuits was not published till after the time of Mr. De L'Isle, he is the more excusable.

35. Marini *hist. Tunq. & Lao*, p. 329, 359.

36. The Chineses in about 1652, and Marini in 1657 or 1658.

37. Editor's note: Ke-moy may refer to the Khmu (or Khamu) ethnic group of northern Laos.

38. Choisy, *voy. de Siam* [1687], p. 563.

39. Kaempfer, p. 27.

40. Editor's note: The peoples whom the compilers identify as 'Lahos' are the Shan and Lü, whose territories were farther up the Mekong and never part of the Lao kingdom of Lan Sang. Nor was the territory of Lan Na, with its capital at Chiang Mai.

41. Editor's note: Obviously the Chinese did not describe the Lao kingdom of Lan Sang because their route did not take them through any part of Lan Sang.

42. Marini, p. 337.

43. By unicorns, probably, are to be understood rhinoceroses.

44. Editor's note: This phenomenon of salt rising to the surface and covering the fields was noted by nineteenth-century travellers, particularly in the west-bank area north of the confluent of the Mun River and the Mekong. Up-river, however, salt was relatively scarce. Luang Prabang depended particularly on the salt works near the watershed of the mountains to its south-west (in the upper extremity of the Nan River basin). There were also important salt works around the watershed that now forms the boundary between the upper Ou River of Laos and the La River of China, although both sides of that watershed line were part of the Lü kingdom of Sipsòng Panna and did not belong to Lan Sang.

45. Marini, *hist. Tunq. & Lao*, p. 323, 335, & seq.

46. Ibid. p. 337 & seq.

47. The Gnay are a nation bordering on China, with which they have much commerce. Marini, p. 331. They seem to lie on the north-west part of the upper Lao.

48. Editor's note: The compilers are referring to the small, heavy-limbed hornless deer *Moschus moschiferus*. Musk is extracted from a sac beneath the abdominal skin of the male. The romanisation in the 1666 French edition is *ye hiam*, which may be Marini's Italian romanisation of a southern Chinese dialect. The mandarin term is *she xiang* and refers to the product itself: musk. The Chinese character *she* contains the 'deer' element and refers to the deer-like animal, whereas the Chinese term *xiang* refers to the product's 'fragrance'.

49. Marini, p. 337, & seqq.

50. Editor's note: Although this description might seem to be a fanciful traveller's tale, the writers were probably referring to the *pa bük*, or giant Mekong catfish.

51. Ibid. p. 341.

52. Kaempfer. ubi supr. p. 26.

53. Marini, p. 348, & 359.

54. The like may be said with regard to his account of Tong-king; also Borri's [1631], of Kochin-china; in short, the voyages of Alexander De Rhodes, and other missioners, into those countries.

55. Gio. Philip. Marini, a Jesuit, published several relations in Italian, in five books; among which those of *Tonquin* and *Lao* have been translated into French, and published in 1666. From a note of Mr. La Croze, *hist. du Christ* [1724], p. 51, the account of Lao seems to have been written by [Giovanni Maria] Leria, a Jesuit; for we have not seen the Italian of Marini.

56. De Faria, *Asia Portug.* [1695] vol. ii. p.11.

57. Editor's note: This is a description of Vientiane, adapted from Marini (1666), although Luang Prabang and Champasak were independent Lao capitals in 1759. The compilers had no inkling that the old kingdom of Lan Sang had become divided in or about 1707 and, shortly after that, divided again, with the formation of the kingdom of Champasak in the south. The latitude of Vientiane (which is 18 degrees 7 minutes) was measured accurately by Leria or one of his companions in the 1640s.

58. Or the Menan Kong; which, according to the Chinese journal, afterwards enters Kamboja, as if at no great distance.

59. Marini, p. 341, & seqq.

60. Or terminating with an *s*, Laos, Laus, Lahos, to denote more precisely the plural in our language. The country itself is also called Laos.

61. Editor's note: The compilers in 1759 had no information about the real northern Lao kingdom, with its capital in Luang Prabang. Everything in this section is about the Tai-speaking territories farther up the Mekong (Lan Na, Shan territory and Sipsòng Panna), which were not part of the Lao kingdoms. Some information in the next section likewise may be taken from accounts about these other Tai-speaking territories.

62. Editor's note: Chiang Mai and Chiang Saen were part of Lan Na. The upper limits of the kingdom of Siam were much farther south, near or below the latitude of Vientiane itself. It seems unlikely that Kyang-hay (seven days from the Mekong) was Chiang Rai.

63. *Moang, Mohang, Muhang*, or *Mong*, signifies also kingdom sometimes, in the language of these countries.

64. Du Halde, ubi supr. p. 61.

65. By Lang, perhaps, is to be understood Leng.

66. This must be but a small circumference, and no way consistent with the length of eight stages; since we are told these *senes*, or cords, are but of eight fathoms each. [Editor's note: The *sen* is an old Tai measure of distance equal to about 40 metres. The numbers given in this account show that some other measure was used. If 8 fathoms (48 feet) is correct, the *sen* here was about 14.6 metres, and 400 *sen* would have been 5.85 km. This measurement may refer to the circuit of the city walls of Chiang Tung.]

67. Editor's note: The kings of Chiang Tung during this period are listed in Mangrai (1981: 251). The dates in his chronicle are confused, but the ruler mentioned by the Chinese appears to be King Ingham, who succeeded when King Athit Racha (also known as Suriya Racha) died in early 1651.

68. Marini, p. 62, & seq.

69. If this be not an interpolation of the missioners, Vi-nan must be a different province or district from that of Yun-nan.

70. Ibid. p. 64, & seq.

71. According to this explanation, the name of Lahos, or Laos, is peculiar to this province; and from thence extended to the whole country.

72. Editor's note: These names appear in a 1687 document by envoys from this little kingdom ('Description du royaume du Laos' 1832: 416). Many of the spellings in the 1759 English edition are different from those of the French version. The geographical description shows clearly that this town was the capital of the Lü kingdom, Sipsòng Panna. The site at that time was west of the Mekong and slightly south-west of the present-day site of Chiang Rung.

73. The name of the city or province is here omitted; but what it should be we cannot determine, excepting perhaps Lan-chang, the country of elephants.

74. Perhaps the oxen; which of the country of Koko Nor between China and Tibet, are famous for their fine hair.

75. Marini, p. 62, & seq.

76. It is observable, that the Lahos are no-where called Lanjans through all this journal.

77. Marini, ibid.

78. There seems to be some mistake here; for there is not room for so large a country in these quarters.

79. Marini, p. 63, & seq.

80. Ibid. p. 345–350. In one place, De Faria says the Laos are very good-natured; but, in another, that they are very brutal and uncivilized: he allows however that they are honest, and have no thieves among them. See [Faria (1695)] *Portug. Asia*, vol. iii, p. 178 and vol. ii, p. 12.

81. De Faria says, their colour is white, and the women very beautiful. *Portug. Asia*, vol. iii, p. 178.

82. Kaempfer, p. 26.

83. Marini, p. 345, & seq.

84. Ibid. p. 343, & seq.

85. We are told by our author, p. 451, that sodomy, the great vice of Asia, is quite unknown to them; and yet some authors, as Fitch [1599], who was among the Lanjans, assure us otherwise; and that they wore bells inserted in their privities, like the Peguers, and other neighbouring nations, in order to prevent that crime. But this story of the bells is suspicious.

86. De Faria tells us, that they eat vermin; and that the people of Tongking despise them on that account. *Portug. Asia*, ubi supr.

87. Marini, p. 347, & seqq.

88. De Faria, vol. iii, p. 178.

89. Ibid. vol. ii, p. 12.

90. Editor's note: The practice of tattooing from the waist to the knee, or even to the ankle, was the custom of men in Lan Na and in lower-Mekong Lao towns.

91. Kaempfer, *Japan*, vol. i, p. 27.

92. Marini, p. 351, & seqq.

93. Ibid. p. 351.

94. Marini, p. 354, & seq.

95. Da Cruz, ap. Purch. [*Purchas His Pilgrimes*] vol. iii, p. 168 [see Cruz (1953)].

96. This perhaps was Jangoma which was taken about the year 1672 by the Siameses from the Lanjangs, to whom this remark more particularly relates.

97. Kaempfer, *Japan*, vol. i, p. 26.

98. Ibid.

99. Marini, p. 376, & seqq.

100. Marini, p. 378, & seqq.

101. Named Pon, Ta, Bo, Bà, Mi, Savan.

102. Marini, p. 380, & seqq.

103. Marini, p. 382, & seqq.

104. Almost the same thing is said of Sommona Kodom [Gautama the Buddha], by the Siameses. See hereafter [a subsequent chapter in the *Universal History*] the history of that lawgiver.

105. Marini, p. 385, & seqq.

106. Marini, p. 388, & seq.

107. If they cannot have these things by the indulgence of their religion, they find ways to obtain them; and by their licentious way of living become odious to the orientals, as hath been often remarked from the writings of the missioners themselves; so that our author may be suspected, as to what he says here, and in other places, upon the same subject.

108. Marini, p. 389, & seqq.

109. Marini, p. 391, & seqq.

110. Is this worse than the evasion of Popish priests; who, when the diseased people, after praying to their saints, find no relief, to solve the objection, pretend it is because they had not faith.

111. Marini, p. 394, & seq.

112. Marini, p. 395–399.

113. Ibid. p. 341.

114. Marini, p. 401, & seqq.

115. Editor's note: The Carthusian order was founded in 1086 by St. Bruno, who established his monastery in the Chartreuse valley near Grenoble in France. St. Romuald founded the Camaldule order in 1012.

116. Marini, p. 405, & seqq.

117. This was customary among the Roman priests, according to the sarcasm of Cicero: *Capite et superciliis semper est rasus, ne unum pilum boni viri habere dicar* [Their heads and eyebrows are always shaved—not a single manly hair to be noted].

118. Marini, p. 408, & seqq.

119. May not the same be applied to the Romanists [Catholics]?

120. This is not probable, since the religion of Shaka was in the world 1000 years before Christ: more probably therefore, that the church of Rome borrowed this, and many other ceremonies, from thence.

121. One would think our author is reflecting on those of his own religion; since this is as much the case with them as the Lanjans.

122. This Jesuit draws a frightful picture of them; as it were to exceed what is reported of the Romish [Catholic] monks and hermits, in these parts of the world.

123. Marini, p. 412, & seqq.

124. Marini does not explain what sort of printing is in use with the Lanjans. [Editor's note: Marini was referring to Buddhist texts on palm-leaves, which were copied by hand. Mechanical reproduction by printing presses was not introduced until more than two centuries later.]

125. Marini, p. 415, & seq.

126. Marini, p. 419, & seqq.

127. Marini, p. 416, 421, & seqq.

128. Marini, p. 427, & seq.

129. This, which the Romish [Catholic] clergy would have pass, and, among the laity, does pass, as almost an infallible proof of the holiness both of the priest and his religion, in their church; is here treated by the Jesuit as it ought to be, that is, no proof at all.

130. Yet remember, for all these signs of religion and piety, that they are idolatrous priests, and of profligate morals: so that a sanctified outside may be consistent with a wicked heart, and is no proof of goodness.

131. The Romish [Catholic] priests are more indulgent, and give much more extensive dispensations.

132. Marini, p. 430–436.

133. See the conformity more at large in Loubere's relation of Siam, p. 135.

134. Mr. La Croze says, they differed in this point only.

135. See *new gen. collect. of voy. and trav.* vol. iv. p. 461 [Green (1757)].

136. Alex. de Rhodes thinks, Shaka came from Siam; Navarette [1962] says, from Ceylon.

137. *Relat. of Siam*, p. 136 [La Loubère (1693)].

138. Knox [1681], *hist. Ceylon*, aliquo loco.

139. La Croze, *Chret. des Ind.* p. 500.

140. Loubere, par. i. c. xxii. p. 130 [La Loubère (1693)].

141. See La Croze, ubi supra.

142. Clem. Alex. Strom. [Titus Flavius Clemens, known as Alexandrinus and as Clement of Alexandria]. 1.i. p. 529. edit. Potteri. ap. La Croze [1724], p. 492.

143. Lib. i. adv. Jovin [treatise by Saint Jerome published in Latin (AD 393) with the title *Contra Jovinianum* (Treatise against Jovinian)].

144. Who are the followers of Tatian, and Justin Martyr.

145. Clem. Alex. ubi supra.

146. Lib. xv. [see Strabo (1916)].

147. Ziegen Balg. ap. La Croze *Chret. des Indes* [1724], p. 493, & seqq.

148. Ibid. p. 497. It seems not a little odd to us, that the end of Wishtnû's sixth incarnation should be to preach down the religion of Budda, and yet that he should personate him, or assume his form, in the ninth, as if he found no fault with Budda, but his worshippers.

149. Pons [1743] ap. *Lettr. Ediff.* tom. xxvi. p. 247.

150. La Croze, ubi supra, p. 497, 499.

151. Mr. Loubere [La Loubère (1693)] informs us, in his relation of Siam, chap. iii. that the year 1689, beginning in December 1688, was the 2233 from Sommona Kodom's death. [Editor's note: The calendar year common to South-East Asian Buddhist countries began on 10 April 1688, ended on 9 April 1689 and was the year BE 2231. The year itself did not begin in December, although the month known to the Lao and Thai as the 'first' lunar month began in November and ended in December 1688.]

152. Marini *hist. de Tunq. & Lao*, p. 358, & seq.

153. Marini, p. 346, & seq.

154. Ibid. p. 349.

155. Marini, p. 370, & seqq.

156. Marini, p. 357, & seqq.

157. Marini, p. 361, & seqq.

158. Marini, ubi supra, p. 356.

159. Editor's note: This information is obviously oral history recorded by Leria at Vientiane in the 1640s. After the collapse of Burmese power at Pegu at the end of the 1590s, contemporary European observers remarked on the depopulation of the Pegu countryside at that time. Some of the deserted villages must have been places where the Lao had been forced to settle in the 1570s, as captives of the Burmese. *The Chiang Mai Chronicle* (Wyatt and Wichienkeeo 1995: 124) records the movement of Lao people from Pegu across Lan Na territory towards Lan Sang in 1598/9. Prince Damrong (1914: 672–3) thought this flight was part of a bigger movement of Lao captive labourers out of Burma, Chiang Mai and Ayutthaya and back to Lan Sang.

160. Marini, p. 366, & seqq.

7

THE QUY HOP ARCHIVE:
VIETNAMESE-LAO RELATIONS REFLECTED IN BORDER-POST DOCUMENTS DATING FROM 1619 TO 1880

TRAN VAN QUY

Quy Hop is the name of a historic border post in the mountainous western part of Nghe-tinh Province. It is also one of the names of the trail that has been used since ancient times to cross the mountains between the northern coast of Vietnam and Laos. Quy Hop was formerly an important frontier district (*chau*) on the Vietnamese-Lao border. When it was still an administrative unit, its territory encompassed part of present-day Quang-binh District, part of Huong-khe District and some hamlets scattered in the Truong Son mountain chain, which separated the Vietnamese settlements on its eastern side from the Lao settlements to the west of the cordillera. Quy Hop ceased to be a territorial unit after the Vietnamese revolution of 1945, when frontier districts were eliminated from the administrative system.

Today, the Quy Hop post is in the district (*huyen*) of Huong-khe. The site of the old post, on the right bank of the Tiem Stream (Rao Tiem), was also once the site of the Cho Tiem market place. On the opposite side of the stream was the Cho Gia market, which is still a rural market place today. The latter market is in the hamlet of Trung Thanh, which is part of Huong Vinh village, and it is 10 kilometres from the town of Huong-khe, the site of the Chu Le railway station.

Across the present international boundary from the former border post are the old Lao administrative centres of Kham Muan and Kham Koet, in the basin of the Kadin and Theun Rivers. From

239

Quy Hop, the Lao hamlet of Maka[1] is a three-day walk along the historical foot-path—known also as the Trim Treo trail—and Tha Khaek on the Mekong is only an additional two days' walk away.

THE BORDER-GATE POST

The history of Quy Hop can be traced back to the eleventh century, under the Ly dynasty of Vietnam. From the fifteenth to the nineteenth centuries, the border post was under the supervision of a Vietnamese commander (*tong binh*). The local troops (*tho binh*) were organised under a system of conscription handed down from father to son. They made their living by tilling paddy fields in the village and extracting whatever goods and money that they could from the traders passing back and forth across the border.

In addition to his duties related to the border post, the Vietnamese commander was concurrently the governor (*phu dao*) of the frontier district and the mandarin (*tong su*) in charge of Lao affairs. In his capacity as a mandarin, he was responsible for transmitting orders to the heads of the various Lao administrative units within the kingdom of Vientiane. Such orders came either from the central government or from the governor of Nghe-anh, who was the imperial Vietnamese delegate (*Do doc Dinh Nhat hau*) responsible for supervising relations between Vietnam and the Lao kingdom of Vientiane, which was treated by Vietnam as a vassal state.

THE ARCHIVE

The chest of documents found at Quy Hop contains official archives from generations of officials who held this multi-purpose position of post commander, governor and mandarin. The chest was discovered in 1974 in the family temple of Duke Tran Phuc Hoan. The duke, who died in the eighteenth century, was a remarkable officer who managed to make the Trim Treo trail a secure and reliable avenue of communication for economic and military purposes. A temple dedicated to the duke and his wife still stands at

Quy Hop. It is said that a temple in his honour still exists on the Lao side of the border, too. Many of the duke's descendants distinguished themselves in the resistance that was waged against the Thai by the Vietnamese-Lao alliance at the end of the eighteenth century.

The people who are responsible for maintaining the family temple of Tran Phuc Hoan report that the archive was once larger than it is now. Only half of the original documents have survived. Over a period of many years, the other half was used to roll joss-sticks and cigarettes.

Since 1981 the present author has published numerous articles about the discovery of the Quy Hop documents and their importance to the study of the region's history.[2] The documents are dated, and there is considerable continuity in the items. The oldest piece is dated 1619, in the reign of Vinh To (1619–28), and the last one is as recent as 1880. Almost all of the materials are official documents that deal with the public functions of the successive officials who served as post commander, governor and mandarin. The documents include written orders, mandates and notices from higher authorities—from the prefecture, the province and the central government's Ministry of Finance during the Le (1418–1788), Tay-son (1788–1802) and Nguyen (1802–1945) dynasties. Also included are royal edicts of the emperors Canh Thinh (1792–1802), Thieu Tri (1841–7) and Tu Duc (1847–83). Many types of documents, originating from lower levels, are in the form of requests, reports and registries of tax-payers and taxes. The correspondence between Vietnamese and Lao authorities is particularly abundant.

Considering the rarity of provincial documents from the period encompassed by this archive, the quantity of documents is impressive. There are altogether 300 items (a total of 700 pages) written in Vietnamese using the *nom* script, which is a script based on Chinese characters that are modified to transcribe the Vietnamese language. Items in the Lao language and script have likewise been preserved. All Vietnamese pieces were written with a brush using Chinese ink, on a special paper known as *giay gio*, which was manufactured in Vietnam from the bark of *Aquilaria crassna*.

The documents preserved at Quy Hop date from the times of many emperors who reigned over Vietnam during the two and a half centuries that the archive encompasses. These emperors include Vinh To, Ao Khanh, Vinh Huu and Canh Hung of the Le dynasty; Thai Duc, Quang Trung and Canh Thinh of the Tay-son dynasty; and Gia Long, Minh Mang, Thieu Tri and Tu Duc of the Nguyen dynasty. An uninterrupted series of items records events during the reign of Canh Hung (Le Hien Tong, r. 1740–86) of the Le dynasty. The documents bearing dates from 1802 to 1880 provide a rich source of information about the early part of the Nguyen dynasty.

All documents in the Quy Hop archive are primary sources. Many items bear the original seals in red ochre, affixed to a fine quality paper that was reserved strictly for use by mandarins alone. Although some items are copies rather than the original documents, they are copies made first-hand for official use, which leaves little doubt that the texts were completely and accurately reproduced.

The documents are concise and deal with a broad range of subjects, including military, economic, administrative, political, diplomatic and financial matters, as well as aspects of everyday life and local customs. Some examples of these subjects include references to the system of local troops (*tho binh*); payments of taxes; preparations for a military campaign; lists of exiled citizens; the reception of Lao missions; trade with the Lao; an offer of elephants; tribute received from the Lao in the form of their local products; and sales of elephants, cattle and paddy fields. Among the local administrative duties reflected in the archive are papers dealing with village regulations, inheritances, local grievances and even sharing fish that were raised in the common ponds. Social and community issues are likewise revealed in papers that deal with problems such as selling children for purposes of adoption and with rituals such as festivals dedicated to the tutelary spirits.

For the historiographical study of the traditional *nom* system of writing in Chinese characters, these documents offer a unique opportunity, because of the colloquial words they contain and their references to indigenous names that are unknown today, including some Lao names. Nearly all the documents are in the *nom* script. Some items are written in mixed Chinese and *nom*. The writers, who lived during a span of three centuries, represent many professions. Duke Pham Dinh Trong, for example, was a physician. Some writers were highly educated intellectuals, such as the great mandarins of the Trinh administration. Others, including scantly educated officials and barely literate labourers, reflect the lower levels of literate society, whose writings are characterised by whimsical styles and script.

The archive contains many texts from the period of the Tay-son rulers, who exercised power from the 1770s to 1802. In general, texts dating from this period are scarce in Vietnam, because of the revenge taken by Emperor Gia Long (r. 1802–20), who founded the Nguyen dynasty. The first discovery of important Tay-son texts was made more than forty years ago by Hoang Xuan Han at the family temple of La-son Phu-tu (Hoang 1950). The Quy Hop site is the second such discovery and is the more important of the two, because the Quy Hop archive contains three times as many Tay-son documents as the archive of La-son Phu-tu.

The extant documents in the Quy Hop archive are crammed with chronological details that are valuable for researchers. As a local archive, they provide a virtual encyclopaedia of facts and events relating to a rural society that has almost vanished today. No similar treasury of documentary materials has been found, thus far, that contains such a considerable volume of material, offers such richness of detail and provides a perspective on such a long period of Vietnamese history.

TRADING RELATIONS WITH THE LAO

The Quy Hop archive contains the best collection of historical materials discovered thus far that deal with Vietnamese-Lao relations. It provides rich details and many clues to events in Lao history that are unchronicled elsewhere. For instance, it documents the determined resistance, with Vietnamese collaboration, pursued by the Lao against Thai military intervention in the latter part of the eighteenth century. This movement was organised and led by King Nanthasen's (r. 1781–94) brothers, who established a stronghold in the mountainous Phac-bat area.[3] These names, like some other Lao names that appear in the following pages, are transcribed phonetically in this study from the Chinese and *nom* scripts that are used in the original documents.

Among the many Lao administrative divisions with which the Vietnamese had direct contact, prior to the destruction of the Lao capital in 1828, the important ones are mentioned in the archive according to the Vietnamese version of their names. Not all these names have been identified, but a few identifications seem obvious from the context of the documents. The name Tran Ninh was still in use well into the present century. It is the Vietnamese name for Siang Khwang—the Phuan kingdom in the plateau region north-west of Vinh, which was treated by Vientiane as a vassal state. The place called Lac Hoan is almost certainly a Vietnamese rendering of the Lao 'Lakhòn', which is a shortened, modified name for Nakhòn Phanom. It is logical that this name appears frequently in the records, because the powerful governor of this town once controlled not only a long stretch of the Mekong above and below the town but also much of the left-bank hinterlands that lie immediately west and south-west of Quy Hop. Trinh Cao is difficult to identify, other than as a town on or near the Mekong in the Nakhon Phanòm region.

Among the Quy Hop documents are three official Tay-son texts concerning the expansion of trade with the Lao kingdom. The first text is an order amending the tax regime at Quy Hop, which was called literally the 'border gate' leading to and from the Lao kingdom. This text, written in the reign of Thai Duc, is dated 1 September 1787. It was written in Chinese by Ho Tuong Quan, the imperial delegate and administrator of Huong-son District.[4] The document conveyed the following instructions to the officials at Quy Hop:

> The first step towards peace for the country is to loosen the constraints on trade. You are therefore instructed to abolish the usual payment of visa fees on people as well as the payment of tax on grain.

The second official text, likewise in Chinese, is dated 30 November 1792 (the seventeenth day, tenth month, fifth year of the reign of Quang Trung). In this document, Du Loc Hau, the imperial delegate, who was also the deputy governor of Nghe-anh Province, sent the following instructions to two officials in Quy Hop:

> When the inhabitants of the regions beyond Quy Hop bring their pigs to sell, they pass through your border post. I would like each of you to buy three pigs for me and to send them to me at the provincial office. Your costs will be reimbursed.

The third text includes instructions to lower the taxes on imported water buffaloes. It is in the form of a mandate from the imperial delegate and governor of Nghe-anh—Do Doc Dinh *quan cong* (Duke Dinh, Admiral)—and it is addressed to an official of the central government's ministry of finance who was posted to Quy Hop. The mandate is dated 19 April 1795 (the first day, third month, third year of the reign of Canh Thinh) and bears a red seal. It says that

> The price of a buffalo has been 15 ligatures[5] up to the present time, and buffaloes have been taxed at a rate of 1.5 ligatures each. The regulations are hereby changed as follows. Buffaloes shall be divided into two categories: big buffaloes shall be priced at 10 ligatures, and others shall be priced at 7 or 8 ligatures. The tax shall be calculated at 10 per cent. Small buffaloes following their mothers shall be free of tax in order to encourage trade.

According to the *Viet Su Thong Giam Cuong Muc* (1957 xix: 55), famine struck the province of Nghe-anh in 1777. In response, the mandarin of the province, Nguyen Khan, proposed to the central government that the border of Quy Hop be opened to free trade. The chronicles note that this proposal was approved. The official taxes were thereafter paid only once, at a specified place along the commercial route, and they were acknowledged by an official receipt that local officials could not avoid issuing. The officials continued in an unrestrained way, however, to extract 'visa fees' from traders and to confiscate portions of their goods in transit.

Trade through Quy Hop thus continued to be obstructed by the 'visa fees' and the confiscation of merchandise. The Quy Hop border establishment consisted of the principal post (at present-day Cho Tiem) and also a line of subordinate posts dotting the forest along the Trim Treo trail. Only 5 kilometres from the principal post, the subordinate post of Dong Ngang was erected for the purpose of collecting the 'visa fees', and another post at Dong Tuan was 10 kilometres farther along the trail. This line of posts enabled the petty officials and their soldier-guards to 'pillage' the caravans of traders to a certain extent. Ten years prior to the opening of the border, Nguyen Khan, the co-governor of Nghe-anh Province, realised that it would be desirable to open the border crossing at Quy Hop to a freer system of trade, but he did nothing to carry out his idea.

Nguyen Van Hue—the general and populist hero of the late eighteenth century, who had just come to occupy Nghe-anh—eliminated the obstruction by an almost radical measure. The September 1787 text focused on the problem of winning the hearts of the people with a policy of developing trade with Vietnam, as well as on providing an economic basis for the Vietnamese-Lao alliance.

The second Tay-son era text mentioned above demonstrates that the border crossing of Quy Hop ceased to be isolated and that trade along this route was flourishing in the early 1790s. Pigs sold at Quy Hop must have been cheap and plentiful, because a provincial mandarin issued orders to have them purchased six at a time. Since the mandarin ordered such purchases at Quy Hop, and since transport of the pigs down-river from Quy Hop took two days and nights, it is reasonable to conclude that pigs were relatively inexpensive at the border post. Otherwise, the mandarin would not have bothered to place such an order.

The third Tay-son text is more explicit. By the time this text was written, Nguyen Van Hue had become emperor (Quang Trung, r. 1788–92), and Quy Hop had become an important centre of trade. It had a permanent tax office, headed by an official from the Ministry of Finance. The development of trade with the Lao kingdom had become state policy decreed by the emperor and reinforced by his successors, in actions such as the 1795 reduction in the import tax levied on water buffaloes from the Lao kingdom.

It is clear that this policy was mutually advantageous for the economies of the two countries. From the viewpoint of the Lao who lived in adjacent areas—across the mountains in the territory of the kingdom of Vientiane—a policy of free circulation through the border post allowed them to export a variety of animals, including pigs, horses, buffaloes, elephants, monkeys and bears. They were also able to export goods that were gathered or produced in the Lao kingdom, such as ivory, rhinoceros horn, bones of tigers and other wild animals, opium, grain, beeswax, honey, tree resins, *Aquilaria crassna* bark (for paper-making), cardamoms and fine fibres used for sewing straw hats. In turn, the Lao imported from Vietnam a variety of products, including salt, silk and other textiles, large knives, metal ploughing implements, copper pots, paper, ink and medicines. Such products were used by all classes among the Lao, and in addition many luxury items were imported for use by the upper classes.

Quy Hop was clearly an important market place for goods traded between the lowlands of Vietnam and the Lao kingdom, and among villages on the slopes of the cordillera. Communications from Quy Hop east to the port of Hoi Thong (present-day Ben Thuy, near Vinh) were easy. From this point, foreign traders, especially the Chinese who had resided for many generations in various trading centres of Vietnam, could reach Quy Hop. There they siphoned off, at its source, some of the wealth of the trade in valuable products of Lao origin. Thus, for more than two centuries, products of the Vientiane kingdom were exported via Quy Hop and then went by ship to lands across the sea, wherever the Chinese and other foreign merchants traded.

THE HISTORIC TRIM TREO TRAIL

Quy Hop was linked directly to Lao territory across the cordillera by the Trim Treo trail. It was easy to walk and to lead (or ride) horses and elephants along this trail, which led to the site of present-day Tha Khaek on the Mekong. From that point, it was easy to travel by boat to Vientiane and other Lao market towns along the river, or to go overland across the broad plain that led west towards the Thai kingdom. Merchandise from Vietnam, China and other countries (including imports from Europe) was carried along this trail, destined for numerous parts of Laos and other inland states farther up the Mekong.

Three or four historical trails lead from the coast of Vietnam across the cordillera and down to the banks of the Mekong. Among these, the route through Quy Hop offered the easiest passage and was best endowed with resources essential to travel in the past. The Trim Treo trail via Quy Hop follows the Xan Stream (Rao Xan), which is an upper branch of the Ngan Sau River of Vietnam, until it reaches the watershed in the mountains. It then follows the crest of the mountains for a certain distance, before turning down along the Nòi River (Nam Nòi, a tributary of the Theun) on the Lao side and continuing across to the town Yommarat. This route was the most convenient corridor of communication discovered by the Vietnamese and Lao, to link the South China Sea and the interior of South-East Asia.[6]

This particular trail winds through the mountains at a comparatively low elevation. The nearby peaks are much higher: Trim rises 800 metres above sea level, Treo Ma more than 750 metres and Treo Con 700 metres. The trail is not as rugged as the other routes through the cordillera.[7] Most important, in the past as well as the present, buffaloes, elephants and horses could be grazed and watered easily along this route, which winds past grassy hillsides and shallow mountain streams. The fact that other trails across the cordillera were less well endowed with these natural advantages helps to explain why economic activities were concentrated along the Quy Hop route. For these reasons, the Vietnamese chronicles[8] note that Lao caravans, whenever they were headed towards destinations in Vietnam, always used the trail by way of Quy Hop.

About twelve centuries ago, Jiadan (730–805), a Chinese invader who lived during the time of the Tang dynasty, reached the country of the Ai Lao people, which is believed to be the precursor of the Lao kingdom. In his account of the route that he followed, he wrote that he arrived in this land along 'a mountainous trail west of old

Nghe-anh'[9]—almost certainly the one later known as Trim Treo, which passes through Quy Hop. Numerous modern scholars have attempted to identify this famous trail. Among them are the French scholars Henri Maspero and Paul Pelliot, the German Adolf Bastian, the Dane Erik Seidenfaden, the Chinese Hoang Thinh Chuong and the Vietnamese Dao Duy Anh. Although many theories have been proposed, the conclusion reached by Dao (1964: 198) seems to be the only one that is correct, although a few minor refinements in his description are necessary.

Dao concluded that the trail ran through the scrub forest of Quy Hop, rather than following the route of modern Highway 8, which leads to the Kaeo Nüa mountain pass. Contrary to Dao's assumption, however, the trail began at Quy Hop and not at Vu Quang. It should be noted, moreover, that French and even contemporary Vietnamese cartographers have persisted in spelling this name 'Phu Quan', which is incorrect. This error is a century old and is the result of poor transcription by French cartographers when they attempted to record the historic name Vu Quang. It is on an upper tributary stream of the Ngan Sau (which is marked 'Rao Xan' on modern maps) and not on the Ngan Truoi.

The trail itself was accurately described by Le Quang Dinh, the minister responsible for the armies of Emperor Gia Long, in his textbook on military geography, which was issued in 1806 with the title *Nhat Thong Du Dia Chi* ('General Geography of Unified Vietnam').[10] The soldiers posted in those days at Quy Hop must have trod every inch of this trail through the forested mountains, and they measured the distances along the trail with a standard Vietnamese measuring rod (called a *tam*), which was 3.2 metres long. Although their data can be taken only as an approximation by modern standards, their systematic measurements give precise information about a trail that was relatively long.

The distance from the main post at Quy Hop to the subordinate post at Dong Ngang was 2,994 rods (9.6 kilometres). After a crossing a shallow stream that was nearly 10 metres wide (3 rods), the soldiers proceeded an additional 1,957 rods (6.3 kilometres) before reaching the hill-slopes of Dong Ngang. The total length of the trail from Quy Hop to Con-pha-vinh,[11] on the Lao side of the mountains, was 44,990 rods (144 kilometres). While traversing this route, the soldiers, traders and other travellers had to make a total of 64 crossings of streams and rivers. The military geography even recorded the widths of the waterways, indicating that travellers had to cross a total of 487 rods (1,558 metres) of water along the way.

VIETNAMESE-LAO ALLIANCE, 1792–3: PLANS FOR A TAY-SON CAMPAIGN AGAINST THE THAI

Historical works on the Tay-son period have neglected the important role of Quy Hop and its commercial exchanges with the interior of South-East Asia. Three documents in the archive deserve special attention, because they were written during the Tay-son period and reveal numerous facts about relations with Laos that were previously unknown to scholars. These documents are an important resource for research into the Vietnamese-Lao alliance against the Thai during this period.

One letter was written in Lao script by Chao Chiam and is addressed to the governor of Nghe-anh. Chiam is identified in the correspondence as the youngest brother of the king (Nanthasen, who reigned at Vientiane 1781–94) and appears to have been the future King Anuwong (who reigned 1805–28). The original letter was relayed to the governor and no longer exists. But a copy of the translation in *nom* script was retained by the Quy Hop commander and preserved in the archive. The copy is dated, according to the Lao calendar, 'the eleventh day of the moon in the eleventh month of the animal-year [rat], the era-year 154 [Lesser Era 1154]', which probably corresponds to 26 September 1792.

The words of the Lao are sincere, simple and spontaneous. But the sentences (at least in the Vietnamese translation) are long and difficult to understand. The complex composition in Vietnamese probably reflects the very imperfect understanding that the two sides had of each other's languages. There are also some lacunae and undecipherable words, indicated by dots in the quotation below. The key passage from Chao Chiam's letter is as follows:

On the last occasion, I instructed [the Lao officials] Phia Chan-the-pha and Phia Man-kha-thi to escort Phoc-na-khi[12] to visit your excellency and to report that the Vientiane kingdom has been invaded by the Thai. The king [Nanthasen]—who is confined to the capital, subject to restraints and prevented from taking any initiative or action—told me to take command of the affairs of the kingdom and to organise a resistance against the Thai from the mountainous region of Phac-bat. . . .[13] Your excellency despatched eight soldiers from the post of Quy Hop to bring us written orders with four dragon-design robes, four turbans, two skirts and four gift boxes.

We three brothers [the Lao king and his two younger brothers] and Sam-pha-mat [the governor of Nakhòn Phanom][14] agree with the contents of your letter. We are very happy with it. I have been designated to come and pay homage to your excellency. Unfortunately, I am in charge of the affairs of the kingdom, and if I come in person to pay homage to Your excellency in Dai Viet [Vietnam],[15] the Thai will surely become aware of it. The Thai will then surely behead our relatives, our women and our children, and they will massacre our compatriots. Thus we dare not wear the dragon-design gowns or the turbans you have bestowed on us, for fear of being killed by the Thai. For the same reason, the correspondence your excellency addresses to us, if intercepted by the Thai, will create difficulties for us.

Concerning your military detachment, which is now camped in Tran Ninh [Siang Khwang], we beg you to withdraw these forces. For if your forces remain there, the Thai will force the king in Vientiane to launch an attack [against them], which would be an act of disloyalty [by the Lao] towards the court of Dai Viet. To keep faith, I have given orders to my representatives to take an oath before your excellency in my name. As our big-brother country, may Dai Viet demonstrate its fraternal affection for us, as in the past, and may it come to our aid for the repatriation of our relatives and the men, women and children who are being held in the Thai kingdom.[16]

We beg the great army of Dai Viet to come and to defeat the Thai. If the army should arrive by way of Châu Ba Dong,[17] I will go to meet it, since I am in Phac-bat. If it comes from the direction of Lac Hoan [Nakhòn Phanom] and passes through. . . , it will be received and escorted by the chief of Lac Hoan and Sam-pha-mat. In the direction of Müang . . . Ba Dong, the escort is entrusted to Thoc . . . Bon, who will organise the passage along the Mekong. The movement of the army from Tran Ninh [Siang Khwang] towards Vientiane is, for mercy's sake, to be postponed, because the Vientiane king is still there [in the capital]. In the event that he is forced by the Thai to attack you, it will not be a voluntary act against Dai Viet.

The promptest arrival of the great army is crucial. The twelfth lunar month [mid-December 1792 to mid-January 1793] is the most favourable time. You should inform me by written ordinance about the date and directions of the arrival of the great army, and with this information I can make preparations to receive it. In combat, the Lao and the Thai could easily be mistaken, each for the other. And therefore, I ask you to decide about means of avoiding any trouble in such a circumstance.

Another letter was written by the governor of Nghe-anh Province and is addressed to three Lao officials: Chao Na (maybe Prince Inthasom), Chao Chiam (maybe the future King Anuwong) and Chao Sam-pha-mat (probably the governor of Nakhòn Phanom). A copy of this letter in *nom* script is preserved in the Quy Hop archive and is dated 16 November 1792.[18] The original letter was translated into Lao, before being forwarded to the Lao authorities. It provides a unique record of the official Vietnamese attitude concerning events along the Mekong, in response to the recent arrival of Thai forces in Vientiane's territory:

A couple of months ago, you sent an ambassador and a deputy-ambassador, who reported that the Thai invaded the fortress of Vientiane. You expressed also your distress at not being authorised to come to the [Vietnamese] capital Phu-xuan [Hué] to beg the court to send the [Vietnamese] army [to the aid of Vientiane]. These assertions are incorrect.

At that time, I sent seven men to Lac Hoan [Nakhòn Phanom] and Trinh Cao, to gather intelligence about the situation. But you had no reliable guides for them. My men were led astray among the caves and forests, and they could not make reliable observations concerning the piratical Thai. We have to be cautious, because every military mission is costly for the country.

This time I am sending four soldiers. You will have to escort two of them to Vientiane, so that they can reconnoitre and observe the Thai. Then you will escort these four soldiers back, together with the intelligence information gathered by them. I will analyse it, and I will then write to you again, so that you can store up enough food for the passage of the great [Vietnamese] army.

The third Tay-son period document is a brief notation, written in *nom* script by an officer at Quy Hop to his superiors on 23 December 1792.[19] It describes the reception given to three groups of Lao officials, who had just arrived with a 'message of extreme urgency concerning the situation with the piratical Thai'. The minute says:

The delegation [from] . . . comprises Chao Ma-phu and Chao Ma-miat, accompanied by a number of lower ranking officials (*phia*) and their followers, officers and soldiers—26 people altogether. The delegation [from]. . . comprises two people. The delegation from Trinh Cao comprises Governor Cat-van-but, the commander, the deputy governor, lower-ranking officials, interpreters and their followers, officers and soldiers—13 people altogether.

The post of Quy Hop presented brocaded official gowns to Cat-van-but, the commanders and the governors. Others received five *thuoc* of fine fabrics [1 *thuoc* = 0.4 metre] and 10 ligatures of silver.

It is clear that this minute refers to representatives from the three zones of resistance in the Lao kingdom, who were on mission to seek military aid in Vietnam to combat the Thai invasion of their country.

The last document is a copy of a letter from the imperial delegate (the *Do doc Dinh Nhat hau*) of the Tay-son emperor and is addressed to Chao Chiam and the chiefs of villages in the Lao kingdom. The original text is dated 22 December 1792,[20] and an additional date (24 December 1792) was added by the Quy Hop post commander to the copy in the archive (in *nom* script). The following passage from this letter indicates that a Vietnamese army was preparing for a major and imminent campaign across the mountains, for the purpose of driving the Thai from Vientiane and away from the banks of the Mekong:

> Today, I have instructed, Lang Nhat Hau, the commander of Quy Hop, to lead thirty trail-blazers to gather intelligence in the field about the affairs of the Thai, in preparation for military action. Afterward, the great rear guard will follow them. We have resolved to annihilate the foreign invaders, so as to re-establish peace in your land.
>
> I would like you to care for this advance party and to assist them in amassing provisions for the great army that will follow. Then, you will send men to co-operate with Lang Nhat Hau to prepare the trail for the attack to be launched against the rear flank [of the Thai forces]. Please deploy all of your forces for this challenging campaign, so that your native lands can rekindle their fires and so that your hamlets and villages can regain the prosperity enjoyed in the times of your ancestors. I have faith and confidence in you.

The Quy Hop archive regrettably does not provide any further information about the progress of the campaign. The immediate results of the campaign, which must have been set in motion early in 1793, are reflected in the contents of five brief and concise letters that have survived at Quy Hop. All bear dates in August 1793, were written by Lao officials in charge of five Lao regions and are addressed to the imperial delegate. The original letters were written in Lao and were translated into Vietnamese by the chief of the hamlet of Tu Cam. Only one text in Lao has been preserved in the archive; the others are copies of translations in Vietnamese.

The governor of Trinh Cao, named Cat-van-but, reported on an inspection mission by his men and a Vietnamese official:

> Some days ago, I sent my men on a tour to inspect the area of Lung-Khong.[21] They observed nothing. This time, Thong Yai, who was sent by Your Excellency on a mission around the local districts, likewise encountered no [Thai] pirates. He visited us on the fifth day

of the seventh month [11 August 1793]. I have the honour to report
to you by this modest and respectful note.

Another report, written by Chao Ap-la-sa (possibly the *chao
uparasa*, the Lao heir apparent), is even briefer:

> No [Thai] pirates. The countryside is secure, thanks to the beneficence
> of Your Excellency. If pirates do appear around here, I will inform
> the chief of the hamlet.

A Lao official whose name is not recorded wrote in the same
vein on 9 August 1793:[22]

> The chief of the hamlet has charged his men with the responsibility
> of escorting your excellency's two representatives, who have come to
> reconnoitre at Chau But. There is nothing to report. The countryside
> is secure. If pirates do appear, I will inform you in writing.

There is also a note, written by Chao Phoc-na-khi, reporting that

> The entire kingdom is peaceful. In Vientiane, there are no pirates. If
> the pirates do appear, I will inform you in writing.

Although this file is very incomplete and provides no details of
the campaign waged by the Vietnamese army down to the Mekong,
the extant documents demonstrate the basic facts. A major campaign
took place early in 1793, by which time the last Tay-son emperor,
Quang Trung, was already dead. The campaign was conducted by
the Nghe-anh governor, who was concurrently the imperial delegate
reponsible for Vietnamese-Lao relations, and it ended with a victory
for the Vietnamese forces.

CONCLUDING REMARKS

Trade along the Trim Treo trail was flourishing at the end of the
eighteenth century, and the movement of merchandise was

substantial in both directions through Quy Hop. The volume of trade explains why the Ministry of Finance at the imperial court established a permanent office on the border to collect taxes. It also explains why, in a district as isolated as Quy Hop, two local markets were able to operate so close to each other. One was held nine days each month at Cho Tiem, the site of the Quy Hop border post itself. The second market was at Cho Gia, a mere 300 metres from Quy Hop and separated from Quy Hop by only a shallow stream, the Rao Tiem, which is easy to wade across. The market was held six days each month at Cho Gia—which even today is one of Huong-khe District's large market places and still attracts Lao customers.

More than two centuries ago, the people of the Vientiane kingdom were partially sealed off in their land-locked territory, because of the closed-door policy of the Le dynasty and its Trinh lords in Vietnam. The policy of the new Nguyen dynasty (under Gia Long, who became emperor in 1802) was likewise basically antagonistic towards cross-mountain trade. The Tay-son rulers alone were able to find a satisfactory solution by opening the border at Quy Hop to trade between the two countries. This measure provided the economic basis for the political alliance between the Tay-son and the Lao in the late eighteenth century. The alliance was short-lived, however, because the Tay-son rulers remained in power only briefly.

NOTES

1. The trail can be located on most maps in reference to the approximate coordinates of this village: 105 degrees 31 minutes east longitude and 17 degrees 56 minutes north latitude.

2. Editor's note: See for example Tran 1984 and 1985. Complete bibliographical details are not available to the editor, but other publications in Vietnamese by Tran Van Quy include an article on the documents of the Tay-son period, discovered at Quy Hop, in *Tap Chi Nghien Cuu Lich Su* (Journal of Historical Research, Hanoi, vol. 2, February 1981, pp. 3–4, 84–86, 93); an article on Vietnamese-Lao trade during the Tayson period, based on the unpublished Quy Hop documents, in *Tap Chi Van Hoa Nghia Binh* (Cultural Review of Nghia Binh Province, Qui Nhon, vol. 13, January 1986, pp. 22–4); a paper in Vietnamese presented at the Symposium on the Bicentenary of the Liberation of Phu-xuan, Hué, August 1986; and an article on newly discovered evidence concerning Vietnamese-Lao relations in the Tay-son period, in *Tap Chi Lich Su Quan Su* (Journal of Military History, 14 February 1987).

3. Editor's note: Passages in the documents, together with the identification of Lac Hoan as Nakhòn Phanom, suggest that Phac-bat was somewhere in the mountainous area of the Kadin River basin, possibly in the vicinity of the town of Kham Muan.

4. This district encompassed present-day Huong-son and Huong-khe Districts. Huong-khe was detached and became a separate district in 1867.

5. In the old Vietnamese coinage system, bronze coins (each with a hole in the centre) were strung on bamboo cords. A ligature was a bound set of 600 of these coins, valued at 1 *quan*. As time passed, 1 *quan* came to be worth 3.75 grammes of silver. The value of a buffalo was therefore about 52.25 grammes of silver (a little more than 2 Spanish silver dollars).

6. Editor's note: See the chapter by Tatsuo Hoshino, which describes a trail in this area a thousand years earlier. The two descriptions are remarkably alike.

7. Two nearby passes, which were chosen for the construction of modern roads, are the Kaeo Nüa pass (modern Highway 8) and the Muya (Mugia in French transliteration) pass (modern Highway 15).

8. See for example *Viet Su Thong Giam Cuong Muc* (vol. 20, p. 55, referring to the year 1777) and *Dai Nam Nhat Thong Chi*.

9. Editor's note: Professor Tatsuo Hoshino (letter to the editor, 6 March 1995) questions the use of the toponym Nghe-anh during the ninth century, because the name Nghe-anh was given to the site only in the year

1036. The reference could not come from Jiadan (730–805) himself but might be a misidentification by Henri Maspero.

10. A manuscript of this work, in *nom* script, is preserved at the Institute of Han Nom, under catalogue number VHV 176, leaf 30.

11. This site may be Kuan Phawang village, at the foot of the limestone hills, about 15 km from Tha Khaek, along Highway 8 to Yommarat (Gnommalat in French transliteration).

12. Editor's note: Phoc-na-khi may be a Vietnamese rendering of the rank (*pha*) and title (*na khi*) of a Lao official. A Vientiane commander known as the Pha Nakhi was killed during military operations at Chiang Mai in 1797 (*Phongsawadan yò müang wiangchan* 1969: 143).

13. Editor's note: The Lao document indicates that this area was close to the Quy Hop post and adjacent districts (Châu Ba Dong). Judging from the old communications routes, Lao resistance must have been organised in the hilly country between the Mekong and the cordillera, in the Theun River basin or the Bang Fai River basin.

14. Editor's note: In the long quotation from the 26 September 1792 Lao document, Sam-pha-mat is mentioned in connection with Lac Hoan (Nakhòn Phanom). This name appears to be a Viet-namese rendering of the title of the governor of Nakhòn Phanom, which was Somphamit.

15. Editor's note: The name Vietnam was not used prior to 1804, when Emperor Gia Long coined it. To avoid an anachronism, the old name Dai Viet is used in the translation.

16. Editor's note: This is a reference to captives taken from Vientiane, after the Thai conquest in the late 1770s, and forcibly resettled in the Chao Phraya basin.

17. Ba Dong is the collective name used in reference to three small frontier districts (*châu*) of Quy Hop.

18. Editor's note: The date given in the document is in the Vietnamese lunar calendar: the third day of the tenth lunar month of the fifth year of the reign of Quang Trung. The corresponding date in the Lao lunar calendar was the third day of the first Lao lunar month, or 16 November 1792.

19. Editor's note: The Vietnamese lunar date specified in the document is the tenth day of the eleventh Vietnamese month of the fifth year of the reign of Quang Trung. The corresponding date in the Lao lunar calendar is the tenth day of the second Lao month, or 23 December 1792.

20. Editor's Note: The Vietnamese lunar calendar date given in the document is the ninth day of the eleventh month of the fifth year of the reign of Quang Trung.

21. Editor's note: This supposed toponym might actually be a verb, mistranslated by the Vietnamese officials. *Lòng khong* in Lao means 'to go by boat down the Mekong'. This phrase might therefore be translated as follows: 'Some days ago, I sent my men on a tour down the Mekong River to inspect the area.'

22. Editor's note: The Vietnamese lunar date in the document is the third day of the seventh month of the first year of the reign of Canh Thinh.

THE LAO–TAY-SON ALLIANCE, 1792 AND 1793

Kennon Breazeale

In the preceding chapter, Tran Van Quy discusses a unique collection of historical documents, discovered in 1974 at an old Vietnamese administrative post on the Lao border. Some of these documents provide information about frontier events in 1792 and 1793 that are recorded nowhere else. Using the internal evidence of the documents, Tran argues that a Vietnamese army was sent across the mountains into the Mekong basin in early 1793, that it succeeded in driving Thai forces out of Lao territory along the Mekong and that it carried out its mission with the support and co-operation of the Lao. The present chapter assesses these Vietnamese records from a different perspective and attempts to place them in the context of other evidence concerning relations among the Lao, Vietnamese and Thai during those years. This approach leads to very different conclusions about the sucession of events.

As Tran points out, little contemporary Vietnamese documen-tation has survived from this period, because so many records were destroyed as a result of the Vietnamese civil war, which lasted for three decades and did not end until 1802. Some contemporary Thai documents are preserved in Bangkok, but they, too, are sparse. Most Lao documents were lost when the city of Vientiane was burned in the late 1820s. Other potential sources include the Lao and Thai chronicles (compiled long after these events took place) and a few contemporary observations made by French missionaries (none of whom had first-hand experience in this frontier area). Despite the handicap of finding reliable information about Lao-Vietnamese relations, the present chapter attempts to shed at least a little more light on this subject and on the complex relationships that determined the events recorded in Tran's documents.

THE SETTING OF HOSTILITIES AND ALLIANCES

Up to the 1770s, the Lao of Vientiane communicated officially with the northern Vietnamese kingdom (the region under the control of the Trinh lords in Hanoi) by way of the Quy Hop trail. This trail and the Quy Hop frontier post, which was responsible for relaying official communications to and from the Lao, are described in detail by Tran. Other trails across this part of the cordillera gave the Lao additional means of access to the northern Vietnamese region. Communications with the southern Vietnamese kingdom (the region under the control of the Nguyen lords) were maintained primarily by way of the Ai Lao pass, which is immediately northwest of Hué, the Nguyen seat of government. The mountains south of the Ai Lao pass were inhabited by numerous tribal groups, were almost impenetrable and never served as a practical route to Vietnamese areas south of Hué. For most of the 1600s and 1700s, therefore, the Lao of Vientiane maintained relations with two separate Vietnamese governments.

From the viewpoint of Lao officials in Vientiane, the civil war among the Vietnamese, which began in the early 1770s, resulted in three successive changes in relations across the cordillera, as control of the coastal area passed from one Vietnamese regime to another. In the mid-1770s, when the southern Vietnamese kingdom came under pressure simultaneously from the Trinh to the north and from a rebellion to the south led by the Tay-son brothers, the Nguyen administration abandoned Hué and made Saigon its temporary capital. It lost and regained Saigon several times in a series of struggles with the Tay-son, but maintained continuous control of it from 1788 onward. Meanwhile, Trinh forces took control of Hué in 1775 and held it until 1786, when they were ejected by the Tay-son rebels. During the next two years, the leader of the Tay-son forces in the north eliminated the Trinh administration entirely, forced the Vietnamese emperor into exile in China and proclaimed himself emperor with the regnal name Quang Trung. In 1802, Nguyen forces gained control of the entire coastline and, in 1804, the newly proclaimed Nguyen emperor, Gia Long, gave the name Vietnam to the united kingdom.

After 1775, therefore, the Lao no longer had the option of communicating with two independent Vietnamese governments. At this juncture, the Trinh lords alone controlled the entire northern and central coastline, and all the mountain trails used by the Lao led into Trinh territory. After the 1786-8 transition, this territory was controlled by the northern Tay-son government.[1] From the Lao viewpoint in the early 1790s, it must have seemed likely that this Tay-son administration would remain permanently in power. This impression was reinforced by the fact that Quang Trung was a brilliant military strategist, had undertaken important administrative reforms and appeared to have a long reign ahead of him. Tay-son officials, moreover, were encouraging the Lao to expand their trade with Vietnamese market places near the border and had lowered the taxes imposed on Lao traders.

The question of establishing official contacts with the northern Tay-son court created a dilemma for the Lao in the early 1790s, because of two major political changes during the previous decade and a half. First, a Thai invasion of all the Lao towns along the Mekong in the late 1770s had forced all three of the Lao kingdoms (Luang Prabang, Vientiane and Champasak) to acknowledge the suzerainty of the Thai king. They were thus allied, however reluctantly, with the Thai. Second, the claimant to the throne of the old southern Vietnamese regime, Prince Nguyen Anh, took refuge temporarily in Bangkok in 1783. After he regained control of Saigon in 1788, the Thai king provided material support for the Nguyen cause and continued to do so during the campaigns of the 1790s against the northern and southern Tay-son forces, leading ultimately to the unification of Vietnam. The Lao were thus caught between two opposing power blocks, both of which claimed suzerain rights over the kingdom of Vientiane: the Thai (who were allied with the Nguyen) and the Tay-son (who were allied among themselves and had vowed to destroy the Nguyen). Under these circumstances, the Lao were wary, for fear that their contacts with the Tay-son authorities might come to the attention of the Thai.

The Lao administration in Vientiane was further constrained by its other neighbours. Relations with the Lao kingdom of Champasak, down-river on the frontier with Cambodia, were not friendly, and those with the up-river kingdom of Luang Prabang were openly hostile. Relations with the small Phuan kingdom in the plateau region, immediately north of the city of Vientiane, were tenuous. Phuan rulers often resisted Vientiane's efforts to assert suzerain rights, and the Phuan were occupied with a civil war of their own in the 1790s. Nonetheless, the Lao at Vientiane in the early 1790s judged their neighbours in the Mekong basin to be relatively weak. The only big threat was the Thai kingdom, and the only option for alliance against the Thai was the Tay-son.

NANTHASEN'S BELLIGERENT POLICIES

Aggression by Vientiane against Champasak was one of the factors that brought Thai forces to the middle-Mekong region in the late 1770s and led to the successive submissions of the three Lao kingdoms. Vientiane fell in 1779 to the Thai forces, and the accession of the new king, Nanthasen, was given formal approval by the Thai king in 1781.[2]

During 1782 Nanthasen was occupied with restoring order and inducing the people who had fled during the Thai occupation to return to their homes. He also had to collect taxes from all the major towns of his kingdom, to be sent as tribute to Bangkok. In the process, he was required to reassert Vientiane's traditional rights as suzerain of the Phuan king, thereby obliging the Phuan also to send tribute to Bangkok.[3]

The first decade of Thai suzerainty did not lead to any improvement in Vientiane's relations with its Lao and Phuan neighbours, and during the second half of the 1780s Nanthasen pursued a policy of hostile aggression, which continued into the early 1790s. He succeeded in crippling his old adversaries up-river by securing

Bangkok's permission to attack Luang Prabang. After capturing the city, he took King Suriyawong and the senior Luang Prabang princes to Bangkok. There, they faced charges that they were maintaining relations with the Burmese, who had been waging war against the Thai kingdom for more than two decades. This coup created an interim administration at Luang Prabang from about April 1788 until about March 1792.[4] It was headed by a Lao official who was under the influence—possibly even the direct control—of Vientiane and who was in no position to oppose Nanthasen.

After dealing with Luang Prabang, Nanthasen turned his attention north, summoned the Phuan ruler, King Somphu, and held him under house arrest in Vientiane for about three years. During this period, the Phuan kingdom fell into disorder, when a rebellious faction established an independent power base on the western edge of the plateau. Forces from Vientiane were sent up—ostensibly to restore order, but also to plunder. Thousands of Phuan prisoners were carried away by the Lao, and some Phuan villagers fled east down the mountains, into the Vietnamese province of Nghe-anh. Because of the interim administration at Luang Prabang, the Phuan could not hope for a Lao alliance to counterbalance aggression from Vientiane, and they turned to the only other potential source of help: the Tay-son emperor.

THE 1792 TAY-SON EXPEDITION TO THE MEKONG

Somphu's brother appealed to Quang Trung, pointing out that the Phuan were loyal vassals of the Vietnamese emperor, too, and not vassals of the Lao alone. After the 1791 rains ended, Quang Trung responded by sending a Vietnamese army across the cordillera into Vientiane territory. The mission of this army was not to take possession of Lao territory but to accomplish more limited objectives: chastising Nanthasen for his aggressive policy and forcing him to release the Phuan king. The route taken by the Vietnamese is not recorded. Since the only known casualties on the Lao side were the forces of Nakhòn Phanom, it seems likely that the operations were limited to the narrow band of territory between the

Mekong and the cordillera, immediately east and north-east of Nakhòn Phanom.[5]

Nanthasen must have reported the invasion to Bangkok and appealed for reinforcements during the dry season, early in 1792. No record has been found, but the appeal can be inferred from the Quy Hop documents, which show that Thai troops were present at the end of the 1792 rainy season, not only in the city of Vientiane but also down-river along the Mekong in Vientiane territory. In fact, when the Tay-son forces were crossing the cordillera, and the alarm was sounded by the Lao early in 1792, Thai forces were already deployed in the Lao towns farther down the Mekong. They were there, however, for reasons entirely unrelated to Vientiane or to the Vietnamese, and had been sent there the previous year to deal with a rebellion.

In 1791, the aged king of Champasak was besieged in his capital. He faced a rebellion by a holy man, who claimed to have miraculous powers and had attracted a large contingent of believers. The king appealed for reinforcements from nearby Yasothòn and from Bangkok, and at some time during the seige he died. A senior Yasothòn official arrived first, in command of a local Lao army, and he succeeded in suppressing the rebels before the Thai forces arrived. The exact time of these events is not known. This drama was apparently unfolding during the dry season and the early rainy season in the first half of 1791, because the Yasothòn commander was appointed in September 1791 as the new king of Champasak.[6]

Troops from Bangkok may not have been involved at all. There is no Thai record of an emergency in the Mekong valley during this period, and possibly a mixed army of Thai, Lao and Khmer soldiers from the provinces around Nakhòn Ratchasima was deemed sufficient. While these forces were still restoring order in the Champasak region after the 1791 rainy season, the Tay-son forces marched across the cordillera in a retaliatory gesture against Nanthasen. Again, a few bare facts are known, and one can only speculate about the Lao response.

Under the circumstances, the only practical course of action open to Nanthasen was to appeal to Bangkok for reinforcements. And to do that, his letter had to be relayed by the governor of

Nakhòn Ratchasima, who had special responsibilities for Mekong affairs and who was already in charge of the lower-Mekong operations. It seems probable that the governor ordered some of his men to move up the Mekong into the area of Nakhòn Phanom and that he sent another contingent directly from Nakhòn Ratchasima to Vientiane. Some men may have been sent from Bangkok. If they were, it was certainly only a small contingent, because there seems to be no record of a mobilisation of central Thai troops for such a purpose.

The few records that have survived suggest that the military action on this occasion was very limited. Various sources estimate the size of the Vietnamese force at 3,000 to 30,000 men.[7] Most estimates are probably exaggerated, and possibly no more than a few thousand men were involved. The Nakhòn Phanom contingent was overcome in the fighting,[8] but no other details are known. One account says that the Vietnamese forces were decimated by fever and ailments while crossing the malaria-infested mountains, and the survivors retreated (La Bissachère 1812: 180).

Meanwhile, another Vietnamese contingent took a route farther north and moved into the relatively more healthful Phuan kingdom in the plateau region. Nanthasen seems to have accepted the Vietnamese chastisement immediately. The Phuan king was released and returned home, to be reinstalled under the supervision of the Tay-son representatives in the plateau.

Thus, during the dry season in the first half of 1792, a Tay-son contingent took up a position in the plateau region, but apparently without a plan to move into Lao territory. At the same time, Thai forces were taking up positions in the Mekong-bank towns of the Vientiane kingdom, but found no enemy to attack. These are the circumstances that are reflected, although not explicitly described, in the Quy Hop documents.

Such armies customarily lived off the land, foraged for food wherever they could find it, seized villagers' supplies of rice and took their other possessions as well. Nanthasen was faced with unruly forces that were occupying his towns and entirely outside his control. He had reigned in Vientiane for only a decade under Thai suzerainty, and during that time he surely must have given thought to the possibilities of throwing off Thai domination. The events of early 1792 may have convinced him that an alliance with the Tay-son was the only glimmer of hope on the horizon.

Judging from the Quy Hop documents, Nanthasen must have sent representatives to Nghe-anh Province almost immediately after the Tay-son withdrawal. Although relations with the Tay-son meant continued submission as a vassal of the Vietnamese, perhaps he knew from experience that the Vietnamese would require only token symbols of submission and, unlike the Thai, would not make onerous demands on him. This theory is speculative but still consistent with the fragments of new evidence provided by Tran.

The Quy Hop documents show clearly that Nanthasen and the Nakhòn Phanom governor were in contact with the Tay-son governor of Nghe-anh Province during the rainy season in mid-1792. Nanthasen placed his youngest brother (apparently the future King Anuwong) in charge of affairs in the hills east of the Mekong, and the Vietnamese encouraged the prince to prepare for resistance against the Thai. These contacts are confirmed in a letter dated 26 September 1792 from the prince, who urged the Vietnamese to withdraw their contingent from Phuan territory and also to send a large Vietnamese army across the cordillera to attack and defeat the Thai forces.

His reason for wanting the troops withdrawn from the plateau was to spare the Lao from being obliged by the Thai to serve as reinforcements, if orders were received to launch an attack into the plateau. Since the Lao would have faced the same problem if a Vietnamese army crossed the cordillera, the Lao must have hoped for a sudden strike by the Vietnamese and Lao against Thai forces on the Mekong, along the Nakhòn Phanom stretch of the river, and a rapid march up-river, leaving the Thai commander in Vientiane too little time to mobilise Lao reinforcements. The Lao plan must therefore have been to await a critical moment at Vientiane and then turn against the Thai while the Vietnamese were approaching the city, instructing any Lao contingents that were sent down-river to let the Vietnamese army pass without obstruction.

At about the same time, late in the 1792 rainy season, the governor of Nghe-anh Province sent seven men by way of the Quy

Hop frontier post with instructions to investigate and report on the military situation in the Nakhòn Phanom area. Their Lao guides were unreliable, however, and the mission failed to accomplish its objective, as shown in the governor's complaint on 21 November 1792. Indicating that a campaign against the Thai forces would be very costly, the governor sent four more men who were to be escorted to Vientiane, where they would assess the positions and strength of the Thai forces and then report to Nghe-anh. Their assessment must have been the deciding factor in any recommendation, positive or negative, made by the governor to the Tay-son court. The governor added that, when a decision was reached, he would inform the Lao, so that they could prepare food supplies to support the Vietnamese forces while they were operating in Lao territory.

A 23 December 1792 record shows that the Lao had already mobilised men in three different areas of the hills between the Mekong and the cordillera, and they were preparing for the arrival of the Vietnamese army. Instructions arrived the next day from a court official representing the new Vietnamese emperor, Canh Thinh. (He succeeded when his father, Quang Trung, died suddenly, shortly after this series of communications with the Lao began.) The court official sent thirty men to gather more military information. He instructed the Lao, meanwhile, to provide enough food for a large Vietnamese force (which was to be sent later) and to prepare for a major campaign to rid the kingdom of the Thai forces, indicating that the Tay-son government was 'resolved to annihilate the foreign invaders'.

At this intriguing point, the Quy Hop documents fall silent. The only other records of these events were written by the Lao in August 1793, stating that Thai forces were no longer on the Mekong. But what happened during the months of January to July 1793?

SPECULATIONS ABOUT THE EVENTS OF 1793

Tran Van Quy postulates that the Thai were driven from the Lao kingdom by joint Lao and Tay-son operations and that the Tay-son campaign in Vientiane territory took place in early 1793, rather than in early 1792 as previously believed. Unfortunately for this theory, other sources—Lao, central Thai, northern Thai and European— all agree that the Tay-son forces invaded during the 1791-2 campaign season: that is, after the 1791 rainy season and during the dry season early in 1792. And even the Quy Hop documents provide no direct evidence that a campaign took place at all in 1793. Moreover, there are no Thai or Lao records of an emergency in the central Mekong region at this time. The most convincing evidence is that no action was taken subsequently by the Thai. Nothing out of the ordinary is recorded during the year 1793 or during most of the year 1794. If the Thai forces had been routed on the Mekong, the Thai court unquestionably would have sent an army to retaliate and to restore Thai influence in this region.

An alternative explanation of events requires only minor speculation to fill the gaps between fragments of contemporary evidence. The Tay-son contingent, weakened by attacks of malarial fever and gastric disorders, probably withdrew immediately after the incursion in early 1792, while the Thai soldiers were moving into the central Mekong towns. The Thai then had no military objective, except to maintain surveillance on Vietnamese activities in the plateau and await orders, in case the Thai court decided to send an army to eject the Tay-son contingent from Phuan territory. It seems likely, moreover, that Thai officials in Bangkok were not paying close attention to Mekong affairs and, instead, relied on the governor of Nakhòn Ratchasima to monitor events.

At this juncture, the Thai court became fully occupied with its long-time policy to regain control of the towns on the upper west coast of the Malay peninsula. This territory had been lost to the Burmese in the mid-1760s and had subsequently been a persistent concern of Thai leaders. An alliance sought by the governor of Tavoy presented an unexpected opportunity to regain control of that coastal area and ensured that the court turned all its efforts in that direction during 1792 and especially in early 1793.[9] A Thai contingent was sent to Tavoy in 1792, and the security of the town was considered so important that King Rama I himself went to Kanchanaburi Province, on the border, in November 1792. He remained there until January 1793, while the heir apparent led the main army across the mountains to take up positions on the coast. Since the Thai mobilisation to the west was planned during a period of at least nine months in 1792, King Nanthasen probably became aware of it. That gave him another factor to add to his calculations. Thai forces were concentrating on the western frontier of the kingdom, and the Thai government would therefore be unable to respond effectively to a sudden strike against the Thai forces remaining in the Mekong-bank towns at the beginning of 1793. Such action would seal the Thai border and inevitably prevent the Lao from trading with the ports of the Gulf coast. But that loss was counterbalanced by Tay-son efforts to lower the trade barriers and encourage the Lao to export their goods across the Vietnamese border.

Thai strategists, for their part, must have regarded the Tay-son presence in the distant plateau area as a minor concern that could be ignored for some time. At that juncture, the Thai court judged both the northern and the southern Tay-son governments to be a greatly diminishing threat. Nguyen forces had destroyed the southern Tay-son fleet at Qui-nhon in August 1792. And Quang Trung, who had been the redoubtable military strategist since the beginning of the Tay-son movement, died at Hanoi the next month. Thus, in late 1792, at the moment when the Lao were urging Tay-son officials to launch a strike with Lao support against the Thai along the Mekong, the Thai were assuming that Nguyen forces were making substantial progress, that the Tay-son were weakened by the loss of the emperor and that the Tay-son were not in a position to offer more than token threats against territory in the Mekong basin. Also, Thai forces had been operating along the Mekong for nearly two full years, under the supervision of the governor of Nakhòn Ratchasima. There was no obvious reason to keep them in the field, and the rice shortage at the end of 1792 must have hastened their departure.[10]

Given these considerations, it seems likely that orders from Bangkok authorised the withdrawal of the contingents from the Mekong after the 1792 rains and that the Thai forces were beginning to leave Vientiane, Nakhòn Phanom and other strategic points by the time that the Tay-son intelligence officers began their assessment during the final weeks of the year. The Vietnamese may have observed the withdrawal, or perhaps they found no enemy forces at all in the places they visited. Thus the alliance with the Lao no longer had any military objective.

AFTERMATH OF THE ALLIANCE

The Quy Hop records show that the Lao princes were exceedingly anxious to maintain secrecy in their negotiations with the Tay-son and to ensure that none of their communications fell into Thai hands. They appear to have succeeded for a while. But within two years, some details of their dealings with Tay-son officials reached the Thai court. The Thai records do not specify who lodged the accusations against Nanthasen and the Nakhòn Phanom governor for conspiring with the Tay-son.[11] Both men were summoned to Bangkok in November 1794 to plead their cases. Unable to refute the charges, they were imprisoned and removed from office.[12]

In early February 1795, Nanthasen's younger brother, Inthasom, left Bangkok with instructions to take charge at Vientiane. During the first half of 1795, King Rama I was examining the case against Nanthasen and had not yet made a final decision. At the end of June 1795, however, when a general amnesty for prisoners in Bangkok was proclaimed, the king specifically excluded Nanthasen. About three weeks later, Inthasom was named to succeed at Vientiane.[13] Nanthasen was imprisoned for life and died in Bangkok.[14]

Nanthasen must have had great expectations at the end of 1792. Down-river, the king of Champasak was dead, his heirs were quarrelling among themselves and an outsider had been placed on the throne. To the north in the plateau, the Phuan were divided into two hostile factions, and King Somphu was held under house arrest in Vientiane. Up-river, Luang Prabang had been without a king for nearly four years. Although King Anurut returned and began restoring the old order during the first half of 1792,

Nanthasen must have seen that Anurut posed no immediate threat to Vientiane.

To the east, the Tay-son had consolidated their control over the Vietnamese coastline and were a power to be reckoned with. Even so, the Tay-son could not be used as allies to strike against Thai territory, because the distance was too great and the burden on the Lao to provide logistical support might have been unbearable. But the Tay-son could be used for the more limited objective of driving the Thai away from the Mekong-bank towns and ensuring that they did not return. After such a success, Nanthasen might then have asserted his claim to be the preeminent monarch of the central Mekong kingdoms and might have induced his reluctant neighbours into a general alliance, to ensure that the Thai could not regain control using the piecemeal tactics they had employed in the late 1770s. This seemed to be Nanthasen's moment in history, and he eagerly sought the alliance with the Tay-son, in spite of the risks.

' Ironically, the results of Nanthasen's alliance were the abrupt termination of his career and a further weakening of Lao authority. Even before his departure from the political stage, the Thai authorised Nguyen loyalists to purchase rice in the Lao towns and provide logistical support for the Nguyen forces fighting their way north up the coast, on the opposite side of the cordillera. In the final year leading to Nguyen Anh's ultimate victory over the Tay-son, during the dry season of late 1801 and early 1802, some Thai troops returned to the central Mekong and apparently crossed the cordillera, obliging the Lao to provide logistical support for them. At the same time, Lao troops from Vientiane were sent against the Tay-son contingent in Phuan territory.[15] Thus, far from attaining the strong position sought by Nanthasen, the Vientiane monarchy was subject to yet more Thai demands and compelled to support the Chakri-Nguyen alliance.

Ultimately, the alliance sought by the Lao with the Tay-son can be viewed as a tale of miscommunication and mis-timing, involving a Thai army and a Vietnamese army, each in search of an enemy but neither encountering the other. Almost certainly, that outcome was a fortunate one for the Lao people. It spared them from the devastation they would surely have suffered if their homeland had become a battleground for an intensified war between the Chakri-Nguyen alliance and the Tay-son.

ABBREVIATIONS USED FOR MATERIALS CITED

TNL R1 Unpublished documents of the First Reign, in the Manuscripts Division of Thailand's National Library, Bangkok.

PP1 *Phongsawadan lan chang tam thòi kham nai chabap doem* [Chronicle of Lan Sang, According to the Original Lao-Idiom Text], in *Prachum phongsawadan phak thi 1* [History Series Part 1] (1963).

PP5 *Phongsawadan müang luang phrabang tam chabap thi mi yu nai sala luk khun* [Chronicle of Luang Prabang, According to the Manuscript in the Ministers' Pavilion (1867 version)], in *Prachum phongsawadan phak thi 5* [History Series Part 5] (1963).

PP11*Phongsawadan müang luang phrabang* [Chronicle of Luang Prabang (1870 version)], in *Prachum phongsawadan phak thi 11* [History Series Part 11] (1964).

PP70a *Phongsawadan yò müang wiangchan* [An Abbreviated Chronicle of Vientiane (October 1893 version)], in *Prachum phongsa-wadan phak thi 70* [History Series Part 70] (1969).

PP70b *Phongsawadan yò müang wiangchan* [An Abbreviated Chronicle of Vientiane], in *Prachum phongsawadan phak thi 70* [History Series Part 70] (1969).

PP70c Chan Ngon Kham, *Phongsawadan müang nakhòn phanom sangkhep chabap phraya Chan ngon kham riap riang* [Abbreviated Annals of Nakhòn Phanom, Version Compiled by Phraya Chan Ngon Kham on 21 November 1914], in *Prachum phongsawadan phak thi 70* [History Series, Part 70] (1969).

NOTES

1. Among the three Tay-son leaders, the youngest (Nguyen Van Hue) became emperor in the north. His elder brother (Nguyen Van Nhac) became emperor of a separate kingdom with its capital in Qui-nhon. A third Tay-son kingdom (under Nguyen Van Lu) was established in the region of the Mekong delta and Saigon. The two southern Tay-son regions are not discussed in this chapter, because the Lao of Vientiane had no direct means of communicating with them. The complex mountain and plateau region of the southern cordillera blocked access to Qui-nhon. And the Mekong route required passing through the Lao kingdom of Champasak and then through the eastern part of Cambodia.

2. One of the abbreviated Lao chronicles (PP70b: 141) gives 27 September 1779 as the day the Thai forces captured Vientiane. Another

abbreviated chronicle (PP70a: 133) says that the king (presumably Siribunyasan) returned to the capital between late November and late December 1780. The exact date of his death is not known. His son, Nanthasen, was taken away with other prisoners in 1779 (Yim et al. 1982: 55). The Thai edict for Nanthasen's accession is dated 29 November 1781. It is recorded in an unpublished list of appointments in the First Reign (TNL R1/1153/3) and in a published extract from the Royal Scribes Department (Yim et al. 1982: 55).

3. TNL R1/1144/7 despatch from the king of Vientiane, 4 August 1782, relayed 16 August 1782 by the governor of Nakhòn Ratchasima.

4. King Suriyawong of Luang Prabang submitted to Thai suzerainty around the end of the 1770s. Some Lao chronicles (for example, PP1: 184) specify 1788/9 as the year Luang Prabang was captured by Vientiane forces. A contemporary Thai record (*Tamnan phra kaeo mòrakot* 1967: 1) shows that King Suriyawong attended court in Bangkok on 20 May 1788 and presented a history of the Emerald Buddha to King Rama I. This evidence suggests that Luang Prabang was captured during the dry season in early 1788 and that King Suriyawong made the journey down to Bangkok during the first half of May 1788. He died in Bangkok in 1791/2 (PP1: 184) and had no son to succeed him.

His younger brother, the heir apparent (*uparat*), was likewise taken to Bangkok and held there for nearly four years (from May 1788 to February 1792). He was then allowed to return to rule Luang Prabang with the regnal name Anurut. The record of his appointment has been preserved and is dated 3 February 1792 (TNL R1/1153/2, list of various appointments in the First Reign). Some other sources give the same year for the appointment (PP5: 343 and PP11: 210).

Some modern authors place the interim administration during the period 1791–5. These dates seem to be based on a misinterpretation of entries in some of the Lao and Thai chronicles.

The first error in reading arises because the Lao year CS 1153 (12 April 1791 to 11 April 1792) appears in some chronicles at the beginning of the passage concerning events at Luang Prabang. Usually, the year refers to the first event mentioned in a passage. In this case, however, the year refers to the major event in the passage, which is the accession of King Anurut in February 1792. The information listed between the date and the major event is merely historical background leading up to the accession: the attack on Luang Prabang and the removal of the king and princes to Bangkok.

The second error and greater confusion arise because the 'king' who was removed from Luang Prabang to Bangkok seems to be identified by some annalists as Anurut. (See Sila 1964: 110 for this error.) When the heir apparent (*uparat*, the future King Anurut) was taken to Bangkok, he was not yet king. Nonetheless, the annalists (and anyone else writing about him after February 1792) refer to him retrospectively, in formal writing style, by attributing to him the highest position he ultimately attained, even during the period prior to his accession. This is a common occurrence in historical documents and is a potential pitfall for the unwary reader.

The chronology of this period is still open to debate, but the dates outlined in these notes are consistent with the present chapter's interpretation of events.

5. A contemporary document, which appears to be from Emperor Canh Thinh (Quang Trung's son and successor) states that Tay-son troops were sent to chastise Nanthasen for his invasion of the Phuan kingdom, which had resulted in a flood of Phuan refugees into Nghe-anh Province (TNL R1/1158/3 letter from the Vietnamese ruler to King Rama I, 16 October 1795). Archaimbault (1967: 576 n. 1) records the Phuan appeal and the resulting campaign against Nanthasen in the year CS 1153 (1791/2). An abbreviated Vientiane chronicle (PP70a: 134) records the defeat of the Nakhòn Phanom governor by the Vietnamese in 1791/2. According to a French missionary report, people in Saigon feared in February 1792 that the Tay-son forces intended to march down the Mekong, gather reinforcements in Cambodia and attack Saigon from the west, thereby destroying the Nguyen administrative and military base (Cadière 1912: 26). Lê (1955: 309) says that partisans of the exiled Lê emperor were in contact with the Lao and Phuan, were operating along this frontier and were an objective of the Tay-son operations. La Bissachère (1812: 180) reported that the invasion took place shortly before Quang Trung's death in 1792, but he does not mention a motive. The Chiang Mai chronicle (Wyatt and Aroonrut 1995: 160) gives 1791/2 as the year of the attack but has no details.

Other sources offer alternative explanations and doubtful details. Hoang (1966: 67) gives no motive but says that Quang Trung sent the governor of Nghe-anh, General Trân Quang Diêu, on this expedition and that Diêu occupied and sacked Vientiane and set up various forts in the kingdom. Hoang's source appears to be Hoa Bang's *Quang Trung Nguyên Huê* (Saigon 1958), but none of these details are plausible. A Vietnamese textbook (cited by Khin Sok 1991: 56) asserts that Nguyen Anh had asked

Rama I for permission to send Nguyen forces through Lao territory into Nghe-anh Province. It seems highly unlikely, however, that the Thai court would have authorised the passage of a large Vietnamese army across this territory.

6. The appointment of Chao Na to Champasak on 22 September 1791 is recorded in a list of various appointments during the First Reign (TNL R1/1153/2). The Yasothòn man, an outsider, seems to have been chosen not only for his administrative skills and military accomplishments but also because the members of the Champasak royal family were divided among themselves and unable to agree on a successor.

7. A sample of the numbers of Vietnamese soldiers includes 3,000 (Thiphakôrawong 1978: 170), 3,000 (reinforced by 3,000 Phuan, Sila 1964: 110, 1996: 169), 5,000 (Lê 1995: 309) and about 30,000 (Cadière 1912: 26).

8. The defeated commander, Somphamit, listed in an abbreviated chronicle (PP70a 1969: 134), was the governor of Nakhòn Phanom. He seems to be the same governor mentioned in the Quy Hop records. Possibly he was taken as a prisoner to Nghe-anh in early 1792 and subsequently used by the Tay-son authorities to open the discussions with Nanthasen.

9. For a summary of the events at Tavoy, see Wenk (1965: 71–81). Wenk was apparently unable to convert the lunar-calendar entries of his sources, and he thus does not give precise dates. At the beginning of March 1792, large numbers of men and barges were mobilised in Bangkok to go to the boat landings in Kanchanaburi Province, where they received a large party of envoys and Buddhist monks, who had come across the mountains from Tavoy (Yim et al. 1982: 30–4).

10. One of the abbreviated chronicles of Vientiane (PP70b: 142) records a shortage of rice at exactly this time, possibly caused by drought and a poor harvest along the Mekong at the end of 1792.

11. The Ngaosrivathanas (1998: 95–6) speculate that the source of the accusations against Nanthasen and the Nakhòn Phanom governor was Vietnamese, pointing out that a Tay-son mission visited Bangkok in early 1794, shortly before a Nguyen mission arrived. This theory is a plausible explanation, although it leaves a long and unexplained gap in time between these early 1794 Vietnamese missions and the 24 November 1794 departure of Nanthasen from Vientiane, after being summoned to court (PP70b: 143). The information concerning the Lao may have been brought by a mission sent by Nguyen Anh in the second half of the year, and the obvious source could have been Nguyen agents who had infiltrated

the Tay-son administration. One should not, however, dismiss Nanthasen's many other enemies as possible sources. King Anurut of Luang Prabang bore a grudge against Nanthasen for his long imprisonment in Bangkok, and Sila (1964: 110, 1996: 169) believed Anurut to be the accuser. In the Phuan region, King Somphu likewise had been a victim of Nanthasen. And on 24 November 1794, a mission from the rebel Phuan faction based on the frontier of Luang Prabang was received at court in Bangkok and asked to be placed under the supervision of King Anurut instead of King Somphu (TNL R1/1156/13 Chao Klang to Chief Thai Minister, 2 June 1794, translated and read at court on 24 November 1794). Either Phuan faction could have been a channel of information from the Tay-son through Luang Prabang to Bangkok. Finally, it is possible that the governor of Nakhòn Ratchasima, who had broad responsibilities for monitoring affairs in the central Mekong region, uncovered some details of Nanthasen's negotiations with the Vietnamese.

12. See Thiphakòrawong (1978: 207–8) and PP70a: 134. The governor was punished with a hundred lashes and allowed to redeem himself by going on a campaign to Chiang Mai to fight the Burmese. He died en route (PP70c: 207–8).

13. Inthasom's 2 February 1795 departure from Bangkok, an appeal by the Thai heir apparent to spare Nanthasen's life and the 30 June general amnesty (which excluded Nanthasen and others implicated with him) are recorded by Thiphakòrawong (1978: 208, 213). The edict naming King Saiya Setthathirat (Inthasom) is dated 23 July 1795 and is recorded in TNL R1/1153/2 (a list of various appointments in the First Reign).

14. According to a passage in Sila (1964: 110), Nanthasen and the governor 'stood trial for two years, during which King Nanthasen died', but this is a mistranslation. The original text is less precise about the time and says only that they 'fought the case during two years, and he [royal pronoun, hence Nanthasen] died in Bangkok' (Sila 1996: 169). In the contemporary way of reckoning time, the first year of the case was CS 1156 (the 1794 summons to Bangkok), and the second year was CS 1157 (12 April 1795 to 11 April 1796). Nanthasen was still alive early in the second year (when the June 1795 amnesty excluded him), but the year of his death has not yet been identified.

15. Thipakòrawong (1978: 199) records that Rama I approved a request in 1793 by Nguyen Anh to send some men to the Lao towns to organise food supplies for his campaign, and edicts were sent to facilitate this work. Lê (1955: 319) says that Nguyen Anh sent a request in the spring of 1798, asking Rama I to send an army through the Lao towns towards

Nghe-anh, for joint operations with Nguyen forces, which would march up from the south. The Thai and Lao annals provide some support for this conclusion, although not in 1798.

In February 1799, Nguyen Anh sent a request to Bangkok, asking for Lao and Khmer troops to harass the Tay-son in Nghe-anh from the rear (presumably by marching up the Mekong, crossing the cordillera and attacking outlying posts). Meanwhile, Nguyen forces would attack from the south (Thipakòrawong 1978: 226–7). Ordinarily, Nguyen Anh's forces sailed up the Vietnamese coast each year, catching the seasonal winds that begin in late May. Rama I realised, however, that an army operating in the cordillera in June would be caught in the annual rains, which usually began about that time, and that too many men would be lost because of resulting fevers and disease. He therefore gave orders for 5,000 Khmer troops to assist the Nguyen, not in Nghe-anh but in the assault on Qui-nhon (which fell during the 1799 attacks).

The Thai chronicles do not record a response concerning the request for Lao forces, but the basic proposal seems to have been accepted in a modified plan. One Lao chronicle records the arrival of 20,000 Thai soldiers at Nakhòn Phanom in 1801/2, for operations against the Vietnamese at a battle site identified only as Tha Sida (PP70b: 143)— obviously a river landing called Sida by the Lao, and possibly in the river basin leading down to Vinh. Another Lao chronicle shows that Vientiane Lao forces were fighting the Vietnamese during the same season in Phuan territory. Thus, during the campaign season leading to Nguyen Anh's victories in June and July 1802, both Lao and Thai forces seem to have been in the field, attacking outlying positions on the Tay-son western frontier, while Nguyen forces moved north up the coast.

MILLENARIAN MOVEMENTS IN LAOS, 1895–1936: DEPICTIONS BY MODERN LAO HISTORIANS

Bernard Gay

What are the rôle played and the place occupied by historical research in Lao society since decolonisation and the proclamation of the country's independence in 1953? History, a long-neglected field, has become a subject of national concern since 1975. The change occurred in 1974–5, after the short-lived Provisional Government of National Union was formed in April 1974. When the communist party assumed total power in December 1975, the Lao People's Democratic Republic (Lao PDR) superseded the Kingdom of Laos.

During the entire period of the monarchy and revolutionary war from 1945 to 1975, only slight interest in the study of history was shown by the pro-Western Lao élite who retained control of the administration in Vientiane. The lack of development of a Lao history curriculum, even for purposes of elementary-level teaching, was exacerbated by the fact that the Ministry of Education relied on French teachers, who were neither trained in history nor knowledgeable about the country's past. They did not even have a command of the Lao language adequate to draft history textbooks for Lao secondary schools. In the portion of the country controlled by the revolutionary Pathet Lao party, the historical pamphlets that were issued aimed only at glorifying the great deeds performed by the revolutionary forces in their struggle against the 'imperialism' of America and its allies.

Since its founding, the government of the Lao PDR has devoted its attention to drafting both a national history and a history of the Lao revolutionary party. In order to paint such a vast historical canvas and carry out the ambitious plan to encompass the entire period from prehistoric times to the end of French colonial rule, the official published version will be chronologically divided into three parts. Thus far, only the third volume (Thongsa et al. 1989) has appeared in print. It begins with the arrival of the French in Laos during the 1880s and ends with the last days of the French administration. Its principal theme is the struggle for independence.

Among the episodes of Lao history in the nineteenth and twentieth centuries, the popular movements that unfolded in the centre and south of the country between 1895 and 1936 have been a primary focus of investigation and analysis by modern Lao historians. These movements are well worth examining, both for their subject matter and for their analyses, which are illustrative of certain trends in contemporary Lao historiography. The first part of the present study is devoted to the events that took place between 1895 and 1936. This part relies essentially on work conducted in the French archives and in the field in southern Laos. Full documentation of the source materials cited in this part of the study can be found in Gay (1987). The second part of the study examines the representations of these events by Lao historians.

French archives are a rich source of primary materials on the Lao millenarian movements that began in 1895 and continued almost to the end of the colonial era. Three major phases can be distinguished by place and by time. The first phase consists of demonstrations on the Bòlawen (Bolovens) plateau in southern Laos, between 1895 and 1898. A more intense and longer-lived series of contestations was enacted in the same region between 1899 and 1936. The third phase encompasses the disturbances that erupted in Savannakhet Province and continued there and elsewhere from 1899 to 1903.

FIRST PHASE, 1895–8

In 1895 and twice in 1898, the fertile Bòlawen plateau was the focus of excitement provoked by individuals who called themselves holy men: the *phu mi bun*, meaning literally persons with Buddhist merit. These public demonstrations were not widespread and affected only villages inhabited by some of the Proto-Indochinese ethnic minorities. The disturbances were sparked off by two individuals who were Lao—the ethnic group that was politically and socially predominant in Laos but not strongly represented in the troubled area. The two Lao men were apparently strangers to the plateau area, and both were former Buddhist monks. By posing as magicians and pretending to have great magical powers, they imposed themselves on the gullible villagers, who were animists rather than believers in Buddhism.

The Lao man who initiated the movement in 1895 is known as Ong Thòng. (*Ong* is an honorific. His assumed name, Thòng, means 'gold' or 'golden'.) He was born in Bangkok and represented himself to the villagers as 'a son of the king of Vientiane, inspired by the gods'. He made himself the de facto governor of the district of Dasia and asserted that he was responsible for stopping the spread of a cholera epidemic. In recompense, the inhabitants of villages that he had 'spared' from this plague were exhorted to pay sums of money to him. The government authorities, not surprisingly, took a dim view of his activities and his interference in local administration. But when they arrested him, he managed to escape. His escape was interpreted by the villagers as a miraculous occurrence, which reinforced his reputation as a person who could exercise extraordinary powers. This monk-magician reappeared in 1901 as one of the protagonists in the Bòlawen movement, which he helped to lead from 1901 to 1910.

Another movement arose also in 1895, in an area neighbouring the Bòlawen plateau but centred on Kham Thòng Yai, a minor administrative centre in the river basin of the Se Dòn. This movement was led by another holy man—known as Ong Khao, probably because he wore robes of white (*khao* in Lao)—who was assisted by a faithful lieutenant known as Ong Dam (*dam* meaning

black) and ten followers. Kham Thòng Yai was one of the crucibles
of millenarian activities from 1901 to 1910. During the violent
events of 1902, which spread through the Lao-speaking towns on
the right bank of the Mekong under Thai control, holy men known
as Ong Khao and Ong Dam were among the leaders. A man called
Ong Dam was arrested in the Bòlawen area at Ban Chalang on 31
January 1902. Ong Khao first came to public attention in 1894,
when he dispensed 'justice' in the tribal area around Ban Dasia. This
holy man performed his ceremonies using objects stolen from the
Catholic mission in the Kontum plateau area. After escaping the
first time from the agents of the princely ruler of Champasak, he
was arrested again. Once released, he abandoned the claim that he
possessed magic power. Also associated with this movement was a
man named Kaen, who was from Phaya Fai and likewise claimed to
have supernatural powers. He exhibited his powers to the local
populace for some time, but then he was arrested and fell into
obscurity.

SECOND PHASE, 1899–1936

The second major phase of millenarian movements was centred on
the Bòlawen plateau and lasted from 1899 to 1936. More than
thirty authors have made studies of these events: a series of
confrontations that were among the most momentous and long-
lasting encountered by the French colonial authorities in Indochina.

Historians have previously regarded 1900 or 1901 as the starting
point of this phase of Lao millenarian movements. But in fact, the
incidents began in 1899, when the local Lao authorities first warned
the French administration about the activities of a certain Nai Mi.
Nai Mi belonged to the Ngeh ethnic minority,[1] was a son of a village
head of Ban Chakam and acquired a reputation as a healer. As his
renown spread among the villages, his 'miracles' drew a large
number of people, to whom he distributed candles that were
supposed to ensure happiness. According to information gathered
by French commissioner J.-J. Dauplay, Nai Mi was formerly a
monk, had become literate in Pali and Lao, had been instructed in

sacred Buddhist texts and had once performed a pilgrimage to a sacred Buddhist site in Bangkok. In February 1901, Nai Mi proclaimed himself (or perhaps was recognised by his entourage) to be a holy man (*phu mi bun*), and he adopted the name Ong Kaeo (*kaeo* meaning 'precious gemstone'). He had ceremonial buildings erected on two mountains—Phu Tayin and Phu Takao—and invited the populace to attend a traditional Lao religious festival (*bun*). Up to this time, the colonial authorities paid no attention to him, despite the reports made by local Lao officials.

The mountain-side ceremonies, which drew together thousands of people of heterogeneous political and cultural backgrounds, immediately became a source of anxiety for the French authorities. Among the themes of Ong Kaeo's public discourses were religious topics tinged with Buddhist eschatology. One general belief, which is common to all areas where Theravada Buddhism prevails, is that Theravada Buddhism itself will last for 5,000 years and will be succeeded by another form of Buddhism. (The origin of this belief is a very late and apocryphal prophesy attributed to Buddhagosa.) In a letter written in May 1901, Ong Kaeo announced that the 5,000 years marking the end of Buddhism had already elapsed and that a holy man had become manifest. In another letter, he presented himself as the supreme head of a new religion that had just come into existence.

Although these notions were probably incomprehensible to the French, and to most other people who were not Buddhists, Ong Kaeo adopted them into his religious synchretism, which also made use of other beliefs that are deeply entrenched in all communities in the region. These beliefs include the existence of individuals who have supernatural powers and can perform miraculous acts, such as resuscitating the dead, healing all kinds of illness, transforming ordinary stones into gold, becoming invisible, flying through the air, ensuring agricultural abundance and dispensing amulets that bestow invulnerability on the bearers. While presenting himself as one such person, Ong Kaeo incorporated a political motive into his message to the people. He proclaimed himself a king or ruler (*chao somdet*) and simultaneously called upon the French to withdraw to their homeland.

Early in 1901, the movement was still a peaceful one. In February, for example, Ong Kaeo received a French trader in a friendly way. Suddenly, around March or April 1901, Ong Kaeo became bellicose. Assertions advanced by contemporary observers to explain this change are numerous and contradictory. The Catholic missionaries and some French officials, however, perceived the fatal combination of beliefs and exercise of authority that was at work. The deep-seated belief of the populace that Ong Kaeo was a person with supernatural powers, juxtaposed with the intrusion of the forces of law and order into the area where Ong Kaeo displayed his miracles, transformed a relatively innocuous local drama (one of many that have doubtless been played over the centuries) into a movement with a hostile objective. Official interference precipitated open and radical confrontation, aimed at the local Lao officials and the French colonial authorities.

Commissioner Remy and the Lao governor of Saravane attempted on 15 March to apprehend Ong Kaeo at Nòng Mek and to put an end to his public performances and religious activities. Their failure to capture him drew the attention of a far greater audience than Ong Kaeo alone could ever have attracted. Once again, an avoidance of arrest was equated, in the minds of the people, with proof of miraculous powers. Those who believed in his miracles, along with others who had remained skeptical thus far, now became fully convinced of his powers. They willingly placed themselves under his command, and he sent them on several forays against local police posts. Their lack of success in these attacks did not prevent them from continuing to believe in the powers of their holy man.

Dissension between French officials at different posts—a characteristic of bureaucracy throughout the colonial period— enabled Ong Kaeo to remain on the run for years and to evade the patrols sent out by commissioners at Pak Se, Saravane and Attapeu to arrest him. The ineptitude of such officials encouraged him all the more to pursue the tactics of guerrilla war and, from the safety of his forest refuge in the mountains, to launch an ambush against anyone who ventured into the mountains in search of him. Ultimately, it took a blockade of the Bòlawen plateau to put an end to his activities. He was captured and he died on 10 November 1910—killed (so the officials reported) while trying to escape.

After the death of Ong Kaeo, one of the lieutenants of his movement, named Kommadam, officially remained a rebel but concurrently cultivated good relations with the head of the minor French administrative post that was responsible for keeping him under surveillance. Kommadam maintained a low profile until 1925 and then declared himself 'Lord of the Khòm'. (The title that he assumed, *Chao Phaya Khòm*, implied in Lao that he presided over the spirits of a vanished race, the Khòm, who are imagined to be the builders of the ancient stone temples of Champasak and other towns.) He claimed to have magic objects in his possession, to be omniscient and to have been sent by the heavens to establish a kingdom of upland tribal peoples. The tribal peoples in part of the Bòlawen plateau acknowledged and believed in his claims. His following swelled between the years 1930 and 1936—a period in which the effects of the global economic recession became progressively felt in Laos. In spite of regular pursuit by Lao officials, he maintained a guerrilla resistance on the Bòlawen plateau for a whole decade. Finally, in September 1936 a military unit succeeded in killing him.

THIRD PHASE, 1899–1903

The third phase of millenarianism centred on Savannakhet Province and is often called the 'Phò Kaduat' revolt. During 1899 the Mekong River was criss-crossed by 'preachers' who originated in Laos. (According to Thai reports, however, they came from the little administrative centre of Khong Chiam on the Thai side of the river.) They announced the coming of a holy man and foretold dire misfortunes that would befall anyone who failed to obey his orders. They also prophesied that a catastrophe would occur during the second week of April 1902; that it would last seven days and seven nights; and that it would be followed by a Golden Age for all who expiated their sins according to the holy man's commands. These prophesies spread throughout Savannakhet Province.

Disturbances developed rapidly, which necessitated the despatch of a unit of the local gendarmerie from Sepon. On 30 November 1901, at the village of Ban Huai Büng, the headman and his wife Mae Bing (the self-proclaimed queen of the tribal peoples) were arrested. Also arrested, at Ban Talai, were Phò Bing and his wife—another Mae Bing, who was popularly recognised as the mother of all holy men. French attempts to restore law and order produced no tangible results, and the agitation continued to mount with increasing fervour. A similar millenarian movement was concurrently in progress on the Thai side of the Mekong during March 1902. It was crushed as a result of swift action by Thai military forces.

On the Lao shore, in fulfilment of a Lao oral tradition, a holy man known as Ong Pha Chan (*pha chan* signifying 'the moon' in Lao) presented himself to the people and performed ceremonies with active assistance from the head of the monastery in Ban Sida. His given name was Adoni, and he was also known as Phò Kaduat (literally 'Father Kaduat'). He invited everyone to venerate a statue of the Buddha, which he claimed had fallen from the heavens. People from more than 120 villages were convinced that this miracle had indeed occurred, and they flocked to his ceremonies, where they received from the holy man a selection of incantations (*mantra*) and magic verses (*gāthā*). These, they were assured, would make them invulnerable.

The French authorities, fearful of incipient guerrilla insurgency, responded by sending an armed force to deal with the problem. This attempt, in turn, provoked a violent response from the massed villagers, and the violence spiralled to the point of frontal attacks between the opposing forces. Finally, in December 1902, the movement began to collapse. By that time, most of the leaders had been arrested or killed.

MILLENARIAN NATURE OF THE MOVEMENTS

The movements described above were millenarian. The term millenarian in the Lao context has a typological dimension above and beyond the historical Judeo-Christian meaning of this term, in the sense that in Laos it refers to a combination of destruction and ensuing regeneration. It therefore carries a dual religious message: the end of the world as we know it, and the re-appearance of a past Golden Age. This end of the world, followed by the rebirth of an era of bliss and prosperity, can take any of several forms. It can be perceived as either distant or near, or as determined (or not determined) by some sacred text that specifies the moment of the great day and its duration (limited in time or eternal). The return of a Golden Age, which is often mentioned in creation myths, may be perceived as collective, universal or restricted to a group; it is sometimes preceded by a natural cataclysm and always brings about radical change. The notion of returning to a Golden Age generally combines multiple aspirations, including the religious (to purify the faith), the political (to found or re-establish a political order, a dynasty, an ethnicity or national independence) and the socioeconomic (to proclaim equality, justice and prosperity). It is often linked with the coming-to-earth of an exceptional person, such as a divinity, messiah or prophet.

A perusal of southern Lao history reveals evidence of such movements and their leaders in 1578–9, in 1791 (Chiang Kaeo), in 1819–20 (Sakiat Kòng) and around 1850 (Mò Ha). These four movements have all the aforementioned characteristics, as did the Bòlawen movement between 1899 and 1910. The striking religious aspects in the Bòlawen case are its predicted end of the fifth Buddhist millennium (thus fulfiling the earlier prediction that Theravada Buddhism would end) and the arrival of a holy man—both of which are documented in Ong Kaeo's May 1901 letter. In a June 1901 letter, Ong Kaeo represented himself as the supreme head of a new religion that would supersede Theravada Buddhism. Then he announced the return to a Golden Age, in which rice (the Lao staple of life) would grow by itself in the fields without cultivation—a theme found in written and oral legends of most South-East Asian countries. At the same time, passing himself off as a miracle worker, he performed feats of magic and organised religious ceremonies. At these gatherings, in return for gifts, he distributed amulets to confer invulnerability and beeswax candles to ensure happiness and prosperity.

Complex religious ingredients are present in the Savannakhet Province movement between 1899 and 1903. The end of the world was announced for the month of April 1902, at which time the earth was supposed to be immersed in total darkness for seven days and seven nights. Anyone hoping to survive this scourge would have to adhere scrupulously to a set of prescriptions (taboos on certain foods, an interdiction against using money, an exhortation for virgin girls to marry), to perform a pilgrimage to the most sacred stupa in the region (the That Phanom on the Mekong) and to obey the instructions of the holy men when they appeared. The coming of the holy men was heralded, and the names of two of them in particularly (Phò Kaduat and Ong Buddha) were announced. Finally, a Golden Age was predicted, which would take concrete form through the restoration of the Lao kingdom of Lan Sang, the appearance of a universal monarch (an *avatār* of a future Buddha) and the departure of all foreigners (meaning the Thai and the French).

The movement directed by Kommadam from 1926 to 1936 likewise had a religious component. Kommadam represented himself as a holy man who was endowed with magic powers. He claimed he was sent to earth by celestial spirits, to destroy the society that was imposed on the peoples of the Bòlawen region under Lao tutelage. His mission was to replace the prevailing order with an indigenous Khòm kingdom, which would ensure happiness for all the Proto-Indochinese peoples.

INTERPRETATIONS OF THE MOVEMENTS

Three-fourths of the studies published about these movements have been written by foreign historians. Studies conducted by Lao are primarily literary (Kathay Don Sasorith) or are overtly political (party members of the Neo Lao Haksat or authors writing officially for the Lao PDR) or attempt to be scientific (Thongsa et al., Mongkhol Sasorith, Sa Nhanh Dongdeng and Chanthi Saignamongkhoun). Their goals are thus different.

Kathay Don Sasorith in his book *Pour rire un peu* (1947) tries merely to be anecdotal. But his account of Kommadam's cordial relations for many years with a local French official provides insights and information that help to explain why this unruly chief had no trouble with the French until 1925.

By contrast, a book that has some political agenda to orient it will endeavour to integrate its interpretation of these millenarian movements into an anti-colonial context and to link the movements with the broader struggle waged by the Lao people for their independence. For example, Kaysone Phomvihane places Ong Kaeo, Kommadam and Phò Kaduat among the five great heroes of Lao history since the fourteenth century.

Among the authors who attempt to be scientific in their approaches to the history of millenarian movements, a distinction has to be drawn between those few who have some training in history and those who have none at all. It is also important to distinguish between authors who are obliged to present the official viewpoint and those who are not. Finally, a distinction should be made between writings that are based on field research—collecting testimony directly from the actors in these dramas, and drawing upon the traces of them imprinted on the collective memory—and writings that are limited solely to the ideas that can be formulated while working in an office.

How do Lao writers present the millenarian movements? Lao views of the genesis and the termination of the phenomena outlined above can be divided into four trends. According to Lao authors, the movements are (1) purely political, (2) political with recourse to manipulation of magic and religious beliefs, (3) religious and political or (4) social and superstitious.

The school of thought that presents these movements as having a purely political origin is headed by two major figures who have examined the Bòlawen and Savannakhet movements: one schematically (Phoumi Vongvichit 1968) and the other with brevity (Kaysone Phomvihane 1975, 1976 and 1978). Phoumi Vongvichit, a member of the Politburo of the ruling party and acting president of the Lao PDR until 1991, anchors the origins of the movements within the aims and methods of French colonisation. He argues that the colonial system needed to keep the people in ignorance (and hence in misery), in order to exploit and pillage natural resources, and that this system used weapons of division, repression and obscurantism. He does not precisely describe these brutal methods but asserts that the people were forced to react against them. The people thus took arms against excessive exactions, including heavy taxation, forced labour and requisitions of goods.

For Kaysone Phomvihane, general secretary of the Communist Party until his death in 1992, these movements are firmly rooted in the traditions of heroic struggle waged by the Lao people against foreign aggressors, which can be traced back to the founding of the first independent Lao kingdom more than six centuries ago. It is notable that the heroes he cites prior to the struggle against French colonialism are King Setthathirat, who resisted the first Burmese invasions in 1569–70, and Chao Anuwong, who fought for independence against the Thai in 1827–8. This portrayal of history implicitly acknowledges that the Lao had good relations with their other neighbours, including the Chinese, Vietnamese and Cambodians.

A second school of thought gives prominence to the political facets of the movement, while also acknowledging that the manipulation of popular cultural and religious beliefs is a subsidiary explanation. This is the marxist school of the Committee for Social Science Research (Thongsa et al. 1989). If its position were accepted and officially endorsed by the political decision-makers, this endorsement would represent a step forward in taking into account the role of mentalities and religious beliefs in the march of history. Building on the analysis of Phoumi Vongvichit, this school of thought draws upon evidence that reveals the oppression and exploitation of national resources by the colonial regime. It completes the picture by mentioning two other factors leading to the revolts: the famine of 1902, which decimated numerous villages in Savannakhet Province, and the system of slavery, under which the population of the Bòlawen plateau had suffered during more than a century of Thai rule.

To these political, social and economic causes, this school of thought adds the manipulation, by leaders of the Bòlawen and Savannakhet movements, of popular belief in magic and the millenarian expectation of the coming of a universal ruler (known as Phaya Thammikarat), as a means of gaining the trust of the population and provoking them to rise against the authorities. According to this school of thought, this strategy had been devised and agreed upon by all the heads of the insurrection on both banks of the Mekong when they met at Khemmarat in 1900. Curiously enough, some members of this school even say that contemporary French authors identified Phò Kaduat and Ong Kaeo as the foretold universal ruler.

A third school accords equal importance to religious factors and to the political goal of independence. The attention of this school is concentrated only on the movement in Savannakhet, although this focus is never explained. This school of thought is represented by the Collectif for World Peace, a marxist-controlled organisation, which issued a booklet through the publishing house of the Pathet Lao in 1953. The theme is also portrayed by Sa Nhanh Dongdeng in his biography of Phò Kaduat published in 1974.

The last trend is represented by Mongkhol Sasorith (1973), a researcher educated in France who has progressive views. He attributes social and superstitious origins to the movement led by Ong Kaeo and social ones to the Savannakhet movement. Referring to the reconstruction of Laos undertaken by French colonisation, he explains these movements in terms of civil oppression exercised by the Lao against the peoples of the mountains—oppression that had caused numerous revolts in the past. Whereas the Lao acknowledged symbolically that the upland peoples were the indigenous inhabitants of the land, the Lao nonetheless imposed on them heavy taxes, harsh forced labour and multifarious other exactions. This existing near-enslavement was exacerbated by additional demands from the central colonial authorities, including more taxation, services and requisitions. To this list of grievances, Mongkhol Sasorith adds a dimension not mentioned by other writers: the arrogance, the brutality and the incomprehension of some French colonial officials. Another difference is that he adopts the viewpoint of a colonial author, citing—among various reasons for Kommadam's defiance of the French—the prohibition by French authorities of the traditional practice of slave hunting, which was a source of appreciable revenue in southern Laos. Finally, Mongkhol Sasorith notes that Ong Kaeo used numerous superstitions to strengthen his leadership as a holy man, which he defined as

a kind of Messiah who, having received from the spirits certain special powers (which rendered him invulnerable and capable of making miracles), was entrusted with the mission of ruling over men and ensuring justice among them. (Sasorith 1973: 146–7)

These four views put forward by Lao authors, on the genesis of the movements in the Bòlawen plateau and Savannakhet Province, require some comment. The authors trace the movements etiologically only to frustrations and grievances: economic (tax pressure and natural catastrophes that generate misery), social (ethnic enslavement and exploitation) or political (vicissitudes of political power and rejection of colonial authority). The human factor is never directly taken into account as a possible motive force behind these movements. For ideological reasons, Lao historians have presented these movements as anti-colonial revolts and have refused to take into account their genesis. In this way, they avoid reference to the irrational beliefs that marxism condemns. Finally, by studying these movements only in their second phase, when transformed into armed struggles, Lao researchers are able to point to a national resistance against the colonial system in southern Laos.

On the other hand, certain hesitations and variations are notable within the marxist perception of these movements, especially with regard to the importance of religious and cultural factors in their emergence. These factors were perceived as central to the 1953 study by the Collectif for World Peace, but they have since been reduced to subsidiary causes and are portrayed simply as a tactic adopted by the leaders of the movements. The successive shifts in emphasis demonstrate the evolution of marxist thought in Laos, which started with a far-from-orthodox ideological interpretation that can be attributed to a lack of ideological training. A rigid marxist position then came to the fore, based on rejection of irrationality, although it soon returned to a tentative effort to take account of factual realities. It is interesting that the only researcher (Mongkhol Sasorith) who discusses the superstitions inherent in these movements was educated in France.

Archival and published documents demonstrate that none of these movements began as insurrections against the colonial system. Whether in the Bòlawen plateau region or Savannakhet Province, a long period elapsed between the moment when a miracle worker initiated a movement and the moment when the movement was transformed into an insurrection against colonial power. Moreover, it was only when colonial administrators decided to arrest a miracle worker—and failed—that the movement became radicalised, bellicose and opposed to the colonial power. To this the archives bear witness.

The gap that exists between the actual course of events earlier in this century and its representation in subsequent writings is created by the dogmatism of the authors and, in particular, by a materialist vision of reality that minimises and often ignores the psychological, religious and cultural variables influencing these movements. These constraints permitted the authors to envisage only one aspect of the appearance and repression of these movements. This blinkered portrayal of events was reinforced by an ideological concept of what history *had* to be like, if it were to be shaped according to the desired tradition of the national struggle to safeguard (or recover) independence and of the march of societies towards socialism. These reductionist histories, mutilating reality, led to the creation of a gallery of heroes, who are more civic models than historical persons, and to the perpetuation, against hard facts, of an illusion of ethnic cohesion and harmony. In re-appropriating these episodes of their national past, contemporary Lao historians have tailored them to the dimensions of an official history.

NOTES

1. Concerning the Ngeh minority, see Lebar et al. (1964: 144).

LAOS MAPPED BY TREATY AND DECREE, 1895–1907

KENNON BREAZEALE

The familiar shape of Laos emerged on modern maps between 1895 and 1907. This study provides a brief introduction to the complex process of defining Laos territorially in relation to the five neighbouring countries, during the first decade and a half of French colonial rule. It does not attempt to examine the political negotiations among the four governments (British, Chinese, French and Thai) that carved up the interior of mainland South-East Asia through international agreements. That subject and some of the technical aspects of demarcation have been documented by numerous authors.[1] Since earlier works have already described the general historical context in which French Laos came into existence, this study investigates the series of legal instruments that determined the modern boundaries. It also raises some debatable issues that clearly deserve more detailed investigation.

EARLY TECHNICAL SURVEYS

Prior to the mid-1890s, no one had any clear idea about the configuration that Laos would take on the map. In published maps of the mid–nineteenth century, few places in Laos were marked with any precision, and even the physical features of the Mekong valley were only roughly known. The Ernest Doudart de Lagrée mission up the Mekong River during 1866–7 produced the first map

(Garnier 1873) based on a brief scientific survey. Further details were added by explorers, such as Etienne Aymonier (1885, 1895, 1897) and Paul Neïs (1885), who visited Laos during 1883 and 1884.

Technical surveys on a more comprehensive scale were carried out separately by French and by Thai officials beginning in the mid-1880s. The first map based on their efforts was prepared by the Thai survey department, under the direction of James McCarthy, and was published in 1888. The French surveys were coordinated by Auguste Pavie, who arrived in Laos in 1887. His regional map was printed for French government use in 1893 and served as a primary reference for the French diplomats and colonial officials who negotiated the definitive western boundaries of Laos. Other published maps (such as Pelet 1902) were not detailed or accurate enough to meet the needs of negotiators. The Pavie maps—including an atlas that appeared in 1903—although incomplete and inaccurate in some respects, were the best ones available to the joint commissions that carried out demarcation work along the Chinese-Lao boundary during 1896–7 and the Lao-Thai boundary during 1905–7.

In examining the diplomatic negotiations and administrative decisions that determined the final configuration of Laos on the map, it is important to bear in mind that the geographical service of the Indochina government had barely begun the great task of making technical surveys in Laos at the time that the boundary lines were drawn. Its detailed maps were not completed until later. Indeed, for much of Laos, maps showing precise boundary lines were never compiled at all.

LEGAL STATUS OF LAOS AS A FRENCH COLONY

When the Government of Indochina was established in 1887, the French colony (Cochinchina) was the only political unit that had a defined boundary. On behalf of the governments of the French protectorates—Cambodia and Annam (Central Vietnam)—France reserved all their historic claims to territory in the interior. After the

1867 Franco-Thai treaty[2] divided Cambodia and attempted to define a common boundary between the French and the Thai spheres in Cambodia, French diplomats and colonialists adopted a policy of avoiding any international agreements that implied French recognition of a boundary elsewhere in the Mekong valley. This policy was maintained in the Franco-Thai treaty of 1893, which enabled the French to take control of the left-bank of the Mekong but was specifically worded to avoid any reference to a boundary.

French administration in Laos did not come into existence on the basis of an agreement with an indigenous government.[3] Laos was therefore unlike the other constituent states of French Indochina (including Tonkin, which belonged to Annam but was administered separately as a protectorate). In the protectorates, treaties with the Vietnamese and Cambodian governments were ratified by the French parliament, provided the legal basis for French rule and bound France to the treaty terms. By contrast, during 1893 and 1894, individual commissionerships were created in the principal Lao administrative centres by order of the governor general of Indochina. Once French control was established and the cooperation of local Lao leaders was secured, this string of posts was combined into two regional military commands by order of the governor general in June 1895. The northern provinces were placed under a commandant for upper Laos, and the remaining provinces came under another commandant for lower Laos. The two halves of Laos were combined by decree of the governor general in February 1899, and an April 1899 decree by the president of the French republic gave the head of the unified colonial service in Laos the title of resident superior, making him equal in rank to his counterparts in Annam, Cambodia and Tonkin. By a separate presidential decree later the same year, the colonial officials in Laos were incorporated into the Indochina civil service.

The powers of the Indochina government were flexible enough to allow considerable local variation in the structure of administration, without approval from the French parliament. Not surprisingly, French colonial administration in Laos evolved according to the pattern already established in the three protectorates. Unlike the administrators of a French colony, the civil service in Laos carried out its functions to the extent permitted by a meagre budget, supplemented by the administrative efforts of Lao leaders in each province. The resulting administrative structure was thus moulded by fiscal necessity into a hybrid between the protectorate model and the colony model.

Although there was no indigenous Lao government, officials in Paris assumed from the outset that Laos must be a protectorate, and they regularly used this term in correspondence up to 1911. In that year, however, a presidential decree redefined the powers of the governor general, and the applicability of the term 'protectorate' in the case of Laos was debated at length. The French colonial and foreign ministries concluded that Laos was a 'colony' under French law and that French laws applicable to French colonies in general were therefore in force in Laos.[4]

Only after the Laos representative advisory council was created in 1920—followed by an elected assembly in 1923 and the promulgation of the Lao law code—did technical issues bring the question of legal status to the fore. What was the legal basis for establishing and enforcing the law code? If Laos was a colony where French law should prevail, to what extent could it be governed lawfully as though it were a protectorate? In response to the governor general's request for a definitive decision to resolve such problems, the Supreme Colonial Council in France considered all the legal arguments, and its conclusions were printed in the government gazette (*Journal Officiel*, 5 June 1930). The council's opinion is the only published official statement on the subject, and it concluded that Laos in its entirety was a French colony.[5]

The publication of these findings placed the Indochina government in an extremely awkward position with respect to its policy in Luang Prabang. For internal administrative convenience and for reasons of prestige in dealing with British Burma, China and Thailand, French colonial authorities consistently treated the hereditary rulers of Luang Prabang as kings, thereby creating the illusion that the historic territory of Luang Prabang was a protectorate of the French republic. A protectorate convention was, in fact, signed by the Lao king in 1895 and his successor signed two additional conventions in 1912 and 1914. These documents were countersigned, however, only by the residents superior of Laos, and a fourth was signed in 1917 by the governor general himself. None of these documents was submitted to the French parliament, and they were not recognised by the government in Paris as international agreements. When the Supreme Colonial Council declared that the protectorate conventions were internal Indochinese arrangements, which had no validity in French law, the king of Luang Prabang protested vigorously. From an administrative point of view, the Indochina government was anxious not to make any changes that would diminish the status and authority of the king, who was a symbol and instrument of stability in a region that would have been difficult and costly to govern as a colony. Such considerations made it necessary to shelve discreetly the government's initial plan to adopt the council's opinion into a presidential decree, which would have made explicit the legal status of Laos.[6] The existing misconception was thereafter perpetuated, and the Indochina government continued to treat Luang Prabang as an 'internal' protectorate. The governor general and the colonial minister gave the king numerous reassurances that his domain was indeed under French protection and would continue to receive all honours due to a protected kingdom. No such recognition was extended, however, by any higher French authority, and the French government took great care to restrict overt recognition to the governor general's office alone.

The legal status of Laos was the subject of a thesis submitted by François Iché to the University of Toulouse. Iché previously served as a magistrate in Champasak Province and was familiar with all aspects of applying French and local law in the different states of Indochina. While he was conducting his research, officials in the colonial ministry in Paris helpfully guided him through all the unpublished conventions and other documents that supported the ministry's policy towards Luang Prabang. Iché, who was returning to the Lao civil service, obligingly made a carefully reasoned argument that the agreements between colonial officials and the king of Luang Prabang were legal, even if never ratified by parliament. His arguments therefore supported the ministry's position that Luang Prabang enjoyed a special protected status and that the rest of Laos was unquestionably a French colony (Iché 1935: 155, 179, 185).

Considering the subtleties and ambiguities involved in applying French law in Laos, it is not surprising that the legal powers exercised by colonial officials in fixing some of the boundaries were likewise ambiguous. Since Laos was a colony and not a protected state, its territory belonged to France, and the French parliament had absolute power to cede any portion of Laos or to acquire additional territory for Laos through negotiations with other independent governments or with the protectorates of Indochina. The international boundaries of the colonial period were defined by treaties between the French government and the governments of Britain, China and Thailand. The following sections provide an overview of how the northern and western limits of Laos were defined in these international agreements. They also discuss how the internal boundaries with Cambodia and Vietnam, within the Indochina Union itself, were added to the map by colonial officials, exercising powers that had only an ambiguous legal basis.

BOUNDARIES WITH BURMA AND CHINA

The first boundary segment of modern Laos to be determined by international agreement is one of the most remote: the China-Laos line, tentatively defined in the Sino-French convention of June 1895 (see fig. 4). This agreement provided for the extension of the demarcation work on the China-Vietnam line, which had been in progress since 1885. The second boundary was fixed by the British-French declaration of January 1896 along the thalweg of the Mekong River, to divide British Burma from French Indochina. The thalweg is the line that follows the lowest part of a valley and roughly defines the middle of a river.

The demarcation of the Lao boundary with China originated in the 1885 Sino-French treaty, which provided for a joint commission to investigate (and mark, wherever possible) the boundary between Chinese and Vietnamese territory. The initial findings of the commission were incorporated in a delimitation convention in

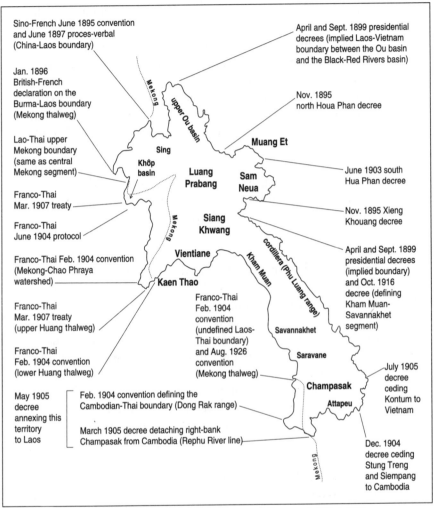

Fig. 4. Lao Boundary Segments by Treaty and Decree, 1895–1907

1887. The westernmost point mentioned in these two agreements was the Black River basin, and the westward extension of this line was left open to further negotiations. Demarcation work proceeded slowly across the China-Vietnam frontier, however, since the French army in Tonkin was still struggling during those years to bring this turbulent region under effective French control.

By late 1893, the boundary was marked only as far inland as the Red River, and demarcation work was suspended temporarily, so that the terrain between that point and the Mekong could be explored in greater detail.[7] Also at this time, French officials were gradually taking up positions in the Lao territories east of the Mekong, which the Thai government had renounced by treaty in October 1893. As a temporary administrative expedient, all of the Lao territories bordering on Yunnan Province were placed under the jurisdiction of the French resident superior in Tonkin—an arrangement that unified the technical, military and political aspects of delimitation in this little known region.

A plan to erect border markers from the Red River west to the Black River by mid-1894 was devised but then suspended, while the French foreign and colonial ministries reconsidered the extension of this line even farther west to the Mekong, in the light of conflicting British, Chinese and French claims in the upper Mekong valley. In October 1894 the French foreign minister outlined a policy to seek a rational boundary that would serve the long-term interests of Indochina. Pointing out the lesson already learned from earlier delimitation decisions, which had not taken small administrative units fully into account, he indicated that definitive agreements on the exact line from the upper Black River basin to the Mekong should avoid arbitrary divisions of existing political entities. Since the tentative line across the Black River basin cut through the territory of a French ally, he insisted on renegotiations with China to keep all the lands of the local ruling family intact.[8]

West of the Black River, however, the French foreign minister and the colonial under-secretary both preferred geographical to political unity, so that the entire Ou River basin could be retained by Indochina.[9] The western watershed of the upper Ou was the only physical feature that seemed to provide a simple definition for purposes of demarcation as far as the Mekong. Although the proposed line required a cession of territory by China, including two small Lü governorships in the upper Ou basin, it left the populous and economically most important part of the Lü princely state (Sipsòng Panna) within the borders of China. It supported

China's historic claim to the remaining Lü territory east of the Mekong and gave Indochina a north-western boundary that conformed to the contours of basic geographical features.

In October 1894 the Chinese government agreed in principle on the proposed western extension of the common frontier line, and the two governments prepared to carry out the demarcation work as quickly as possible.[10] In December 1894 and January 1895 three survey groups arrived in the area to verify different segments of the border. They failed to reach conclusive agreements and referred to their governments the findings concerning the upper Black River territory desired by France and the exact line along the western watershed of the Ou basin that would leave China in possession of two important commodities: some of the salt pits, which were vital to the Lü populace, and the gardens of Ibang, which produced a tea highly prized by the court in Beijing.[11]

Before the detailed survey reports and maps were received, however, the French minister in Beijing signed an additional delimitation convention in June 1895, which defined the extended line to the Mekong and provided for immediate demarcation. To complicate matters further, the British and French were embroiled in a dispute over a small tract of trans-Mekong territory. One month prior to the signing of the Beijing convention, British troops occupied part of the territory that the French were trying to acquire from China. The demarcation work of the Sino-French commission in this area therefore had to be postponed until the dispute, which arose in 1893, was resolved.

Early in 1893, when a British-Thai commission completed the demarcation of the Burmese-Thai boundary from the Salween east to the Mekong, one trans-Mekong state—Chiang Khaeng—was claimed by both governments. The inhabitants of this state were partly Shan and partly Lü. The ruler was a cousin of the Chiang Tung (Kengtung) prince and a relation of the Sipsòng Panna prince by marriage. From his capital at Sing, on the east bank, he governed some rice-growing lands west of the Mekong, but most of his domain was east of the river. The British government renounced its claim to Chiang Khaeng, on condition that the Thai government could not cede the territory to China or France.[12]

Having reached this agreement with the Thai, and assuming that a similar British claim to Sipsòng Panna would be renounced in favour of China, British officials in early 1893 were expecting the joint British-Thai delimitation work to continue. The British and Thai governments envisaged a line between Burmese and Thai territory that would run northward along the Mekong (possibly with a slight deviation west of the river) to the point where the Burma-China boundary reached the Mekong. Since the territory east of this line would be Thai, and since Bangkok had no diplomatic relations with Beijing, the Foreign Office in London suggested that its diplomats in China could act as intermediaries for the demarcation of a common Sino-Thai boundary. Such a line would have kept intact all the political entities that existed at the time, since it would have extended eastward from the Mekong and along the southern limits of Sipsòng Panna, ending at a point on the *eastern* watershed of the Ou basin.

This well-constructed scheme would also have created a comfortable buffer of Thai territory between British and French colonial possessions. But it came unstuck when the Thai government was forced by a French ultimatum to renounce all territorial claims east of the Mekong. Even before the Franco-Thai treaty was signed in October 1893, the British and French governments began talks on the territorial implications for the upper Mekong. Both governments wanted to avoid a common boundary between their respective colonial empires. During 1894 and 1895, in search of a combination of territories that would create a Thai-controlled buffer, a joint commission investigated all possible north-south border lines that could be drawn west and east of the Mekong, but no combination could be found that was acceptable to both sides. After negotiations collapsed, British troops from Burma crossed the Mekong in May 1895, to the great consternation of the French government, and established a garrison in Sing.

Undaunted by this turn of events, the French minister proceeded to sign the delimitation convention in Beijing a month later. Pending further negotiations with Britain, the French tried to keep the terms of the convention secret, especially since they were still attempting to arrange the demarcation of the contested territory, even though they had lost control of it for lack of any French troops or officials to post there.[13] The British-French dispute was resolved by a joint declaration in January 1896, which designated the thalweg of the Mekong as the border between Burma and Indochina. A French official reached Sing in May 1896 and took possession of the upper Mekong tract for the colonial government. At this point in time, the Mekong was the only border of Laos that had been precisely defined, since the Sino-French demarcation work was still suspended.[14]

While the French representative was en route to Sing, the governor general's office made an embarrassing discovery in the terms of the prematurely concluded Beijing convention. When the document was signed, the French had made only cursory surveys, and they did not know the precise path of the Ou River watershed line. As a result, there were several contradictions between the text of the convention and the appended maps. The text described an east-west line from the Mekong, following the watershed south of the La River basin (which was awarded to China), and by early 1896 the cartographic service of the French colonial ministry had begun to print maps of the definitive boundary showing this line.[15] Not until April 1896, however, did Indochinese officials receive the results of an accurate survey, which revealed that the little stream adjacent to Sing flowed not westward into the Mekong (as previously reported) but northward into the La itself.[16] Having gained possession of Sing from the Thai, then having lost and regained control of the town in the dispute with Britain, the French now realised that they had signed away their rights to this coveted territory in a diplomatic agreement with China.

To avoid formal renegotiation of the convention itself, various internal contradictions between the text and appended maps had to be resolved on a point-by-point basis by the joint boundary commission.[17] In the end, the definitive line was drawn to the north of Sing, as the French wished. The border markers along the China-Laos line were erected by the commission in early 1897, and the final reports were signed in late March. On the first of April, along the trail between the upper Ou River and the Chinese town of Simao, the last marker was put in place.[18] The delimitation process was completed in June 1897, when the final procès-verbal was signed by the chiefs of the joint commission.

BOUNDARIES OF LAOS WEST OF THE MEKONG

When formulating the 1893 Franco-Thai treaty terms, French officials in Paris selected the Mekong as the sole geographical feature that provided an indisputable line of reference. The clause by which the Thai government was forced to renounce all territorial claims beyond the Mekong was an improvisation by the French government in response to the unanticipated opportunity (provided by the 1893 gunboat incident near Bangkok) to demand a huge territorial concession. In the haste of the moment, no consideration was given to the division of existing political entities. Along the lower Mekong, the capital of Champasak was on the west bank, although most of the lands and populace of this princely state were on the opposite side of the river and therefore passed under French control. In the north, Luang Prabang was similarly divided. Its capital was on the east bank, but part of its territory lay between the river and the mountain range to the west.

Subsequently, yielding to pressure from the French for the reunification of Luang Prabang, the Thai government renounced all rights to the right-bank Lao lands in the upper Mekong in the 1904 Franco-Thai convention. For most of its length, the western boundary of Luang Prabang, as defined in the convention, followed the crest of the mountains that form the watershed line between the Chao Phraya and Mekong basins. The upper and lower extremities of this line, however, were modified in stages during the next three years. At the southern end, the February 1904 convention defined a line that began at the Hüang-Mekong confluent and followed the thalweg of the Hüang River as far as the Tang (a left-bank tributary stream). The line then followed the thalweg of the Tang to its source and the main watershed line. Near the northern end, the boundary ran from the watershed line to the source of the Khòp River and then followed the thalweg of the Khòp for its entire length to the Mekong.

After further negotiations, which resulted in additional territorial concessions by the Thai government, the boundary line was modified by a protocol in June 1904. According to the redefined boundary, the line ran along the Hüang as far as the Man (a right-bank tributary), continued along the thalweg of the Man to the watershed above its source, and then followed the watershed line northward. At the upper end, instead of running from the watershed to the Khòp River, it continued along the crest of the mountains and then down to the Mekong along the next ridge. Under the new arrangement, the Thai government ceded the remainder of the Khòp valley and the portion of Dan Sai district that was on the left bank of the Man River. In the Franco-Thai treaty of 1907, Dan Sai was retroceded to Thailand by reverting to the Hüang River line originally proposed by the French. The definitive line, defined in the delimitation protocol of this treaty, specified a boundary following the thalweg of the Hüang for its entire length. The 1907 protocol also redefined the line above the Khòp and awarded to Luang Prabang an additional sliver of territory along the right bank of the Mekong. The net result of all these adjustments is that the definitive western boundary of Luang Prabang is defined in five separate segments specified in the 1904 convention, 1904 protocol and the 1907 treaty.

A comparison of published and unpublished maps that were available in 1904 reveals that neither the French nor the Thai negotiators had enough knowledge of the geographical features of the Khòp and Hüang basins to define the desired line accurately. The June 1904 protocol attempted to award to Luang Prabang a long sliver of land north of the Khòp confluent. This stretch of the Mekong was inaccessible from the Thai side, because the land drops steeply from the watershed down to the river. Existing maps, based on the Pavie surveys, show a single long ridgeline, parallel to the Mekong and west of this entire tract, and the negotiators attempted to describe this ridge in the text of the protocol. But in the field, the surveyors discovered a short, intervening ridge immediately above the Khòp confluent. Strict application of the protocol definition would have shifted the boundary point on the Mekong considerably far south of the point actually intended, leaving the inaccessible sliver of land within the Thai borders. The surveyors' findings therefore had to be incorporated into another redefinition in the 1907 treaty.

The original Hüang River decision was likewise based on inadequate knowledge of local geography. A sketch map, compiled for reference by French negotiators to compare the conflicting French, Lao and Thai versions of the Luang Prabang boundary, clearly indicates that the French claimed the entire left bank of the principal waterway (now known to be the Hüang) to its source, including the town of Kaen Thao.[19] Only in 1906 did the first reasonably accurate map become available to the negotiators.[20] The 'Tang' (or 'Tane') River specified in the 1904 convention cannot be identified with certainty on any map. The published maps (McCarthy 1888, Pavie 1903 and Pelet 1902, among others) all give the impression, moreover, that the Man and Hüang are a single river and that the waterway now known to be the upper Hüang had a different (but not yet specified) name. The mysterious 'Tang' most likely was a local name for the northern branch of the upper Hüang, which became the definitive boundary. This supposition is supported by the McCarthy map, on which the name Huaytang ('Tang Stream') appears as part of the name of a village near the source of the Hüang. The texts of the February 1904 and March 1907 documents seem to refer to different waterways, whereas in fact the intended line was the same in both cases.

The 1904 and 1907 agreements also defined the right-bank boundary between French and Thai territory in the lower Mekong. The French objective was not to reunite the lands of the historic Lao kingdom in this area, however, since the ruling prince of Champasak (whose capital was on the right bank) continued to acknowledge Thai suzerainty after 1893 and had no independent relations with French colonial authorities. Immediately after the prince's death in 1901, the Thai government began to transform Champasak into an ordinary Thai province, on the grounds that the heir-apparent (who was never consecrated as a dependency prince) was unpopular and lacked the respect of local leaders.[21] Not all of the little towns in this area belonged to Champasak. Up to 1904, the Thai territory immediately south of the Dong Rak range was administered from Ubon as part of Isan Circle. It included the remnants of the Champasak prince's domain, two separately administered towns on the lower Mekong and two small towns (Cheom Ksan and Melouprey) slightly to the west but in the Great Lake basin.[22] When the Thai government ceded this territory, the new boundary was defined not in reference to Champasak but in terms of a longer line across northern Cambodia, following the watershed of the Dong Rak mountains and ending at the Mekong up-river from Champasak.

Joint surveys were carried out during the next several dry seasons, and maps produced by the boundary commission in both the lower and upper Mekong were printed in 1906.[23] In the delimitation protocol of the 1907 treaty, the line already verified to the west of Champasak was adjusted slightly, by defining the precise point on the Mekong where the line ended. An additional protocol was signed in May 1908, which provided for the preparation of definitive maps of the Indochina-Thai boundary,[24] and these maps were published jointly between 1909 and 1912 by the Thai army map department and the cartographic service of Indochina.

AMBIGUOUS MEKONG BOUNDARY

In the course of all these agreements, two stretches of the Mekong continued to separate Laos from Thailand. Most of the international boundary between these two countries today is formed by these two long stretches of the river. It is often assumed (Prescott 1975: 429) that these segments of the boundary were fixed in 1893, but the Franco-Thai treaty of 1893 purposely made no reference to a boundary. The treaty stated only that the Thai government renounced all territorial claims beyond the river and all claims to the islands in the river. On the right bank, moreover, the Thai government remained in control of the hinterlands, but severe restrictions were placed on Thai authority inside a zone 25 kilometres wide, which extended the entire length of the Mekong. Thai soldiers were prohibited from entering the zone, and since most senior provincial officials of the central government were army officers (and the others never risked travelling without an armed escort), they were unable to exercise full authority over local administration in the zone.

The renunciation clause in the treaty was composed by French officials and imposed on the Thai government as a condition of settling the gunboat incident. At the time of the treaty, the limits of French territorial claims had not yet been determined, and the advocates of French colonial expansion expected, at a future date, to gain control of much additional territory in the Mekong valley. Maintaining a long-established policy of leaving themselves an entirely free hand in future boundary negotiations, the French government in 1893 carefully avoided any terminology that could be interpreted either as a boundary or as French recognition of Thai sovereignty on the right bank.

The Thai renunciation of claims to all islands in the Mekong was interpreted by the French, moreover, as a renunciation of rights to the river itself. By late 1893, as Thai officials withdrew from the left-bank territories and the Mekong-bank towns, and moved inland behind the 25–kilometre limit, the French began to take possession not only of the left bank but also the river. The importance of the river is reflected in the French president's statement when introducing the treaty to the Senate in Paris. He jubilantly proclaimed that, upon ratification of the treaty, 'the waters of the river . . . become exclusively French'.[25]

The realisation of French dreams of taming the central and upper Mekong seemed imminent in 1894 and 1895, when a steamer service was launched and a French naval gunboat reached the upper Mekong to undertake a thorough hydrographic study. But soon after the turn of the century, the Mekong-mania that fuelled French territorial fervour in the 1890s began to dissipate amidst the stark realities of administering Laos and developing it commercially. The navigable stretches of the Mekong were divided in several places by cataracts and long stretches of rapids, which necessitated heavy government subsidies to maintain a steamer service on each navigable stretch, plus facilities for trans-shipment around the unnavigable ones. In terms of communications and other administrative costs, Laos was a drain on the budget of the

Indochina Union, and it was already clear by the turn of the century that existing and potential forms of taxation in this impoverished region could not produce enough revenue to pay for its skeletal colonial administration. Expectations of commercial development were dampened by the fact that Lao consumers were too poor to buy imported French goods, and most of the forest and mineral resources were so inaccessible that even a rapacious developer would be hard pressed to exploit them profitably. By the time the negotiations for the 1904 Franco-Thai convention were completed, the inflated myth of riches in the interior had been punctured, and the momentum for further French territorial acquisitions in the central Mekong basin had subsided.[26]

French visions of great transport networks in the Mekong valley persisted, however, and the determination that only the French and the Thai should be involved in the construction and operation of large public works (such as railways) was a major factor in subsequent French negotiations with the Thai government. This goal was partly achieved in the April 1904 British-French declaration, in which Britain agreed to raise no objections if France sought exclusive concessions from the Thai government in the Mekong valley. In the Franco-Thai convention of February 1904, the Thai government accepted the principle of exclusive privileges for the French in public works and, in return, France formally recognised Thai sovereignty over the right-bank lands.

The illusion that the Mekong was already a defined boundary is reinforced by the subtle terminology in the 1904 convention clause that describes the line west of Champasak. This line extends from the Great Lake in Cambodia north to the mountains and then along the Dong Rak range to a point on the Mekong. The clause ends with the statement: 'Up-river from this point, the Mekong remains the boundary of the Kingdom of Siam, in conformity with the first article of the 3 October 1893 treaty.' Since the 1893 treaty article was expressly constructed so that the Mekong was *not* an international boundary, what does this statement mean?

Both sides accepted that a territorial limit had to be specified in the convention, but they could not agree on the exact position of the line. The French government insisted on French sovereignty up to the shoreline on the Thai side, so that France could exercise undisputed authority in all matters relating to commercial traffic, policing and other river management. Since the Thai government was unwilling to make this concession, the 1904 clause provided a compromise. It formally established a boundary, for the first time, without attempting to define the line. The phrase 'in conformity with the first article of the 3 October 1893 treaty' is not an attempt to declare, retroactively, that this boundary existed since 1893. On the contrary, it allowed the French to continue interpreting the 1893 article in the sense of French sovereignty up to the Thai shoreline, while allowing the Thai government to interpret the same article in a different sense.

The omission of any reference to Indochina or to Laos in this article of the 1904 convention is significant, because the text refers only to the outer limit of Thai sovereignty and not to a common line between Thai and French territory. From the French viewpoint, this subtle solution maintained the status quo by recognising Thai sovereignty only up to the line that the French interpreted as the boundary, without explicitly defining that line. The French foreign and colonial ministers were in agreement that the convention made no concession with regard to the exact line but upheld the French claim to sovereignty over the river.[27] This solution also made it unnecessary to apply, along the Mekong itself, another article that required joint verification of the boundary between Thailand and Indochina.

In the succeeding years, the absence of a precise boundary definition posed few practical problems for administration at the provincial level on either side of the river. But it did create a bizarre patchwork of French territorial claims on the right bank. The shoreline theory meant that the boundary changed (always to the advantage of Laos) whenever the river-bed shifted. Thus, if the river cut a new channel through an outcrop of land on the right bank, thereby separating a piece of land from the shore, the new island became part of Laos. Outcrops of land that were attached to the right bank in the dry season but became islands during the flood season were treated as part of Laos in all seasons. If an island near the Thai side became permanently attached to the Thai shore, as the result of silting in a narrow channel, the former island, together with the former channel, continued to belong to Laos, and the boundary line thereafter followed the former shoreline. Fortunately, no one lived on these low-lying parcels of land, which were exposed annually to flooding, and the disputes that did occasionally arise were mostly about seasonal land-use rights.

The 1904 convention enabled the French government to persist for another two decades in its interpretation that the 1893 treaty gave France exclusive possession and management of the waters of the Mekong. In practice, the Thai government accommodated the shoreline theory but never formally recognised it. Only in the course of negotiations leading to the 1926 Franco-Thai convention did the French relent and agree to the thalweg as the definitive boundary.

LAOS-VIETNAM BOUNDARY

Territorial changes between Laos and the other constituent states of Indochina were made by decree of the governor general. The only precisely defined Lao boundary segments that appear in such decrees are the Rephu River line (with Cambodia) and one portion of the cordillera line (with Vietnam). Although the boundary between Laos and Vietnam follows or is close to watershed lines for most of its 2,100-kilometre length, the lack of published documents long defeated efforts to study the process by which this line was determined (Prescott 1975: 481). An extensive search for unpublished French documentation on the Laos-Vietnam boundary was made by Bernard Gay (1989). He provides a perceptive analysis of how some segments of the boundary came into existence, through French cartographers' efforts to map the locally accepted political and ethnic dividing lines. He describes how the local authorities on each side of such borders dealt with their counterparts on the other side, in the absence of a precise line between their respective spheres of authority. And he argues that, with the exception of the segment defined in 1916, in an effort to clarify jurisdiction over tribal groups, the plan to carry out precise surveys was never implemented, partly because of the prohibitive costs.

When the basic structure of French administration was established in June 1895, the territories under the commandants of upper and lower Laos were defined roughly in terms of jurisdiction over specified Lao towns. The watershed of the cordillera was a convenient line that naturally divided central Vietnam from central Laos. Farther north, however, two states had been dependencies of both Vietnam and Luang Prabang. Several territorial changes were made in these two states, in search of a practical division of authority based on ethnic considerations and existing political units. Siang Khwang (the former Phuan princely state) was incorporated into upper Laos in November 1895. But the Hua Phan state (a group of Lao frontier towns) underwent a series of transmutations.

French administration in the Hua Phan towns began in October 1893, when this territory was annexed by decree to the adjacent military command in Tonkin. The northern Hua Phan towns (including Müang Et) in the upper Ma River basin were transferred to Laos in November 1895. The southern Hua Phan towns (including Sam Nüa) in the upper Sam River basin were transferred from Tonkin to Annam in March 1894, by a letter of agreement from the governor general, but this decision was rescinded by a January 1895 decree, which transferred them to Laos. The decree, however, was voided by an August 1896 decree, which annexed them once again to Annam. When the unified administration of French Laos was established in 1899, the Hua Phan towns were the only Lao political unit bordering on Vietnam that remained divided.

Manoeuvres by Vietnamese officials to retain the entire Sam River basin within their borders arbitrarily separated the people of the Hua Phan state, and after a few years it was evident that the watershed line was an impractical boundary. The Lao officials of Sam Nüa and nearby towns objected vehemently to the provincial Vietnamese authorities, and by the turn of the century they were demanding reunification with Laos, threatening otherwise to abandon their towns and move the entire populace across the watershed.[28] In June 1903, to stem the flow of villagers, who had already begun to move across the border into Laos, the governor general issued a decree that transferred the southern Hua Phan towns once again and reunited them with the rest of Hua Phan Province.

Early the following year, French Laos reached its maximum territorial extent, at least in theory, after the acquisition of the right-bank Luang Prabang territory. But by the end of 1904, even before the Franco-Thai convention was ratified, the southern Lao boundaries with Vietnam and Cambodia began to take their final form. In the process, the territory administered by the resident superior at Vientiane was greatly reduced.

After the unified administration was established in 1899, efforts had been made to create French posts in the vast and almost impenetrable region of mountains and plateaus around the trijuncture of present-day Cambodia, Laos and Vietnam. At that time, all of this territory was part of French Laos. One experiment quickly ended in failure: the idea of creating a single central authority over the many tribal peoples who inhabit the region. Even in the best of times, Laos had neither the financial nor the human resources necessary for such a task. And from about 1901 onward, in some of the tribal areas and along the Mekong itself, millenarian movements and other forms of resistance began to plague the colonial government. In search of a more practical system, a new policy was implemented in 1904 and 1905 which shifted the financial burden and administrative responsibilities in much of this southern territory to other governments of the Indochina Union. As a result, the boundaries of southern Laos were completely redrawn.

Since the isolated plateau region was thought to be more accessible from Vietnam, it was detached from Laos in two stages. Darlac was placed under the jurisdiction of the Annam resident superior by decree of the governor general in November 1904. An administrative centre was established in the northern part of the region (Kontum Province), and it was transferred to Annam in July 1905. Although the entire plateau region was separated territorially from Laos, only Kontum Province was integrated territorially into Annam. Darlac, on the other hand, acquired a kind of independent status as an autonomous unit within the Indochina Union, governed by the Annam resident superior. In the 1920s the imperial government in Hué began to press the Indochina government to incorporate Darlac into Annam, and its territorial integration was finally approved by a decree of the French president in 1932. During all this time, French maps created the illusion that it was actually part of Vietnam.

CAMBODIA-LAOS BOUNDARY

On the Mekong side, the lower reaches of the rivers that flow down from the plateau were controlled by Stung Treng and Siampang. Both towns were transferred from Laos to Cambodia by decree of the governor general in December 1904. This cession was intended as a means of improving general administration and was part of a broader plan to establish a single large province, which would extend the length of the Cambodian-Lao boundary and encompass a large area with a heterogeneous population.

In the February 1904 Franco-Thai convention, the Thai government ceded a block of territory that was south and east of the Dong Rak range, comprising the right-bank portion of a Lao princely state (Champasak) and some small towns that were claimed by Cambodia. An internal boundary within the ceded territory was fixed in March 1905 by decree of the governor general. The 1904–5 decrees thus made possible the creation of an enlarged Stung Treng Province by combining some of the right-bank lands acquired from Thailand (Thalabarivat, Cheom Ksan and Melouprey) with the left-bank territory (Stung Treng and Siampang) that was transferred from Laos (see Figure 5).

The line was designated as the northern limit of Cambodia, and it followed the Rephu River, from its source in the Dong Rak range to its confluent with the Mekong. The river is known by various pronunciations of its name: Nam Rephu (Lao), Tonle Repou (Khmer) and Selamphao (Lao and Thai). The river was a clearly defined geographical feature that was easily understood by the local populace, and it had long been acknowledged as a provincial limit. By a decree of May 1905, the right-bank territory north of the Rephu was formally incorporated into Champasak Province, which up to that time had consisted only of the French territory on the left bank.

No attempt was made to reconstitute the Champasak princely state as a political or territorial entity. The 1904 convention and

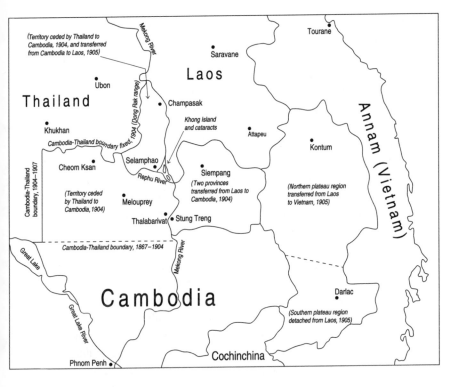

Fig. 5. Southern Lao Boundaries Redrawn, 1904–5

1905 decrees ignored the territorially overlapping Lao administrative system that existed prior to 1893 and imposed instead a geographical division that was consistent with French concepts. Several modern provinces thus inherited portions of the former princely state. Champasak town and five of its former satellite towns (subordinate governorships) were incorporated in the enlarged Champasak Province, together with two other satellites (both formerly under the jurisdiction of the Khong Island governor). The redrawn boundaries left three of Champasak's former satellites in Thailand (since they were on the opposite side of the Dong Rak range), one (Thalabarivat) in Cambodia and three in Saravane Province.[29]

The transfer of left-bank territory to Cambodia in 1904 was officially justified by the claim of the royal government in Phnom Penh that all the towns constituting the enlarged province of Stung Treng had once belonged to Cambodia. According to the Champasak version of history, however, the modern sites of Stung Treng, Siampang, Khong and Attapeu were mere villages under Champasak control prior to the 1827–8 Lao-Thai war. About 1830 they were detached from Champasak, elevated in status to provincial towns and supervised until 1893 by the interior ministry in Bangkok.[30] The Thai government justified these changes as the best means of restoring order after the 1827–8 war and of maintaining stable administration during the 1833–47 Thai-Vietnamese war, in an area that was inhabited by Khmer, Kui, Lao and tribal peoples.

Both Melouprey and Selamphao were officially established in 1843 at their modern sites.[31] Local leaders in both places received instructions from the Thai government the previous year to bring people from the forests and settle them around these town sites.[32] In addition to Lao and Kui, the settlers probably included some Khmer families, who took refuge in this area because of protracted warfare in Cambodia between the Thai and Vietnamese. They may also have included tribal people, who were regularly brought from the mountains and traded as slaves. Since the predominant ethnic group of Melouprey was Kui—whom the Thai regarded as more closely related to the Khmer than the Lao—Melouprey was placed under the jurisdiction of the Khmer governor of Khukhan Province. In Selamphao—a Champasak satellite on the right bank of the Mekong, immediately above the mouth of the Rephu River—the populace was mixed Lao and Kui, like the rest of the right-bank populace all the way up to Champasak town (Aymonier 1885: 7, 43–4).

By establishing a new satellite town and resettling farmers along the right bank of the Mekong, as far south as the cataracts at Khong Island, the princes of Champasak consolidated their control over most of the land along the river banks. During the 1870s two more satellite towns were established north of Selamphao,[33] and the agricultural lands available to the three governorships must have been inadequate for their expanding populations. Immediately south of the Rephu River, however, extensive annual flooding below the cataracts rendered the land unsuitable for rice farmers. Part of the Selamphao population therefore moved much farther down the Mekong and settled opposite Stung Treng. In 1885 the Thai government officially recognised Thalabarivat as a new satellite of Champasak, to govern these resettled villagers.[34] By the turn of the century, therefore, migration and population growth had considerably changed the ethnic composition and political control of this sparsely populated area, and Lao villages had spread down the right bank as far as Stung Treng. On the opposite side of the Mekong, early French explorations show that the Stung Treng populace was predominantly Lao in the 1860s, although some Chinese, Vietnamese and Khmer also lived and traded there (Mourin d'Arfeuille 1872: 468). At the turn of the century, the Khmer accounted for a negligible proportion of the lowland population on the left bank and had begun to adopt the Lao language and customs, in part through intermarriage.[35]

French officials, when contemplating the desirability of a new boundary line across southern Laos, were largely ignorant of the past century of evolution in local administration and the recent demographic changes that had taken place in this area. Factors such as the predominantly Lao population on the left bank and Champasak's control of the mixed Kui and Lao population on the right bank were outweighed by administrative and political considerations. A boundary line near the cataracts at Khong Island had the advantage of rational management of the river transport system. The stretch of the Mekong that is navigable from the sea could thus be placed within the borders of Cambodia, whereas the trans-shipment facilities (including the light railway across Khong Island, which served the navigable stretch above the cataracts) would continue to be the responsibility of Laos. General French policy towards the royal government of Cambodia was better served by combining much of this territory into one large province and presenting it to the Khmer king. Perhaps most important, the Phnom Penh treasury could afford to pay for improved administration and communications, especially in the mountainous areas east of Stung Treng.

The governor general brushed aside the objections of his subordinates in Laos and seized upon a historical justification, anachronistic though it was, for combining most of this territory into an enlarged province and placing it under Cambodian administration. The Rephu River had been acknowledged by the Kui and Lao as the dividing line between their respective settlements around Melouprey and Khong Island only a generation earlier,[36] and this waterway was declared the new boundary in 1905. On the opposite bank of the Mekong, the new boundary between Cambodia and Laos continued around the northern limits of Stung Treng and Siampang and then extended eastward towards the plateau region, to the point that is now the trijuncture of Cambodia, Laos and Vietnam.

LEGAL TANGLES AND THEIR RESOLUTION

The nature of the powers exercised in redrawing the internal boundaries of Indochina is not just a historical question but a topic of continuing interest, since no definitive line existed in many places until near the end of the twentieth century.[37] The territorial delineation of Laos reflects the exploration and discovery by Europeans of the interior of the peninsula, which was still in progress when modern boundary lines were inserted on the map. Demarcation began before basic surveys had been made in many areas, and much of the terrain was barely known. Treaty negotiations were carried out on the basis of very imperfect maps, including those produced by the Pavie mission, and errors in such maps hampered on-the-spot efforts by surveyors to verify lines that had been chosen in faraway government offices. The demarcation process also reflects general misconceptions up to 1911 about the legal status of Laos and the French search for a coherent administrative policy in the course of establishing French control.

Four international agreements determined the status of the territory in northern Laos that did not belong to Luang Prabang. Thai rights to this area were renounced in 1893, and British claims were renounced in 1896. The terminology of the agreements with both of these governments left France with a free hand throughout the left bank. But the 1895 Sino-French convention was more specific. It stated that

'The common boundary of Yunnan [i.e., the Chinese empire] and Annam [i.e., the Vietnamese empire] between the Black River . . . and the Mekong is drawn as follows. . . . The territory of the Eight Salt Pits [near the *western* watershed of the upper Ou basin] remains assigned to Annam.'

At the time the convention was signed, this boundary was treated as an extension of the line already marked across the frontier between Yunnan Province and Tonkin, and China explicitly ceded to the Vietnamese government the upper Ou basin (part of Sipsòng Panna, a Chinese dependency state) and other left-bank territory north-west of Luang Prabang.

This territory was acquired from China on behalf of the Vietnamese government under the terms of the 1884 Franco-Vietnamese protectorate treaty, which states that 'France undertakes to guarantee henceforth in their entirety the states of His Majesty the King of Annam.' The Vietnamese authorities, in signing this agreement, certainly never intended that France should convert territory that had been acquired on behalf of Vietnam into a French colonial possession. The Laos-Tonkin border was never fixed precisely, and no agreement between France and Vietnam ever transferred any of this undefined territory to Laos. The distinction between the northern provinces and the rest of Laos was not important during the early years of French rule, when Laos as a whole was assumed to be a protectorate acquired on the basis of historic Vietnamese and Cambodian rights. After 1911, however, one criterion for reclassifying Laos as a colony was the absence of any treaty or other binding agreements with the Vietnamese or Cambodian governments. In reaching that conclusion, however, French authorities overlooked the status conferred by treaty on the northern provinces. As time passed, these provinces were simply assumed to be an integral part of Laos, because the map makers showed them that way.

A similar anomaly arose in the south-west corner of Laos. At the time of the negotiations leading to the 1904 Franco-Thai convention, the French based their territorial claim in this area on historic Cambodian rights. The convention therefore stated that the Dong Rak range (part of which forms the western boundary of present-day Champasak Province) is 'the border between Siam and Cambodia'. Compounding the contradictions between French intentions, terminology and eventual action, the governor general issued a decree in March 1905 that divided the newly acquired territory along the Rephu River, stating that this line is 'the boundary between the Kingdom of Cambodia and the Kingdom of Bassac (Laos) on the right bank of the Mekong'. This text implies that the two kingdoms were of equal status. Yet Bassac (a short form of the name Champasak) was never officially treated as a kingdom by the French, had no recognised status as a political entity within Laos and neither administered nor claimed part of the territory north of the Rephu River. The Rephu-line decree referred to Champasak as a Lao territory but made no provision for its incorporation into Laos. Its western boundary (the Dong Rak range) had, moreover, been defined as the Cambodian-Thai boundary. To clarify the status of this territory, a second decree was issued in May 1905, which made no reference to old Champasak as a political entity. Instead, it simply enumerated the towns on the right bank north of the Rephu and annexed them to the new (left-bank) Champasak Province of Laos.

When the southern boundaries of Laos were redrawn, the northernmost segment of the Dong Rak line became the Lao-Thai border. Thus, a diplomatic agreement ratified by two nations was modified by an act of the governor general, in effect ceding to Laos a portion of territory that was defined by international agreement as Cambodian, but without any authority from either the French parliament or the Cambodian government. No clause in the 1863 Khmer-French treaty establishing the protectorate implied that France had the power to cede Cambodian territory. And in signing the treaty, King Norodom certainly never intended to empower French officials (colonial or metropolitan) to give away any of his domain.

Where did the governor general get the authority to make such sweeping changes? All of the big territorial transfers affecting Laos were made at a time when the governor general's powers were not yet fully defined. During this period, the basic law by which the French parliament conferred his powers in general terms was contained in two presidential decrees issued in 1887 and 1891. Although these decrees were cited as the source of authority for transferring territory between the states of Indochina, the decrees contain no provision for such changes. Nor were such powers granted in the 1911 presidential decree that redefined the governor general's powers and responsibilities. Authority to make territorial modifications was not explicit in any law.

By transferring Siampang and Stung Treng from Laos to Cambodia, and by transferring Kontum from Laos to Vietnam, the governor general ceded territories of a French colony to French protectorates. By transferring to Laos some of the territories defined in the 1895 Sino-French convention and the 1904 Franco-Thai convention, he ceded protectorate territories to a French colony. In some cases, he acted without consulting even the colonial minister, who was the authority in Paris to whom the governor general was responsible. The subject of the legality of such changes was broached within the colonial ministry in 1907 when the governor general annexed to Cambodia the rich western provinces ceded by Thailand to France (not to Cambodia), but no action was taken at that time. Subsequently, French colonial officials and the governments of the protectorates simply assumed that the redrawn boundaries were definitive. After all, the map makers showed them that way.

Not until 1915 did a colonial inspection mission officially question the legality of the entire series of territorial mutations in Indochina.[38] The inspectors discovered that French legal documents concerning the boundaries of Laos were a tangle of contradictions and arbitrary decisions taken without authority. The French parliament responded with legislation to provide a statutory basis for the governor general's actions. A presidential decree was issued in September 1915 that ratified the earlier decrees but restrained the governor general from executing any further territorial changes without first receiving authorisation from Paris.

By this time, the French government had decided that Laos was legally a colony. Parliament, moreover, had absolute powers to dispose of a colony's territory, since it belonged outright to France. Accordingly, the cessions from Laos to Cambodia, Thailand and Vietnam were perfectly valid. But the French parliament unilaterally changed its own bilateral treaty engagements: that is, the Chinese cession of upper Laos to Vietnam and the Thai cession of Champasak to Cambodia. And it did so without the agreement of the Vietnamese and Cambodian governments. This arrogation of powers is a mystery that perhaps could be unravelled only by a legal scholar thoroughly trained in the intricacies of French constitutional law.

One of the documents mandated by the 1915 legislation was the 1905 decree that fixed the boundary between Cambodia and Champasak at the Rephu River. An unintended result of the 1915 decree is that it recognised the Rephu as the southern boundary of the Kingdom of Champasak—not of French Laos. After this right-bank territory was incorporated into Champasak Province, the historic capital ceased to be an important administrative centre, although the royal family continued to live there. The colonial authorities established the provincial capital at a new site up-river and preferred to ignore Champasak town and the old élite. Official dealings with the Champasak royal family contrasted starkly with the many public gestures, made by the Indochina government in subsequent years, to promote an image of Luang Prabang as a protectorate and kingdom. Since the French government itself avoided any acknowledgement of the status of Luang Prabang, and in view of the great subtlety with which the latter policy was carried out, it is ironic that the Rephu River decree was ratified in the 1915 legislation. No one seems to have noticed the exact wording of the governor general's decree, which refers to Champasak as a kingdom. In effect, the French government, while taking such great care to avoid recognition of the northern Lao kingdom in official documents, had already acknowledged the existence of the southern one in an act of parliament.

Among the boundary changes that resulted in a diminution of territory for French Laos, all but one were ratified in the 1915 decree. (The exception is Dan Sai, which was ceded to Thailand in the 1907 treaty, already ratified by parliament.) The 1915 decree was far from comprehensive, however, in its treatment of Lao territorial acquisitions from other states of Indochina. It ratified only the transfers of the southern part of Hua Phan Province and of Siang Khwang Province from Vietnam and the transfer of right-bank Champasak from Cambodia. The authors of the 1915 decree overlooked the November 1895 decree that transferred the north Hua Phan towns from Vietnam to Laos, and they made no attempt to deal with most of the Laos-Vietnam boundary.

The line between the upper Ou basin and Vietnam is not specified in any decree. This boundary can be traced back to the French military occupation of the upper Black River basin, in alliance with the local ruling family. A provisional line was drawn between areas controlled by French and Thai troops in late 1888, in a written agreement between a senior Thai commissioner and the French.[39] Although this agreement was a temporary expedient, pending the anticipated boundary settlement, the line was accepted locally as a dividing line between Laos and Vietnam, and it was not contested by provincial authorities on either side.

In contrast to upper Laos, where political entities remained intact after the 1827-8 Thai-Lao war and during the Thai-Vietnamese war in the 1830s and 1840s, the central Lao territories east of the Mekong were devastated by depopulation campaigns and political collapse. When the French began to carve rough administrative circumscriptions out of this part of Laos in 1893 and 1894, they adopted Vietnamese territorial definitions and established a system of provincial commissionerships, each headed by a French colonial official who governed with the mediation of the Lao élite. The French acted in consultation with, and with approval from, the government in Hué, but the Vietnamese agreed from the outset that Vietnamese officials would play no rôle in this system.[40] The governor general decided in 1894 that the limits of administrative units in this part of Laos should follow the watershed of the cordillera as closely as possible, to avoid any unexpected difficulties.[41] This mountain barrier physically divided the Lao from the Vietnamese, and once the French gained control of the Lao provinces, the watershed continued to be the generally accepted dividing line. Ultimately, an exact definition was given (in an October 1916 decree) to only one segment of the cordillera. The rest of the long common boundary between Laos and Vietnam, together with the portion of the Cambodia-Laos boundary that is east of the Mekong, came into existence as a result of efforts by Indochina's cartographers to fill in the remaining gaps on their maps.

Our modern conception of Laos as a political entity originates in the June 1895 decree that created a hierarchy of more than two dozen French administrative posts in upper and lower Laos. The basic provincial structure was formally approved by the French parliament in the 1899 presidential decrees, which created a unified administration for Laos and integrated the colonial officials of Laos into the Indochina civil service. The 1899 decrees do not mention boundaries, but they can be interpreted as a form of parliamentary sanction of the approximate boundaries of provinces in existence at that time. The decrees can therefore be regarded as statutory approval of the existing, although imprecisely defined, Lao boundary with Vietnam.

Once the framework of French administration in Laos was established, all of the major territorial modifications were made while Paul Beau was governor general (from 1902 to 1907). Shortly after Beau's arrival, a rift occurred with Armand Tournier (resident superior of Laos 1899–1903), which seems to have run far deeper than a disagreement over administrative policy. Tournier served in Laos from the beginning of French rule and was the commandant of lower Laos from 1895 to 1899. He was proud of his achievements and a passionate opponent of the plan under consideration during 1902–3 to dismember Laos and annex it piecemeal to the three adjacent protectorates. A confrontation with Beau placed Tournier in an untenable position and made it impossible for him to remain in the Indochina civil service. He went on home leave in February 1903 and eventually retired at the end of 1906, still holding his title as resident superior of Laos (BOC 1906: 807).

After Tournier's departure, French administration in Vientiane seemed to be cast adrift. An attempt was made to appoint a new resident superior in late 1903 (BOC 1903: 1,008), but he never took up the post. George Mahé (a civil service inspector) served as interim chief in Vientiane, but he had not yet been confirmed as resident superior by 1906, when he went on extended home leave. The extraordinarily long interim administration finally ended with the arrival of Fernand-Ernest Lévecque (resident superior 1906–9).

Under the Beau regime, the long-term interests of Laos and its culturally diverse population were weakly represented in the deliberations of the Indochina government. All cessions of Lao territory were made during this interval. Efficient administration and ancient rights were cited as justifications for the changes. But the cavalier treatment meted out to Laos might be attributable in part to egotism and clashes of personality. An investigation into internal colonial-establishment politics and rivalries is not within the scope of this chapter, but such factors should be taken into account in future research. The delimitation of Laos is a subject that deserves far lengthier and more detailed treatment than this brief introduction can provide. A definitive work, however, will have to await the writing of more comprehensive studies of pre-colonial administration, demographic change in the frontier areas and the political history of French rule in Laos.

APPENDIX

ABBREVIATIONS AND ACRONYMS FOR SOURCES CITED BELOW

AOM = Archives d'Outre-Mer (French colonial archives), Aix-en-Provence

BOC = *Bulletin officiel des Colonies* (Official Journal of the Colonies)

FO = Foreign Office Papers, Public Record Office, London

IAF = Indochine, ancien fonds (Indochina archives, old series, to 1920, deposited in the Archives d'Outre-Mer), Aix-en-Provence

INF = Indochine, nouveau fonds (Indochina archives, new series, largely post-1920 but also containing pre-1920 documents, deposited in the Archives d'Outre-Mer), Aix-en-Provence

JOIF = *Journal officiel de l'Indochine française* (Official Journal of French Indochina)

MAE = Ministère des affaires étrangères (archives of the Ministry of Foreign Affairs, Quai d'Orsay, Paris, now renamed the Ministère des relations extérieurs, or Ministry of External Relations); NS = *nouvelle série* (for Siam, comprising mostly post-1896 documents)

TNA = Thai National Archives, Bangkok

TNL = Thai National Library, Manuscripts Division, Bangkok

TREATIES LISTED IN CHRONOLOGICAL ORDER

Full texts of international agreements are in Reinach (1902 and 1907), except as otherwise noted. Tuck (1995) provides English translations of Thai-French international agreements, and Prescott (1975) provides English translations of border-related clauses. Texts of the protectorate treaties concluded between Luang Prabang and representatives of the Indochina government are in Iché (1935).

11 August 1863 Cambodian-French protectorate treaty

15 July 1867 Franco-Thai treaty dividing Cambodia and defining a common boundary

6 June 1884 Franco-Vietnamese protectorate treaty

9 June 1885 Sino-French treaty

26 June 1887 Sino-French delimitation convention

3 October 1893 Franco-Thai treaty

20 June 1895 Sino-French delimitation convention

3 December 1895 convention between Luang Prabang and the Indochina government
15 January 1896 British-French declaration
13 February 1904 Franco-Thai convention
8 April 1904 British-French declaration concerning Siam
29 June 1904 Franco-Thai protocol
23 March 1907 Franco-Thai treaty and boundary protocol
25 August 1926 Franco-Thai convention concerning Indochina (Sayre 1928)

DECREES LISTED IN CHRONOLOGICAL ORDER

All *arrêtés* (decrees of the governor general) were published in the *Journal officiel de l'Indochine française* (JOIF). The *décrets* (presidential decrees) were approved by the French parliament and published in both JOIF and the *Bulletin officiel des Colonies* (BOC).

17 October 1887 *décret* defining the governor general's powers (BOC 1887: 784-6)

21 April 1891 *décret* further defining the governor general's powers (BOC 1891: 308-10)

14 October 1893 *arrêté* creating the Müang Et military post and placing the Hua Phan state under the jurisdiction of a Tonkin military territory (JOIF 1893 2: 478)

14 January 1895 *arrêté* rescinding a 2 March 1894 letter (which had authorised the transfer of Sam Nüa and other south Hua Phan towns to Annam) and transferring these towns instead to Laos (JOIF 1895 2: 42)

1 June 1895 *arrêté* creating a hierarchy of administrative centres and placing upper Laos and lower Laos under separate Commandants Superior (JOIF 1895 2: 278-9)

22 November 1895 *arrêté* incorporating Siang Khwang into upper Laos (JOIF 1895 2: 735-6)

30 November 1895 *arrêté* transferring the north Hua Phan towns (including Müang Et) to upper Laos (JOIF 1895 2: 736)

29 August 1896 *arrêté* transferring Sam Nüa and other south Hua Phan towns from Laos to Annam (JOIF 1896 2: 907)

6 February 1899 *arrêté* uniting the administration of upper and lower Laos under a Resident Superior and abolishing the posts of Commandants Superior (JOIF 1899 2: 133-4)

19 April 1899 *décret* changing the status of the Commandant Superior of Laos to a Resident Superior (BOC 1899: 464–5)

16 September 1899 *décret*s creating the Indochina civil service and unifying the colonial personnel of the constituent states (BOC 1899: 1,240–51).

15 June 1903 *arrêté* transferring Sam Nüa and other south Hua Phan towns from Annam to Laos (JOIF 1903: 696)

22 November 1904 *arrêté* separating the southern plateau region (Darlac) territorially from Laos and placing it under the administrative control of the Annam Resident Superior (JOIF 1904: 1,446)

6 December 1904 *arrêté* transferring Stung Treng and Siampang from Laos to Cambodia (JOIF 15 December 1904: 1,500)

28 March 1905 *arrêté* defining the right-bank boundary (Rephu River) between the kingdoms of Champasak and Cambodia (JOIF 6 April 1905: 453)

16 May 1905 *arrêté* annexing right-bank territory acquired from Thailand to Champasak Province in Laos (JOIF 25 May 1905: 692)

4 July 1905 *arrêté* establishing the northern plateau region (Kontum) as an autonomous province and transferring it territorially to Annam (JOIF 1905: 912)

20 October 1911 *décret* redefining the governor general's powers (BOC 1911: 1,294–6)

20 September 1915 *décret* requiring territorial changes between constituent states of the Indochina Union to be approved by the colonial ministry and ratifying eleven *arrêté*s that had previously made such changes (JOIF 1915: 1,815–6)

12 October 1916 *arrêté* defining the exact eastern boundaries of Kham Muan and Savannakhet Provinces (JOIF 1916: 1,673)

12 April 1932 *décret* approving a 30 April 1929 *arrêté* integrating Darlac Province into Annam (JOIF 1932: 1,858)

NOTES

1. See for example Chhak (1966), Duke (1962), Fourniau (1989), Goldman (1972), Prescott (1975), Reinach (1901), Tuck (1995) and Winichakul (1994).

2. Full citations to all international agreements and other legal documents are provided before the notes to this chapter.

3. Auguste Pavie served as a temporary commissioner on mission to deal with frontier affairs in 1895–6. In December 1895 he concluded an agreement with the king of Luang Prabang to establish a protectorate. He was not authorised to make such an agreement, and it was never recognised by the government of France as an international agreement. The document was used by the Government of Indochina, nonetheless, as a basis for its internal relationship with Luang Prabang within the Union of Indochina.

4. INF 1111. Foreign minister to colonial minister, 22 November 1911, and undated draft reply; colonial minister to vice president of the State Council, 15 December 1913.

5. AOM Conseil Supérieur des Colonies 29. Report to the colonial minister (Supreme Colonial Council session 1928–1929), 30 December 1929 (pp. 71–3). This is the detailed report of the council.

6. INF 614(2). Moretti inspection report, 3 January 1936.

7. IAF B12(15). Cable, Pavie to foreign minister, 5 March 1894.

8. INF 694. Hanotaux to Delcassé, 1 October 1894.

9. INF 693. Develle to Delcassé, 1 June 1893.

10. IAF B12(15). Jusserand to colonial under-secretary, 13 November 1894; memo., 19 November 1894. INF 694. Gérard to foreign minister, 10 October 1894.

11. INF 694. Delcassé to foreign minister, 8 January 1895; Nisard to Chantemps, 6 February 1895; Hanotaux to Chantemps, 27 April 1895.

12 . The Chiang Khaeng agreement was in the form of an unpublished exchange of notes. See FO 628/15/216 Devawongse to Jones, 11 April 1893; FO 17/1177 Jones to Rosebery, 12 April 1893 and minutes 23–25 October 1893. Chiang Khaeng was never delineated, and it never appeared as a political entity on published maps of French Laos. FO 925/2334 outlines Chiang Khaeng in a map titled 'Skeleton Map Shewing Approximately the boundaries between China, Siam and Burma and French Indo-China', War Office, Intelligence Division No. 1107, June 1895. Lafont (1998: 259) reconstructed the map in detail by using local annals and other records.

13. INF 691. Hanotaux to Chantemps, 14 Oct. 1895.

14. INF 694. Hanotaux to Chantemps, 12 July 1895; cable, governor general to Colonies, 12 September 1895.

15. INF 694. Geographical service to political affairs department, 9 January 1896, and enclosed map, 'Carte des frontières sino-annamite' (map of the Sino-Vietnamese frontier).

16. INF 695. Rousseau to colonial minister, 25 April 1896.

17. INF 695. Hanotaux to Lebon, 11 July 1896; Lebon to foreign minister, 27 October 1896; Rousseau to colonial minister, 31 October 1896.

18. INF 694. Doumer to colonial minister, 14 May 1897.

19. MAE NS Siam 26 Governor general to colonial minister, 3 January 1903 and appended map. This sketch map compares the various lines under discussion based on French, Lao and Thai proposals. The French claim extended the length of the waterway now known to be the Hüang and its northern branch. The Thai proposal was a line up the Hüang as far as the 'Tane' (a short left-bank stream below Kaen Thao town) and then up the Tane to the watershed. The journal *Asie française* published a map in 1906 (reproduced in Duke 1962 facing page 262) placing the 'Tang' in precisely the latter position but showing it as a long river running down from the watershed line between the Mekong and the Chao Phraya. No such river exists, and the 1906 map is illogical since Kaen Thao was acquired by Luang Prabang as a result of the February 1904 convention.

20. MAE NS Siam 79 contains the first fairly accurate map of the Hüang basin, compiled and printed to illustrate the findings of the 1905–6 Franco-Thai delimitation commission.

21. TNA R5.M57/22. Instructions of Prince Damrong to Luang Chindarak, 5 May 1900; M57/14 report of Chindarak to Damrong, 17 July 1900. The vacuum in temporal and spiritual authority caused by the death of the aged Champasak prince, and the efforts to convert the remnants of the principality into an ordinary province, must have been important factors contributing to the outbreak of violent millenarian movements during the next two years. For an account of those events, see the chapter by Bernard Gay.

22. Melouprey and Cheom Ksan were under the jurisdiction of Khukhan—a town north of the mountains. In 1904 Khukhan was the seat of a Khmer governorship but is now a district in Sisaket Province. Farther west, a third town (Chong Kal) was under Sangkha, a Khmer governorship that is now a district in Surin Province. The line defined in the 1904 and

1907 delimitation protocols split several of the existing administrative units that straddled the mountain range.

23. Some of the findings of the 1905–7 joint demarcation are in MAE NS Siam 77 (reports) and 79 (printed maps).

24. MAE NS Siam 72. De Margerie to Pichon, 29 June 1908. NS Siam 75. Procès-verbal, 4 October 1909.

25. NFI 615. Report of the 2 February 1894 Senate session.

26. For a masterly account of the struggle within French political circles relating to these territorial questions, see Tuck (1995, especially chapters 7–9).

27. AOM Siam 87. Delcassé to Doumergue, 5 January 1903.

28. IAF A30(107). Administrative reports by Armand Tournier for April–May 1902 and June-August 1902. *La Dépêche coloniale*, 15 June 1903.

29. A map in Breazeale (1975: 341) identifies all of the towns listed in the governor general's May 1905 decree and the former Champasak satellite towns that were east of the Mekong. 'Pasah' in the decree is a misprint for the name of Champasak town, which was known also by its shortened form, transliterated by the French as Bassac or Pasak.

30. TNA R5M62.1/34. Despatch, Prince Yuttitham to Phitsanuthep, 13 July 1892.

31. TNL R3/1205/160. Instructions of Maha Amat to various governors, 22 July 1843.

32. Instructions from interior minister Bòdin to Maha Amat, 15 October 1842, published in *Thesaphiban* [Journal of the Interior Ministry] 15/86 (May 1913): 80.

33. TNL R5/270/2 (old catalogue). Memorandum on the establishment of the Saphang Phupha governorship, 9 September 1879. R5/270/4 (old catalogue). Memorandum on the establishment of the Munlapamok governorship, 7 October 1881.

34. TNL R5/271/2 (old catalogue). Edict establishing Thara Bòriwat (Thalabarivat), 24 July 1885.

35. IAF A30(107). Tournier to Beau, 6 November 1902.

36. TNA R5M62.1/34. Prince Phichit to King Rama V, 15 May 1892.

37. For the Lao-Vietnamese accords on delimitation, which were finally completed and ratified in 1991, see Gay (1995: 17).

38. INF 654. Roume to colonial minister, 18 July 1915.

39. TNA R5M2.12.kai.Luang Prabang 8. Despatch from Prince Mahin, 12 March 1889.

40. INF 836. Cable, governor general to colonial under-secretary, 21 August 1893.

41. IAF A30(99). Chavassieux to colonial under-secretary, 28 April 1894.

REFERENCES

Aijmer, Goran. 1979. 'Reconciling Power with Authority: An Aspect of Statecraft in Traditional Laos'. *Man* (London) 14: 734–49.

Les annales du Laos (Luang Prabang, Vientiane, Tran-Ninh et Bassac) [Chronicles of Laos: Luang Prabang, Vientiane, Tran-Ninh (Siang Khwang) and Champasak]. Hanoi, 1926. This title is cited by Paul Le Boulanger, D. G. E. Hall and others, but apparently no such book appeared in French. A hand-written work in Lao, with the same title (*Phongsawadan haeng pathet lao khü luang phabang wiang chan müang phuan lae champasak*), was printed in 1926 and reissued in 1967 by the Education Ministry, Vientiane.

Archaimbault, Charles. 1967. 'Les Annales de l'ancien royaume de S'ieng Khwang' [The Chronicles of the Old Siang Khwang Kingdom]. *Bulletin de l'Ecole française d'Extrême–orient* (Paris) 53 (2): 557–673. In French.

———. 1973. *Structures religieuses lao (rites et mythes)* [Religious Structural Elements of the Lao: Rituals and Myths]. Vientiane: Vithagna. In French.

Aymonier, Etienne. 1885. *Notes sur le Laos* [Notes about Laos]. Saigon: Imprimerie coloniale. In French.

Aymonier, Etienne. 1895 and 1897. *Voyage dans le Laos. Mission Etienne Aymonier* [Journey in Laos. The Etienne Aymonier Mission]. Two volumes. Paris: Leroux. In French.

Barbosa, Duarte. 1921. *The Book of Duarte Barbosa. An Account of the Countries Bordering on the Indian Ocean and their Inhabitants, Written by Duarte Barbosa, and Completed About the Year 1518 A.D.*

Edited by Mansel Longworth Dames. Works Issued by the Hakluyt Society, second series, vol. 49. London: Hakluyt Society.

Barros, João de. 1946. *Ásia de João de Barros. Dos feitos que os Portugueses fizeram no descobrimento e conquista dos mares e terras do Oriente. Terceira Década* [Asia, by João de Barros: The Deeds of the Portuguese in the Discovery and Conquest of the Seas and Lands of the East, Third Decada]. Reprinted from the 1563 edition and edited by Hernaní Cidade and Manuel Múrias. Lisboa: Agência Geral das Colónias. In Portuguese.

Barthélemy, P. de. 1898. 'Le Laos'. *Bibliothèque illustrée des voyages autour du monde par terre et par mer* [Illustrated Library of Journeys around the World by Land and by Sea] 44. In French.

Bastian, Adolf. 1866–71. *Die Völker des östlichen Asien* [The Peoples of East Asia]. Six volumes. Leipzig: O. Wigand. In German.

Blair, Emma Helen, and James Alexander Robertson. 1903–9. *The Philippine Islands, 1493–1898.* Fifty-five volumes. Cleveland, Ohio: Arthur H. Clark Company.

Bocarro, Antonio. 1876. *Década XIII da História da ändia* [Thirteenth Decada of the History of India]. Edited by Rodrigo José de Lima Felner. Lisboa: Academia Real das Sciencias. In Portuguese.

Boisselier, Jean. 1965. 'Récentes recherches archéologiques en Thaïlande' [Recent Archaeological Research in Thailand]. *Arts asiatiques* [Asian Arts (Paris)] 12: 153–4. In French.

Borri, Cristoforo. 1631. *Relatione della nuova missione delli PP. della Compagnia di Giesu* [Accounts of the New Missions of the Fathers of the Society of Jesus]. Roma: n.p., 1631. In Italian. English translation published with the author and title Christopher Borri, *An Account of Cochin-China.* London: n.p., 1732.

Breazeale, Kennon. 1975. Integration of the Lao States into the Thai Kingdom. D.Phil. thesis, University of Oxford.

———. 1979. 'Thai Provincial Minority Elites: Aspects of their Expansion on the Eastern Borders in the Nineteenth Century'. In *Proceedings of the Seventh Conference of the International Association of Historians of Asia* 23: 1,667–91. Bangkok: Chulalongkorn University Press.

Brébion, Antoine. 1910. *Bibliographie des voyages dans l'Indochine française du IX au XIX siècle* [Bibliography of the Journeys in French Indochina from the Ninth to the Nineteenth Centuries]. Saigon: Schneider. In French.

Bressan, Luigi. 1998. 'Introduction.' In *A New and Interesting Description of the Lao Kingdom (1642–1648). G. F. de Marini,* pp. vii-lxvi. Translated and edited by Walter E. J. Tips and Claudio Bertuccio. Bangkok: White Lotus Press.

Briggs, Lawrence Palmer. 1950. 'Les missionaires portugais et espanols au Cambodge 1555–1603' [Portuguese and Spanish Missionaries in Cambodia, 1555–1603]. *Bulletin de la Société d'études indochinoises* [Journal of the Society of Indochinese Studies (Saigon)] 25 (1): 5–29.

Brown, MacAlister, and Joseph J. Zasloff. 1986. *Apprentice Revolutionaries: The Communist Movement in Laos, 1930–1985.* Stanford: Stanford University Press.

Cadière, Léopold. 1912. 'Documents relatifs à l'époque de Gia-Long' [Documents Pertaining to the Period of Emperor Gia-Long]. *Bulletin de l'Ecole français d'Extrême-orient* 12 (7): 1–82. In French.

Camões, Luiz Vas de. 1950. *The Lusiads of Luiz de Camões.* Translated from the 1572 Portuguese (Lisbon) edition and edited by Leonard Bacon. New York: The Hispanic Society of America, 1950. Retranslated from the 1572 edition, edited by William C. Atkinson and published with the title *The Lusiads.* Harmondsworth, Middlesex: Penguin, 1973.

Campos, Joaquin José António de. 1983. *Early Portuguese Accounts of Thailand. Antigos Relatos da Tailāndia.* Lisboa: printed by the Imprensa Municipal de Lisboa [Lisbon City Press] for the Câmara Municipal de Lisboa [Lisbon City Council]. In English and Portuguese.

Cardim, António Francisco. 1646. *Première partie. Relation de la province du Iapon. Escrite en Portugais par le Père François Cardim de la Compagnie de Iesus, Procureur de cette Province. Traduitte et reveuë en François* [Part One. An Account of the Ecclesiastical Region of Japan. Written in Portuguese by Father Francisco Cardim of the Society of Jesus, Procurer of This Region. Translated and Revised in French.] In António Francisco Cardim and Francisco Baretto, *Relation de ce qui s'est passé depuis quelques années, iusques à l'an 1644 au Iapon, à la Cochinchine, au Malabar, et en plusieurs autres isles et royaumes de l'Orient compris sous le nom des Provinces du Iapon et du Malabar, de la Compagnie de Iesus. Divisée en deux parties, selon ces deux provinces* [An Account of What Has Happened for Some Years up to 1644 Japan, Cochinchina, Malabar and Several Other Islands and Kingdoms of the Orient Included in the Japan and Malabar Ecclesiastical Regions of the Society of Jesus], pp. 1–182 Two parts, dated 1646 and 1645, in one volume. Paris, Mathurin Henault et Iean Henault, 1645–6.

Ce Fu Yuan Gui. Edited in 1,000 volumes by Wang Qin Ruo and others in AD 1013. Qing era edition, edited in 240 volumes by Li Si Jing and others; Hong Kong: Zhonghua Shuju, 1960 (12 volumes). Song era (Seikado) edition; Tokyo: Toyo Bunko, 1978 (79 volumes). Song era edition; Beijing: Zhonghua Shuju, 1989 (4 volumes). In Chinese.

Chamthewiwong [The Chronicle of Cham Thewi (Queen Cham)]. For the Pali text and a translation in French, see George Coèdes (1925), 'Documents sur l'histoire politique et religieuse du Laos occidental', *Bulletin de l'Ecole française d'Extrême-orient* (Hanoi) 25 (1–2): 141–71. For an English translation, see Donald K. Swearer and Sommai Premchit, *The Legend of Queen Cama: Bodhiramsi's Camadevivamsa, a Translation and Commentary.* Albany: State University of New York Press, 1998.

Chamberlain, J. R. 1972. 'The origin of the Southwestern Tai'. *Bulletin des Amis du royaume lao* [Journal of the Friends of the Lao Kingdom (Vientiane)] 7–8: 233–44.

———. 1991. 'The Efficacy of the P/Ph Distinction in Tai Languages'. In J. R. Chamberlain, ed., *The Ram Khamhaeng Controversy.* Bangkok: The Siam Society.

Chan Ngon Kham, Phraya. 1969. *Phongsawadan müang nakhòn phanom sangkhep chabap phraya chan ngon kham riap riang* [Abbreviated Annals of Nakhòn Phanom, Version Compiled by Phraya Chan Ngon Kham on 21 November 1914]. In *Prachum phongsawadan phak thi 70* [History Series, Part 70], Khurusapha reprint series, vol. 44, pp. 204–17. Bangkok: Khurusapha, 1969. In Thai.

Chanthi Saignamongkhoun. 1977. *Pawat phò kaduat* [Biography of Phò Kaduat]. Kaeng Kok: n.p. In Lao.

Chaumont, Alexandre de. 1686. *Relation de l'Ambassade de Mr le Chevalier de Chaumont à la Cour du Roy de Siam* [A Relation of the Embassy of Monsieur de Chaumont, Knight, to the Court of the King of Siam]. Paris: Seneuze et Horthemels.

Chhak, Sarin. 1966. *Les frontières du Cambodge avec les anciens pays de la fédération indochinoise: le Laos et le Vietnam (Cochinchine et Annam)* [Cambodia's Frontiers with the Former Countries of the Indochinese Federation: Laos and Vietnam (Cochinchina and Annam)]. Paris: Librairie Dalloz. In French.

Choisy, Abbé François-Timoléon de. 1687. *Journal du voyage de Siam fait en M.DC.LXXV et M.DC.LXXXVI.* Paris: S. Mabre-Cramoisy. Reprinted with the title *Journal du voyage de Siam fait en 1685 et 1686 par M. l'abbé de Choisy, précédé d'une étude par Maurice Garcon.* Paris: Editions Duchartre et Van Buggenhoudt, 1930. Edited by Dirk van der Cruysse and published with the title *Journal du voyage de Siam fait en 1685 et 1686.* Paris: Fayard, 1995. Translated by Michael Smithies and published with the title *Journal of a Voyage to Siam 1685–1686.* Kuala Lumpur: Oxford University Press, 1993.

Christie, C. J. 1979. 'Marxism and the History of the Nationalist Movements in Laos'. *Journal of Southeast Asian Studies* (Singapore) 10: 146–58.

Chum Chitamet, ed. 1967. *Nangsü khun bòrom rasathirat* [The Book of Khun Bòrom the Great: The True Ancient Version]. Vientiane: Literary Committee of the Kingdom of Laos. In Lao.

Clifford, Hugh Charles. 1904. *Further India: Being the Story of Exploration from the Earliest Times in Burma, Malaya, Siam and Indochina.* London: Lawrence and Bullen Ltd.

Coedès, George. 1944. 'Une nouvelle inscription d'Ayuthya' [A New Inscription from Ayutthaya]. *Journal of the Siam Society* (Bangkok) 35 (1): 73–76. In French.

Coedès, George. 1937–66. *Inscriptions du Cambodge* [Inscriptions of Cambodia]. Eight volumes. Hanoi and Paris: E. de Boccard. In French.

Collectif for World Peace. 1953. *The Liberation Struggle of the Pathet Lao.* Samneua: The Pathet Lao Propaganda.

Condominas, Georges. 1968. 'Notes sur le Bouddhisme populaire en milieu rural lao' [Notes on Popular Buddhism in a Rural Lao Setting]. *Archives de sociologie des religions* [Archives of the Sociology of Religions (Paris)] 1–2: 25–6, 81–110, 111–50. In French.

'Conventions et traités entre la France et le Siam relatifs au Laos (1893–1947)' [Conventions and Treaties between France and Siam Relating to Laos (1893–1947)]. *Péninsule—Etudes interdisciplinaires sur l'Asie du sud-est péninsulaire* [Peninsula: Interdisciplinary Studies on Peninsular South-East Asia (Metz)] 16–17 (1988): 9–178. In French.

Cortembert, E., and Léon de Rosny. 1862. *Tableau de la Cochinchine* [Tableau of Cochinchina]. Paris: Armand Le Chevalier. In French.

Cruz, Friar Gaspar da. 1953. 'Treatise in Which the Things of China Are

Related at Great Length, with Their Particularities, as Likewise of the Kingdom of Ormuz. Composed by the Reverend Father Gaspar da Cruz of the Order of Saint Dominic.' Translation of the 1569 Portuguese edition, in Charles Ralph Boxer (translator and editor), *South China in the Sixteenth Century, Being the Narratives of Galeote Pereira, Fr. Gaspar da Cruz, O. P., Fr. Martín de Rada, O.E.S.A.* Works Issued by the Hakluyt Society, second series, vol. 106. London: Hakluyt Society.

Curtis, Lilian Johnson. 1903. *The Laos of North Siam.* Philadelphia: Westminster Press.

Da Tang Xi Yu Qiu Fa Gao Song Zhuan [Biographies of Eminent monks Who Went to the Western Countries in Search of the Law]. Edited by Wang Bang Wei. Beijing: Zhonghua Shuju, 1988. In Chinese.

Da Tang Xi Yu Ji [Diary of a Journey to the Western Countries during the Great Tang Period]. See Xuan Zhuang.

Dabin, G. 1885. 'A Missionary's Journey through Laos from Bangkok to Ubon'. *Journal of the Straits Branch of the Royal Asiatic Society* (Singapore) 15: 103–17.

Dai Nam Nhat Thong Chi [Geography of Vietnam]. 1966–8. Translated from Chinese; 5 volumes. Hanoi: Editions des sciences sociales. In Vietnamese.

Dai Viet Su Ky Toan Thu [Complete Annals of Dai Viet]. 1971–3. Translated from the 1675 Ngo Si Lien et al. version. Four volumes. Hanoi: Nhaxuatban khoahocxahoi. In Vietnamese.

Damrong Rajabhubap, Prince, ed. 1914. *Phra ratcha phongsawadan chabap phra ratcha hatthalekha (phim khrang thi 2) kap kham athibai khòng phra chao barommawongthoe krom phra damrong rachanuphap* [Royal Chronicles, Royal Autograph Version (Second Edition), with Commentary by Prince Damrong Rachanuphap]. Bangkok: Thai Press

Dao Duy Anh. 1964. *Dat Nuoc Viet Nam Qua Cac Doi* [The Territorial Configuration of Vietnam in Various Historical Periods]. Hanoi: Editions des sciences sociales. In Vietnamese.

'Description du royaume de Laos et des pays voisins, présentée au roi de Siam en 1687, par des ambassadeurs du roi de Laos' [Description of the Kingdom of Laos and Neighbouring Countries, Presented to the King of Siam in 1687 by the Ambassadors of the King of Laos]. 1832. *Nouveau journal asiatique* [New Asian Journal (Paris)] 10: 414–21. In French.

Deuve, Jean. 1985. *Le Royaume du Laos 1949–1965: Histoire événementielle de l'indépendence à la guerre américaine* [The Kingdom of Laos, 1949–65: Historical Chronology from Independence to the American War]. Paris: Ecole française d'Extrême-orient. In French.

Dhida Saraya. 1985. 'Si thep khü si chanasa'. *Müang boran* [Muang Boran Journal (Bangkok)] 11(1): 63–76. In Thai with an English summary titled 'Sri Thep [Śrī Dēva] Was Sri Canaça [Śrī Canāśapūra]'.

Dommen, Arthur J. 1971. *Conflict in Laos: The Politics of Neutralization.* Revised edition. New York: Praeger.

Du Halde, Jean Baptiste. 1735. *Description géographique, historique, chronologique, politique et physique de l'empire de la Chine et de la Tartarie chinoise, enrichée des cartes générales et particulières de ces pays, de la carte générale et des cartes particulières du Thibet et de la Corée.* Paris: P. G. Le Mercier, 1735. Published in English translation with the title *The General History of China. Containing a Geographical, Historical, Chronological, Political and Physical Description of the Empire of China, Chinese Tartary, Corea [Korea] and Thibet.* Four volumes. London: J. Watts, 1736.

Duke, Pensri Suvanij. 1962. *Les relations entre la France et la Thaïlande (Siam) au XIXe siècle d'après les archives des affaires étrangères* [Relations between France and Thailand (Siam) in the Nineteenth Century, according to the Foreign Affairs Archives]. Bangkok: Librairie Chalermnit. In French.

Dupont, Pierre. 1943. 'La Dislocation du Tchen-la et la formation du Cambodge angkorien (VIIe-IXe siècle)' [The Dismemberment of Zhen La and the Formation of Angkorian Cambodia (7th–9th Centuries)]. *Bulletin de l'Ecole française d'Extrême-orient* (Hanoi) 43: 17–55.

Eredia, Manoel Godinho de. 1930. 'Eredia's Description of Malaca, Meridional India, and Cathay.' Translated from the 1613 Portuguese manuscript *Declaração de Malacca* with notes by J. V. Mills. *Journal of the Malayan Branch of the Royal Asiatic Society* (Singapore) 8 (1): 1–203.

Faria e Sousa, Manuel de. 1695. *The Portuguese Asia, or the History of the Discovery and Conquest of India by the Portuguese, Containing All Their Discoveries from the Coast of Africk [Africa], to the Farthest Parts of China and Japan.* Translated from Portuguese and abridged by John Stevens. Three volumes. London: C. Brome. Reprinted in

3 volumes by Gregg International Publishers, Farnborough, United Kingdom, 1971.

Fell, R. T. 1988. *Early Maps of South-East Asia*. Singapore and New York: Oxford University Press.

Fitch, Ralph. 1599. 'The Voyage of Mr Ralph Fitch, Merchant of London, to Ormus, and so to Goa in the East India; to Cambaia, Ganges, Bengala; to Bacola and Chonderi, to Pegu, to Jamahay in the kingdom of Siam, and back to Pegu, and from thence to Malacca, Zeilan, Cochin, and all the Coast of the East India, Begun in the Year of our Lord 1583, and ended 1591'. In Richard Hakluyt, ed., *Principal Navigations, Voyages, Traffiques and Discoveries of the English Nation*, vol. 2, 1599. Reprinted in John Pinkerton, ed., *A General Collection of the Best and Most Interesting Voyages and Travels in All Parts of the World; Many of Which Are Now First Translated into English by John Pinkerton*, vol. 9, pp. 406–25. London: Longman, Hurst, Rees, Orme, and Brown, Paternoster-Row; and Cadell and Davies in The Strand, 1811. Reprinted in Richard Hakluyt, ed., *The Principal Navigations, Voyages, Traffiques and Discoveries of the English Nation*, vol. 5, pp. 465–505. Glasgow: James MacLehose and Sons, 1904. Edited by J. Horton Ryley and published with the title *Ralph Fitch: England's Pioneer to India and Burma*. London: T. Fisher Unwin, 1899.

Floris, Peter. 1934. *Peter Floris, His Voyage to the East Indies in the Globe 1611–1615: The Contemporary Translation of His Journal*. Edited by W. H. Moreland. Works Issued by the Hakluyt Society, second series, vol. 74. London: Hakluyt Society.

Folliot, Professeur. 1889. 'Examen des anciennes frontières entre le Siam et l'Annam, d'après la carte de Monseigneur Taberd, et des empiétements des siamois sur le territoire annamite' [An Investigation of the Old Frontiers between Siam and Annam, according to the Map by Monseigneur Taberd, and the Siamese Encroachments on Annamese Territory]. *Bulletin de la Société d'études indochinoises* [Journal of the Society of Indochinese Studies (Saigon)] 1889 (2): 21–4. In French.

Fourniau, Charles. 1989. 'La frontière sino-vietnamienne et le face à face franco-chinois à l'époque de la conquête du Tonkin' [The Sino-Vietnamese Frontier and the French and Chinese Face to Face during the Period of the Conquest of Tonkin]. In Pierre-Bernard Lafont, ed., *Les Frontières du Vietnam: Histoire des frontières de la péninsule indochinoise* [The Frontiers of Vietnam: History of the

Frontiers of the Indochinese Peninsula]. Paris: Editions l'Harmattan. In French.

Fraisse, André. 1948. 'Voyages d'autrefois au Laos' [Journeys in Past Times to Laos]. *Bulletin de la Société d'études indochinoises* [Journal of the Society of Indochinese Studies (Saigon)] 23 (2/2): 123–44. In French.

Freeman, John H. 1910. *An Oriental Land of the Free, or Life and Mission Work among the Laos of Siam, Burma, China and Indo-China.* Philadelphia: Westminster Press.

Gagneux, Pierre-Marie. 1972. 'Vers une révolution dans l'archéologie indochinoise: le Bouddha et les stèles de Thalat, Vientiane' [Towards a Revolution in Indochinese Archaeology: The Buddha and the Commemorative Stone Slabs at Rat Landing, Vientiane]. *Bulletin des amis du royaume lao* [Journal of the Friends of the Lao Kingdom (Vientiane)] 7–8: 83–105. In French.

———. 1980. 'La frontière occidentale du royaume de Lan-Xang: quelques documents' [The Eastern Frontier of the Lan Sang Kingdom: Some Documents]. *Péninsule—Etudes interdisciplinaires sur l'Asie du sud-est péninsulaire* [Peninsula: Interdisciplinary Studies on Peninsular South-East Asia (Metz)] 1: 3–21. In French.

Galvano [Galvão], Antonio. 1862. *The Discoveries of the World, From Their First Original unto the Year of Our Lord 1555.* Works issued by the Hakluyt Society, first series, no. 30. London: Hakluyt Society, 1862. In Portuguese, from the 1563 manuscript, with an English translation.

Garnier, Francis. 1873. *Voyage d'exploration en Indo-Chine affectué pendant les années 1866, 1867 et 1868 par une commission française présidée par M. le capitaine de frégate Doudart de Lagrée et publié par les ordres du Ministère de la Marine* [Journey of Exploration in Indochina Carried out during the Years 1866, 1867 and 1868 by a French Commission Headed by Frigate Captain Doudart de Lagrée and Published at the Order of the Ministry of the Navy]. Two volumes and an atlas. Paris: Hachette. Reprinted without the atlas in a single volume by Hachette, 1885. In French.

Gay, Bernard. 1987. *Les mouvements millénaristes du centre et du sud Laos et du nord-est du Siam, 1895–1910* [Millenarian Movements in Central and South Laos and in the North-East of Siam, 1895–1910]. Four volumes. Paris: Centre d'histoire et civilisations de la péninsule indochinoise. In French.

———. 1989. 'La Frontière vietnamo-lao de 1893 à nos jours' [The

Vietnam-Lao Frontier from 1893 to Our Own Times]. In Pierre-Bernard Lafont, ed., *Les Frontières du Vietnam: Histoire des frontières de la péninsule indochinoise* [The Frontiers of Vietnam: History of the Frontiers of the Indochinese Peninsula], pp. 204–32. Paris: Editions l'Harmattan. In French.

————. 1995. *La Nouvelle frontière lao-vietnamienne. Les Accords de 1977–1990* [The New Lao-Vietnamese Boundary: The 1977–90 Agreements]. Paris: Editions l'Harmattan. In French.

Gerini, G. E. 1909. *Researches on Ptolemy's Geography of Eastern Asia.* London: Royal Geographical Society.

Gogoi, Padmeswar. 1968. 'Early history of the Tai: the Ngai-Lao kingdom'. In Padmeswar Gogoi, ed., *The Tai and the Tai Kingdoms; with a Fuller Treatment of the Tai-Ahom Kingdom in the Brahmaputra Valley.* Gauhati, India: Gauhati University.

Goldman, Minton F. 1972. 'Franco-British Rivalry over Siam, 1896–1904'. *Journal of Southeast Asian Studies* (Singapore) 3 (2): 210–28.

Goldstein, Martin E. 1973. *American Policy toward Laos.* Rutherford, New Jersey: Fairleigh Dickinson University Press.

Green, John, ed. 1745–57. *A New General Collection of Voyages and Travels.* Four volumes. London: Printed for T. Astley. Volume 4 (1757) is subtitled *Description of China, of Korea, Eastern Tartary and Tibet: Travels through Tartary, Tibet, and Bukharia, to and from China, 1246–1698.*

Groslier, Bernard Philippe. 1958. *Angkor et le Cambodge au XVIe siècle d'après les sources portugaises et espagnoles* [Angkor and Cambodia in the Sixteenth Century, according to Portuguese and Spanish Sources]. Annales du Musée Guimet, Bibliothèque d'études, vol. 63. Paris: Presses Universitaires de France.

Grossin, Pierre. 1933. *Notes sur l'histoire de la province de Cammon (Laos)* [Notes on the History of Kham Muan Province (Laos)]. Hanoi: Imprimerie d'Extrême–orient. In French.

Guillot, M. E. 1894. 'La France au Laos et la question du Siam' [France in Laos and the Question of Siam]. In *Grandes Conférences de Lille* [Great Conferences in Lille]. Lille: L. Daniel. In French.

Gunn, Geoffrey C. 1988. *Political Struggles in Laos (1930–1954).* Bangkok: Editions Duang Kamol.

Gutzlaff, Charles. 1849. 'The Country of the Free Lao'. *Journal of the Royal Geographical Society* (London) 19: 33–41.

Hafner, James A., Joel M. Halpern and Barbara Kerewsky-Halpern, eds. 1983. *River Road through Laos: Reflections of the Mekong.* International Area Studies Occasional Paper no. 10. Amherst: University of Massachusetts at Amherst. Reprinted in 1986.

Hamilton, Alexander. 1727. *A New Account of the East Indies, being the Observations and Remarks of Captain Alexander Hamilton.* Two volumes. Edinburgh: John Mosman. Reprinted with the title 'A New Account of the East Indies, Being the Observations and Remarks of Capt. Alexander Hamilton, Who Spent His Time There from the Year 1688 to 1723', in John Pinkerton, ed., *A General Collection of the Best and Most Interesting Voyages and Travels in All Parts of the World; Many of Which Are Now First Translated into English by John Pinkerton*, vol. 8, pp. 258–522. London: Printed for Longman, Hurst, Rees, Orme and Brown, Paternoster-Row, and for Cadell and Davies, 1811. Edited by William Foster and published in 2 volumes with the title *A New Account of the East Indies.* London: Argonaut Press, 1930.

Hase, Johann Mathias. 1744. Map titled 'Asia secundum legitimas' (first published in Nuremberg). Reproduced in Egon Klemp (1989), *Asia in Maps from Ancient Times to the Mid-Nineteenth Century*, plate 13. Leipzig: Acta Humaniora, 1989.

Haudricourt, André-Georges. 1972. *Problèmes de phonologie diachronique* [Problems of Diachronic Phonology]. Paris: Société pour l'étude des langues africaines. In French.

Hoang Ngoc Thanh. 1966. The Tay-Son Period in Vietnamese History (1778–1802). M.A. thesis in history, University of Hawaii.

Hoang Xuan Han. 1950. *La-son Phu-tu* [A Biography of La-Son Phu-tu]. Paris: Minh Tan. In Vietnamese.

Hoshino, Tatsuo. 1976. *Pour une histoire médiévale du moyen Mékong* [Towards a Mediaeval History of the Central Mekong]. Paris: Mémoire de l'Ecole des hautes études en sciences sociales. Reprinted by Duang Kamol, Bangkok, 1986. In French.

———. 1990. *Dakuryu to Mangetsu* [Muddy Rivers and a Full Moon]. Tokyo: Kobundo. In Japanese.

Humphreys, Arthur Lee. 1989. *Antique Maps and Charts.* London: Bracken Books.

Hutchinson, E. W. 1940. *Adventurers in Siam in the Seventeenth Century.* London: Royal Asiatic Society.

Iché, François. 1935. *Le statut politique et international du Laos français, sa condition juridique dans la communauté du droit des gens* [The Political and International Status of French Laos: Its Legal Position in the Context of People's Rights]. Toulouse: Imprimerie moderne Paillès et Chataigner; Paris: Librairie Arthur Rousseau. In French.

Ireson, Carol J., and W. Randall Ireson. 1991. 'Ethnicity and Development in Laos'. *Asian Survey* (Berkeley) 31: 920–37.

Ji Gu Dian Shuo Yuan Ji [Records of Old Yunnan]. Edited by Zhang Dao Song in the late Song era. Xuanlantangcongshu edition, Shanghai: Jinghua Inshua, 1941. In Chinese.

Jinakalamalini [The Garlands of the Epoch of the Conqueror]. For the Pali text and a French translation, see George Coèdes (1925), 'Documents sur l'histoire politique et religieuse du Laos occidental', *Bulletin de l'Ecole française d'Extrême-orient* (Hanoi) 25 (1–2): 36–140. For an English translation, see N. A. Jayawickrama, *The Sheaf of Garlands of the Epochs of the Conqueror: Being a Translation of Jinakalamalipakaranam of Ratanapanna Thera of Thailand*. Pali Text Society Translation Series no. 36. London: Luzac and Company, 1968.

Jing Zhenguo, ed. 1985. *Zhongguo guji zhong you guan Laowo ziliao huibian* [Collection of Chinese Historical Documents on Laos]. Henan: Zhongzhou Gujichubanshe. In Chinese.

Jiu Tang Shu [Old Tang Dynasty Annals]. Edited in 200 volumes by Liu Xu and others in AD 944. Beijing: Zhonghua Shuju, 1975 (16 volumes). Shanghai: Shanghai Gujichubanshe and Shanghai Shudian, 1985 (16 volumes). In Chinese.

Jumsai, Manich. 1971. *History of Laos*. Second edition. Bangkok: Chalermnit Press.

Kaempfer, Engelbert. 1727. *The History of Japan*. Translated from the German manuscript by John Gaspar Scheuchzer. Two volumes. London: Printed for the translator, Impr. Hans Sloane. Reprinted in 3 volumes with the title *The History of Japan, Together with a Description of the Kingdom of Siam 1690–92*. Glasgow: James MacLehose and Sons, 1906.

Katay, Thao. 1947. *Pour rire un peu: Histoires vécues* [For a Little Laughter: Stories Lived Through]. Bangkok: Lao Issara. In French.

Kennedy, Victor. 1970. 'An Indigenous Early Nineteenth Century Map of Central and Northeast Thailand.' In Tej Bunnag and Michael Smithies, eds., *In Memoriam Phya Anuman Rajadhon*, pp. 315–49. Bangkok: The Siam Society.

Khin Sok. 1991. *Le Cambodge entre le Siam et le Viêtnam (de 1775 à 1860)* [Cambodia between Siam and Vietnam, from 1775 to 1860]. Paris: Ecole française d'Extrême-orient. In French.

Knox, Robert. 1681. *An Historical Relation of the Island Ceylon, in the East Indies.* London: R. Chiswell.

La Bissachère, Pierre Jacques Lemonnier de. 1811. *Etat actuel du Tonkin, de la Cochinchine et des royaumes du Cambodge, Laos et Lactho* [Current Situation of Tonkin, Cochinchina and the Kingdoms of Cambodia, Laos and Lactho]. Two volumes. Paris: Galimani, 1812. Reprinted in 1 volume by Gregg International Publishers, Westmead, England, 1971. In French.

La Croze, V. 1724. *Histoire du christianisme des Indes* [History of Christianity in the Indies]. The Hague: Frères Vaillant et N. Prévost. In French.

La Loubère, Simon de. 1691. *Du royaume de Siam, par M. Simon de La Loubère, envoyé extraordinaire du Roy auprès du Roy de Siam en 1687 et 1688.* Two volumes. Paris: Chez la veuve de Jean Baptiste Coignard, 1691. Translated from French by A. P. Gen and published in two volumes with the title *A New Historical Relation of the Kingdom of Siam.* London: Printed for Thomas Horne, Francis Sandler and Thomas Bennet, 1693. A facsimile of the 1693 edition was issued with the title *The Kingdom of Siam.* Kuala Lumpur and Singapore: Oxford University Press, 1969.

Lach, Donald F. 1968. *Southeast Asia in the Eyes of Europe.* Chicago: University of Chicago Press.

Lafont, Pierre-Bernard, translator and editor. 1998. *Le royaume de Jyn Kh_n. Chronique d'un royaume tay lõe2 du haut Mékong (XVe–XXe siècles)* [The Kingdom of Chiang Khaeng: Chronicle of a Tai Lü Kingdom on the Upper Mekong, Fifteenth to Twentieth Centuries]. Paris: Editions l'Harmattan.

Lamdap nithan müa pha phuthachao dai khao ma yiap nai din müang luang lan sang ('Sucession of Tales from the Time when the Lord Buddha Trod the Ground of Müang Luang Lan Sang'). A facsimile of the 1874 Lao manuscript was published in Phinith (1987: 353–410), with a translation in French.

Langlois, C. 1836. 'Remarques sur la notice (sur le Laos) de M. Pallegoix' [Comments on M. Pallegoix's Notes about Laos]. *Bulletin de la Société de géographie* [Journal of the Geographical Society (Paris)] 6: 59–65. In French.

Le Boulanger, Paul. 1931. *Histoire du Laos français. Essai d'une étude chronologique des principautés laotiennes* [History of French Laos. Towards a Chronological Study of the Lao Principalities]. Paris: Librairie Plon. Reprinted by Gregg International Publishers, Ltd., Farnborough, England, 1969. In French.

Le May, Reginald. 1926. *An Asian Arcady: The Land and Peoples of Northern Siam.* Cambridge: W. Heffer and Sons. Reprinted by Houghton Mifflin Company, Boston, Massachusetts, 1927.

Le Quang Dinh. 1835. *Nhat Thong Du Dia Chi* [General Geography of Unified Vietnam]. Published in *nom* script in Hué in the reign of Minh Mang. In Vietnamese.

Lê Thành Khôi. 1955. *Le Viêt-Nam, Histoire et civilisation: Le Milieu et l'histoire* [Vietnam, History and Civilisation: The Setting and History]. Paris: Editions de Minuit. In French.

Lebar, Frank M., Gerald C. Hickey and John K. Musgrave. 1964. *Ethnic Groups of Mainland Southeast Asia.* New Haven, Connecticut: Human Relations Area Files Press.

Lefèvre-Pontalis, Pierre-Antonin. 1914. 'Wen-tan' [Wen Dan]. *T'oung Pao* (Leiden) 15: 382–90. In French.

Lejosne, Jean-Claude, trans. and ed. 1986. *Le journal de voyage de G. Van Wuysthoff et de ses assistants au Laos, 1641–1642* [The Journal of Geebaerd van Wusthof and His Assistants in Laos, 1641–2]. Brussels: Editions Thanh-Long. In French.

Lévy, Paul. 1974. *Histoire du Laos* [History of Laos]. Paris: Presses Universitaires de France. In French.

Linschoten, John Huyghen van. 1885. *The Voyage of John Huyghen van Linschoten to the East Indies; from the Old English Translation of 1598.* Edited by Arthur Coke Burnell. Works issued by the Hakluyt Society, first series, vol. 70. London: Hakluyt Society. Reprinted by Burt Franklin, New York, 1964.

L'Isle, Guillaume de. ca. 1750. 'India di la del Fiume Ganges overo di Malacca Siam Cambodia Champa Kochinkina Laos Pegu Ava &c.' [Map of India from the Ganges River to Melaka, Siam, Cambodia, Champa, Cochinchina, Laos, Pegu, Ava, etc.]. Reproduced in R. T. Fell, *Early Maps of South-East Asia*, pp. 76–7. Singapore and New York: Oxford University Press, 1988.

Lorrillard, Michel. 1995. Les chroniques royales du Laos: Contribution à la connaissance historique des royaumes lao, 1316–1887. Doctoral thesis (thèse pour le doctorat de régime unique), Ecole pratique des hautes études, Paris.

Luce, Gordon H. 1960. 'The Tan (97–132 A.D.) and the Ngaï Lao'. In *Journal of the Burma Research Society: Fiftieth Anniversary Publications*, no. 2, pp. 201–38. Rangoon: Burma Research Society.

McCarthy, James. 1888. Map of Siam. *Proceedings of the Royal Geographical Society* (London) 10 (3): facing p. 188.

McGilvary, Daniel. 1912. *A Half Century among the Siamese and the Lao.* New York: Revell.

Maitre, Cl. E. 1909. 'Préface: Note sur l'histoire de la cartographie indochinoise' [Preface: Note on the History of Indochinese Cartography]. In Lucien Louis Joseph Gallois and C. C. de Chabert-Ostland, *Atlas général de l'Indochine française* [General Atlas of French Indochina]. Hanoi: Imprimerie d'Extrême-orient. In French.

The Man Shu (Book of the Southern Barbarians). 1961. Translated from Chinese by Gordon H. Luce and edited by G. P. Oey. Southeast Asia Program Data Paper no. 44. Ithaca, New York: Southeast Asia Program, Cornell University.

Mangrai, Sao Saimöng. 1981. *The Padaeng Chronicle and the Jengtung State Chronicle Translated.* Michigan Papers on South and Southeast Asia no. 19. Ann Arbor, Michigan: Center for South and Southeast Asian Studies, University of Michigan.

Manguin, Pierre-Yvès. 1972 *Les Portugais sur les côtes du Viet-Nam et du Campa: Etude sur les routes maritimes et les relations commerciales, d'après les sources portugaises (XVIe, XVIIe, XVIIIe siècles)* [The Portuguese on the Coast of Vietnam and Champa: A Study of Maritime Routes and Commercial Relations, according to Portuguese Sources (16th, 17th and 18th centuries)]. Paris: Ecole française d'Extrême-orient.

Marini, Giovanni Filippo de. 1663. *Delle missioni de'Petri della Compagnia di Giesu nella provincia del Giappone e particolarmente de quella di Tumkino.* Roma: Nicolo Angelo Tinassi. In Italian. Translated into French and published with the title *Histoire nouvelle et curieuse des royaumes de Tunquin et de Lao. Contenant une description exacte de leur origine, grandeur et éstendue, de leurs richesses et de leurs forces, des moeurs et du nature de leurs habitants; de la fertilité de ces contrées et des rivières qui les arrosent de tous cotes et de plusieurs autres circonstances utiles et nécessaires pour une plus grande intelligence de la géographie* [A New and Interesting History of the Kingdoms of Tonkin and Laos, containing an exact description of the origin, size and breadth, their resources and powers, the customs and character of their inhabitants, the fertility of these lands and the rivers that irrigate them on all sides, and many other matters useful and necessary for a greater knowledge of geography]. Paris: Gervais Clouzier, 1666. A facsimile of the section on Laos in the 1666 French edition, with an interpretation in Lao by Houmpanh Rattanavong, was published with the title *Pathet lao nai sum pi k. s. 1640—Relation nouvelle et curieuse du royaume de Lao, traduite de l'Italien du P. de Marini Romain* [Laos about the Year A.D. 1640— A New and Interesting Account of the Lao Kingdom, Translated from the Italian of Father de Marini of the Roman Church]. Vientiane: Sathaban Khonkhwa Sinlapa Wannakhadi lae Phasasat [Institute for Research in the Arts, Literature and Linguistics], 1990. A translation in English by Walter E. J. Tips and Claudio Bertuccio was published with the title *A New and Interesting Description of the Lao Kingdom (1642–1648): G. F. de Marini.* Bangkok: White Lotus Press, 1998.

Martini, Martino. 1655. *Novus Atlas Sinensis.* Amsterdam: Joan Bleau.

Maspero, Henri. 1918. 'La frontière de l'Annam et du Cambodge du VIIIe au XIVe siècle' [The Frontiers of Annam and of Cambodge from the Eighth to the Fourteenth Centuries]. *Bulletin de l'Ecole française d'Extrême-orient* (Hanoi) 18 (3): 29–36.

Mercator, Gerard. 1636. *Atlas or a Geographicke description, of the Regions, Countries and Kingdomes of the World, through Europe, Asia, Africa and America, represented by new and exact maps.* Amsterdam: Henrici Hondij [Henry Hondius], 1636. Facsimile reproduction published with the title *Mercator-Hondius-Janssonius Atlas or a Geographicke Description of the World.* Two volumes. Amsterdam: Theatrum Orbis Terrarum, 1968.

Meyer, Roland. 1931. *Le Laos* [Laos]. Hanoi: Imprimerie d'Extrême-orient. In French.

Miche, Jean-Claude. 1852. 'Geography of Cambodia'. *Journal of the Indian Archipelago and Eastern Asia* (Singapore) 6: 173–8.

———. 1854. 'Excursion au pays des laos' [An Excursion to the Land of the Lao], *Nouvelles annales des voyages et des sciences géographiques* [New Chronicles of Voyages and Geographical Sciences (Paris)] 1854: 155–60. In French.

Mongkut, King. 1924 *Prachum prakat ratchakan thi si phak phanuak* [Collected Proclamations of the Fourth Reign, Supplementary Volume]. Bangkok: Royal Institute. In Thai.

Morga, Antonio de. 1971. *'Sucesos de las Islas Filipinas' by Antonio de Morga*. Translated from Spanish and edited by J. S. Cummins. Works Issued by the Hakluyt Society, second series, vol. 140. Cambridge: Hakluyt Society.

Mouhot, Henri. 1864. *Travels in the Central Parts of Indochina (Siam), Cambodia, and Laos, during the years 1858, 1859 and 1860*. Two volumes. London: John Murray. Edited and abridged by Christopher Pym and reprinted with the same title; Kuala Lumpur and New York: Oxford University Press, 1966. Reprinted in one volume with the title *Travels in Siam, Cambodia and Laos, 1858–1860*. Singapore and New York: Oxford University Press, 1989.

Mourin d'Arfeuille, C. 1872. 'Voyage au Laos: Notes sur le voyage au Laos, fait en 1869 par M. d'Arfeuille, lieutenant de vaisseau, et M. Rheinhart, capitaine d'infanterie de marine, inspecteur des affaires indigènes' [Journey to Laos: Notes on the Journey to Laos Made in 1869 by C. Mourin d'Arfeuille, Navy Lieutenant, and M. Rheinhart, Naval Infantry Captain and Inspector of Native Affairs]. *Revue maritime et coloniale* [Maritime and Colonial Review (Paris)] 32: 465–79. In French.

Munlasatsana (tamnan munlasatsana) [Munlasatsana (a chronicle written by Phra Phutthapukam and Phra Phutthaya in the fifteenth or sixteenth century)]. 1976. Bangkok: Soemwit Bannakhan. In Thai.

Navarette, Domingo. 1962. *The Travels and Controversies of Friar Domingo Navarrete 1618–1686, Edited from Manuscript and Printed Sources by J. S. Cummins*. Works issued by the Hakluyt Society, second series, vol. 119. Cambridge: Hakluyt Society.

Neïs, Paul-Marie. 1885. 'Voyage au Laos (1883–1884)' [Journey to Laos (1883–4)]. *Bulletin de la Société de géographie* [Journal of the Geographical Society (Paris)] 7e série 6: 372–93. In French.

Népote, Jacques. 1986. 'Le voyage de Van Wuysthoff au Laos (1641–1642): Les Contextes' [The Journey of van Wusthof to Laos (1641–2): The Context]. *Péninsule—Etudes interdisciplinaires sur l'Asie du sud-est péninsulaire* [Peninsula: Interdisciplinary Studies on Peninsular South-East Asia (Metz)] 13: 8–42. In French.

Ngaosyvathn, Mayoury, and Pheuiphanh Ngaosyvathn. 1988. *Chao anu, 1767–1829: pasason lao lae asi akhanae* [Chao Anu, 1767–1829: The Lao People and South-East Asia]. Vientiane: Editions LPDR. In Lao.

———. 1998. *Paths to Conflagration: Fifty Years of Diplomacy and Warfare in Laos, Thailand, and Vietnam, 1778–1828.* Studies on Southeast Asia no. 24. Ithaca, New York: Southeast Asia Program, Cornell University.

Ngo Si Lien et al. 1984–6. *Da Yue Shi Ji Quan Shu* [Complete Annals of Dai Viet]. Compiled in 1675 in 19 volumes. Edited by Chen Jing He in 3 volumes. Tokyo: Toyogaku Bunken Center. In Chinese.

Ortelius [Abraham Ortelis]. 1571. 'Indiae Orientalis, Insvlarvmqve adiacienti vm typus' [Map of India, East Asia and Adjacent Islands]. Reproduced in Bernard Gay, *Le Bassin du Mékong, Images du Passé —The Basin of the Mekong River, Images of the Past* (Paris: Descente du Mékong – Inalco, 1996), p. 129.

Osborne, Milton. 1975. *River Road to China: the Mekong River Expedition 1866–1873.* New York: Liveright.

Pallegoix, Jean-Baptiste. 1836. 'Notice sur le Laos' [Notes about Laos]. *Bulletin de la Société de géographie* [Journal of the Geographical Society (Paris)] 6: 372–93. In French.

Pavie, Auguste. 1898. *Mission Pavie* [Mission of Auguste Pavie in Indochina], vol. 2. Paris: E. Leroux. Volume 2 contains translations of several Lao historical works: 'Histoire du pays de Lan-Chhang (Hom Khao)' [History of the Land of Lan Sang (The White Umbrella)], pp. 1–77; 'Abrégé de l'histoire du pays de Lan-Chhang (Hom khao)' [An Abbreviated History of the Land of Lan Sang (The White Umbrella)], pp. 79–94; 'Chronologie de l'histoire du pays de Lan-Chhang (Hom khao)' [Chronology of the History of the Land of Lan Sang (The White Umbrella)], pp. 95–102; ' Histoire du Pra-Bang' [History of the Prabang Image], pp. 103–17; and 'Fragments de l'histoire du Lan-Chhang' [Fragments of the History of Lan Sang], pp. 125–42. In French.

———. 1903. *Mission Pavie, Indo-chine: Atlas, notices et cartes* [Mission of Auguste Pavie in Indochina: Atlas, Notes and Maps]. Paris: Augustin Challamel. In French.

Pelet, Paul. 1902. *Atlas des colonies françaises* [Atlas of the French Colonies]. Paris: Librairie Armand Colin. In French.

Pelliot, Paul. 1903. 'Le Sa–Pao' [The Title 'Sa-Pao']. *Bulletin de l'Ecole française d'Extrême–orient* (Hanoi) 3: 665–71. In French.

———. 1904. 'Deux itineraires de Chine en Inde à la fin du VIIIe siècle' [Two Itineraries from China to India at the End of the Eighth Century]. *Bulletin de l'Ecole française d'Extrême–orient* (Hanoi) 4: 131–413. In French.

Petithuguenin, Paul. 1949. 'Auguste Pavie diplomate. La question franco-siamoise des états laotiens (1885–1896)' [Auguste Pavie, Diplomat: The Franco-Siamese Question Concerning the Lao States, 1885–96]. *Revue de l'histoire des colonies françaises* (Paris) 35: 200–30. In French.

Phinith, Saveng, translator and editor. 1987. *Contribution à l'histoire du royame de Luang Prabang* [Contribution to the History of the Luang Prabang Kingdom]. Paris: Ecole française d'Extrême-orient. In Lao and French.

Phomvihane, Kaysone. 1975. Rapport général au Congrès national des représentants du peuple [General Report to the National Congress of the People's Representatives]. Unpublished report. Vientiane. In French.

———. 1976. *Rapport général au Congrès national des représentants du peuple* [General Report to the National Congress of the People's Representatives]. Vientiane: State Publishing House. In French.

———. 1978. *Pathet lao* [The Lao Nation]. Vientiane: State Publishing House. In Lao.

Phongsawadan haeng pathet lao khü luang phabang wiang chan müang phuan lae champasak [Chronicles of Laos: Luang Prabang, Vientiane, the Phuan Kingdom and Champasak]. Printed in a handwritten version in Hanoi, 1926. Reprinted in 1967 by the Education Ministry, Vientiane. In Lao.

Phongsawadan lan chang tam thòi kham nai chabap doem [A Chronicle of Lan Sang, According to the Original Lao-Idiom Text (the Pracha Kitchakòrachak manuscript)]. In *Prachum phongsawadan phak thi 1* [History Series Part 1], Khurusapha reprint series, vol. 2, pp. 134–85. Bangkok: Khurusapha Press, 1963. In Lao (printed in Thai script).

Phongsawadan müang luang phrabang [Chronicle of Luang Prabang (1870 version)]. In *Prachum phongsawadan phak thi 11* [History Series Part 11], Khurusapha reprint series, vol. 10, pp. 135–236. Bangkok: Khurusapha Press, 1964. In Thai.

Phongsawadan müang luang phabang [Chronicle of Luang Prabang (version ca. 1900)]. Vientiane: National Library, 1969. In Lao.

Phongsawadan müang luang phrabang tam chabap thi mi yu nai sala luk khun [Chronicle of Luang Prabang, According to the Manuscript in the Ministers' Pavilion (1867 version)]. In *Prachum phongsawadan phak thi 5* [History Series Part 5], Khurusapha reprint series, vol. 4, pp. 315–69. Bangkok: Khurusapha Press, 1963. In Thai.

Phongsawadan yò müang wiangchan [An Abbreviated Chronicle of Vientiane (October 1893 version)]. In *Prachum phongsawadan phak thi 70* [History Series Part 70], Khurusapha reprint series, vol. 44: 131–7. Bangkok: Khurusapha, 1969. In Lao (printed in Thai script).

Phongsawadan yò müang wiangchan [An Abbreviated Chronicle of Vientiane (ca. 1857)]. In *Prachum phongsawadan phak thi 70* [History Series Part 70], Khurusapha reprint series, vol. 44: 138–52. Bangkok: Khurusapha, 1969. In Lao (printed in Thai script).

Phothisane, Souneth. 1998. The *Nid_n Khun Bòrom*: Annotated Translation and Analysis. Ph.D. thesis in history, University of Queensland.

Pietrantoni, Eric. 1957. 'La population du Laos en 1943 dans son milieu géographique' [The Population of Laos in 1943 in Its Geographical Setting]. *Bulletin de la Société des études indochinoises* [Journal of the Society of Indochinese Studies (Saigon)] nouvelle série 32: 223–43. In French.

Pinkerton, John. 1802. *Modern Geography. A Description of the Empires, Kingdoms, States, and Colonies; With the Oceans, Seas, and Isles; In All Parts of the World: Including the Most Recent Discoveries, and Political Alterations. Digested on a New Plan.* London: T. Cadell and W. Davies, Strand; and T. N. Longman and O. Rees, Paternoster-Row.

———, ed. 1815. *A Modern Atlas from the Latest and best authorities, exhibiting the various divisions of the World, with its chief Empires, Kingdoms, and states, in sixty maps, carefully reduced from the largest and most authentic sources.* London: Printed by T. Bensley for T. Cadell and others.

Pinto, Fernão Mendes. 1614. *Peregrinaçam de Fernão Mendes Pinto em que la conta de muytas e muyto estranhas cousa ....* Lisboa: Pedro Crasbeeck, 1614. In Portuguese. Translated into English by Henry Cogan and published with the title *The Voyages and Adventures of Fernand Mendez Pinto, a Portugal, During his Travels for the space of one and twenty years in the Kingdoms of Ethiopia, China, Tartaria, Cauchinchina, Calaminham, Siam, Pegu, Japan, and a great part of the East-Indies.* London: Printed by J. Macock for Henry Cripps and Lodowick Lloyd, 1653; reprinted 1663 and 1692. A slightly abridged reprint of Henry Cogan's translation was published with the title *The Voyages and Adventures of Ferdinand Mendez Pinto during his Travels for the space of one and twenty years in the Kingdoms of Ethiopia, China, Tartaria, Cauchinchina, Calaminham, Siam, Pegu, Japan, and a great part of the East Indies.* London and New York: T. F. Unwin, 1891. A new translation by Rebecca D. Catz was published with the title *The Travels of Mendes Pinto.* Chicago and London: University of Chicago Press, 1989.

Pires, Tomé. 1944. *The Suma Oriental of Tomé Pires and the Book of Francisco Rodriguez.* Works Issued by the Hakluyt Society, second series, vol. 89. London: Hakluyt Society.

Polo, Marco. 1929. *The Book of Ser Marco Polo, the Venetian, Concerning the Kingdoms and Marvels of the East.* Translated from Italian and edited by Henry Yule. London: J. Murray.

Pons, Père. 1743. 'Lettre du Père Pons, missionnaire de la Compagnie de Jésus, au Père Du Halde de la même Compagnie' [Letter from Father Pons, a Jesuit Missionary (in India), to Father Du Halde, 23 November 1740]. In *Lettres édifiantes et curieuses, écrites des missions étrangères, par quelques missionnaires de la Compagnie de Jésus* [Inspiring and Interesting Letters Written from the Foreign Missions by Some Missionaries of the Jesuit Order], vol. 26, pp. 220–56. Paris: Chez P. G. Le Mercier et Chez Marc Bordelet. In French.

Pracha Kitchakòrachak (Chaem Bunnag), Phraya. See *Phongsawadan lan chang tam thòi kham nai chabap doem.*

Pramuan Wichaphun, Phraya. 1939. *Phongsawadan müang lan chang lae lamdap sakun sitthi saribut ratcha trakun lan sang wiangchan* [Chronicle of Lan Sang and the Lineage of the Siddhi Sariput Branch of the Lan Sang (Vientiane) Royal Family]. Bangkok: n.p. In Thai.

Prescott, J. R. V. 1975. *Map of Mainland Asia by Treaty.* Melbourne: Melbourne University Press.

Prevost, Antoine François, ed. 1747–80. *Histoire générale des voyages* [A General History of Voyages]. Twenty-five volumes. The Hague: P. de Hondt. In French.

Pruess, James B., trans. and ed. 1976. *The That Phanom Chronicle: A Shrine History and Its Interpretation.* Southeast Asia Program Data Paper no. 104. Ithaca, New York: Southeast Asia Program, Cornell University.

Purchas, Samuel, ed. 1905–7. *Hakluytus Posthumus or Purchas His Pilgrimes, Containing a History of the World in Sea Voyages and Lande Travells by Englishmen and Others.* Reprinted from the

1625–6 London edition. Twenty volumes. Glasgow: James McLehose and Sons.

Reinach, Lucien de. 1901. *Le Laos* [Laos]. Two volumes. Paris: A. Charles. In French.

———. 1902. *Recueil des traités conclus par la France en Extrême-orient, 1684–1902* [Compilation of the Treaties Concluded by France in the Far East, 1684–1902]. Paris: Ernest Leroux. In French.

———. 1907. *Recueil des traités conclus par la France en Extrême-orient, 1901–1907* [Compilation of the Treaties Concluded by France in the Far East, 1901–7]. Paris: Ernest Leroux. In French.

———. 1911. *Le Laos* [Laos]. Paris: Guilmoto. In French.

Rhodes, Alexandre de. 1651. *Dictionarium Annamiticum Lusitanum et Latinum* [Vietnamese-Portuguese-Latin Dictionary]. Rome: Typis Sacrae Congregationis.

Richard, Jérôme. 1778. *Histoire naturelle, civile et politique du Tonquin* [Natural, Civil and Political History of Tonkin]. Two volumes. Paris: Chez Moutard. In French. Translated anonymously and published with the title 'History of Tonkin' in John Pinkerton, ed., *A General Collection of the Best and Most Interesting Voyages and Travels in All Parts of the World; Many of Which Are Now First Translated into English by John Pinkerton*, vol. 9, pp. 708–71. London: Longman, Hurst, Rees, Orme, and Brown, Paternoster Row; and Cadell and Davies, 1811.

Rochet, Charles. 1946. *Pays lao: Le Laos dans la tourmente, 1939–1945* [Lao Country: Laos in Torment, 1939–5]. Paris: Vigneau. In French.

Rosny, Léon de. 1872. *Variétés orientales* [Asian Variedness]. Paris: Maisonneuve. In French.

Sa Nhanh Dongdeng. 1974. *Sük phò kaduat* [Father Kaduat's War]. Vientiane: Khamphan Prasaisitthidet. In Lao.

Sanson, Nicolas. 1669. 'L'Asie' [map of Asia, published in Paris, 1669]. Reproduced in Egon Klemp (1989), *Asia in Maps from Ancient Times to the Mid-Nineteenth Century*, plate 12. Leipzig: Acta Humaniora, 1989.

Sasorith, Katay Don. 1959. 'Historical Aspects of Laos'. In René de Berval et alia, *Kingdom of Laos: The Land of the Million Elephants and of the White Parasol*, pp. 24–31. Saigon: France-Asie.

Sasorith, Mongkhol Katay. 1973. Les Forces politiques et la vie politique au Laos [Political Forces and Political Life in Laos]. Doctoral thesis (doctorat d'état en science politique), Université de Science Politique, Paris. In French.

Sayres, Francis Bowes, ed. 1928. *Siam: Treaties with Foreign Powers 1920–1927*. Norwood, Massachusetts: Plimpton Press.

Schafer, Edward H. 1967. *The Vermilion Bird: T'ang Images of the South*. Berkeley and Los Angeles: University of California Press.

———. 1970. *Shore of Pearls*. Berkeley and London: University of California Press.

Seidenfaden, Erik. 1922. 'Complément à l'inventaire descriptif des monuments du Cambodge pour les quatre provinces du Siam oriental' [Complement to the Descriptive Inventory of Cambodian Monuments, for the Four Provinces of East Siam]. *Bulletin de l'Ecole française d'Extrême-orient* (Hanoi) 22: 55–99.

Siam and Laos as Seen by Our American Missionaries. 1883. Philadelphia: Presbyterian Board of Publication.

The Siam Repository. Annual, 1866–73 (Bangkok).

Sila Viravong, Maha. 1957. *Phongsawadan lao* [Lao History]. Vientiane: Ministry of Education. In Lao. Translated by the U.S. Joint Publications Research Service and distributed in 1959 by that agency in typewritten form. A facsimile of the typewritten version was published with the title *History of Laos*. New York: Paragon Book Reprint Corporation, 1964.

———. 1992. *Prawattisat lao* [Lao History]. Translated into Thai by Sommai Premchit from a manuscript in Lao completed by the author in 1985 (a revised version of his 1957 book). Chiang Mai: Social Research Institute, University of Chiang Mai. Reprinted by Matichon Press, Bangkok, 1996. In Thai.

Sila Viravong, Maha, and Nouan Outhensakda. See Thep Luang and Mongkhun Sitthi.

Smuckarn, Snit, and Kennon Breazeale. 1988. *A Culture in Search of Survival: The Phuan of Thailand and Laos*. Yale University Southeast Asia Studies, Monograph Series no. 31. New Haven, Connecticut: Yale Center for International and Area Studies.

Stevensen, Charles. 1977. *The End of Nowhere: American Policy toward Laos since 1954*. Boston, Massachusetts: Beacon Press.

Strabo. 1916. *The Geography of Strabo, with an English Translation by Horace Leonard Jones, A.M., Ph.D., Based in Part upon the Unfinished Version of John Robert Sitlington Sterrett, Ph.D., LL.D.* Eight volumes. London: William Heinemann; New York: G. P. Putnam's

Sons. In English and Greek. A Latin translation of the manuscript, written in Greek ca. 7 BC, was first published in Rome in 1472 and was reprinted many times. Book 15 of the manuscript (on India, Ceylon and South-West Asia) is contained in vol. 8 of the 1916 translation.

Stuart–Fox, Martin. 1981. 'Reflections on the Lao Revolution'. *Contemporary Southeast Asia* (Singapore) 3: 41–57.

———. 1983. 'Marxism and Theravada Buddhism: The Legitimation of Political Authority in Laos'. *Pacific Affairs* (Vancouver) 56: 428–54.

———. 1986a. *Laos: Politics, Economics and Society.* London: Frances Pinter.

———. 1986b. 'Politics and Patronage in Laos'. *Indochina Times* 70: 1–7.

———. 1997. *A History of Laos.* Cambridge: Cambridge University Press.

———. 1998. *The Lao Kingdom of Lān Xāng: Rise and Decline.* Bangkok: White Lotus Company.

Stuart–Fox, Martin, and Rod Bucknell. 1982. 'Politicization of the Buddhist Sangha in Laos'. *Journal of Southeast Asian Studies* (Singapore) 13: 60–80.

Sugimoto, Naojiro. 1956. *Tonan Ajia Kenkyu Ichi* [Studies on South-East Asia, Volume One]. Tokyo: Gannando. In Japanese.

Sui Shu [Sui Dynasty Annals]. Edited in 85 volumes by Wei Zhi and others, AD 636–56. Beijing: Zhonghua Shuju, 1975 (6 volumes). Shanghai: Shanghai Gujichubanshe and Shanghai Shudian, 1985 (6 volumes). In Chinese.

Swanson, Herbert R. 1984. *Khrischak Muang Nua: A Study in Northern Thai Church History.* Bangkok: Chuan Printing Press.

Sylvestre, J. 1889. *L'Empire d'Annam et le peuple annamite* [The Empire of Annam and the Annamese People]. Paris: F. Alcan. In French.

Taberd, Jean-Louis. 1837. 'Note on the Geography of Cochinchina'. *Journal of the Asiatic Society of Bengal* (Calcutta) 7: 319.

Tachard, Guy. 1686. *Voyage au Siam des Pères Jésuites envoyés par le Roi aux Indes et à la Chine* [The Voyage to Siam of the Jesuits Sent by the King to the Indies and China]. Paris: Seneuze et Horthemels. In French.

Tai Ping Huan Yu Ji [Geography of the Taiping Reign Period]. Edited in 200 volumes by Lu Shi during the Taiping Xingguo period AD 976–84. Edited in 30 volumes by Chen Lan Sen and others in 1793. Chongrenyueshi edition, Nanjing: Jinling Shuju, 1882 (36 volumes). Tapei: Wenhai Chubanshe, 1963 (2 volumes). In Chinese.

Tai Ping Yu Lan [Encyclopaedia of the Taiping Reign Period]. Edited in 1,000 volumes by Li Fang and others in AD 984. Taipei: Xinxing Shuju, 1959 (Sibucongkan 3 Pian edition, 12 volumes). In Chinese.

Tâm Quach-Langlet. 1989. 'La perception des frontières dans l'ancien Vietnam à travers quelques cartes vietnamiennes et occidentales' [The Perception of Frontiers in Old Vietnam, Reflected in Some Vietnamese and Western Maps]. In Pierre-Bernard Lafont, ed., *Les frontières du Vietnam: Histoire des frontières de la péninsule indochinoise* [The Frontiers of Vietnam: History of the Frontiers of the Indochinese Peninsula]. Paris: Editions l'Harmattan. In French.

Tamnan phra kaeo mòrakot [A Historical Account of the Emerald Buddha]. 1967. Cremation volume for Nang Chan Thammakasem. Bangkok: Fine Arts Department. In Thai.

Tan Qixang, ed. 1982. *Zhongguo Lishi Dituji* [A Historical Atlas of China, Volume Five]. Shanghai: Cartographic Publishing House. In Chinese.

Tang Hui Yao [A Tang Dynasty Reference Book]. Edited in 100 volumes by Wang Bo and others, ca. AD 961. Jiangsu Shuju, 1884 (Wuyingdian Juzhenshu edition, 24 volumes). Beijing: Zhonghua Shuju, 1955 (3 volumes). Shanghai: Shanghai Gujichubanshe, 1991 (2 volumes). In Chinese.

Thep Luang, Maha, and Maha Mongkhun Sitthi, compilers. *Nithan khun bòrom rasathirat* [Tales of King Bòrom the Great]. Edited by Sila Viravong and Nuan Uthensakda. Vientiane: Saeng Panya Kanphim, 1967. In Lao.

Thesaphiban. The provincial administration gazette of the Ministry of Interior, Bangkok. Monthly from 1906. In Thai.

Thiphakòrawong, Chao Phraya. 1978. *The Dynastic Chronicles, Bangkok Era, First Reign.* Translated from Thai and edited by Thadeus and Chadin Flood. Volume 1. Tokyo: Centre for East Asian Cultural Studies.

Thongsa Sayavongkhamdy, Bunkong Thongsavat, Daeng Phomsavan, Souneth Phothisane, Singthong Singhapanya and Viangvichit Sutthidet. 1989. *Pawatsat lao lem sam 1893 thüng batchuban* [History of Laos, Volume Three: From 1893 to the Present Day]. Vientiane: Sathaban Khonkhwa Wittayasat Sangkhom [Committee for Social Science Research], Ministry of Education. In Lao.

Toye, Hugh. 1968. *Laos: Buffer State or Battleground?* London: Oxford University Press.

Tran Van Quy. 1984. 'Mot So Van Ban Thi Tay-son' [Some Unpublished Official Papers of the Tay-son Period]. *Bao Nhan Dan* [The People' s Daily], 22 April 1984, p. 2. In Vietnamese.

———. 1985. 'Unpublished Documents on the Reign of Quang Trung'. *Vietnamese Studies* (Hanoi) 6 (76): 143–5. This journal is also published in a French-language edition: *Etudes vietnamiennes* (Hanoi).

———. no date. Muc Luc Tu Lieu Quy Hop [Catalogue of the Documents in the Quy Hop Archive]. Unpublished manuscript, Institute of Han Nom, Hanoi. In Vietnamese.

Tsukiyama, Jisaburo. 1961. 'Togo (Tu hu)'. In Jisaburo Tsukiyama, *Ajia Rekishi Jiten Dai Shichikan* [A Historical Dictionary of Asia], vol 7, p. 123. Tokyo: Heibonsha. In Japanese.

Tuck, Patrick. 1995. *The French Wolf and the Siamese Lamb: The French Threat to Siamese Independence 1858–1907.* Bangkok: White Lotus.

Universal History. 1759. *The Modern Part of an Universal History, from the Earliest Account of Time. Compiled from Original Writers. By the Authors of the Antient Part, Vol. 7.* London: Printed for S. Richardson, T. Osborne, C. Hitch, A. Millar, John Rivington, S. Crowder, P. Davey and B. Law, T. Longman and C. Ware.

Vajirañan National Library. 1915–21. *Records of the Relations between Siam and Foreign Countries in the Seventeenth Century. Copied from Papers Preserved at the India Office.* Five volumes. Bangkok: Council of the Vajirañan National Library.

Viet Su Luoc [Abridged History of the Viet]. See *Yue Shi Lue.*

Viet Su Thong Giam Cuong Muc [General History of Vietnam]. 1957. Compiled in Chinese in the 1870s; translated into Vietnamese and published in 20 volumes. Hanoi: Editions de l'Histoire. In Vietnamese.

Vliet, Jeremias van. 1910. 'Translation of Jeremias van Vliet's Description of the Kingdom of Siam, by L. F. van Ravenswaay', *Journal of the Siam Society* (Bangkok) 7 (1): v-viii, 1–108. Translated from the 1692 (first) Dutch edition; the manuscript was compiled in 1638.

Vliet, Ieremi [Jeremias] van. 1938. 'Van Vliet's Historical Account of Siam in the Seventeenth Century'. *Journal of the Siam Society* (Bangkok) 30 (2): 95–154. Translated by W. H. Mundie from the 1647 Dutch manuscript.

Vongvichit, Phoumi. 1968. *Le Laos et la lutte victorieuse du peuple lao contre le néo-colonialisme américain.* Hanoi: Editions du Neo Lao Haksat,

1968. In French. Translated and published with the title *Laos and the Victorious Struggle of the Lao People against U.S. Neo-Colonialism.* Hanoi: Neo Lao Haksat, 1969.

Wachirayan [Wachirayan Journal (Bangkok)]. Monthly, 1884–1905.

Wenk, Klaus. 1968. *The Restoration of Thailand under Rama I, 1782–1809.* Tucson: University of Arizona Press.

Winichakul, Thongchai. 1994. *Siam Mapped: A History of the Geo-body of a Nation.* Honolulu: University of Hawaii Press.

Wolters, O. W. 1968. Ayudhya and the Rearward Part of the World. *Journal of the Royal Asiatic Society of Great Britain and Ireland* (London) (1968): 166–78.

————. 1982. *History, Culture, and Region in Southeast Asian Perspective.* Singapore: Institute of Southeast Asian Studies.

Wong, Sik/Sek Ling. 1954. *Yue Yin Yun Hui* [A Chinese Syllabary Prounced according to the Dialect of Guangdong]. Hong Kong: Chung Hwa Book Company (Zhonghua Shuju). In Chinese.

Wusthof, Geebaerd van. 1669. *Vremde Geschiedenissen in de Koninckrijcken van Cambodia en Louwen Lant, in Oost-Indien, Zedert den Iare 1635, tot den Iare 1644, aldaer Voorgevallen* [Distant Journey in the Kingdom of Cambodia and the Lao Country, in East India, from the Year 1635 to the Year 1644, and What Happened There]. Harlem: Pieter Casteleyn. In Dutch.

———— [Gérard van Wusthof]. 1871. 'Voyage lointain aux royaumes de Cambodge et Laouwen par les néerlandais et ce qui s'est passé jusqu'en 1644' [Distant Journey to the Kingdoms of Cambodia and Laos by the Dutchmen and Events There up to 1644]. Translated from Dutch and edited by Francis Garnier. *Bulletin de la Société de géographie* [Journal of the Geographical Society (Paris)] 6e série 2: 249–89. In French.

————. 1986. *Le journal de voyage de G. Van Wuysthoff et de ses assistants au Laos, 1641–1642* [The Journal of Geebaerd van Wusthof and His Assistants in Laos, 1641–2]. Translated and edited by Jean-Claude Lejosne. Brussels: Editions Thanh-Long. In French.

Wyatt, David. 1984. *Thailand: A Short History.* New Haven, Connecticut: Yale University Press.

Wyatt, David, and Aroonrut Wichienkeeo. 1995. *The Chiang Mai Chronicle.* Chiang Mai: Silkworm Books.

Xin Tang Shu [New Tang Dynasty Annals]. Edited in 225 volumes by Ou Yang Xiu and others in A.D. 1060. Shanghai: Shangwu Yinshuguan, 1937 (Bainaben edition, 40 volumes). Beijing: Zhonghua Shuju, 1975 (20 volumes). Shanghai: Shanghai Gujichubanshe and Shanghai Shudian, 1986. In Chinese.

Xuan Zhuang. 1985. *Da Tang Xi Yu Ji* [Diary of a Journey to the Western Countries during the Great Tang Period]. Edited by Ji Xian Lin and others. Beijing: Zhonghua Shuju. In Chinese.

Yim Panthayangkun, Thòngsüp Suphamak, Sathit Semanin, Tri Amattayakun, Manit Wanliphodom, Chaliao Chansap and Kunlasap Ketmaenkit, compilers. 1982. *Prachum mai rap sang phak thi 1 samai krung thonburi* [A Collection of Instructions Received from the King, Part 1: The Thonburi Period]. Bangkok: Khana kammakan phicharana lae chat phim ekkasan thang prawattisat samnak nayok ratthamontri [Committee for Investigating and Publishing Historical Documents, Office of the Prime Minister]. In Thai.

Yuan He Jun Xian Tu Zhi [Description of the Yuanhe-Period Geography: Prefectures and Districts]. Edited in 40 volumes by Li Ji Fu, AD 806–19. Jiangsi Shuju, 1874 (Wuyingdian Juzhenshu edition, 16 volumes). Nanjing: Jinling Shuju, 1880–2 (edited by Yan Guan, 8 volumes). Tokyo: Toyo Bunko, ca. 1970 (Beijing Library edition, 8 volumes). Beijing: Zhonghua Shuju, 1983 (2 volumes). In Chinese.

Yue Shi Lue [Abridged History of the Viet]. Three volumes. Shanghai: Shoushangecongshu, 1922. Shanghai: Shangwu Yinshuguan, 1937 (Congshujichengchupian edition no. 3257). Tokyo: Toyo Bunko, 1960 (Beida edition). In Chinese.

Yule, Henry. 1857. 'On the Geography of Burma and Its Tributary States, in Illustration of a New Map of Those Regions'. *Journal of the Royal Geographical Society* (London) 27: 54–108.

Yunnan Zhi [Official History of Yunnan]. See *Man Shu*.

INDEX